The COMPOSITE ART of ACTING

The COMPOSITE ART of ACTING

Jerry Blunt

The Macmillan Company, New York / Collier-Macmillan Limited, London

To my students,
who have been such excellent teachers,
and to Betty

Foreword

Whenever man wishes to make any one of his activities noteworthy, he raises that activity to the institutional level. Centuries ago the dramatic establishment was among the first to be so honored. It has maintained itself, with varying fortunes, from that time forward. In some instances it has needed all of its sturdiness to survive.

In the full stretch of its history, however, there has never been so much wrong with the theatre that fine acting could not go a long way to cure. Among the factors that make it an outstanding institution, none is more critical than the night after night playing of all its actors on all its stages.

Presently our theatre shows a response to the strain of the last three or four decades. But it is a viable institution for all that. And the evidence promises an encouraging turn. If and when the present potential becomes actual, it will be in large part because fine acting will supply the artistry required in any great theatre.

Artistry is a superstructure raised over a foundation of basic competence. When competence is present, artistry is promised.

Acting is a composite art. Artistry in a whole endeavor is possible only when artistry is also present in each of the parts. To act, an actor must move and speak; pantomime and voice are essential components of this art. Basic competence must be won in each before artistry in either or in the amalgam of both can be achieved.

Now is the time, when our theatre is edgy with promise, to master the foundation studies out of which the composite art of acting grows. The development of fine acting could be the capping action in the emergence of that new theatre we so strongly desire.

BASIC COMPETENCE

Artistry is the working result of a dramatic instinct disciplined into full power by basic competence in the parts that comprise it.

Basic competence is crammed with mastered details, the organization of which precludes uncertainty, and gives a clear direction to all work undertaken. With it the actor knows how to begin each separate task. From it he draws confidence to sustain every effort. Because of it he enjoys the respect of his fellow artists. With it, when he stands on stage, there is a sense of rightness in his presence; he belongs where he is, and there will be no doubt in the minds of his viewers about his fitness for his place.

Basic competence denotes ability in an actor to perform the necessary first actions of his art. These lie:

1. In the area of individual development:
   To free himself psychologically for dramatic expression under theatrical conditions,
   To acquire a comprehension of the nature and the meaning of the dramatic experience,
   To acquire an operative theatre sense,
   To develop the ability to draw information from primary source materials,
   To have a thorough knowledge of the dramatic form;
2. In the area of specific practice:
   To master the fundamentals of dramatic action: definite, economic, and meaningful movement, as well as preliminary, arrested, and suspended movement,
   To master the fundamentals of vocal action: theatre strength and quality, flexibility of tone, skill of articulation, and tonal awareness and control,
   To achieve synchronization of line and movement,
   To ground himself soundly in rehearsal techniques.

Competence is the authoritative companion of artistry. Without basic competence artistry may be imagined but cannot be realized. On the other hand, when stability of knowledge is welded to certainty of practice, the creative potential of a player has its best hope of realization.

ARTISTRY

Dramatic creation is a recognizable process. It is founded upon an actor's ability to:

1. Understand those portions of the human story that come within his compass and on which he will base his comprehension of characters and situations,

2. Translate what he has come to understand into the language of the stage—that is, into meaningful dramatic action,
3. Develop the power to involve both himself and his audience in the dramatic experience.

When an actor creates well, he affirms man's capacity as the most expressive of all living creatures, as well as his own position as one of the most expressive of all men. Artistry in expression is an accomplishment beyond craftsmanship, but it cannot exist without it. When achieved, artistry is the outcome of inspiration and application. It is the overt demonstration of its creator's finest hopes. It fulfills the desire of those witnesses who cannot themselves achieve it. It richly rewards all who become involved in the dramatic experience.

The actor's powers of expression are unique. They cover a great range and possess tremendous force. By intensive training they can be developed to remarkable reaches of artistry.

Although he has other personnel and theatrical aids to help him, the actor is the drama's master interpreter. As the prime agent of expression in the theatre, his mind and body must be trained to reveal the depth and power and versatility his art demands. As the prime mover in the creation of the dramatic experience, he must assume a great responsibility. The dramatic experience is a shared experience, and as he is willing to give himself to his art, so must he in equal measure be willing to share that giving.

The theatre today needs demonstrable artistry in acting to make it again what it has been at its best, and what it can once more become.

J. B.

Guidelines for Use

The book is divided into four sections with separate but related subject content. The material in Part I, "The Dramatic Experience," is pertinent to the other three parts to the extent that it provides a *raison d'être* for the whole work. What is expressed there gives foundation to each of the other sections.

When acting is taught as a whole, ignoring the parts, its expressive potential is compressed into a lesser compass. Unless later practice discovers the lost areas of learning, an entire professional life can be marked by a less qualitative accomplishment than might otherwise have been possible.

Pantomime is too seldom taught as an acting discipline in our acting classes, and voice training has, in many instances, been surrendered to our increasingly distant cousins in the speech department, where a different orientation prevails. The teaching of movement and voice in drama classes, conducted under theatre conditions and controlled by dramatic specialists, is urgently needed.

If separate classes in pantomime and voice cannot be conducted in a present curriculum pattern, the recommendation is made that an Acting I class balance assignments between these two disciplines. As a matter of practical benefit, it is suggested that the student be directed in a program of voice development before undertaking studies in pantomime. If a beginning is made in voice production (Part III, Chapters 10 through 12), the student has a basis for continuing on his own when his attention moves to the opening chapters on pantomime. Thereafter, balanced progress can be achieved by alternation of emphasis.

In the large number of institutions that require six but offer twelve units in acting, more time and greater concentration is gratifyingly possible, permitting the student to master his basic competence in movement and voice before progressing into the fuller form of acting.

Some instructors will want to make their own way through the book, teaching different classes in different ways. By linking chapters from all Parts in new sequences, they will be able to make the material serve their individual needs.

The selection of practice material for a text in acting poses a special problem. On the one hand, choosing scenes from a limited number of plays permits concentration that leads to studies in depth. On the other hand, there is need for multiple contacts with those masterworks, past and present, that form the heritage of every student of the theatre. The solution sought here was to find a balance between the two approaches.

Three plays, *Hamlet* by Shakespeare, *The Imaginary Invalid* by Molière, and *She Stoops To Conquer* by Goldsmith receive special emphasis. Familiarity with each of these will be of benefit to the student. In addition, since the selections cover sources from the Greeks to the present day, sound knowledge of dramatic literature would be most helpful.

Because the physical activity of acting—that is, demonstrations, exercises, and performances—is heavily concentrated in Parts II, III, and IV, the contents of Part I are set down in essay form, intended to correspond to lecture work in an acting class. Reading and discussion assignments are the purpose here.

The Appendix has a double function. It is offered as a reference work as well as a source of study and practice for those who wish the additional information it provides.

Thanks are expressed to Midge Quennell for illustrations and Marie Sanchez for charts.

Contents

Part IV. *Acting*

Appendices

Part I

The Dramatic Experience

Chapter 1

Expression

Acting is the oldest of the arts. It evolved out of man's desire for a distinctive type of expression. His need for communication was the forcing factor. Before he drew, wrote, danced, or sang, man created the dramatic manner from which the formal act of acting grew.

Organized and disciplined, acting became an honored profession in the theatre of the Greeks. Thus it possesses ancient dignity as an organic part of an institution that was formed before the basic philosophical concepts of the western world were enunciated, before the oldest church was established, and before the oldest judicial system was created. Lifelike in all its aspects, acting is the most pertinent and the most humanly revealing of all the extraordinary actions men term arts.

Acting is a composite art—composed of parts, endowed with a manner, and possessing a purpose. Before the theatre existed, even before the dramatic process was formally organized, the parts were formed, the manner was shaped, and the purpose was in operation. Each actor bears a responsibility to acquire basic competence in each of the parts, to become practiced in the manner, and to understand the purpose.

The Components of Acting

Acting is composed of two parts: pantomime and voice. Pantomime is dramatic expression made evident by positions and movements of the body. Voice is dramatic expression projected by the human tone. Acting is the full form that results from a synthesis of the two.

When functioning as an independent unit, each of these parts can initiate the dramatic process and produce a dramatic experience. Therefore each of them is a discipline in its own right. Before an actor can achieve mastery of the composite art he must be competent in performance in each of the separate forms.

The Dramatic Manner

In the beginning, before the dramatic process could function, it was necessary that an unusual kind of action be created. It had to be one that solved the problem of how to catch and then hold the attention of others as long as the experience was in progress. Fortunately man had within himself a faculty for creating the kind of action needed. This faculty was his dramatic instinct.

The dramatic instinct is rooted in an absolute need to express, and in a sureness within each individual that what must be expressed is important, not only to himself, but also to those around him. Prompted by his dramatic instinct, man evolved the wonderfully efficient form of expression we call the dramatic manner.

In spite of many variations, there is no mistaking this unique type of communication. Compounded of urgency and attractiveness, it has been noteworthy in all places on the globe and at all times and among all peoples. Were a person on a street corner in Chicago or Oslo or Peking to move and speak in this certain way, each onlooker, if asked to describe what he saw, would select the particular word that in his language signified *dramatic*.

This mode of expression has many varying forms, called styles. Each style derives its distinction from the wish of an actor to express himself in a specific way. Since there are many styles in practice today, there is a great variety of ways in which a dramatic experience can be achieved.

THE PURPOSE OF ACTING

The purpose of acting is to produce a dynamic condition that involves all participants with extraordinary intensity. This dynamic condition is the dramatic experience. When the dramatic process, initiated by actors and accepted by an audience, culminates in a commonly felt response, a dramatic experience is born. It is at once the aim and the end of all dramatic activity.

Acting is but one part of the dramatic experience, integral and necessary; and the dramatic experience is but one branch of the large, unique, and important type of human activity called expression.

EXPRESSION

Man is the most expressive of all animals. This quality in him is one of the basic causes for the predominant position he occupies in the life of this world.

His expressiveness is a precious thing. The health of his present personal and group life is dependent upon it. It is the means of release for his thoughts, emotions, and physical sensations. When his expressiveness fails to function or functions badly, the resultant repression and incoherence can cause disruption and violence within him, or between him and other persons and groups. But when expressiveness functions well, it guarantees that one part of his makeup is contributing properly to the health of the whole.

Expressiveness has made possible man's enjoyment of the practicalities of science and the beauties of art. Most important of all, it is the means whereby he makes known to others his sense of relationship to everything in his environment.

Although expression, many-faceted and flexible, is so widely used that it proves its usefulness every day of our lives, its functions can be reduced to two. The first is utilitarian. Its task is to fulfill the communication needs required by the business of living. We talk about our work or our homes, about what we have eaten and how we will clothe ourselves—in short, about the routines of daily life. Were man a work-creature who was content merely to survive, his communicative needs would cease with utilitarian expression.

Once the operational requirements of our lives are satisfied, however, the unused stock of expression is released to serve our creative impulses. We are left free to make other statements and to wonder about them, to express opinions about tides and temples, to see the point of a joke, and to search for the meaningful relationships that exist between man and man.

A human being is and always has been provoked by his surroundings, so much so that he must continually probe and continually comment. This kind of activity results in the creation of ideas and feelings. But ideas and feelings have only partial value when contained within a person. Freely released, they become the foundations for our fields of knowledge—philosophy and religion, science and education, and the wonderful world of art.

It is with this last form of expression, the world of art, that this book is concerned. Art is an action in which a statement about the ordinary in life is made in an extraordinary manner; it is a dynamic experience in which contained knowledge and feeling are released to effect a desired response in another person. Art is a form of expression and art is expressiveness.

To enable him to participate in the exciting activity of art, man has two basic means of communication: he can express himself by using his corporeal body or he can express himself by using objects—making artifacts such as ornaments or instruments and handling or moving them.

When he uses himself, he has four communicative resources at his disposal: position of body, movement of body, tone of voice, and words—

exactly the same means of expression an actor employs in his work. From these four resources, used separately or in combination, the number of communicative patterns that can be made is infinite. From them the art forms of drama, dance, music, and oral literature were created. When man employed objects as a means of expression, the arts of sculpture, painting, architecture, instrumental music, and written literature were born.

Each form of expression, utilitarian or artistic, self-expressive or expressive through objects, serves man in a fulfilling way. A variety of expressive forms is possible, but the use of only one form most concerns us now.

Dramatic Expression

Man is more noteworthy for his human than for his animal condition. Twin characteristics of his human condition are that he must learn and he must comment. In both cases his action is the same: he observes, he reacts to his observations by thinking and feeling, and then he expresses his reactions to the outside world.

Sometimes his comment is a duplication of a fact, a statement that two and two are four or that rain fell during the night or that the grain market went up two points. In other instances the comment is directly related to, but unlike, the fact. It is at once a distortion and an interpretation, a statement that expresses how the commentator feels about the subject, what thoughts and emotions and sensations it engenders in him.

When some ancestor of ours first picked up a charred piece of wood and sketched the outlines of an animal on the walls of his cave home, he was commenting on a fact of ordinary life in an extraordinary way. When another man first raised voice in song because the wonder of a morning was too great to be contained in ordinary speech, he was performing the same kind of act as the fellow in the cave. Each was expressing himself in an artistic manner, one with the aid of an object, the other in pure self-expression.

Probably before either of these actions occurred, an earlier ancestor had in some way learned how to reveal his thoughts and feelings in another extraordinary manner. He didn't sing his feelings or draw his thoughts; he only moved and spoke in a way related to a normal manner of expression, yet one that was not normal at all. Somehow he had found that by distinctiveness of action he could make usual expression unusual, and that with it he could catch and hold the attention of others. In short, he discovered the dramatic manner.

The extra vitality that is in all art was there from the beginning. The movements and tones used were easily recognized. They were man's habits; he had used them all his life. But as he now employed them they were different. They contained contrast to add attractiveness and conflict to add interest, and the elements of timing and emphasis were employed in a style of attack and pause that was arresting, commanding. When he moved and spoke, perhaps he marveled at the convenience he had discovered: he was entirely self-contained, a unit of communication that could perform anywhere, any time. All that was required was the presence of two persons, the performer and someone to watch and listen.

So effective was this form of expression, it became a valued practice. It was so distinctive that a name was given to it. it was called acting. It was man's first nonutilitarian form of communication, which is another way of saying that acting must have been the first art form evolved by man.

THE DRAMATIC EXPERIENCE

The dramatic experience is dramatic expression made whole and brought to completion. Containing all the fundamental ingredients, it is the core of drama. It is the result of the presentation of the greatest play or the smallest class exercise. Its successful initiation is the aim of all theatrical labors. It is what the actor creates and what he offers to his society. It is the foundation of the institution we call theatre.

The motivation for the dramatic experience is the same as the motivation for all expression. Man, curious about all portions of the human story and deeply touched by its pertinence to him, must investigate that story. This causes him to form opinions and to develop feelings that must be expressed. In order that his comment will not be wasted, the actor insures the attention of his onlookers by moving and speaking in the extraordinary manner we have called dramatic.

Now why, out of the many modes of expression open to him, does the actor choose this particular way to achieve the response he desires? Does he have an innate faculty that prompts him to express himself dramatically rather than in some other artistic form? It is safe to assume that he does.

The Dramatic Instinct

Each evening throughout the land groups of people move into theatre auditoriums where they wait expectantly for the dimming of the house-lights and the raising of the curtain. Backstage are other persons who arrived earlier to ready themselves and the stage for the evening's work. Why are the people there, those out front and those backstage? Of the many things the members of either group might have done on that particular evening, why did they choose to come to the theatre? Those who work there need to know the answer to this basic question.

The reason for the presence of the people in the theatre building is that there is a universal instinct for the dramatic that lives, and has always lived in varying degrees, in all peoples on the globe. This dramatic instinct,[1] functioning in man as a conscious or subconscious drive, indicates his belief that his conceptions are worthy of more than usual expression and that by the use of the dramatic he can provoke thoughts and stimulate emotions that lift him and his viewers out of the realm of the commonplace and let all share a rare experience. This unique impulse has been operating from the time the first crude dramas were played around campfire circles down to the time of tonight's opening.

Most people possess the dramatic instinct in some degree. Those in whom it is strongest naturally seek out the work areas of the theatre, there to find the most satisfactory release possible for their compelling urge. Others, lacking as strong a motivation, file into the auditorium seats. Both degrees of the dramatic instinct are necessary, each one a complement to the other, psychologically and artistically.

The dramatic instinct thus impels the two main actions of the dramatic experience: the act of releasing and projecting, and the act of receiving and absorbing. These actions establish the necessary partners in the dramatic experience: the doer and the perceiver, the actor and the audience. The first is the active partner, initiating the creation with all the resources he can command. The second is the passive partner, receiving the creation to the fullest of his capacity. To the latter there comes a single strong pleasure, that of escaping from commonplace thoughts and feelings while held in the grip of an intensified experience. To the creator, however, there is a double gratification, for added to the sensation of release is the particularly human pleasure of receiving a favorable response to an outlay of effort. It is for both of these gratifications that the actor strives, each being essential to his creativity.

The basic reason, then, for the meeting of the doers with the perceivers that has kept the dramatic institution functioning down through

---

[1] The appropriateness of the term instinct may be questioned by those who insist upon a restricted meaning for the word. They, with reason, would limit its application to the natural and unreasoning actions of insects and animals. In recent years studies in psychology and the life sciences have emphasized this use. But terms are the property of no special group, and instinct is a viable word with a long history of diversified employment. Here, instinct signifies a natural aptitude or knack, or better yet, an innate drive or impulse.

the centuries is to provide an extraordinary experience for persons on both sides of the footlights, honest and in depth, lasting from first curtain rise to last curtain fall and, in memory, beyond.

Whatever the type of production, whether it is serious or comic, the experience must be honest, taking its motivation honestly from the materials involved. And it must possess a staying power strong enough to remain and return in memory in the hours and days and months that follow the event.

If the dramatic experience is honest and intense, each person present will feel impelled to do two things: each will want to talk to others of the experience just enjoyed, and each will wish to return to the theatre for more of the same experience. Economically, these are the simplest, strongest, and most basic reasons of all for the presentation of a play.

SUMMATION

A need to be expressive in an extraordinary way is the basic motivation for all that is dramatic. Dramatic instinct prompted the evolvement of the dramatic manner. From the dramatic manner, with its unique ability to catch and hold the attention of others, the art of acting was to grow. It is the act of acting that initiates and sustains the dramatic experience.

The dramatic experience has two participants, the actor and the audience, and two main actions, projecting and receiving. Each participant and each action is indispensable to the other. All the drama the world has known is but an enlargement and refinement of this relationship and practice.

Chapter 2

The Dramatic Form
and the Theatre

THE DRAMATIC FORM

If the dramatic manner was to have more than impromptu use, if it was to be extended and refined into an action capable of expressing a series of coherent thoughts and feelings, a form had to be developed to discipline its use. Whether the users of the dramatic manner created the form that evolved or borrowed it from their nascent fellow artists, the master storytellers of ancient times, we do not know. We do know that by the time history was put on permanent record a similar form was in use by both. From that day to this the form has been an effective means whereby a discipline is applied to the contents—the thoughts, actions, and emotions—of the dramatic experience.

ORGANIZATION

The dramatic form is a unit with three parts: a beginning, a middle, and an end—or in today's terms, an introduction, body, and conclusion.

The psychological motivation for each portion of the unit is easily discernible. The creator, be he actor or playwright, has a foreknowledge of what is to happen in the coming dramatic experience; the perceivers, the audience, have not. Therefore, the first thing the creator must do is inform the audience of the conditions that exist at the beginning of the experience—where, when, who, what, why—so that what is to follow will be understood. This, the *introduction*, provides the necessary expository material. After the opening situation is established, the creator, by some kind of *inciting incident*, involves his *protagonist* (and his audience) in a conflict. The motivation for the protagonist's action is that he, like all persons everywhere, has a desire to fulfill, a goal to attain. His involvement in a conflict comes from the fact that someone else, an *antagonist*, or some other force, either seeks to attain the same goal, or wishes to keep him from doing so. The strivings of the contending parties intensify the action until a decisive point of win or lose for one party or the other is reached. This is the *climax*, the time when the conflict is resolved in favor of one or the other, and victory is matched by defeat. After the climax come the *concluding statements*, which give a summation of the experience. Only then is the audience released from the hold of the drama to return to a normal state of being.

Tying each part tautly to the succeeding one is the element of *desire*, evident with equal intensity on both sides of the conflict.[2] Human desire can focus on any attainable thing, material or spiritual (in some plays it even seeks to make the unattainable concrete enough to be attained), and is the drive that energizes the actions of protagonist and antagonist alike. It is a line that runs through a play from introduction to conclusion and can be traced by the cutting edge of the conflict. In dramaturgical terms it is often called the *spine* of the play.

Organization, it is said, breeds organization. When the time came for the drama to be put into recognizable shape, it was also time to organize the workers into functional groupings. No one man, however protean, could adequately handle all the divisions of the drama. For although the actor came first, and at first his subject materials were simple, the very number of things to be said and the number of persons who wished to say them, or aid in the saying, became so great that a separation of labor was necessary. Thus the organization of the play form was accompanied by an organization of personnel. Out of this division of labor came our present grouping of participants in the dramatic effort—actor, playwright, director, scenic designer, stage manager, and so on.

The dramatic form that easily contains the activity of so many persons is a logically developed and psychologically sound unit. From time to time its length may vary from a mere sketch to that of one, three, or five acts; its contents may change from comedy to tragedy, or its manners from realistic to antirealistic points of view, but the basic structure does not change; it cannot be changed without a change in the dramatic experience itself.

Centuries ago when Thespis or Aeschylus, or some unknown who did not make the history books, first shaped the dramatic experience into the organized form of a play and saw its effect upon an audience, he must have known what the drama was for. Today we would define that form as an organized dramatic experience extended into an action of the length and cohesiveness necessary to express a basic idea or feeling. So effective did this organization of the dramatic experience become that man felt impelled to provide housing for it. He did so, and the house, given the stability of a permanent setting and the dignity of a name, so proved its worth that it became one of his finest creations.

[2] See chart, Part IV, Chapter 21, "Tempo and Climax," p. 335.

THE THEATRE

A theatre is both a physical structure and an institution. Born of the need to provide a home for the dramatic experience, it has sustained itself since its birth because that need persistently asserts itself in each new generation.

The theatre as a physical structure was first created by taking advantage of an accommodation of nature. A hillside curve at the foot of the Acropolis in ancient Athens answered the demand for a favorable physical relationship between actor and audience. As the number of participants in the dramatic experience grew, the size of the theatre was increased. But although it encompassed more and more of its natural surroundings, the structure still answered to the needs of the communal bond that is the core of the dramatic experience.

When the theatre left its natural accommodations to be housed indoors some two thousand years later, it was that same communal need, as much as tradition, that dictated the relationship between the stage and the auditorium.

The theatre as an institution is as old as the theatre as a physical structure. Not only did the dramatic experience motivate the creation of a specific building, it promoted those special responses that endowed that building with an institutional spirit, as varied as its creators' impulses to expression and as strong as their mental and physical and emotional strength could make it.

The theatre has been a remarkably variable institution. At certain times it has been accepted by the society in which it exists as one of the great institutions of that society. At other times it has been wholly rejected by the society around it. When this has been true, the theatre has ceased to function as an institution. In the full swing of history, however, it has never ceased to function for long. The pressing need to be dramatically expressive has always asserted itself, at which point the theatre has come into being once more; it has even been resurrected by the very society that condemned it in the first place.

As a physical structure the theatre has had many shapes. The Greeks drew the first. In all the periods that followed, theatre people either created a new one or imitated one already established. Once set, the form of its theatre was not varied by any period in any appreciable degree—until the modern period came into being. Then, in a rash of eclecticism and originality, the people of modern times both accepted and broke the traditions of the past by employing any shape, new or old, they thought suitable to their needs. As a result, flexibility never before imagined is possible today.

Through the centuries two standard types of theatre shapes have evolved: the circle and the wall. One was the product of a primitive, the other of a sophisticated, society. In the first the actor was located at the center of a circumference of human beings. In the second the player acted with his back against a wall, and all his viewers were grouped in a solid phalanx before him. A third kind of theatre, the horseshoe, is an in-between type, using features of both the others. This last form was much used during the Renaissance, and is increasingly favored today.

The first form, the circle—arena, or theatre-in-the-round—discloses its origin in its shape. The clan circle, bespeaking group strength and solidarity in the unbroken circumference, bespeaking also group interest in its internal life, was a tight band that excluded all that was alien. The focus of attention was always on the core of the circle. With their backs to the world, the clan stared inward to the center, where the known and the unknown, the meanings and the mysteries of the tribe were unfolded. Intimacy, solidarity, concentration—an involvement that ringed and contained the dramatic experience—were the attributes of the circle theatre.

The opposite staging, the wall—the proscenium—came later, when more security had come to society and the protection of the clan was no longer required. Increased security meant an increase in the number of onlookers, and intimacy had to give way to enlargement. Subtleties gone, the performers all faced one way so that the viewers, placed opposite, might directly receive and directly share the dramatic experience. An advantage not possible in the earlier theatre came with this new arrangement. The upstage wall that defined the stage area gave opportunities for decoration. It was only natural that this space should be used to represent the scene of the action. Thus the contrivances of illusion were introduced and exploited.

The horseshoe stage, shaped between the extremes of the other two, was the theatre of the Elizabethans. Here the audience could somewhat enclose the action and thus feel a stronger sense of contact, while at the same time recognition was given to the requirements of an art form in which the performers must appear and disappear within the framework of illusory action. Recognition had also to be given to the fact that the mechanics of artistic illusion required some space for housing.

Whatever the variance of shape, the theatre exists today as the people who work there and the people who come there would have it exist, with the variety and the strength and the depth they are capable of creating and appreciating. The theatre of tomorrow, the theatre of those who are in training today, will exist on exactly the same terms.

Chapter 3

The Actor and the Audience

THE ACTOR

Everyone is a potential actor. In prehistoric times everyone probably did act, but only in the way that most children and many grown-ups act today—incidental players, we might call them, which indicates that then as now individuals did not wish to contain their thoughts and feelings.

Later, in primitive times, a half-actor came into being. The chief, priest, or witch doctor, functioning as a representative of all the tribe, enacted magical or religious ceremonies that were markedly dramatic in nature. Then, with the Greeks, society required the presence of a full-fledged actor, one who stood forth boldly for what he was, a professional player practicing his art within the discipline of an established dramatic form.

THE ACTOR'S ROLE

The actor plays a key role in the presentation of the dramatic experience, which is born in his action. When he performs before an audience, the whole theatre quickens with life and the institution realizes its function.

An actor is a doer. His place of work is a stage, bare of furnishings most of the time. His period of work is divided into two successive steps: the preparation period, which is the time of study and rehearsal, and the presentation period, which is the time of performance. An individual is judged a fine, an average, or a poor actor not by his ability to write or read or talk about acting but by his ability to perform his work successfully during the preparation and presentation periods.

THE ACTOR'S INTEGRATION

When an actor stands on a stage, surrounded by a setting and in a radiance of light, and moves and speaks within a created illusion, he is no ordinary being. He is a complex and intense physical and psychological integration, unique because his livelihood depends upon his ability to create an artistic whole out of many diverse elements. His concern, as broad as the stage and as deep as the auditorium, cannot be for himself alone.

He expresses his integration in his onstage actions, some of which are very lifelike, some of which are more theatre-like. The closer the theatrical need is to its life counterpart in manner and degree, the more the actor uses himself in lifelike terms. The farther away the theatrical need is from its life counterpart, the more the actor employs his totality in theatrical manners and intensities. As he moves from character to character and play to play, he uses both lifelike and theatre-like practices. Realism balances theatricalism. Hamlet matches Harlequin.

An actor is a pressure performer, never laboring except in a crucial time. He does his work in an atmosphere of unrelenting urgency, a concomitant of his enlargement. An error made under pressure is an error magnified. A thousand and one thoughts and experiences have been catalogued and correlated by the controlling mechanisms of his brain, so that in the pressure of each mounting moment of the play's growth he may perform his varied actions with the ease and spontaneity and intensity his art demands.

To achieve his full integration within the confines of the intense experience of acting, an actor must function in several ways: first as a *receptive agent*, sensitive and responsive to his environment, then as a *screening agent* who selects the useful and rejects the useless, then as an *organizing agent* capable of shaping a dramatic creation, and finally as a *releasing agent* who, with the unfolding moments of a rehearsal's or play's progress, performs as required.

An actor is a many-faceted person. He is one individual who must seem to be many individuals. A vitality of body and alertness of mind must show in reflexes capable of instant response to acts properly or improperly done. His sensitivity, set at trigger tension, must alert him to messages of caution or encouragement from all his surroundings. He must be keenly responsive to the growing creation he and his fellows intend to use to enmesh an audience. To be all these things, to do all these things is not easy. The fine actor makes them seem so.

The Actor's Attributes

Certain attributes can be listed as among those most beneficial to the actor.

The Dramatic Instinct • This is an essential qualification for all who would go into the profession of acting. It is just as easy to say that the actor must possess dramatic ability or talent. These are the terms most commonly used. They are good words, but the term dramatic instinct goes deeper and means more.

Dramatic instinct varies in intensity from individual to individual. In some persons it is strong and close to the surface. In other individuals it is weaker. In still others it is strong but hidden, covered with inhibitions. It may disclose itself in different ways: in one case through a penchant for the fun we call comedy, in another by a continual favoring of serious material. In some fortunate individuals the dramatic instinct bears around the full circle, making them equally capable in any dramatic genre. But it must be there in some form and with some strength, or the aspiring individual will never be more than a craftsman.

The dramatic instinct has certain clearly defined characteristics. Its core impulse comes from a need to release, to perform. This is matched by a pressing desire to share the performance with others. It contains a strong sense of conflict. It has vitality, both physical and spiritual. An honest ego hunger is part of it, for it strongly desires its efforts to be approved. It contains a sense of largeness. Enlivened by the basic art impulse, it has a need to go beyond the usual so that an act of expression can reveal significance in both the trivial and the profound. There is a touch of actuality in it, and a touch that goes beyond actuality into the realm of what might be. Within it are elements for which words cannot be found.

The Ability to Acquire Skills • The dramatic experience is an extraordinary action, just as the theatre is an extraordinary place and the audience an extraordinary group of people. These facts deny the actor the ease of being ordinary in his acting.

The basic competence on which all artistry rests is founded in good part on acting techniques. A technique or skill signifies an act of manipulation of oneself or of an object in order to accomplish a dramatic aim. Skill grows from controlled, repeated, and corrected actions. It is the result of experience and criticism.

With any skill or technique the aim is to achieve mastery; and mastery is the result of practice and yet more practice. The value of an acquired skill lies in this: that when mastery has been achieved, the action involving the skill can be performed without conscious thought, thus leaving the player free to concentrate upon his more creative acts. Technique is of greatest value when it can be forgotten.

Sound techniques or skills are the means whereby the creating artist organizes his abilities so that he may derive maximum benefit from them. Technique balances inspiration. It gives an actor command of his dramatic creation. No matter what the variance of pressures from performance to performance, technique is a control unit capable of guaranteeing steadiness and consistency.

Many as the skills are that must be acquired, the new player is not left entirely on his own. Each generation of actors inherits techniques that have been proven in countless performances. Techniques are durable, and with proper use they continually improve.

Intelligence • The scope and variety of today's productions are unmatched in all theatre history. The play-reading the actor attends tomorrow may be for a Shakespearean tragedy or for a modern problem play, for a revival of *She Stoops To Conquer* or for a frothy, sophisticated piece. Today's actor has a great variety of opportunity; therefore he has a great many obligations. No matter what sort of play he is in, every moment he is on stage he has to say something to the audience. It follows that he should know what he is talking about.

Memorization of lines is one of the less critical actions on the actor's list of duties. Memorization is a mental exercise requiring some intelligence, yet a boy who can memorize a speech from *Hamlet* may be a long way from understanding what he has put "within the book and volume" of his brain. Intelligence is required to grasp the thought content of a line as well as the background conditioning out of which the thought grew.

This is not to say that a careful memorization of lines is not important, or that lines should not be memorized exactly; they should be, and with fidelity to each author. But the act of memorization itself should be a subsidiary act (unless passages with difficult technical terms or unusual wording confront the actor), a bonus resulting from the comprehension that comes from thorough study.

The interpretation an actor gives any role can be no more thorough or significant than his comprehension of the character and its environment. It is true that certain aspects of an interpretation will be experienced emotionally and that others will come in the form of physical responses, but the principal concepts that make up an interpretation are the result of intellectual action. The basic concepts for the creation of such widely divergent characters as a Hamlet or a Harvey are determined in large part by the mental capacity and ability of the player.

An actor matches wits with each of the playwrights he plays. The fact that a playwright originated the thought to be expressed does not guarantee that an actor can project that thought by mere repetition of the playwright's words. He must comprehend them as well. It is no light obligation he assumes, that he use his intelligence to match that of a Euripides or a Shakespeare, of an Ibsen or a Shaw.

Imagination • Creative imagination is the supreme activity of the human mind. By it man has been able to make the leap from what is to what ought to be. To do so, a person must use his imagination to proceed from a series of known facts to a series of supposed facts or conditions. These facts or conditions may be close to or far removed from the point of departure.

In some occupations the exercise of imagination is rare. In the profession of acting it is a workaday practice. Where others, as a rule, move from fact to fact, the actor moves from fact to fancy.

Dramatically, the imagination creates a visual image of a thing, a person, or an action that, because it was only suggested in the original, is new to the creator. For example, a description of a prop causes the actor to form an image of that prop long before the article itself appears. In the same vein a group of stage directions is nothing more than a set of conditions out of which the actor must conceive an action. Using these directions as a basis, he imagines the course of action he will follow before he actually does so.

Imagination, the integral portion of the actor's creativity which shapes a concept or a course of action in advance of the event, guides and directs. It conceives interpretations, creates characters, and works out dramatic action in a way that provides the actor with a clear objective, a determinable goal toward which to progress.

Imagination offers that first view of character so necessary to an actor. An imaginative act creates the character image, only partial at first but steadily growing as study progresses. Prince Hamlet, emerging from bits and pieces, will appear in the actor's mind before he is shown by the actor's body; otherwise the characterization will be a chancy one indeed.

Sometimes imagination is thought to be functioning only when reality has been left far behind and flights of fancy have taken over. This concept requires a discussion of the two kinds of imagination that function for all of us: fictional and factual.

1. *Fictional imagination.* Fiction denotes something already removed from fact. If the basis for an act of imagination, itself a mental act beyond fact, rests on fiction, the result is twice removed from the original source. Thus if an actor, creating a character in a pantomime, based his conception not upon what he knew out of his own experience but upon what he had gleaned from someone else's conception, the basis for his creation would be fictional. It is possible that his act could be soundly creative. On the other hand, the process described above is the main source of the cliché and the stock characterization. Many of our dramatic gangsters, prostitutes, and western heroes are so produced.

Fictional imagination operates from assumed rather than proven facts, or from assumptions that are false rather than true. Often fictional imagination creates images that are more a projection of a wish than of sound reasoning, images out of which daydreams are made.

Fictional imagination, if used in the study of primary source material, can have truly deleterious effects: romanticisms and dramatic half-truths, resulting in overly sentimental and melodramatic acting. It is all too easy to allow this kind of imagination free rein in the theatre.

2. *Factual imagination.* As used in the present context, factual imagination operates from a basis of comprehended knowledge. It functions as freely as the other kind, as freely as the imagination must operate, but it is logical, based upon fidelity to primary sources. Factual imagination is related to truth, not fugitive from it. All great playwrights have written on this basis. In this respect the extent to which creative imagination is stretched is not the critical factor in the soundness of its use; the degree of truth in the relationship to primary sources, actions, or facts determines the quality of the product. The characterization of the Stage Manager in *Our Town* is factually sound; so is Hamlet, and so is Peter Pan.

Factual imagination requires more study and greater certainty of comprehension than fictional imagination does. The extra time and effort are responsibilities a good actor willingly assumes. From their assumption will come a sense of strength and authority to support each imaginative act.

Sound dramatic instinct has a strong portion of factual imagination mixed in with its other parts. When the imagination functions with individuality and distinction and in association with truth, it is a sign that a truly creative actor is at work.

Sensitivity • Through his senses an actor establishes contact with the world around him. Through his senses communication with that world is possible. From himself and the world around him the actor gathers all the materials he is to use in his acting.

As an artist, the actor needs sensitivity more than the average person. One of the functions of the artist is not only to survey the society in which he lives in order to discover the significance of each facet of human endeavor, but also to translate that significance into understandable terms for the benefit of those who do not possess his unique ability to perceive nor his ability to put his perception into a tangible art form.

One fact about our sensory apparatus is seldom touched upon. It is not only through intellect that we comprehend the world around us, nor is it by intellect alone that we understand the subject material of a play. We understand hunger by hunger, touch by touch, the delights of the eye by the use of the eye; and we understand love by love. We understand *about* these things with our intellect, but the body also has a way of knowing—without cerebration.

Our senses act and react and the activity is known to us; it leaves its imprint. When a sense has been employed, the experience makes a record of the event in whatever part of the body was involved. This record may be consulted later by recall of the sense data: thus we remember hurt and hunger, health and good tastes, the feel of wind on the face, and what it is like to laugh and cry.

Theatre Sense • A theatre sense affirms the basic communal nature of drama. Innate or acquired, it is essential to good acting. Through it a player effects an amalgam of himself with his material, his fellow players, and his audience. A theatre sense contains awareness of space and time and persons as integral parts of one experience. It is alert to capacities to create and to receive.

Clara Morris, an American actress of three generations past, anticipated our terms when she said: "It is the delicious sixth sense of the actor which permits him to know in the instant before it forms what the coming reaction is to be." To pluck from the air the knowledge that full-throated laughter will fill the theatre before the laughter itself has come is one of the rewarding excitements of acting. Equally rewarding is the sure knowledge of an audience-wide emotional response even before the emotive point in a passage has been reached. When an actor knows that he "has them," it is his theatre sense that tells him so.

A Capacity for Hard Work • In the profession of acting there are hours and days of labor. Before the gratification of a merited curtain call ever comes to the player, weeks of rehearsal will be conducted under the unrelenting pressure a production date always imposes. To sustain the long hours, to endure the burden of repetition as a scene is done over and over again, to bear the offstage waiting—all this demands physical and nervous stamina in abundance.

If a company has a marked capacity for hard work, it realizes a benefit from the rehearsal period that can be obtained in no other way. And in the daily rehearsal stint, concentrated work stretched over the hours produces a momentum that literally accumulates benefits as it moves along. For the conscientious actor there is no escape from the large amount of hard work involved in his professional labors.

Physical Appearance • Good height and nice physical proportions are an asset to any actor. Each should strive to develop and use whatever physical advantages he has.

Where there is too much variance from the norm in height and weight, something of a limitation is imposed upon the scope and variety of parts available. The person who is too short or who is overly tall, or who has a problem with weight, should bear this in mind and work to develop his potential within the limits of his capability. Such a person, however, will do well to recall that in the long history of the stage there have been many players who made a good physical appearance a matter of relative unimportance when it was measured against true greatness in acting.

THE AUDIENCE

An audience is in the theatre because it has its proportionate share of the dramatic instinct and wishes its proportionate share of the dramatic experience. It is the necessary other half of the theatre's human complement, the receptive, malleable part, willing and waiting to be acted upon, welcoming the experience. Larger only in physical size to the stage personnel, it comes into the theatre seeking participation and identity, willing to suspend for a time a belief that only reality is dependable, substituting the conviction that truth and beauty can be created by man as well as by nature.

THE ACTIVE AUDIENCE

An audience is the principal reacting agent in the theatre. Its response has both an outer and an inner orientation. The outer involves such obvious demonstrations as laughter, applause, and tears. The inner is the more active, so active indeed that could we but glance inside a spectator at any time during a performance, we would see multiple mental, sensory, and emotional reactions flare into being, touching and augmenting each other before dying to make way for others. All art, to be art, must create a response in the perceiving noncreator before the experience can come into being.

Because of this inner activity, audiences are capable of performing some of the actor's work for him. One of the most energetic activators of response in any art is the power of suggestion. No thought or emotion sent out by the players retains its original shape when it strikes its target in the audience. As soon as the message reaches its mark, a process of growth occurs within the spectator. Thoughts and emotions immediately enlarge themselves in direct proportion to the force of the suggestion. This is the perceiver's way of sharing in the dramatic experience. Without an opportunity for such participation, his seat in the auditorium is sure to remain empty.

Many engaging and appealing subjects are presented in the theatre.

But unpleasant events also take place onstage, and evidently the audience comes to see as much of one as it does of the other.

Yet in life we avoid unpleasantness when we can. We dislike pain, and we would escape from sadness and sorrow. We dread the shock of disappointment or death and deplore feelings of despair. But in the theatre all of these and many more are employed continuously as subject materials for our plays. Indeed, the greatest dramas of all time are filled with just such matter.

This is a question for both portions of the theatre, the stage and the house, to ask and to answer: Why do we seek, even with avidity, these experiences of frustration and defeat, of denial and agony? What is pleasant in the Oedipus story, with its incest and the physical agony of self-inflicted blindness? Is the island of loneliness on which Hamlet dwells attractive enough to make us wish to share it with him? Is it entertaining to witness Blanche DuBois in *A Streetcar Named Desire* break contact with reality to retreat to the seemingly safe world of insanity, or to watch the pathetic disintegration of a family in *Long Day's Journey into Night?* But we go to the theatre, all of us behind the curtain and out front, and have been doing so for centuries, to witness the very things we would avoid in life. Why?

In the theatre we enjoy without having to pay for the enjoyment; we satisfy in abundant measure our insatiable appetite to experience multiple life situations without risk. The tears we shed for Hamlet are easy payment because no real Hamlet died. Stopping short of reality, we stop short of permanent suffering. We enjoy everything in the experience but the terrible cost of it, even to the extreme of dying with Juliet or Romeo while treasuring the life within us. Thus we can participate in the fullest and most dreadful experience with safety, and can release ourselves, give ourselves completely over into the experience, because what we do is in the nonbinding realm of make-believe.

The Audience and the Theatre Sense

A theatre sense keeps a player in immediate contact with all elements of the dramatic experience, including actor-audience relationships.

The audience is a teacher. As a responsive mass, the people in the house constantly instruct the players about the effectiveness of all that transpires on stage. In building his library of acting experience, an actor benefits by being receptive to each bit of instruction that comes from out front. Consequently, one of his principal tasks is to learn to read audience responses. He does this best in either of two vantage points: onstage or at the back of the house.

When at work onstage a player can sense responses of all kinds, small as well as large. Those manifested by overt action—such responses as laughter and tears—are relatively easy to read. In addition, the applause at scene ends or act breaks can tell an actor much about the success of his playing. Polite applause differs from friendly applause, and both differ from the kind of handclap that identifies itself with the play in attitudes varying from subdued appreciation to energetic enthusiasm.

Subtle reactions, attitudes a member of the audience experiences during performance without an outward show, are sometimes difficult to detect. In the beginning, a player may have trouble reading these; but it is a mass response that occurs out front, so a reaction that may be subtle when restricted to one individual becomes more obvious when registered as a group experience. In addition, a player knows from personal observation that he can detect changing attitudes in a companion even though no outward show of any kind is made. All persons are sensitive in this respect, the actor most of all. Indeed, a theatre sense can be developed to the extent that a player is aware of subtle reactions from individual seats scattered at random throughout the auditorium.

The rear of the house presents a learning post for an actor second in value only to the stage area itself. To an alert observer, the backs of heads are uncommonly expressive. From the back of the auditorium a player can see stage performance and audience reaction as one unified action. The entire dramatic experience is directly before him. Observing performance after performance of the same play, he has an opportunity to assimilate the very essence of the theatre sense.

When this occurs, the player will realize that this is an understanding that embraces his whole being. He will grasp certain elements of the theatre sense in a rational manner; consequently he will be able to talk about them and explain them to others. He will experience additional elements emotionally. Involvement will be one of these, an inclusion so strong he will thereafter comprehend what it is like to be multiplied by all the people in the house. He will sense other things, grasp intangibles in such a way that he becomes as aware of the mass consensus as if the audience spoke aloud and in chorus. When he knows these things, he will know what the soldier knows about battle after the battle is over, or what the surgeon knows about the unknowable in life after he has seen and felt it come and go in the operating room.

In his way the actor will know about the dramatic experience. Perhaps his present knowledge will associate itself with an earlier knowledge and he will find himself with a dim sense of race consciousness, grasping what group closeness meant long ago when his drama was first forming.

He will understand that his particular kind of expression is one that can pry open and possess. He will know when an active element awakens an inactive one and imposes its will upon it, and he will understand the fusion that follows. He will take this knowledge to every audition and rehearsal and performance for the rest of his life, making him one of those who hold a secret that has special properties.

Chapter 4

The Acting Process

Preparation to act and acting itself are part of one process. The process, indigenous to all methodology, passes through three coordinated phases:

1. *Comprehension,* in which the source materials of acting are gathered, assimilated and comprehended—an intellectual process, requiring time for study.

2. *Translation,* in which the comprehended materials are translated into meaningful dramatic action—a physical process, requiring rehearsal time.

3. *Creation,* in which meaningful dramatic action is released and projected so that an audience may share in the dramatic experience—a physical and spiritual process, occurring at performance time.

COMPREHENSION

THE NATURE OF KNOWING

There is a difference between *knowing about* a subject and *knowing* the same subject, and the difference is a matter of both time and degree. Knowing about comes first in the learning process, but knowing possesses the greater depth and substance. To an actor, knowing about is a preliminary action necessary to accomplishment; but to the same actor, knowing is doing.

A serious musician learns about music in general and his instrument in particular even as he addresses himself to the practice of it. He continues the process of learning about his subject as a preparatory step to each new phase of his practical study. As his mastery of the parts builds into artistry in the whole, his *knowledge* encompasses and surpasses, in depth and scope, his *knowledge about* his subject.

An identical pattern is followed in the study of acting. In Part I of this book we learn about the process of being dramatic—why acting came into being, for what purpose it is used, how it has been organized, and

25

what returns its practice can offer. In Parts II, III, and IV the concentration will be upon knowing—knowing as doing.

The subject content of the *knowing about* phase, comprehension, is best indicated by defining two terms: *assimilation,* meaning to take up and incorporate—that is, to gather needed information and to arrange it, organized, in its proper place in the brain; and *comprehension,* meaning to understand the significance of the facts that have been accumulated and arranged.

There are three steps in the phase we call comprehension.

1. The first is concerned with the assimilation of such general information as is required to signify that an actor is expert in his knowledge about his subject. This involves nothing less than a study of the culture out of which the dramatic process grew and in which it presently functions: an involvement, in short, that indicates a need for what is termed a liberal education, with its disciplines of thought, its interrelation of subject to subject and of period of time to period of time.

2. The second step is less broad in nature but is in no way small or limited. It is concerned with the acquisition of theories and facts directly related to the act of acting, a process that is immediately in progress.

3. The third step deals with the problems of preparing a specific acting project. To this accomplishment much of the material to come is directed.[3]

The Actor's Educational and Cultural Background

Gone is the day when an actor could exist with a limited amount of knowledge in a narrow field of endeavor. Every play he is associated with will deal with some aspect of present or past culture; therefore he must know as much as possible of the conditioning factors that surround his efforts. The range of parts for which he can compete would amaze such an old stager as Colley Cibber of eighteenth-century London. If the common-sense dictum that the player must know what he is doing when he creates any one of many varied characters is accepted, it follows that the actor must take whatever opportunity is offered him to gain the best educational and cultural background possible.

---

[3] In acting, assimilation has taken place when the thought impulse and the physical action following it are unified, the thought and the act being two integral parts of one process. It is only for purposes of study that they are treated separately. This separate treatment presents a problem of which the actor should be aware. When taken out of the classroom or rehearsal hall and organized in book form, the divisions between the interrelated steps of comprehension, translation, and creation suggest a separation that sometimes is artificial and contrary to actual practice. When this is known in advance, the forced separation can be tolerated.

Man is the proper study of mankind, and in no case is this more apt than for people of the theatre, whose preoccupation is with man's own story. The actor is a humanist in the most challenging sense of the word, the present and past doings of his fellows holding the core of his interest. It is important to the player, whose concern is with the already organized ideas set forth in a play, to be able to make background studies in history and literature, social customs, costumes, and any other subject that comes within his compass.

THE ACTOR'S PREPARATION

To initiate the actual process of acting by moving and speaking dramatically, the actor has two sources to guide him and prompt his practice:

1. The impulses of his dramatic instinct, which, more unconsciously than consciously, impel him to move in this manner and to speak with that interpretation.[4]

2. The thoughts—we call them theories—he has gathered from observation or instruction, which give him a definite direction in moving and speaking.

Although the theory aspect must of necessity be emphasized in a book such as this, both sources are employed in every phase of the actor's work and are taken account of in the pages ahead.

Primary Sources • The process of comprehension is immediately concerned with sources of information. Of the many available, one source is basic. Always original in nature, it is called a primary source.

If a historian were doing research on Napoleon and came across letters written by the hand of his subject, he would label such information primary source material. Were he to study what someone else said about those letters, he must label such information secondary source material. The actor, like the scholar, recognizes primary material as the basic source of information; there is as much truth in art as there is in scholarship, albeit of a different kind. In acting, the reference is not to letters and documents as much as it is to acts and facts in nature, which is the ultimate reference point for all art.

Each actor is his own best primary source. The very process of living creates a solid continuity of experience that stretches unbroken from his birth to the present moment. This block of experience comprises a rich account on which drafts can be drawn at will, if he knows what his

---

[4] It should be noted that dramatic instinct is not infallible. Depending upon previous conditioning, it is possible that its promptings can produce as much bad work as good.

account holds. Each actor leads a particular existence, which is one portion of the total human story. Fed into each separate portion is a constant stream of experiences that match in kind the experiences of parallel lives. An intimate knowledge of the experiences accumulated in his own account is the means of understanding the contents in the accounts of his fellows. But he must first know what is held in his own.

For the actor, the use of primary-source material is constant. His intellect and his sense memory are his research agents. Using them he can pry back into his record of experiences to obtain present readings of past thoughts and emotions, the significance of which he might not have noted at the time of their occurrence. Lacking a past specific experience to fit a present specific need, he can rely upon other experiences similar in kind, doing the transposing himself.

Closely related to the actor's own primary source is the reservoir of experiences contained in the lives of those persons with whom he has been intimately associated—his family and his friends. Although these lives might mirror in detail much of his own, they will also contain material that can serve to extend his.

Secondary Sources • The actor also turns to sources outside himself and his associates to gain information. Every theory or motivated idea that aids good practice in acting is relevant and worth seeking. These ideas can come from association with actors whose abilities and skills are well developed. They can be found in classrooms where competent teachers serve as guides. They can be gleaned from the many good books in the field.[5]

Plays themselves often provide good secondary source material and, on occasion, material that has primary source value. Shakespeare and the great Greek playwrights are cases in point: much about manners, family relationships, or other such instructive matter can be found in their works. In this sense, plays differ in value: Jonson is much more revealing of his time than the slightly earlier Marlowe. In addition to the above, an author's description of a character or a set or his instructions for stage business are always of direct and immediate use to the player.

Works dealing with the lives of famous actors and actresses of former times, many of which are unfortunately out of print and sometimes difficult to obtain, will reward careful study. To read Colley Cibber on the art of Thomas Betterton is to read about acting great enough to serve for any time or any period. To discover what close observers had to say about the wonderful versatility and the unusual power possessed by David

[5] Few in number at first, books and textbooks on acting have appeared with increasing frequency in the last decade, until now the number is sufficient to require a separate, comparative study and cannot be given full treatment here. At the head of any list, of course, must stand the work of the master, Constantine Stanislavsky.

Garrick is to discover an inspiration that needs no more than the next rehearsal period to be put to use.

In this connection it is now almost axiomatic that every acting student be thoroughly grounded in all phases of theatrical history. It is important for him to know plays and playwrights and theatres from the past to his own day, and for him to know about the cultures that produced them.

The Specific Project

The last phase of the comprehension period occurs when a specific project has been chosen for presentation purposes. It may be a minor project, such as a scene done as a class assignment, or a major one—a full-length play designed for public presentation. Whether the project is minor or major, a simple yet adequate approach can be followed by the actor in each case. This approach can be developed into a habitual action so strongly established the actor automatically follows it whenever a new project is undertaken. Research is the matter of this approach.

Research • The play, the character, and the situation are the subject matter that motivate the institution of a program of research.

It is at once obvious that certain parts and certain plays, such as pieces designed for an evening of light and superficial entertainment, require little or no research. But as the pieces and the characters grow in strength and scope and depth, the research requirement placed on the player also grows. In the form of a series of questions, here are points with reference to playwright, character, and situation that could properly motivate research.

1. Is there anything in the life of the playwright that will provide a fruitful subject for research, whether for general or for specific bits of knowledge?

2. Is it as necessary to study the lives of some playwrights as it is those of others? With no disrespect to present-day authors, is it as necessary to study the life of George M. Cohan as it is to study the life of Shakespeare, of George S. Kaufman as of Molière?

3. Is there anything in the times and the conditions under which the playwright composed his work that can become usable knowledge for the actor?

4. Is there any knowledge to be gained from the form of the author's composition—verse or prose, original or derivative, neoclassical or romantic—that will aid the actor's creation and delivery?

5. What is established about environment in the play itself? What is said about the character by the playwright and by the other characters and what, in specific detail, does the character say and do?

6. Is the character fictional or historical, and how much of the truth of the actor's portrayal is dependent upon his knowledge of the character, its background, and place in time and locality?

7. Is the nationality of the character (Cyrano, Eliza, Medea) a matter of importance in interpretation?

8. Does the character's age differ from that of the player, and does the difference require additional information?

9. Does the character's occupation require any special knowledge or skills that must be demonstrated to the audience during performance?

10. Is the character's personality of sufficient variation from that of the player creating the role to demand an increase of the player's comprehensive knowledge?

11. Will the clothes worn by the character demand special handling?

12. Will the properties used by the character—swords, drinking glasses, needlework frames, laboratory instruments, and so forth—also demand special knowledge and special handling?

13. Must the character believe in certain subjects not commonly accepted today, such as elements of the supernatural—for instance, witchcraft, a belief in the divine right of kings, predestination, and so forth?

14. What customs of conduct are usual for the character but unusual for the actor?

15. Does the setting of the play cause climate to be an important factor in its development?

16. Do buildings and furniture, their materials and construction, have a bearing upon the character's actions?

17. Is the set itself, a scene in a court of law, a battlement, an old attic, one with which the player is thoroughly familiar?

These questions and others become increasingly important to the actor as he undertakes to present truthfully scene after scene and play after play. As the scope of his interests grows, so will the areas of his research grow, his investigations leading him to a close and penetrating study of himself and those primary sources around him, as well as taking him into the stacked shelves of libraries to utilize the information gathered there.

A general, but not invariable, line of procedure for each research project might follow a course such as this:

1. A study of the whole script, not just the actor's part, for the information it provides.

2. A study of the life, the times, and the conditions of composition of the playwright.

3. A study of the historical setting or settings of the play, together with all pertinent factors related thereto—that is, dress, manners, social position, and so on.

4. A study of the historical character as recorded in the pages of history with the appraisal of its characteristics as given by various writers. If the character is fictional, a study of a similar character who actually lived can be of equal value.

The Use of Facts • Because dramatic work is more than a factual representation of history, facts themselves are not interpretive elements. They form only the basis for an interpretation. Every creative artist distorts the basic facts from which he begins his work in some manner. His act of distortion, if his work is honest, is not a bad act from the standpoint of morality or truth, for the distortion indigenous to any act of interpretation is a proper and necessary function of the art process. Each artist has a fundamental right to his own variation; his work becomes a poor work in this respect only if his distortion is unwarranted or too radical. But the facts he has uncovered are aids and not ends in themselves.

Intent • Before any member of a group begins his research, a unified concept regarding the purpose behind the scene or play to be done must be established in the minds of all. Only then will each individual know what specific experiences he is to look for among his primary sources, and what kinds of information he is to seek in his other research.

Because there is always a purpose behind any dramatic project, there is always some kind of intent present. This fact does not mean that the intent must be profoundly significant. The reasons for doing a scene or a play can be as varied as the different kinds of dramatic expression, as varied as the reasons that prompt individuals of all kinds to want to be dramatically expressive. Frivolous or profound, the important thought in this context is that the actor needs to know and be able to state clearly just what the intent is.

The play *The Imaginary Invalid* by the French playwright Molière provides an illustration of how a production's intent influences the research that must follow. Several legitimate variations of intent in presentation are possible with this play.

One production may present the piece as a socially satiric comedy, much as it is performed by the *Comédie Française* today. Another might emphasize the play's relationship to the Italian *commedia dell'arte* by giving it a lusty staging in broad farce; research would indicate that employment of such a style would be historically proper.

Action and line delivery, which in the first production derived their

motivations from less broad characterizations and less sweeping interpretations, would lose their restraint with the change of emphasis to permit comic *lazzi* (individual bits of stage business) and the knockabout
of slapstick. The character of the costumes worn would undergo a
change, and so would the wearing and handling of them. Even the
makeup and wigs would have to be altered, and yet the essential characteristics of each genre portrayed would still adhere to fact.

To strengthen the point regarding intent, another kind of production
of *The Imaginary Invalid* can be suggested: to present the piece as a historical play in its own time and setting, mounted, dressed, and acted as
a French Renaissance comedy, as we today think it might have been
done by the people of the seventeenth-century Parisian stage.

With this purpose in mind, the focus of attention in the research to
follow alters radically from either of the preceding suggestions. Who
were the players in Molière's company? What was the style of acting
then in vogue? Where was the greater emphasis placed, upon stage
movement or delivery of lines? What was the relationship of players to
other players, of players to audience? How was the stage constructed, and
what were the seating arrangements for the audience? What kinds of
scenery, properties, and lights were used?

Three productions have been suggested, each with a distinct individuality. Three purposes have supplied a slight or a radical variance of approach to the problem of research. Much of the information assimilated
would be useful in all three productions; some of it would have a specialized application; all of it would serve to increase and give substance
to the work of the actor.

The following plays, period and modern, are suggested as suitable
sources for those who would implement the theory content of this section
with practical projects: *The Crucible,* by Arthur Miller; *The Devil's
Disciple,* by G. B. Shaw; *The Rivals,* by R. B. Sheridan; *The Road to
Rome,* by Robert E. Sherwood; *Golden Boy,* by Clifford Odets; *The
Chairs,* by Eugene Ionesco.

TRANSLATION

The translation period is the time when comprehended knowledge
and instinctual feeling are translated into meaningful dramatic action.
Essentially a rehearsal period, it overlaps the previous period's work. It
is a period in which the mental and physical faculties of the player are
meshed in coordinated activity. It is a time of learning by doing, when
skills are set as habits and creative abilities are developed along practical
lines.

This is the period that occupies the actor during most of his professional life, in daily rehearsals that stretch into weeks and months and years of activity. The time of study—comprehension—and of performance—creation—are short by comparison.

During this period multiple ideas are translated into action. Some of the ideas are small, so small they can be reckoned trivial. Some are large, as large as human creativity can cause them to be. None are petty, and none are unimportant. All indicate that the translation period is a period of preparation for performance in which each act should be performed in the manner of the final form as much as possible.

As a result of centuries of practice by untold thousands of actors there has been a gradual accumulation of knowledge about the processes of dramatic translation. It is there for today's actor to use. But one thing must be certain: although a creative idea or a bit of technique may have come from someone else, when an actor uses it he must make it as thoroughly his own as though no one else had ever thought of it or practiced it before.

Dramatic Action

It was noted in Chapter 1 how and why dramatic expression came to be used, and something was said about its manner. In the comment was an implication that, in the motivation to be dramatic, the dominant factor is a desire to express oneself in a manner calculated to arrest and hold attention.

Dramatic action is obvious because its basic purpose is to be obvious. In this respect everyone practices it, freely at a birthday party, in a restrained manner at a funeral service, vigorously on a political platform, romantically in a lovers' quarrel. In each of these instances certain constants can be detected. Always there is heightened action, in the sense that a distortion of normal movement is present. Always there is more than usual energy in it, a fact that is true even when the activity is subdued. Always the feeling is intense beyond the average. But does this mean that everyone can act? In an everyday sense, the answer is yes. In a theatre sense, the response is exactly the opposite.

With the organization of the drama into play form and the institutionalizing of the building that houses the activity, there arose, from need, the additions and the limitations that the form of the drama and the shape of the building imposed. These impositions are responsible for the element of convention that is in all acting and indicate why it is that in the proper sense of the word only certain persons can act.

To some, the term convention may be objectionable because it connotes something imposed, restricted. But such additions and limitations are in all art forms. We speak of the conventions of the ballet, classical or modern; yet we feel or see no loss of effect. Painting is a convention in that all painters, regardless of school or movement, must deal with colors put on a surface with an object. Whether anyone who can act— even act well—in a life situation can act well onstage in a professional sense is a moot question. Our answer is yes, if he can become expert in the conventions of acting; if he cannot, our answer is no.

Meaningful Dramatic Action

To all who have experienced it, the gratification of being dramatic is well known. To take a strong dramatic position feels good physically, emotionally, and mentally. The sensation of moving dramatically is most pleasant, and a strong dramatic tone pleases our ears. But the gratification of creating a pleasing action is not sufficient basis, in itself, for what man intended acting to do. The dramatic manner evolved as a means of expressing something besides itself. The subject may be comic or tragic, flippant or profound, yet it must be present to give acting a reason for use. This is the concept that motivates our emphasis on the full phrase *meaningful dramatic action.*

For any kind of action to be meaningful, it must fit a form of expression. No good art form reproduces nature, but all art forms make a comment about it; and the manner of the comment is determined in part by the nature and the shape of the form. Meaningfulness in an art form signifies that a recognizable change from nature has taken place.

This requires the actor to ask, Under the altered conditions of the theatre, what altered movement or tone will be most like the life movement or life tone it is taken from? Or, to break the restrictions of severely realistic acting, What stage movement or tone will most meaningfully express the dramatic concept to be conveyed to the audience?

Because the extraordinary statement of the dramatic experience is made in an extraordinary place, a whole new language of movement and tone is involved, no small part of which is determined by the mechanics of stage delivery, cues, sight lines, and other such considerations. It is to be expected that some parts of the new language will seem strange and awkward, and for that reason the student may be inclined to hold back in his effort. If so, he should recall how unnatural it was to drive a car when first he tried, or how awkward certain steps seemed when he was learning to dance.

For example, one of the first abnormalities to strike the beginning actor's attention is that he cannot speak in a truly conversational tone onstage. The way he will speak, however, is such as to make the audience believe that the talk truly is conversational. He will soon note, too, that he never talks onstage as he does in life. Life talk halts and wanders, is desultory, gets mixed up. On the other hand, stage talk is selected, disciplined speech, even when it creates the illusion of being halting, wandering, and mixed up. One of the fundamental purposes of acting training is to learn to be expressive in the new language of acting, some of which is close to nature and what the player already knows and some of which is far removed from nature and his own experience.

The Means of Expressing Meaningful Dramatic Action

As the actor strives to develop to the full his ability to execute meaningful dramatic action, he must look to his means of expression. In this respect he is fortunate. Topping all other tools of communication is the physical form of the actor himself. As a functioning organism he, with all that is contained inside and all that appears on the surface, is nature's greatest instrument of expression. As in no other instance, the success or failure of his growth will depend upon his capacity to sharpen, focus, control, and vary what he can do with what he is.

Implementing practice in meaningful dramatic movement are the plays of today and of yesterday, already tested for worth, and available by the hundreds. On these pieces and their characters the actor will be constantly employed, in class or in public. So rich is the heritage that the problem becomes merely one of choice.

A player can do no better than to align himself with greatness in this time of growth. No actor can call himself great until his merit has been measured against the quality of the great ones of the past. From the time of the Greeks to our own period, masterpieces have been steadily stockpiled. One of the properties of any masterpiece is that it can sustain multiple ownership. Once they were written and given to the world, *Hamlet* and *Oedipus*, *Cyrano* and *The Imaginary Invalid*, *The Way of The World* and *The Cherry Orchard* were all susceptible to possession by anyone who would make them his. In this case familiarity can breed competence rather than contempt.

Relationships • As human beings, we know the meaning of movement and tone—have known it for centuries, as will be pointed out in detail in the sections on pantomime and voice. And we also know or will learn how to be dramatically effective. But how to combine these two mutually supportive elements so that the audience not only attends on all action, but also is involved in its significance, is the problem we face now. Most problems have keys that unlock their meanings. This one has, and it is to be found in the term *relationships*.

If relationships were threads, each of us would be as trussed as Gulliver was in Lilliput, one thread extending from us to every object or person in our environment. Wholeness is the thought here: we exist completely, in all our parts, and we relate to the whole of our environment as it exists in every part. This is an unalterable condition of living. Our conscious mind is not always aware of this, but other parts of us are, because being aware is one of the facts of existence.

Relationships exist everywhere and all the time, but we are conscious of only some of them. They are the relationships that give exact meaning to our standing in our environment at any given moment. Every object, animate or inanimate, demonstrates this fact. The recognition that relationships exist, together with the ability to act upon the information relationships supply, is one of the reasons for man's survival and progress. We can determine what the meaning of relationships is:

1. By the condition of the object's position. For instance, a tree is healthy and stands erect; or it is old or blasted by a storm and leans; or it has been made to fall or has fallen through death and lies on the ground. A man stands proudly erect; or he crouches by a wall; or he bends in servitude; or he wraps his arms around his body for protection against the cold; or he turns against the wind; or he sprawls grotesquely in death. A bird drowses, a dog sits up on his haunches, a building tilts, a hungry child stands with hand extended. All these positions are recognizable and knowable.

2. By an object's juxtaposition to everything in its environment. A tree is rooted to and in the earth; it bends before the wind; it alters its shape because of a nearby cliff. Inside or outside, a man has a relationship to his home: he sprawls on or he stays off his lawn; he rests his feet on a table or keeps them on the floor; he sits on the edge of a chair or relaxes in its depth; he puts his head down over his food as he eats or he sits erect and brings the food to his mouth. He is related to the persons in his house, and to persons everywhere by his closeness to or his distance from them, by his turning toward or away, and by the intensity of his movement.

3. By how an object or person is touched and handled. A hammer is held and a nail is pounded. One manner of execution would reveal a boy clumsily building his first birdhouse, showing his strength, his expertness and his desire. Another would exhibit a skilled carpenter at work, showing his strength, expertness, and desire. A girl touches a boy, a woman sits in a chair by a fire, a man drives a new car, a student bites on a pencil, an old man pulls on a pipe, a fighter hits—all reveal a mean-

ing growing out of a demonstrated relationship through the manner of contact.

Attitude is a prime ingredient in the establishment of a relationship, and it exists because of the impulse, desire, or intent of its owner. This brings us full circle in our reasoning. An instinct, a wish, or a purpose determines how we feel toward an object or a person. We take a position, make a motion, utter a tone to the other thing or individual, and this, in turn, indicates the relationship that exists. When relationship is made known in theatrical terms, a meaningful dramatic action is born.

The practical projects of translation form the contents of Parts II, III, and IV.

CREATION

The first phase in the act of acting, comprehension, dealt with the assimilation and understanding of the knowledge necessary to learn to act and to make of acting a purposeful human endeavor. The second, translation, spoke of the engaging process whereby the instinct to be expressive could be canalized into the unique form of meaningful dramatic action. These two phases were but preparatory steps for the third, creation. With this the cycle is complete and the aim of all our labors, the dramatic experience, comes into being.

In creating the dramatic experience our concerns are threefold. One, that the preparation has been thorough to the extent that what is to be projected from the stage is properly organized and meaningfully stated in dramatic terms. Two, that the amount of energy contained in the activity is sufficient to meet theatre requirements. Three, that the magnitude of the statement matches the demands of the dramatic form.

THE CYCLE ENDS WITH CREATION

Man cannot be secretive about himself; what he knows will out. Ever since he has been articulate, certain members of his species have been driven by a double impulse. These are the people who have never been able to rest content with the obvious, who must delve under the surface appearance of things for whatever significance lies there. Then they must make a comment on what they discovered. Scholars, we call them, and teachers, and artists; and such is the double power of their drive, they cannot rest content with the mere statement; they must make their comment in the presence and for the benefit of others. And further, they ardently desire that their comment will challenge, stimulate, and please.

The actor, as artist, is one of this group. Not only is he driven to make meaningful the material with which he deals, but he is also compelled to present it to others, for he cannot rest easy when his work is self-contained. He desires these others to hear him, to pay attention to him, and to be impressed by him to the point of belief. He is one whose drive is so strong that he must rely upon man's first and most emphatic means of expression: position, movement, tone, and words.

ONSTAGE

Dramatic creation can come into being any time an actor stands before an audience. Let the audience be small or large, let the situation be in the intimacy of the classroom or on the public stage, let the time be the length of a short scene or of a long play—if the actor can successfully bring into being the necessary dramatic conditions, then dramatic creation is possible.

The call, "Places!" has a strong emotional connotation for an actor. As a preparatory signal to go to work, it always induces an increase of nervous excitement. When this occurs, the player should remember that the heightened emotional state that envelops him is his alone; it does not belong to the character he is to portray. His nervousness is a trade secret, to be shared only with his fellow players.

Experience will teach him that nervousness reveals itself in a raised vocal pitch pattern, a noticeable increase in tempo, and an abnormal increase or decrease of vocal force, and that it additionally manifests itself in muscular tenseness. Aware of these things in advance, the player can overcome them by performing a set of warm-up exercises and by making certain during the long translation period that he has mastered his means of dramatic expression.

UNIFYING THE AUDIENCE

After "Places!" comes the single call, "Curtain!" It opens, and for the actor and the audience creation begins. This is the time the actor acts; before this he has been preparing to act. This is his time of climax. Now he, the creative actor, is a releasing agent, pouring out in controlled and organized form all the thoughts and emotions, the skills and instinctive responses he has selected as pertinent to this particular effort.

To insure that his hopes are thoroughly realized, the actor has two jobs to do at the same time. One is to present the play's introductory material to the audience. He is aware of this and the audience expects it. The other he alone knows about. To do it the actor must compel each member of the audience voluntarily to surrender his individuality, to become one compliant unit of a mass, a mass that is willingly responsive to direction from the stage.

This is a skirmish that must be waged and won by the actor with each curtain's opening. He has on his side his abilities and skills and a foreknowledge of the situation. He also possesses dominance of position, for he is on an accentuated level that is either raised or lowered above or below that of the audience. Furthermore, he stands in a concentration of light, while his viewers sit only in reflected glow. Finally, and of great importance to him, he has the wishes of his audience to sustain him, for the majority of the spectators have come to the theatre in the expectation that this very experience will be theirs. Arrayed against the actor in this skirmish is the inertia of the audience.

Willing though the majority of the audience may be, the players still need a great deal of skill and energy to bring about a surrender of individuality. It requires effort and adroitness to cause the young man in Row 3, Seat 4, to give as much thought to the play as he is giving to the young lady by his side, or to compel the community's social leader, whose new fur stole nestles so conspicuously around her shoulders, to give undivided attention to the play, or to force the businessman to forget about notes due, or to make the housewife stop fretting about the possibility of a stove left going at home. These are the odds the actor works against, and these are the odds he must win against, if the full sharing of the dramatic experience is not to fall short of realization.

There is an incongruity between physical and spiritual fact in the theatre. It was said earlier that an audience should be an extension of the player. In its purely physical sense, the picture of an audience of several hundred persons being an extension of one actor onstage is a disturbingly disproportionate one. Physically the audience becomes a gross appendage, a growth that dwarfs the host; like an ugly wen it distorts proportion and nowhere permits beauty in the relationship.

But the actor is more than a physical fact. He is a creative doer, and the thing he does is of vastly more importance than the mere physical presence of his person on stage. He creates art, and from him emanates an intangible strength greater by far than the latent strength of the physical mass he stands before. What he does brings into being a spiritual force that binds the larger body to the smaller, with no sense of disproportion. Even though he stands on stage hedged by physical abnormalities—the size of the place he is in, the artificial contrivances he and his fellows have devised to aid dramatic illusion, devices that, as physical facts, are often tawdry and ugly—he and the thing he does cause the physical fact to shrink to unimportance. He is a significant being, for he and his actions are the culminating activity of an institution.

Controlling the Performance

Control of the performance demands several things. First, the doers must control the thing being done. A play itself is a complete entity, a planned work carefully prepared for the purpose of achieving a pre-established result. For the result to be realized, each unit of the whole play must be successfully brought off. This means that the illusion must not be broken at any time, characters must be completely maintained, a sequence or scene must be kept to its proper pace, a climax must achieve its exact intensity, and spontaneity of mental and emotional states must motivate business and lines exactly as planned.

Control of the thing being done further means that the actor must be prepared to handle any unplanned occurrence. During the rehearsal period everyone tries to envisage all possible contingencies. The selected action is carefully mapped to include just what is needed; all else is rejected. Then by continual repetition ("All right, let's take this scene over again") the actions are molded into set patterns of movement that will have the security of habit, so much so that the actors hope to move through the whole length of the piece without any untoward happening. But accidents do occur. When a door sticks or a prop needed onstage is not there, it is the player's responsibility to correct the unexpected circumstance. It is quite possible for him to do this—in most instances by adding the correction to his regular business—but only if he is already secure in lines and movement.

Sustaining the Performance

Concentration and energy are the elements an actor employs to sustain a performance. Many good things happen for both players and audience when the well-mounted and the well-prepared play is presented. When all the dramatic elements have been brought into synchronization, when the actors and the audience are one tightly knit unit, even to the point where the audience will shift as one body at the same time, and when each actor knows beyond question that the entire mass of persons out front is a spiritual extension of himself and the audience does not know of the terrible energy of its concentration—when these things are so, then one of the world's great art mediums is functioning as it should.

The amount of energy required to sustain a play properly is considerable; the disproportion between the number of players and the size of the audience demonstrates this. It is no wonder that an actor's supply of mental, physical, and emotional energy is almost depleted by the time the final curtain comes down—but what a wonderful way for it to be spent!

Improving the Performance

For the actor who would constantly improve the quality of his work, the stage is at once a classroom and a laboratory. For him the time the play is on the boards can be the finest learning period of all. As every player knows or will soon learn, no two audiences are exactly alike. This makes each audience a new test. To meet the challenge, the actor draws liberally and energetically from his library of acting experience and, even as he is doing so, is adding new volumes to his library for future use.

There is a division in the learning process when the play is running, when the onstage learning time is matched against the time offstage. When the actor is onstage and before his audience, he is collecting acting answers about every phase of his work. The question being answered by the audience, which the sensitivity of the actor duly registers as the play moves along, is a simple one: is each sequence and each detail within the sequence being presented with maximum effectiveness? Against this question the actor scores the answers, the *yes,* the *no,* and the more troublesome *perhaps.* When affirmative responses come pouring over the footlights, they affirm the rightness of the procedures in the rehearsal period. Each *no* and each *perhaps* does the opposite. All answers, given and received under the unrelenting pressure of public performance, are stated with an emphasis that is unmistakable.

The time between performances is the actor's study period, an offstage learning time. It begins as soon as the final curtain comes down and continues off and on until the curtain next goes up. It is, in a way, a review process. The audience can be the greatest teacher of acting the theatre knows; but as with all good teachers, the lessons profit little if the student does not study them outside of class. The actor, after he has performed, reviews the lesson to discover what he missed and what he gained so that the next performance can be better than the last.

During each rehearsal period a certain amount of expectation grows in the player about the effectiveness of certain lines or the tellingness of particular bits of business. The player anticipates a specific response at the time of performance. He is on the right track, and he must not leave it. Persistently he must follow his expectation through. If the audience's response to one of these particular points is affirmative as anticipated, he has learned something. If it is not, then he sets his analytical powers to work so that he will learn something.

Why did he fail to get the response he expected? Was he in error in the first place in anticipating an effect not legitimately there? Or if he still believes that his anticipation was correct, how did he fail to bring it off? Was it his stage movement? Was his tone faulty? Was his timing off—just a shade too fast or a trifle too slow? Did he give himself away by showing his anticipation? Of all the things it could have been, what was it? Study, discussion with fellow players, more rehearsal—this is the way to better playing. The actor learns one way with one intensity during the rehearsal period. He learns another way with a much greater intensity during performance.

Part II

Pantomime

Chapter 5

The Expressive Body

Pantomime, the first component of the composite art of acting, is movement styled in dramatic action. Artistry in acting is founded in good part on a mastery of the basic competences of pantomime.

INNER AND OUTER ACTION

First the human organism felt. Then it moved. Sensitive to the flow of air or water, to the effect of light and heat and to the presence of other bodies, it shaped its action in response to the various stimuli in its environment. Accordingly we can say that man first experienced feeling, then he experienced movement. He felt for a reason, and the reason related him to his environment.

In like manner, when he moved, he moved for a purpose, and his movement revealed what the purpose was. An inner working of mind or nerves supplied the impulse that put muscles into action. Impulse began and movement ended what was one complete action.

Movement is an outer extension of thought and feeling; thought and feeling are an inner extension of movement. Both parts are indivisibly linked. Each is a terminal for the other.

In life or on the stage, we move, and moving, we explain ourselves. Nothing can be closer to the core of our being than this biologically imposed two-way action. It is in no way strange that nothing is closer to the core of meaningful dramatic movement than this two-way action.

Acting is the process whereby an inner state of being is revealed and made clear by outward action. Complete acting requires that both parts, the internal and external, function when the act is performed, each matching the other in meaning and intensity.

In the practice asssignments of the chapters ahead you will be engaged much of the time in working out pantomimic problems of a technical nature. To this effort you will direct the impulses of your dramatic instinct and the reasoning power of your mind. When, to match the technical assignments, creative pantomimes evolve out of the lesson patterns, it is expected that your creative faculties will be engaged in a commitment of equal intensity, shaping an inner state of being to motivate and accompany the external action.

ACTING AN ARBITRARY FUNCTION

In normal life a strong situation causes an individual to react by shaping a strong response. In acting, the individual player must also shape a strong response, but without waiting for a fortuitous set of circumstances to cause him to react in the manner required. Without the spontaneity a life situation provides, he must be prepared to act at any designated time. To shape circumstances favorable to creation and to bring the necessary inner and outer states into existence is one of the actor's main concerns.

If a message from the mind or the senses can travel to the rest of the body, causing muscles to move, a message from the muscle, going in the opposite direction, can cause the inner complex to respond. Thought or impulse causes movement, movement causes inner response. You, the pantomimist, thus have a two-way road to the achievement of a state of being favorable to creation. You can think a thought or feel an emotion and the muscles respond, or you can take a position or make a movement and the mind or nerves will answer in like manner. These physical facts can be demonstrated.

THE INNER-OUTER ORIENTATION

The first demonstration shows how creation works when moving from the inside out. For this exercise you are asked to set up an inner state of being for each of the following situations. When this state is strongly established, move around the room in the manner the inner condition will indicate.

1. As a superior person in an inferior place.
2. As a shy person in a strange place.
3. As an impatient person in a confining space.

After you have completed these actions, carefully check *what* you did, recalling as exactly as possible *how* all was done—that is, the positions you took and the way the muscles moved—scope and shape, intensity and tempo.

THE OUTER-INNER ORIENTATION

Demonstration number two shows how the act of creation moves from the outside in. To do this problem, you must arbitrarily assume the following positions and movements and then analyze the inner state of being each creates.

1. Legs spread, head turned slightly to the side and abdominal muscles tightened, stand with back and hands tightly pressed against a wall. After standing so, slide along the wall to one side or the other.

2. Arms folded and weight on the heels of both feet, stand with legs spread and torso leaning back. Then, with lips in a thin firm line, slowly shake the head from side to side.

3. Pigeon-toed, with knees bent a little, tuck both elbows close to the torso and clasp the hands across the abdomen. Lower the head and pull the chin in, looking up and out with slightly raised brows. Move from the center toward a corner of the room, backing part of the way.

Check your responses. Which of these inner states came into being:

1. cunning, fearful, secretive;
2. arrogant, thoughtful, obstinate;
3. timid, fearful, cautious?

Was there an overlap of two core conditions? If so, did they seem compatible?

These two sets of problems should demonstrate the relationship between the thought and the act, between the state of being and the expression of that state by movement and position. And it could follow, then, that an inner state of being that is made manifest by outer revelation can be attained in either of two ways. Because of the difference in personalities and backgrounds among actors this is fortunate, for some players will find themselves more suited to one than to the other. On the other hand, the player who practices both works with a double advantage. In a manner of speaking, he can let his *mind think and act* and his *muscles act and think* as he plays both ends against the middle of his problem.

The usual method, practiced since time immemorial, is to have the actor concentrate on a comprehension of the inner state of being necessary to a scene. If he can assume within himself what he comprehends, creating the physical, sensory, emotional, or intellectual state called for, and if his person is flexible enough, he can reveal the content he carries.

READING MOVEMENT

Is to see a movement, in or out of the theatre, also to know the meaning of that movement? We read words on paper and we hear what other people say, and we can easily understand what is read and said. But can we read movement?

The answer is yes. Reading movement was one of the first sensory and intellectual acts of emerging man. It had to be, and for a very simple reason: in a hostile world in which danger could threaten at any moment, man had to know how he stood with that world every second. However, it was not the motionless objects around him that threatened his existence, it was those that moved. Therefore he not only had to be alert to movement, he had to read it as well, noting of everything he observed whether it promised good to him or portended evil.

Man reads movements as surely as he reads words on the printed page. In the thousands of years of his being, he accumulated a body of knowledge about movement that probably is as great in scope and depth as any other body of knowledge he has.

But if we have all this knowledge, and if it functions for us as indicated, how is it that we are not more aware of it? Certainly no one stops every second of his life and asks: "That movement I saw just now, is it going to harm or help me?" The response to the problem is double: no, we do not stop continuously and consciously pose such problems for answers; and yes, we do ask the questions indicated. We ask them because we must. Not to do so whenever we are in the presence of something that moves would deny the prompting of our most elemental impulses and cause disturbances within us of a very disruptive nature.

So long has man lived with his faculty to read movement, however, and so efficient in its uses has he become, that his very sureness permitted him to drop much of his functioning in this respect from the conscious level of his mind down to the subconscious level long ago. It was a bold step, this putting the matter of survival on automatic pilot, as we might say today, but our forefathers did it successfully.

As an actor, you have an immediate and growing need to use your ability to read movement, reversing the trend of the centuries by focusing your knowledge in the conscious rather than the unconscious portion of your brain. By becoming acutely aware of what you instinctively know, you can build a library of knowledge of movement on which to draw for all your professional life.

Pantomime versus Words

If our ability to read movement has shifted its operational locus to the deeper place where habit resides, our awareness of our more recently acquired form of transmitting intelligence has not. Today there is a tremendous preoccupation with words everywhere, generally accompanied by the assumption that they are our principal means of communication. This is not true. Movement is still the great message-giver; it is only our awareness of this fact that has decreased. Of the four tools of expression the actor has—position, movement, tone, and words—three are inseparably connected with movement, it is only the printed word that can be disassociated from it.

With this emphasis upon movement in mind it should be noted, however, that the tens of thousands of words we hear spilled out into the air from human throats and by mechanical devices, and the words we see on paper in every conceivable form of publication, are of unquestionable importance to human communication. Because of the very necessity of their presence, the next main section in the book (Part III, Voice) will give to words their full share of attention.

But to think of words as our main or only means of communication, forgetting the broad and subtle expressiveness of movement, is gross error. We of the theatre compound that error in that we not only disregard the potential of expressiveness that lies in position and movement, but in that we also are unaware of our use of them.

The Forgotten Art

Pantomime is a forgotten art. This is unfortunate, but true, in spite of the fact that it is the taproot from which all stage action grows and takes its strength.

The inspired theatre-conditioned movements of life, which is what pantomime is, belong in the one place where an interpretation of life can so emphatically and distinctively be presented. The longer the art of pantomime is neglected as a field for intensive study, the greater is going to be our theatre's lack for want of it.

Aims

The primary concern of pantomimic study is the development of the human body as an instrument of dramatic expression. To accomplish this aim, it is necessary that the following attributes be acquired: flexibility, strength, control, and awareness.

Only flexibility will permit a variety of expressions for different characters, for differences in subject matter, and for different modes of expression. Strength not only gives solidity and intensity to what is expressed, it enables the actor to meet the enormous physical demands his work imposes on him. Control guarantees to the actor command of his faculties, granting him the ability to do exactly what he wishes to do when he wishes to do it; since players must create by the clock ("It's eight-thirty, places, please!"), control is essential. Awareness is coordinated with and necessary to each of the above three attributes. It designates that mind controls matter by first being aware of what matter is, as well as what it can do. To know what is being done and how it is brought about is the function of awareness. (This point should not be confused with the need for the establishment of techniques that perform best when they are thought of least. Actually, trained awareness has an automatic action in this respect. As long as any mastered technique is functioning smoothly the awareness faculty is dormant, but if the least thing goes wrong awareness acts and the conscious mind immediately is cognizant of the error.)

Exercise is the way to accomplish these aims. Since there is no lack of first-quality exercise material available to the student in physical education classes or in exercise manuals, space has not been allocated to the subject here.

The Basic Instrument

Your physical frame, with its own intangible energy engine inside, is your instrument of communication. To find out what the human mechanism is capable of doing is to discover what it is capable of expressing. No performer has ever been better than his instrument.

In the assignments ahead not only will you develop the ability to make the human instrument perform with dramatic effectiveness in the dissemination of information, you will also learn to make the instrument play, for a telling response, on the senses and emotions of all who see it perform.

The Visible Instrument • The visible instrument is that part of the actor's total complex that the audience sees. Its employment is the only means the pantomimist has of projecting everything he intends to express. Watching, the audience sees positions and movements, noting both what is done—the action of the pantomime—and how it is done— the revelation of how the character feels about what he is doing.

Already speaking the language of mankind, more in a subconscious than conscious way, your visible instrument must be taught how to translate the commonplace language it understands into meaningfully dramatic action. Like two sister tongues that have great quantities of words in common, these two languages have vast amounts of movement in common. What you know in one you will transpose into the other.

The Invisible Part of the Instrument • The visible form is not just a case of flesh and bone that mechanically goes through motions to create a dramatic experience. It is a living organism whose dynamic comes from what we cannot see but know is there. It is the spirit behind the matter that gives life to the whole complex.

Encased within our bodies are states or attributes. Invisible to sight, we are still positive of their presence because we can think them, feel them, or sense them. Indigenous to all are four definite attributes, sometimes overlapping, sometimes intermingled. They are physical, sensory, emotional, and mental states of being.

Each of these we have experienced many times. The *physical* we have felt as fatigue or vitality or pain within muscle or tissue; and we feel physical actions like walking, running, or sitting. The *senses* we employ continuously. We look, listen, touch, taste, smell; we know what it is to be sensorially alive because our nerves, glands, or muscles have made a record of such events and we are aware of the record. *Emotional* states are among our most common experiences; the record here, too, is exceptionally strong—we know when we are happy or frustrated or sad. The fact that we think and create acts of will establishes the presence of a discernible *mental* condition.

Singly or together, any one or more of these states can send out the impulse that puts muscles into expressive action. Singly or together, they can receive messages from an external movement. Any one of them can predominate over the others at any time, or each can be so lax as to be negligible as a force for action. But whatever the proportion of mixture, the inner state and outer action are always in harmony—unless, of course, an individual deliberately sets out to train for contradictions, but that is for the contortionist rather than the actor to do.

In developing the invisible portion of your instrument of expression for use in pantomime, and later in acting, you have a double action to perform. The first is to increase the sensibility of your personal inner states so that they will make of you a person well above average in your capacity to think and feel and act. The capability of stretching yourself to increased depth and scope is an already proven human attribute. The second is to multiply your oneness by spreading your capability to embrace the inner states of other persons, doing so from their point of view. Later, when you pantomime, for example, a student trying to cheat on an examination, it must be his or her thoughts, emotions, sensory or physical acts you create, as nearly as you can judge them to be.

By observation of primary sources, by a continual reading of human actions, week in, week out, you can develop the ability to enlarge your own capabilities to the point where you can break out of the limitation of your point of view and enjoy that of others. When this occurs to you, you will find that you can move with some ease past the restrictions of what you personally like and dislike into an area where your efforts concentrate on inculcating within yourself the thoughts and feelings of others.

THE THEATRE SENSE

A sense of theatre is a state of being. Those who have it are very much aware of the fact. It is a pervasive condition, one that exerts a consistent pressure on every aspect of the work of the pantomimist.

A restatement of several familiar facts is in order. The dramatic experience is an extraordinary action that is created in an extraordinary place where nothing is unimportant. In this place everything must be energized with the drive inherent in the instinct for dramatic expression, and every phase of the experience must be shared.

This is the basis on which a sense of theatre exists. Impregnate everything you do with these concepts.

Your work now begins with the execution of a problem concerned with your awareness of the reason for your presence in the theatre. The following laboratory session is your first assignment in the study and practice of the art of pantomime.

Small groups of students, three or four at a time, are to go on stage. The purpose of the problem is that each is to realize the nature and intensity of the relationship of the stage to the whole surrounding area. Onstage each is to move about, looking in all directions, noting size and distances, and organizing and assimilating a concept of the whole work area and the whole seating space.

When you are onstage, you should know that you are standing in your special work space. Here is where the results of all your labor will be realized; no other place will match this one in importance to you. Physically small compared to the size of the auditorium, your area is yet the dominant space in the whole building, made so by reason of what you will create there. Behind you and to the side is the backstage area, which is the scene of activity of all your fellow workers; there they will move about, performing their essential tasks in support of all that you do. Since none of them appears in person before the audience, all are dependent on you for the life that must come into their work. All that they do complements you. The result is that you should come to regard backstage as an area always strong in support of what you do.

Before you, in the opposite direction, or around you, as the case would be in an arena theatre, are the seats for the people who will come to this special building to share the dramatic experience with you. Unless what you do in the stage area is big enough and intense enough and clear enough to attract and to hold the attention of those in the audience, the dramatic experience cannot come into being.

As you stand center stage and look out over the auditorium with its rows and rows of seats, you should be as strongly sensible as possible that all the space in front of you is your field of influence. Knowing that during performance you can never look directly out into the house as you now are doing, you also know that the physical image, as well as the intangible concept now growing in your mind, is to be associated with every single phase of your acting activity.

You have three relationships that predominate over all others: the partnership you enjoy with the other doers in the theatre; the alliance you create with your stage characters; the union you weld with your audience. Only in you can these relationships come together. Only through you can the theatre sense come into being. Of all persons in the theatre, you are the key figure, but only because the personnel backstage and the audience are indivisibly connected to you.

In this first session on stage, install the theatre sense as a permanent fixture within your dramatic being. Never let it be ineffective. Always keep it operative in every phase of your activity.

Chapter **6**

The Basic Movements

For all that it stands as a distinct discipline, pantomime is not to be thought of as something apart from acting. It is the basic form, the first art of that activity. In a study of pantomime, there is no waste motion or time. The things learned as a pantomimist are the things used as an actor. The actions of a pantomime are the actions of a scene. Neither in stage movement nor in character movement is a change occasioned by a shift from the lesser to the larger art.

Four attributes are generic to all pantomimic movement: dynamic, definite, economic, and meaningful. These four embody the very essence of acting.

There are also three particular kinds of movement: preliminary, arrested, and suspended. The utilization of these three, in both pantomime and scene, is constant.

In each attribute and kind of movement listed above, the dramatic element is strong, as you will sense. Each provides a necessary ingredient that, when present, makes a distinction between the extraordinary quality of acting and the ordinariness of usual life movements. They are basic elements actors from the Greeks on have used as a matter of instinct or of instruction. Many competences rest in their mastery.

STAGE AND LIFE

Stage actions are not the same as actions in everyday life. If they were, nearly everyone would be able to act. At first this fact may not seem to you in accord with previously established ideas. If you have grown up watching the superrealistic actions of motion picture or television productions, it may seem to you that the best acting movements are as lifelike as possible. This is not so. You must realize that in motion pictures and television the camera, an instrument of great magnifying power, enlarges movement, while the microphone amplifies the voice. But these two instruments, wonderful as they are, have limited use dramatically. In the theatre one of them, the camera, is never employed, and the other is called upon but seldom, and then only to meet special problems.

Therefore do not confuse the requirements and practices of one medium with those of another.

In the theatre you are your own instrument of magnification. But you must be cautioned: the degree of magnification necessary is generally much larger than you will at first be prepared to recognize. Indeed, the level of vitality of spirit and magnification of action required for good stage movement is so much increased above normal, it often forms the single, greatest cause of defeat for the young player.

The probable result, as you first attempt to raise your efforts to the level of intensity required, will be that your actions will seem so grossly overdone as to be absurd. You must recognize why this is so, drawing upon your knowledge that all new experiences seem strange, and neither shy from the requirement nor become antagonistic to it. Although it takes its basic patterns from life, the pantomimic process must change both positions and movements to fit the spiritual demands of the dramatic experience as well as the spatial requirements of the theatre building. This means that pantomime, like its fuller sister art of acting, cannot be limited to a process of reproduction. Instead it must be recognized as a convention, an artificial creation, but one that contains the full plasticity of any art form.

BASIC ATTRIBUTES
FOR ALL STAGE MOVEMENT

Dynamic Movement

A lesser term than dynamic will not suffice to meet the first need you face as a pantomimist. The word itself imparts a sense of the burgeoning life in all human movement. This is the exact concept we desire. Compounded in equal parts of inner spirit and outward action, the term can best be compared to the *élan vital* of Henri Bergson, the vital spirit so necessary to all artistic creation, and so specially important in the field of acting.

Every human being has needs. Each need requires a corresponding drive to achieve an answer to the need. The drive, seeking results, generates the power that directs the body into action. From the sense of power generated action in life comes our concept of dynamic movement on the stage. The theatre, where every effort is to be shared with many persons, both requires and welcomes dynamic action as few other institutions do.

The nature of the movements to be made will be as wide in range as the primary sources from which they are drawn. But violent or tender, heavy with meaning or freighted only with fun, each large and small action must contain the dynamic constant demanded of all dramatic movement, which grows out of and emanates from the person of the player himself. Each must have an intensity that is oriented to performance level.

Of your own volition, whenever you are ready to rehearse or present your pantomime to an audience, you are to call the dynamic condition into being. You can do this, simply by willing it so. As you can swing a bat or skip a rope or dig a hole or dance a routine with more or less intensity, so you can create in varying degrees of vitality this basic dramatic condition. Therefore, dynamic movement becomes the first specific attribute to be considered in our study of pantomime.

EXERCISES AND ASSIGNMENTS

1. The first exercise is a study in contrasts. Onstage each pantomimist, in succession, is to perform twice one of the actions listed below, the first time as the action would be done offstage in any ordinary situation, the second time as a dynamic theatre-oriented series of movements.

Be careful not to make the first action so casual it automatically becomes dramatic, or the second so intense it looks overplayed. Note that no highly dramatic actions are listed. From the beginning it should be understood that commonplace situations are the most often used source of supply for all dramatic purposes.

Limit the total number of movements. In all the exercises of this chapter, length can be a hindrance rather than a help.

 a. Look for a pencil among scattered sheets of paper on a desk.
 b. Look for a dropped quarter on a sidewalk.
 c. Raise a window that sticks.
 d. Sweep a room.
 e. Add a column of figures on an adding machine.
 f. Take a turn at batting practice.
 g. Fold towels, dishcloths, and diapers.
 h. Cross an imaginary street.
 i. Select a TV program.
 j. Select a golf club.
 k. Select a piece of costume jewelry.
 l. Sharpen a pencil.

2. In teams, reinforcing the first assignment, let two pantomimists practice and then present one of the actions listed below. As before, perform the exercise twice, once in ordinary movement, then with the dynamic element added. Limit the number of movements. *Think* movement; do not permit lips to form words.

 a. Meet with a handshake at a formal reception.
 b. Meet with a handshake at an informal party.

c. (Teaming a boy and girl) Become aware of each other on a street corner.

d. Play a portion of a game of checkers, chess, cribbage, or perform a similar diversion.

e. Pay a registration fee to a clerk.

DEFINITE MOVEMENT

The second attribute to be considered is as important, as necessary, and as practical as the first. Made habitual, it should serve you all your acting life.

Definite movement does for pantomimic action what punctuation does for writing: it organizes and groups ideas together for better understanding. Movements, like sentences, must express thoughts and convey feelings. If one movement is allowed to slur into the next, it will be as confusing for the perceiver to read as if two sentences were run together without punctuation of any sort. It follows that each movement must have a definite beginning and a definite ending. This is decidedly unlifelike, since all of us slur movement every hour of the day. This is not a fault, for in life we generally are not attempting to express ourselves in an extraordinary manner. It is only on stage that we must do so.

Do not be afraid to exaggerate your action of beginning and stopping movement. This is quite necessary at first. The human tendency to slur will later take all angularity out of your action, leaving you clear and precise in your movements as you would be with well-articulated speech. If you should overdo, common stage sense and your classmates' criticisms will soon put you right again.

EXERCISE

One student is to go onstage and deliberately slur all movements in a series of actions. Those watching are to detect and instruct the performer in the exact degree of separation required to give the movements the distinction needed. Thus the sharpness of the break between movements will be determined by the movement as it appears out front. Clarity of movement is to be coordinated with fluency of movement. As any good actor can prove, these two elements are quite compatible.

Just as each movement needs to be definite, so does the beginning and ending of each pantomime. The suggestion is made that for all pantomimes a simple convention be adopted. Before you begin your action, stand onstage in your opening position with head lowered. When ready to begin, raise you head and initiate your first movement. At the end of the pantomime, reverse the action by stopping your movement and lowering your head for a moment or two before walking offstage.

This convention serves a double purpose. Standing on stage with head lowered while waiting to begin, you can employ the time to shift your thoughts from the acts of preparation—that is, arranging furniture, announcing a title for your work, and so on, to the coming acts of performance. Sweeping from your mind all nonpertinent thoughts, you intensify your concentration on the pantomime to follow. When you have achieved the mental state necessary and are ready to commit yourself to action, you raise your head and begin your movements. By lowering your head at the end of the pantomime, you effect a transition from the created illusion back to a normal state.[6]

ECONOMIC MOVEMENT

One does not expect to see extra words crammed into a sentence. Similarly, an audience does not expect to see unnecessary movements intruded into a pantomime. Not only do such additions add nothing to what is said, to a marked degree they detract from the meaning intended. Economy of movement demands the use of only those actions required for the advancement of the pantomime's basic idea. All other movements are to be eliminated.

The choice of subject materials for any art is based on a process of selection and rejection. A good painter does not include everything he sees in his landscape. He may use much of the natural scene or only a little of it, depending on his purpose, but in either case he would select what he wishes to paint and reject the rest. So is it with the selection of the movements for a pantomime, and so it will be for all the acting assignments to follow.

Personal Mannerisms and Nervous Movement • Personal mannerisms are habits that no longer trouble the conscious mind for motivation. Existing on an impulse cycle of their own, they intrude into the best-planned pantomimes without the owner being in any way conscious of their uneconomical and distracting presence. They are to be eliminated. Practice in front of a mirror can be most helpful in this respect, as can the careful observation of friends.

In addition, small nervous movements of the kind all of us make in reaction to any kind of social pressure must be controlled. Because of the persistent and pervasive nature of these actions, this is sometimes difficult. For all its potential power to annoy, nervous movement has a sound

---

[6] Although definite and economical movements have individual character and purpose, such is the overlap in practice between the two that they can be performed together as one mutually complementary exercise. The practice activity for both will be found at the end of the next section.

psychological basis. In times of tension, pressures mount within us to the point where some form of release is necessary. The activity we call nervous movement, functioning like so many small channels leading away from the pressure area of a dam, provides us with needed release. In normal circumstances it is a healthy action. But on the stage the multiple and competing movements of twitching fingers, jiggling knees, raised brows, and shifting weight can be only distracting.

All movement made on stage will be seen by an audience. It is reasonable to suppose that no actor wishes to disclose his nervous state. But to control it he must first be aware of it. It is no mean feat to order the body to execute one set of actions and at the same time to deny it the performance of another, especially when the denial centers on movements habitually employed to ease an unpleasant condition. Still, the direction must be given and the control instituted.

EXERCISES AND ASSIGNMENTS

1. Group exercise is effective in initiating the practice of definite and economic movement. The instructor calls the action and the class members, spaced around the room or grouped on stage, perform the exercise.

Execute each movement, as called in sequence, with precision. Upon completion, hold it until the next action is indicated. Only those movements asked for are to be performed. The rest of the body is to be in a neutral position.

The scene is a fun house. You are standing in front of an electrical machine with an ordinary door handle on its face. When turned a sufficient distance, a slight electric shock is felt. Here is the action:

a. Standing in front of the machine, move your head slightly (stage action size) from left to right, reading instructions.

b. Look down at the handle.

c. Smile in anticipation.

d. Release the smile as your right hand goes into an imaginary pocket for the necessary coin.

e. Feel for the coin; there is none there.

f. Frown.

g. Slide the left hand into the other pocket.

h. Find the money.

i. Smile.

j. Withdraw both hands.

k. Look at the coin slot.

l. Raise the left hand to that area.

m. Insert the coin.

n. Lower the arm.

o. Take a deep breath.

p. Extend the right hand to the handle.

q. Grasp it.

r. Slowly turn to the right; stop as the turning becomes more difficult.

s. Raise the left hand to overlap the other.

t. Turn again.

u. Shock!

v. Both hands come back to the chest, eyes wide at the same time.

w. Stare at the handle, then smile—the shock was just strong enough to be fun.

x. Both hands again go to the handle.

y. They grasp it and turn.

z. The shock comes, but you hold, and you grin in pleasure.

2. Independent exercises, featuring the stop and go of definite movement and the stringent economy of one action at a time, can be selected from the suggestions below or from original ideas.

Each pantomimist is to perform his choice twice, once with exaggerated stops at the end of each single movement and with a tempo that makes certain that only one movement at a time is being executed, the second time with no more exaggeration than dynamic stage movement requires.

a. In front of library shelves: (1) One pantomimist searches for a particular chapter heading in several books, (2) another places returned books back on the shelves, and (3) a third jots down titles and call numbers in a notebook, rearranging several books as he does so.

b. In front of a slot machine: (1) Play a slot machine. (2) Service a slot machine.

c. Start a car, shift gears, stop, back up.

d. With a package in hand, use a key to open a door, enter, close and latch the door.

e. Walk, see a coin, look to make sure that you are not seen, stoop, pick it up, check again, rise, pocket it, go on.

f. Emulate a big-league pitcher (an almost perfect primary source for dynamic, definite, economic, and meaningful movement).

g. Arrange a flower display.

3. Pantomimes for two, applicable to definite and economic movement. Do not gag.

a. One player performs actions in front of a mirror, the other acts as the reflection.

b. An imaginary photographer's light stands downstage. As one actor poses for a standing photograph, the other becomes his shadow on the wall.

c. One pantomimist is an actor in a television studio, the other his image on the screen.

4. Pantomimes for four, based on the child's game, "Follow the Leader."

a. The leader crosses a small stream, the three others follow in turn, each executing his movements.

b. Leader handles several objects, others imitate in turn.

c. Leader sits, stretches, reads, yawns, scratches, goes to sleep.

MEANINGFUL MOVEMENT

Acting embraces many actions ranging from lifelike to many that are far from natural. The individual actor, the particular play, the size and shape of the theatre, and the intent of the production are determining factors that condition meaningful action. For example, the farcical behavior of Bottom in *A Midsummer Night's Dream* will convey its message to the audience as surely as the restrained movement of an introspective Hamlet. This is true in spite of the fact that each will not only differ radically from the other, but that both will differ from life.

The test of meaningful movement is this: Was the intent of the actor seen and comprehended in full by all members of the audience? When involved in a series of simple action movements, you have little to worry about. But there is always a desire to create actions filled with interesting nuances, and it is in this kind of pantomimic movement that the real challenge to ability lies.

Sight Lines • A sight line is a technical limitation the relationship between stage and house imposes on all meaningful movement. A sight line is the line of vision from any location on stage to any seat in the house. The first obvious requirement is that the movement itself be seen. If you make a facial gesture when your hand is in front of your face, you have broken a sight line. If you are hidden behind a piece of furniture or stand upstage of another player at the time when you hold the center of interest, your sight lines have been blocked. It is your responsibility not to let this happen.

Audience Eye • The surest way to master the problem of sight lines is to develop an *audience eye*. Physically you cannot be out in the house checking your movements at the same time as you are on stage performing them, but visually you can. If you have the power to create and retain visual images in any degree, it should be possible for you to know how you appear on stage to any person in any seat out front. If this faculty does not develop for you immediately, you can activate it by going into the house to see how another person on stage appears from different angles. Retaining the images made, reverse the situation by going on stage yourself where, by using your audience eye, you determine how you appear in various positions.

Meaningful Dramatic Action • Most of the movement created on our stages today is more dramatic than meaningful. This is not surprising.

When strong dramatic instincts seek release through the persons of directors and players, the natural result is bound to be a predilection for strong dramatic movement. But positions and movements that say more strongly than anything else, "Watch me, respond to me, I am dramatic" are, for all their appeal, limited actions.

You, as a pantomimist, will want to be dramatic. That is a basic purpose in your study. If you have a dramatic instinct, and if you profit from your stage exercises, you will be inevitably. But being dramatic is only a first necessary step in the process of acting. If you take no other, your planning for your pantomimes will be more instinctual or impulsive than thoughtful, and your action will be more attractive than revealing. For some actors this is enough.

Make no mistake about the dramatic actor's ability to capture and hold an audience. If he is good, he can do it with ease and power. There, however, his ability stops. Particularly suited to purely emotional releases, he is at a loss to do more than work a temporary effect on an audience. In pantomime or in play there should be more to acting than that.

Simplicity is the keynote in the opening phases of our work, and there are meanings to be revealed in the plainest of patterns. You open a heavy and a light door differently, a familiar and a strange one differently. You sit in an old and comfortable chair in a manner unlike your movement and posture in a new and stiff one. An expensive object is generally handled with more care than a cheap bit of bric-a-brac. You are more at home in your own room than in an unfamiliar meeting place.

Primary Source Material • To increase your ability to be meaningfully dramatic, it is necessary that you identify and associate yourself with your greatest source of knowledge.

As your own best primary source, wherever you are, you are in a laboratory ideally equipped for study. Favored as few other investigators, you are always in a position to conduct a special kind of analytical work. Knowing of the continual interplay between the internal and external forces in your life, you can conduct a firsthand investigation at any time you wish. Self-study is your aim.

With self-knowledge as a base, you can broaden your inquiry into the meaning of movement by the observation of persons around you. Although the full scope of human movement is too vast and complex to permit an easy cataloguing, it is still possible to establish a few simple lines of investigation. Consider, as a key word, *interest*. You can learn about yourself and other persons by questioning whether in any given situation you are interested or disinterested in your surroundings, and to what degree. Your own immediate state of being provides the answer about yourself. In the case of others, unless they express themselves in words, you must be able to read their external actions.

Fortunately for you, learning to read movement, or learning to reread it as the case might be, is a simpler process than learning to read words. For one thing, you will be dealing with foreknowledge. For another, you will be concerned with simple, basic factors, all of which have figured prominently in your own life—action movements, relationships, urgency, need, likes or dislikes, and so on—and the reading in most instances can be swift and sure.

Other key words can also serve to direct your scrutiny: *what, how,* and *why,* for example. *What* is primarily concerned with the action movements you make in the course of a day's activity, and which always form a large portion of your pantomimic action. You cross a room, sit, open a door, scratch an itch, put on a coat, wash dishes, write, run, kneel—all these work movements of your life are the forwarding movements in a pantomime's progress. Scrutiny of basic actions is the easiest part of the observation process. Creation of these same actions in a pantomime is likewise relatively easy.

To make action movements fully meaningful on stage, you must first be careful to make a proper selection, choosing those most revealing of what you wish to say to the audience. It is easy to become careless in this respect, selecting the first idea that comes to mind, instead of running through a full catalogue of possibilities before choosing those most apt for your purpose.

If your first assignment were to be concerned with housework, what type of activity would you choose? Doing the dishes, dusting, sweeping, making beds? The answer is: The action that will be most meaningful for what you want to say. Dishes can be connected with boredom, dusting with an interest in the objects handled, sweeping with vigorous physical action, beds with a desire to rest.

How always accompanies *what.* It reveals how you or anyone feels about what is being done. Observation of the manner of movement is a complex matter involving both positions and type of muscular action. Here again a few simple words can be most helpful in establishing a line of inquiry. When noting how you or another person moves, check the *vitality* of the action to determine the state of health and degree of interest indicated by the doer. Watch the *tempo* of movement to determine likes or dislikes and/or the degree of compulsion in the action. The *size* of a movement can reveal a sense of freedom or of constriction. Other words, each a stimulator of thought, will come to mind as you develop both your manner of observation and your style of creation of meaningful movement on stage.

The ubiquitous *why* is always to be connected with the *what* and the *how*. It establishes the reason for every action, making understandable what is done. In acting, *why* equates with that key word, *motivation*. Motivations take us below the surface of all external action. They make reasonable even the most obtuse acts. They humanize all activity. The question *why* requires an actor to think, it connects a character to his or her background, it explains relationships. In observation of primary sources *why* will be a much-used word. In the planning of pantomimes it is never to be absent.

EXERCISES AND ASSIGNMENTS

1. Perform one of the suggestions below twice, the first time emphasizing the tellingness of straight action movements, the second time adding further meaning by showing how you feel about the actions you perform. To distribute the expressive burden evenly, let your face reveal how you feel (which is one of its most normal functions) during the first half of the second performance, but make the other parts of your body take over that task during the latter half. *Pantomime all props, now and later.*
    a. Tend flowers in a window box.
    b. Hand out gym equipment.
    c. In a display case arrange materials to announce a coming production.
    d. Shave, or put up hair.
    e. Wait for a bus, or ride a streetcar.
    f. Sort laundry.
    g. Wipe dishes.

2. Choose an activity of your own in which the action movements are not automatically familiar, but which you must clearly reveal to the audience. For example, arrange unusual articles on a shelf or mantel. Let there be no question in the minds of the audience what it is you are handling.

3. Select a primary source activity with which you are not familiar and present a portion of it on stage. Examples: work in a tool, pottery, or processing plant; engage in a handicraft occupation.

SPECIALIZED MOVEMENTS

Three kinds of movements—preliminary, arrested, suspended—have a distinctive function in pantomime and acting. Their purpose is to add interest and intensity to stage action. Drawn originally from life sources, they can be observed in the movements of animals as well as humans.

PRELIMINARY MOVEMENT

The first is the most utilitarian. A preliminary movement is the smaller action that precedes a larger main movement; its purpose is to attract the audience's attention and stimulate its interest in the principal movement that follows.

This movement is used constantly and undramatically in daily activity: we look at an object before we reach for it, we place our hands on the arm of a chair before we get up, we stretch before we sleep, we smile before we shake hands, we smell food before we eat, we wind up before we throw a ball, we spit on our hands before we grasp a handle, we touch before we kiss, and in speech we take in a breath before we speak.[7]

EXERCISE

1. A preliminary movement can give distinction to an action that previously had none. In demonstration, let four students go on stage and stand facing front. Without embellishment, each is to perform in turn one of the following actions: shake hands with an imaginary person, turn the combination on a safe, pick up a dollar bill from a table, take a bite from an apple.

After all have performed, each is to repeat the same action, but with a preliminary movement added. The first performer is to wipe the hand against a trouser leg or a dress before the shake, the second to flex the fingers and test the fingertip touch, the third to look anxiously for the bill, see it, then pick it up, the fourth to polish the apple before biting.

2. Three imaginary doors are on stage, one stage right, one up center, and one down left. In a first run-through, a pantomimist is to look for a person who is not on stage. Entering from stage right, he turns, closes the door, scans the room, and then checks the other two doors, looking out of each in turn—all in unembellished movement.

In a second action, the pantomimist is to enter, close the door, turn and scan the empty room. Then, from that position, he is to look sharply at the up-center door, cross quickly to it, open it and look out. A shift of weight will denote failure to see the sought person. Still in the doorway, he is to turn and look at the door down left and, after the preliminary action, cross down to it. He may or may not discover the missing person outside.[8]

---

[7] The intake of breath before a verbal action is the most used preliminary movement in speech. As such it can vie with the action of looking, which is the most used preliminary movement in pantomime.

[8] The above action was taken from a directorial problem in a revival of the play, *Broadway*. Without preliminary movements, the build to a scene of some intensity was lacking, and the stage had some moments of dullness. With preliminary movements a high point of excitement was achieved. The demonstration indicates that dozens of such movements can be put into dramatic harness during an evening's performance.

Intensity and Proportion • No doubt you have already seen that a preliminary movement is an agent of intensity. Did you note, when the above actions were performed for a second time, that the intensity of the main movement was in direct ratio to the strength of the preliminary movement? To demonstrate the point, repeat the apple exercise yourself, but add this action to it: Polish the apple, *look critically at the sheen achieved, smile,* then bite. Was there not greater intensity in the main movement because the preparation was greater?

Dramatic common sense indicates that a proper proportion exist between the preliminary and the main movement. The first action should not be too large or intense for the second. Conversely, the first must not be too small or too lacking in intensity for the next and main movement.

EXERCISES AND ASSIGNMENTS

1. From observation of primary sources select four distinctive preliminary movements and present them in rotation. Place the emphasis upon the preliminary movement, not on the main action to follow. Ideas can be drawn from work, study, or play activities.

2. Experiment before the class with the main movements of each of the above four preliminary movements by showing some below, some above, and some in exact proportion to the size and intensity of the first movement.

3. Based on the model of the pantomime of the doors, create a sequence of your own devising in which you search for a valuable lost object, clean an untidy room, explore a strange place, sort a shipment of unusual ceramic pieces, or inspect a platoon.

ARRESTED MOVEMENT

Less usual in practice than preliminary movement, arrested movements are more heavily charged with dramatic potential than the other two. Even in nonstage use, this unique movement is sometimes starkly dramatic. Perhaps this is because it is the kind of response that is rooted deep, touching the very core of man's primary conflict—the struggle for survival.

Arrested movement is the abrupt cessation of an action, movement that is suddenly stopped and held suspended for a short period of time. The motivation is clear: When we are performing some usual action in line with some usual thought, we suddenly stop our movement, freezing in that exact position while we check the nature of a sound heard, or a sight seen, or something felt or smelled. If the thing that attracted our attention proves to be harmless, we continue what we were doing. If it seems threatening, we generally change our course of action.

Defined, arrested movement means that an action is abruptly halted by an external or internal notification that some new element has entered our environment, signifying that for safety's sake we should stop what we are doing until our senses tell us if danger threatens. If, after checking, we feel that no threat impends, we resume our movement. If the reverse is true, we hold ourselves in a state of suspended action until the danger is further investigated as to nature and degree, whereupon a new kind of action, one responsive to the threat, is initiated.

It is in part because of arrested movement the race exists—quite a significant fact to associate with the movement we are going to employ in making our actions on stage more intense and more meaningful.

Imagine a dog crossing a street, tail swaying, tongue hanging out, trotting along with head held down and mind fixed in a dog's mental state of unconcern. Suddenly it stops, all motion frozen. An approaching car, sensed by sight or by sound, causes whatever dog thoughts are running through the animal's head to be broken off. A new thing in the environment has aroused that most basic of all instincts, the will to survive, focusing concentration on whatever the new thing is, determining if it be threatening or benign.

Visualizing the picture we can recall that after the arrested action there is always a movement of freeze, pragmatically learned long ago when a wrong movement could mean death. In response to this deep-seated instinct our animal stops, holding the body motionless for a moment. Then the head turns, going in the direction of the coming car. Noting that it is still some distance off, our animal's muscles relax, the head drops down, the tongue comes out, and the body sways forward into the former action. Had the car been closer, the animal might have turned back to the curb, or it even could have, in the case of extreme danger, gone into an alert, spread-legged crouch, with the body retracted from the point of danger and held in a position that contains energy in maximum concentration, out of which movement is possible in many directions.

We have reacted with a similar kind of arrested movement many times in our lives, following the same possibility patterns the dog did. Like him, we have recovered and gone on, or turned in retreat. Nor do any of us require so large a threat as an oncoming car to motivate our action. A bee buzzing around head or hand, a cobweb on the face in the night, a sound heard, a movement seen—any one of these and multitudes like them can cause an immediate response.

Not all arrested movements are externally motivated. Some come as internal actions. How many times have you been walking along, your mind on some personal train of thought, when you suddenly stopped in your tracks—you had forgotten something! A remembered thought, intruding upon a wholly different state of mind, will cause as sure a response as any external action, even though there is no obvious threat to safety involved.

An arrested movement is always a preliminary movement; by its nature it cannot be otherwise. The quality is not, however, reciprocal; all preliminary movements are not arrested. As a preliminary movement, arrested movement adds variety to the large body of movements needed and used in all dramatic pieces. Its intensity potential marks it for employment in many a minor and major climactic situation.

EXERCISES AND ASSIGNMENTS

1. In short sequences, with a distinct break between them, present four different examples of arrested movement. In each case, have just enough movement before and after to supply margins for the separate actions.

Choose two of the four for further development to demonstrate the relationship in size and intensity between the arrested movement and the movements before and after. Ideas can be developed from situations involving sight, sound, touch or thought.

2. Create longer sequences featuring arrested action from situations involving danger, surprise, (pleasurable or the reverse), and interruptions.

3. Emphasize arrested movements as some observed animal might do them.

SUSPENDED MOVEMENT

This kind of movement, less common and less used than either of the two just discussed, nevertheless has a distinct range of employment. Suspended movement is mentioned third because it incorporates in its action elements of the two previous kinds: it is always a preliminary action, and very often it utilizes the principle of arrested movement as well. Thus it is a composite, taking something from two others to add to what it has of its own.

Suspended movement is movement temporarily halted and held in suspense while another, intruding action takes place, after which it is resumed again. The key characteristic is that the movement is only suspended, not completely stopped or dropped. An action of this kind gives, in effect, a promissory note to the audience, assuring them that once the interrupting movement is over, the rest of the action will be performed. This dramatic device sustains attention; its action can hold and tighten any dramatic situation.

Most life and stage actions strive for the completion of one effort before moving on to the next. It is nature's way in us of freeing our faculties for full concentration upon each new effort. But sometimes we are involved in an action that can be interrupted without loss while some lesser action is accomplished. Or we can be engaged in an action so important it must receive full attention; therefore any side action must be disposed of before the main action is continued. In either case suspended movement has several dramatic uses.

1. It can be utilized as a break in a major action. Here is an example. Mrs. X is a dress designer of note. She is arranging a drape on a new model when a subordinate enters and asks for a signature on another design. Holding the drape in place with her left hand, Mrs. X uses the right to sign the sketch. That done, she turns again to the model to complete her suspended movement. She could, of course, have stopped the first action, performed the second and then come back to the first again as she carried on her pantomine, but not only would this produce three short and chopped sequences, it would lessen the dramatic impact.

2. Suspended action can be used to intensify and add interest to the final portion of the movement that has been interrupted. Y, who is secretly engaged, receives her ring in a special delivery package. Just as she takes the ring from its box and before she can examine and try it on, her father enters the room. The ring disappears behind Y's back where it is nervously held until the father leaves the room. Her action with the ring after his departure is heightened because the original movement was abruptly halted and held in suspension for a period of time.

3. Suspended movement can be employed to inject variety and distinctiveness into otherwise average actions. B, a father, is bringing home Christmas presents for the children. Cautiously, he sets the packages down on the porch and enters the house to see if all is clear. Going to a closet, he takes off his overcoat and hangs it up, leaving the closet door open after he has done so. Quickly going outside, he gathers up his parcels, hurries across the room and enters the closet, pulling the door shut after him. As he is lifting the packages to a shelf the door swings open behind him. Holding the packages with both hands, he uses a foot to try to hook the handle and bring the door closed.

It can be seen from these examples that suspended movement has a use in both large and small actions. It can also be noted that it is more restricted in nature than either a preliminary or an arrested movement. Obviously suspended movement requires a more special situation than either of the others. But when such a situation presents itself, suspended movement has possibilities of action that should not be overlooked.

EXERCISES AND ASSIGNMENTS

1. Emphasize the suspended movement that might logically grow out of the actions of a secretary near a telephone, a cashier in a ticket office, a stage

carpenter anchoring a stage flat, an actress putting on makeup, a boy friend's relationship with a younger brother, watching a TV program, bait fishing.

2. Create a sequence of your own choosing featuring a suspended action.

SUMMARY ASSIGNMENT

Design and perform a pantomime featuring both the four generic attributes of movement—dynamic, definite, economic, and meaningful—and the three specialized kinds of action—preliminary, arrested, and suspended.

More important than a clever story is your demonstration of mastery of the basic movements discussed and practiced in this chapter.

Chapter 7

Creating the Pantomime

When the dramatic experience was organized by the Greeks, a form was needed to contain the subject material involved. They developed one that was efficient, harmonious, and durable. Relatively short in length and compact in shape, it is the form we use today. Of immediate interest is the fact that it is adaptive, having the ability to contain everything from a five-minute pantomime to a five-act tragedy. This remarkable elasticity permits you, the pantomimist, to use the same organization employed by Sophocles, Shakespeare, and Shaw.

The basic form, discussed earlier in Part I, Chapter 2, has an introduction, a body, and a conclusion. Taken from life patterns, the form mirrors the progression of events as we see them evolving in nature, but with this difference: the artist adds the element of control, which permits him to select from the mass of material available the things that give point to his story and to reject those that do not.

CREATIVITY

The responsibility for creative activity is fairly well prescribed for the actor in the modern theatre. Although responsible for the creation of roles and the interpretation of lines, he is denied, in the bulk of his work, an opportunity to originate basic subject material. It is a serious denial.

In pantomime the missing opportunity is recovered; originality comes within manageable distance. The task of collecting and organizing material and then writing a three-act play would daunt most players, but performing the same function for a pantomime is not at all difficult for them. Shorter length permits sharper focus on the relation of material to form, of part to part, and on the progression essential to dramatic construction.

In pantomime the actor functions in a double role: he creates the original idea himself, and he presents the finished product on stage. In one action he encompasses the whole creative process. He develops his own latent powers and at the same time he grows in comprehension and appreciation of the abilities of the other dramatic creators.

ORIGINALITY

The opportunity to be original does not include a command to be clever. Creation cannot be imposed or true originality compelled. As no plant can be pushed through the soil from below but must grow of its own volition from the loam that nourishes it, so must the growth of your original thought come willingly from your surroundings and experiences.

Originality indicates that an idea is original only in that it *originates* in an individual. It does not indicate that your idea must be new and totally different from the ideas of all other persons. Few ideas have been left undeveloped by authors of any generation.

The creative faculty is neither flamboyant, sensational, or clever. Instead, it has the ability to see, in the abundant mass of material that surrounds us, a simple idea that seems to ask for dramatic expression. It creates less that is new than it selects from what is known.

There will be a balance in the assignments to come. Some will place the requirement of originality squarely upon your shoulders. Others, that you might not spend too much time trying to think up the initiatory idea, will suggest possibilities for you to develop. The important thing for you to remember is that the target for your attack is (1) to originate subject matter fitted to your present needs, (2) to organize your material within the established dramatic form, and (3) to develop the most effective action possible to dramatize that material.

Before we consider the specific parts of the dramatic form, it is necessary to treat two special attributes of that form both in theory and practice. The dramatic constants, *illusion* and *conflict*, are so indigenous to any dramatic structure, and so essential to pantomimic creation, that each must be discussed and practiced separately before we come to the creation of the complete pantomime itself.

ILLUSION

Illusion is dependent upon the willingness of all concerned to accept as true what obviously is not true. Illusion is neither a new word nor a new concept. Its beginning goes back to the time when man took the giant step from absorption in reality to free dreaming about what was yet to be made real. Like children today, he did not conceive of this process as illusion; he thought of it as make-believe, and his dramatic instinct soon had a use for it.

Long, long ago man found that he could express himself better if, instead of using the commonplace utterances of his language, he illustrated what he wanted to say in a series of energized actions aimed at capturing the attention of his fellows. In effect he said to his viewers, "This is important. Watch me and you will see what I mean." And then he *made believe* he was acting out a real thing. The viewers watched willingly because what they saw was far more interesting than the usual kind of communication.

Perhaps what this man of long ago had to say was not very important; it may have been just the reverse. The significant facts are that he was moved to express himself in a strong and compelling manner, that his audience was willing to be involved in what he had to do and say, and that neither he nor they were fooled by his actions; all knew that what he did was a made-up thing, an illusion of real-life situations.

ILLUSION IN ACTION

Illusion is imagination revealed in overt action.

Your aim is to pantomime imaginary objects and settings with such clarity that an audience can visualize what you pantomime as surely as if the objects and places were directly in view. You are asked to plan and execute your pantomimes without the aid of anything other than general stage lighting and the most basic pieces of classroom furniture. The purpose is double: to cause you to work directly on the core concept of illusion as a principal dramatic constant, and to permit you to practice the creation of illusion in the same practical way as you will later in play rehearsal.

It may seem that this is too little, that help in the form of oral explanations or the use of real properties would serve to decrease pressure and free you for greater creativity. The opposite is true. The more you can realize your imaginings in meaningful movement, the greater will be the development of your creative faculties. By your actions alone you can tell the audience who you are, where you are, what you are doing, what time of day or year it is, and what the relevant objects are in your surroundings.

Nor is this all. You can convince your viewers that the chair you sit on is not that kind of chair at all but a rock or a throne, and that your clothes are not regular campus wear but a uniform or a suit of rags. Further, you can make them believe that the motion of your hands indicate that you are holding a cup or handling a hairbrush or a book and that, in addition, it is a particular kind of cup or hairbrush or book.

THE Ws

The problem of illusion is the problem of *who, where, when* and *why* —key words on which you will build your practice. Let us take them in the order of listing.

Who is easily disposed of for now. As a dramatic constant it is synonymous with characterization, and that is a subject of such importance it requires special treatment in a chapter of its own. For the present time, therefore, it is enough that you attempt no more than the use of those character actions most like your own.

Where refers to place or setting, and with this reference the real work in illusion begins. The stage set, and all that it contains, is always a major consideration in pantomime planning. Your first concern is with the creation of a visual image.

Imagination must be fed specific information in order to produce specific results. Let us say that you have to provide a setting for a pantomimic exercise, the subject of which is the finding of a lost object of some value. Select the general area—a laboratory, along a trail, a jeweler's shop, a living-room—and form the image of your set in your mind or as a floor plan on paper in the exact detail, dictated by the following considerations.

Physical Characteristics • Is the place an interior or an exterior location? Is it large or small? Is it square, rectangular, or oval? Is it new or old, light or dark, warm or cold, familiar or unfamiliar, a place of activity or of rest?

Psychological Characteristics • Do you like or dislike the place? Is it safe or does it hold danger? Does it create a special mood or is the atmosphere normal? Does it have a greater impact upon you than you upon it?

Physical Arrangements • Where, in the shape of an exact line drawn on the stage floor, is the outline of your set? What are its exact dimensions and exact relationship to the stage on which you will perform?

Every set must have entrances. In exact stage placement, where are yours? How many and of what kind? How far apart and of what relationship to the rest of the space? What is the exact detail of their construction—that is, wood or metal, heavy or light, swinging which way (the great majority of stage doors are hinged upstage and swing offstage), and what is the shape and workings of the handles? If this is an exterior set, what is the nature of the entrance and how will it be used?

Furniture and Set Pieces • How many pieces of furniture are in the room? How many are needed? What is the nature of the furniture:

delicate or rough, functional or for display, new or used, in good condition or in disrepair? Based upon a meaningful relationship, what is the exact placement of each piece—that is, in what stage area, how close or far from other pieces, and facing in what direction?

Properties • All objects on stage not listed as scenery are properties. There are *hung* props such as those attached to walls, *set* props that are placed on the furniture to dress the set, and *hand* props such as are manipulated by the actors. Of course, any one of the other two can also be a hand prop if it is handled by a player. It is with hand props that we are concerned.

The discipline of the imagination that leads to the creation of an exact visual image and the control of movement that reveals exactly what the image is can be applied as well to pantomiming props as to disclosing a setting. By action alone the property can be created before the eyes of the spectators—created and maintained, because the discipline of retention is as important to a belief in illusion as any other element. Once established, the prop must neither disappear into thin air nor be misplaced or picked up from a spot in which it was never set down. Exactitude of manipulation and placement is a rewarding experience to the actor who masters it.

The line of questioning about properties follows the pattern already established. Let us return to that lost prop, the search for which motivated the visualizing of the first set. What kind of an object is it? What does it look like, and how, using definite, economical and telling movements, can this be revealed clearly to the audience? What does it feel like—is texture important in its handling? What is its shape, its weight, its use? How will you handle it, carry it, and where will you place it? The answers to these questions will tell you what to visualize and what to create in movement.

When you are cast in a play you will be asked to move in rehearsal within a prescribed set long before the set itself materializes and be required to handle props and to imagine lighting effects far in advance of the appearance of either of these items. The mental faculty that can put a door or a window in an exact spot so many feet on stage and keep it there, that can imagine a chair in an exact relation to a fireplace and never vary the position no matter how much come-and-go action plays around it is not only beneficial to your training, it is a requirement of your profession. Great acting is specific even to a matter of inches.

When comes next. Time is not always as critical an item as place in the creation of stage illusion. Often it is sufficient to indicate that the action takes place during an afternoon or that it is "evening, three days later." In this and all similar cases, it is assumed that general lighting would illuminate the stage and that the source need not be made explicit. But when the element of time is important it must be made integral to the action.

Time is associated with one of life's great dichotomies—day and night, light and dark. The ability to see or not to see, therefore, is associated with this element. Note the number of revealing actions that might grow out of this fact: a light is too bright, therefore eyes must be shielded; it is dusk, therefore one must peer closely at objects or focus sharply to see things at a distance; it is night and one must grope to find an object or to locate a path; a reach for the clock with eyes closed indicates early morning; the act of lighting lamps or turning switches on and off are simple and revealing actions in association with time.

Many commonplace actions in relation to the element of time are, when performed, at once revealing. The pocketing of pencil and closing of notebook preparatory to rising signifies the end of a class hour. Setting a table indicates an approaching meal time. A look at a watch, a stretch, and a return to work tells us that it is not yet quitting time. The act of dressing or undressing can apply to stated periods of morning or night. We eat different foods at the various mealtimes: cereal for breakfast, sandwiches at lunch, meat dishes at dinner.

Time, then, has a relative importance in the creation of stage illusion. Though always present, it need not always be emphasized. It should be employed wherever legitimately possible in the assignments at the end of this section.

Why. Simply stated, *why* is the reason for the occurrence of any action. As previously stated, the stage word used for *why* is *motivation*. In the theatre's glossary of terms, motivation must be placed among the items of first and critical importance.

Reason is inherent in all action. In a physical sense nothing happens by chance. Every meaningful act has its purpose and every purpose is backed by a motivation—that is, the reason for the purpose. It follows, then, that motivation and action are indissolubly linked together.

Each exercise on stage is made up of a series of reasonable actions logically developed. Behind each large and small action is a motivation that must be apparent to creator and spectator alike in order for the action to make sense. Fortunately, motivations are come by easily. Psychologically many grow out of either a wish or a drive: one desires, or one is compelled. It is the first of these that pertains in the majority of instances in life as well as onstage. If you follow a logical line of desire, in planning a pantomimic exercise, it is possible to visualize the series of actions that will make up the sequence and, at the same time, be assured of proper motivations. Likewise, forces that compel movement can be found in abundance: one is forced to study, or to dress hurriedly, or to sit still.

Some motivations are the result of actions external to the pantomimist: a telephone rings, causing a startled response followed by a movement toward the instrument; an uncomfortable chair or a tight collar or skirt demands a physical response; a television set requires adjustment; and so forth.

Of course, some motivations will be more difficult to determine than others, but whether small or large, more significant or less so, internal or external in nature, each motivation must be recognized by the pantomimist and made clear to the audience.

EXERCISES AND ASSIGNMENTS

Remember, you still are not creating dramatic pantomimes, nor are you dealing yet with character creation. Simple, direct stage action is indicated.

1. With no more emphasis upon place than is necessary, stand in one spot within reaching distance of three objects, each of which is to be picked up twice in your series of logical actions. As a basis for your pantomime, choose one of the following situations: at a kitchen table, in a machine shop, behind a counter in a store, at a secretary's desk, behind a cashier's window.

2. As a purely technical exercise, emphasize the disciplines of illusion by testing your ability to create and maintain the illusion of imaginary objects. Choose one of the following suggestions and perform it without benefit of the usual introduction and conflict.

　　a. Walk up a flight of steps.
　　b. Climb through a window.
　　c. Pack a packsaddle.
　　d. Rearrange the living room furniture.
　　e. Change a tire.

3. This exercise begins your experience with the creation of an illusion of space, and your problem is to make clear to your audience exactly where you are. The motivation is that you, for a reason you will devise, must inspect an area or a room. You are alone. Do not select a place with which you are unfamiliar, such as a castle dungeon, but choose a place with which you are well acquainted. Show the approximate size, shape, kind of area, and type or extent of use. Determine exact measurements and maintain them.

4. Pantomime the search for the lost object mentioned on page (74) in the area you selected when creating the exact details of your imaginary set.

5. Perform a stage exercise by selecting one condition from each of the three following groups, *a, b, c,* and combine it with the others.

a. A dormitory room, a gate, a bank building, a swampy place, a basement, library steps.

b. Noon, very late night, dawn, early evening, midmorning, late afternoon.

c. Routine work must be done, a crime is to be committed, fatigue is combined with hot weather, a romance begins, one person awaits the arrival of another, an exciting incident has just taken place.

SUMMATION

The study and practice of illusion (1) disciplines the imagination by creating exact visual images, (2) requires that the visual images be formed in practical stage shapes, (3) necessitates correlation between the imaginative faculty and physical movement as the image is drawn in meaningful dramatic action, (4) trains the actor to be aware of all production elements—sets, lights, props, costumes—long before those elements appear in rehearsal, (5) requires a disciplined control of movement to fit the exact requirements of all settings and props, (6) from beginning to end, it permits the actor to train himself in the belief that that which is not so is so.

CONFLICT

Introduction of the element of conflict signifies that it is time to be dramatic—if, indeed, you have not already been so in the previous assignments, for if the dramatic instinct is present in any degree of strength it is difficult to exclude this dynamic element from even the most mechanical of stage exercises. Let us say that it is now time to bring the dramatic constant of conflict into our work consciously, and by so doing to signify that we are ready to think dramatically, to practice being dramatic, and to project a dramatic creation out into the house.

THE NATURE OF CONFLICT

Why is it that from the time of the ancient Greeks down to our own day, the people of the theatre have held that the one indispensable element in any dramatic action is conflict? There must be a sound reason for this continuously held conviction, one that will justify the universal belief that drama is drama only when opposing forces are committed to a common struggle.

To struggle is human. We struggle in our birth. From that time on we strive to exist; we fight, in each generation of men, not only to stay alive as all other animals do, but to live better than any other generation has ever lived before. Obviously, conflict is a concomitant of the human condition. Even as it is impossible to think of human progress without including it in our thought, so it is impossible not to place it at the heart of all dramatic activity.

THE SCOPE OF DRAMATIC CONFLICT

Conflict is evident in every play worthy of the name, from the mighty dramas of Aeschylus down to the lightest farce among this season's offerings. It is present in each scene of every play and in each sequence of every scene. What we call the spine of a drama is not only the line of developing action in each piece, it is the cutting edge of the conflict. Conflict has its birth in a human drive, an impulse, a need, a desire— something that compels a person to struggle, to seek, to strive for an object or a goal. But something happens to the desire in drama as it does in life: a person, an object, or an event stands in the way of the achievement of the need, the desire, or the goal.

You have undoubtedly noted that every pantomime, like every play, must have a strong story line to sustain it. What is that story line other than the description of a conflict? So when we say we have to think up an idea for a pantomime, what we actually mean is that we have to think up an idea for a conflict.

Conflicts can be found in the simplest sources. Unfortunately we have no great pantomimists practicing in America, but can you not imagine what France's great *mime*, Marcel Marceau, would do with as simple a conflict as having to take a pill, or trying to put a loose spring back in its case, or having to sit still while wearing a pair of tight pants?[9] In your own case, think, for example, of the number of conflicts that spring immediately to mind when any situation that is subject to the pressure of time is mentioned: late to dinner, late to work, or late for a date.

THE PRACTICE OF CONFLICT

To develop a sense of conflict and to discover the limitless possibilities inherent in the use of this dramatic constant, you are to select one of the ordinary actions listed below and develop it in a pantomime with a time limit of three minutes.

Here is a working example: The action is to open a door; the development lies in the discovery of every legitimate obstacle that will delay or prevent the opening of that door. Items: you enter with an armload of

---

[9] The basic difference between pantomime and *mime* is that the former generally is like realistic, wordless acting, while the latter is highly stylized, exaggerated, and antirealistic in its creation of character, costume, and makeup.

imaginary packages; standing before the door, you attempt to turn the knob with a partially free hand; the top package slips, you must release your hold on the handle to prevent the package from falling; adjusting the balance of your burden, you free the other hand; turning the knob, you discover that the door is locked; you search for your key with the free hand, but it is not on that side of your person; you must shift the packages to release the other hand; in the last pocket to be explored, you find the key; unable to see clearly, you try to insert it wrong side up; turning it over, you put it in the lock; the mechanism is old, extra effort is necessary to effect the turn; holding the key down with your free hand, you cautiously employ the other to grasp and turn the knob; after another near accident with the packages, the door opens; the packages again held firmly, you straighten the key and attempt to withdraw it from the lock; the force of your pull causes the door to close; repeating your earlier maneuver, you open the door again; this time your foot acts as a stop while the key is withdrawn; using the same foot, you push open the door, but only partially so—it is caught on a rug; turning, you employ your posterior for additional force; suddenly the door gives way, and you enact a backward fall into the room, your packages spilling around you—and we terminate the illustration at this point.

EXERCISE

How much conflict is possible in these actions?
   a. Eating a hamburger.
   b. Combing the hair.
   c. Picking up a piece of gum.
   d. Sewing on a button.
   e. Shuffling a deck of cards.

REPRODUCTION OR REPRESENTATION

Art, or acting, is not a reproduction of the activities and situations of life, it is a representation of them. Were it reproduction, exact repetition or exact mimicry of human actions would be employed, in which case no such body of specialists as actors would ever be needed.

Representation is a different matter. It requires that, out of all the things, ideas, or persons we could choose to express an idea, we select a certain few to represent all the rest. Thus, if I wish to create a story about a certain kind of student, I do not put in the story all the students I can observe who are like the one I have in mind. I select one, the one I believe most suited, and have him represent the others. Further, I do not include in my story all the actions the representative student performs in a day's activity. I choose only those most significant for my purpose.

An act of creation includes the ability to distinguish what is significant in a certain matter from what is insignificant, to determine what is more useful from what is less so, to select what is appropriate from what is not.

The purpose of the key exercise was exploration. It was an exercise in fertility of invention. As such, your sense of proportion had temporarily to be set aside. Obviously, it is not sound dramatic practice to string a multitude of actions on a very thin thread. Such activity could only lead to pantomimes that would be inordinately busy to little purpose. It follows, then, that fertility of invention must be associated with a process of selection and rejection. The pantomimist must choose, from all the possibilities that spring to mind when a project is initiated, those few best suited to his purpose.

ASSIGNMENT

Redo your pantomime of invention, but this time select the one line of conflict that seems to you to be the best for your purpose. Select in turn, from among the many things you did in that exercise, those few actions that will best project your idea to the audience. Strive for a result that will make your pantomime half as long as it previously was.

THE PARTS OF A PANTOMIME

Four separate functions will devolve upon you when you create a complete dramatic form. In turn you will be a dispenser of information, an inciter to participation, a stimulator of physical and psychic energy, and a terminator of the involvement. As a dispenser of information you will naturally concern yourself with the unit most involved in that function, the introduction.

THE INTRODUCTOIN

An audience, at the beginning of a pantomime, is an uninformed body. Its mass mind can be compared to a blank blackboard on which you are to draw the picture of your dramatic idea. It follows that each line drawn by you must be carefully selected so that what should be said first will be said first and the second and third things will follow in proper sequence. Until the people out front have a body of conditioned knowledge to go on, they cannot share in the experience. The purpose of the introduction is to supply them with that information.

In every creative action there is a point of departure for the story, one which is known to the actor in advance and revealed to the audience as soon as possible. Through the centuries there have been, generally speaking, two methods of accomplishing this action; we have added a third in our time.

In one, the action that comprises the story has its beginning with the opening of the play. *Romeo and Juliet* and *Pygmalion* are good examples of this procedure. In the other method, the characters are committed to an involvement and the story is already going at the beginning of the piece. In this case, the audience must join the experience in transit, as it were. *Hamlet, The Doll's House,* and *Death of a Salesman* are instances of the second method. In these, and any similar dramas, the continuous story is intensified with the beginning of the play.

The third, developed mainly in our time, is called the flashback method. In it the curtain goes up on a scene in progress, often a climactic one, after which, by a jump backward in time, the action is reconstructed up to the initial point. This style is greatly favored in motion pictures and television, and is occasionally used on stage. *The Glass Menagerie,* billed as a memory play, is a case in point.

In the planning for your first whole pantomime, you already have a knowledge of *who, where,* and *when* to aid you. From these conditioning words you can gain ideas of how to begin your creation. Let us work out several examples.

If the *who* of the pantomime is chosen, it means that the first information to go out to the audience will be about your character. This would be the case if we had a story about a town loafer who, before he became involved in a conflict, would yawn, scratch himself, and strike at flies with a switch—movements that would reveal *who* before *where* or *when.*

When we select *where* as the motivation for the pantomime's first actions, we thereby intend to reveal information about the place where the action begins before we emphasize anything else. If a pantomimist entered the stage looking for a house number, he could easily stress locale over characterization. Or if time, the *when,* were important, the opening actions could be references to a watch or clock, to light or darkness.

Of course, it should be recognized that no matter which one of the three is chosen, their companions, *what* and *why,* work as necessary conditioning factors at almost the same time. Indeed, the major purpose of the introduction is to project to the audience the information represented by these five key words as soon as good pacing will allow.

When you have presented the conditioning facts properly to your viewers, the next step in your planning must be concerned with the element of involvement.

THE INCITING INCIDENT

The infinitive *to incite* connotes an idea of intense action, a meaning most fit for inclusion in the dramatic experience. As soon as the audience has sufficient understanding of character and situation, they expect the next step, the involving action.

The purpose of this device is to stimulate the audience to a heightened interest in the material made known in the introduction. It need not be an explosive idea or action, but it should at least be stimulating. The appeal can be to the audience's senses or emotions or minds. A complex incident is not indicated. On the contrary, simplicity of idea or action holds a greater promise of success. Whatever the selection, it should grow naturally out of the subject matter and be honestly motivated by the character's personality.

The inciting incident must include a presentation of the pantomime's conflict in clear and succinct terms. The desire or the drive of the protagonist is to be made known, together with whatever element it is that blocks that desire. Imagine a girl of seventeen trying on a new dress in anticipation of a date (introduction) when her mother enters and tells her she cannot go out that evening ('inciting incident'). This circumstance is as simple as its counterpart in *Romeo and Juliet*. Juliet, in love with Romeo, is commanded to marry her cousin Paris. Just as uncomplicated is the inciting incident in another play, *The Taming of the Shrew*. Kate, in love with no one, is informed that she will wed with Petruchio, and the involvement so simply begun is off to a vigorous start. For all its connotation of extremes and for all its necessity, the inciting incident is really a plain device.

THE BODY OF THE PANTOMIME

The body of a play is the bulk of a play. It is equally so in a pantomime. In both the action, which was set up in the introduction and activated by the energizing agency of the inciting incident, is extended and expanded. The conflict is developed and intensified. In the body the character or characters give substance to the piece as they make their way along the cutting edge of the conflict. Situations necessitating increased involvement are carefully chosen by the creator to lend substance to the body of the work.

The number of incidents employed in the body of a pantomime is determined by the overall size of the effort. Proportion and balance are the two controlling thoughts that should operate here. Slight ideas require less size or length than more solid ones, and while it is sometimes enjoyable to extend slightness just for the fun of it, wit or true cleverness must be present to bring it off. Therefore, the degree of seriousness or slightness in the subject, the extent to which the character can be developed and interest in the development maintained, and the possibilities for growth of intensity in the conflict are the postulates for the length of the body of the pantomime.

Running through the middle section, as either a broad highway or a tenuous thread connecting the beginning of the piece to the end, is the line of the conflict. This has been termed the *spine* of the play, and the figure is an excellent one. Whether the line is broad and straight as in *Oedipus* or devious as in *Hamlet*, it must be clearly marked and strongly presented. There is no doubt that you will have occasion to employ both from time to time in your stage efforts. To illustrate how each might work in a pantomime, let us create two separate stories.

The first will be of a middle-aged man who lives in a war-torn city. Catastrophe, in the form of an exploded bomb, has just struck his home. His desire, following the explosion, is to get across the shambles of what was his living room to his injured wife on the opposite side. The pantomime consists of his return to consciousness (introduction), intensified by the remembrance of his wife's position (inciting incident), his struggle to cross the debris-blocked room (body), and his arrival on the opposite side (conclusion). In the body of this piece, the conflict follows one straight line from initiation to completion without deviation.

The second story, the one with a tenuous line of conflict, will involve a young lady who has been forbidden to go out with her boy friend. If, after the parent has commanded her to remain at home (inciting incident), she were to release her frustration by a series of angry movements and then quiet down in remorse for a broken doll, and follow this with another explosion and then another quiet episode, we would have a pantomime with a less direct line of developing action.

THE CRISIS

For any kind of dramatic progression to occur, the actions in the body of a pantomime must increase in intensity as the piece moves forward. When the most intense point in the pantomime has been reached, two dramatic constants, *crisis* and *climax,* evolve out of the material. Both are inventions of the dramatic instinct and serve to put a distinctive cap on the conflict at the same time they mark a termination of the middle part of the dramatic form.

Sometimes confused with each other and often used interchangeably, the two terms are closely linked in concept, and generally in action. The crisis, first in the schematic development, is the action or event that indicates that a time of decision has arrived. It is the incident that triggers the climactic scene. When the conflict has been advanced to a point of crucial intensity, dramatic good sense indicates that the time has come to reveal whether the action will continue as the protagonist desires, be modified, or be wholly changed as the antagonist wishes. When the crisis arrives the climax becomes inevitable. Coming at a time when the opposing forces of the conflict are ready to commit themselves to a decision, it forces the climax.

An example indicates what a crisis is and how it acts. The man who had to cross the debris-filled room could make a pantomime out of the action of steadily climbing over each obstacle in his path until he reached the other side. But his effort would be much more interesting if he introduced a crisis into his action. Let us say that as he moves the last obstacle, a broken table, out of his way, a heavy beam falls directly across his path. The fallen timber, forcing him to a decision, should bring forth the most intense sequence in the piece. He must either give up his desire and admit defeat, or decide to attempt to lift the heavy beam. In the first decision the climactic scene would occur within him, an internal struggle of will against physical weakness. The second decision would manifest itself by a series of overt movements, setting the climax in the external action of trying to lift the timber. In either case the crisis is a recognizable event.

The Climax

The climax is the most distinctive of all parts in the dramatic form. Always defined as the highest point of physical and/or emotional action in a play, the climax is the point toward which everything preceding it builds and after which everything following it declines in suspense and intensity.

Founded in the introduction, forecast by the inciting incident, its eventual presence promised by the conflict, its nature determined by the desire of the protagonist, built toward in the body of the piece, and made imminent by the crisis, the climax arrives as the promised and anticipated culmination of the whole dramatic experience. In play and pantomime the identical pattern is followed, only in the latter form the whole structure is much more plain, simple, and sometimes, as a consequence, stronger.

After the crisis has brought the climax into being, the contending elements in the conflict lock in a final contest. How long the struggle lasts is dependent upon how much is to be settled and how long the extra intensity of the scene can be held, short of evident strain or obvious striving for effect. Whatever the length, the highlight of the scene is that point at which a decision is reached, for or against the protagonist. The quality of this event will be contained in its intensity rather than in its size; like the crisis, the high point is not constituted for length.

The manner of pantomiming a climactic scene is important. There are almost as many ways to do it as there are pantomimic themes. Plots that lose none of their interest for all their simplicity can be cited as examples. Suppose a boy's parents have gone away and he must cook his own breakfast. He puts eggs in the skillet and settles down for a look at the sports page. The odor of something burning sends him into action. The ensuing sequence, in which it is determined whether the eggs can or cannot be saved, is a climax of an obvious sort, filled with rapid action. Or imagine a girl at a party, playing the game of building a steeple out of matchsticks; she arrives at her climactic sequence when she has to place the last few critical pieces. Unlike the first pantomime, her intensity is characterized by slow and exceedingly careful movement. On the other hand, a young man about town, suffering from a too riotous evening the night before, must force himself to drink a concoction calculated to settle his stomach. The decisive point in the pantomime is reached when, after an internal struggle, he decides one way or the other about taking the stuff. A proper climax will be achieved when the means match the matter, and it will be the player's judgment that will decide the issue.

Minor Climaxes

So far all comment has indicated that only one climax is allocated to a pantomime. Such is not the case. With tension-generated conflict, what is more natural than the growth of minor climaxes? Left to themselves as they occur in nature, tensions seesaw up and down and back and forth in an unpredictable manner. Organized and controlled to produce a dramatic effect, they manifest themselves in those variable high points that give viability to a dramatic work of art. Therefore, minor climaxes and their associate unit, the crisis, will be found as regular features in all types of dramatic pieces, including those formed by the pantomimist.

The Conclusion

The function of the conclusion is to let the audience know the outcome of the conflict. After a climax has been reached, the best practice is to conclude the piece as rapidly as a proper sense of proportion will allow. But one of the objectives of any dramatic effort is to arouse a healthy feeling of curiosity in its viewers, and that curiosity cannot be left unsatisfied. The pantomimist must therefore do more than terminate his action, he must also untie the threads of the plot and let the audience know how the story comes out.

If the protagonist wins, the action continues in the direction his desire indicated as far back as the introduction. If the antagonist, or elements of antagonism, triumph, then the action will bend in the direction indicated by the nature of the opposing desire or obstacle. If a clear-cut decision is not reached in favor of either the protagonist or antagonist, a modified change of direction is indicated. But in any case, even though the intensity of the climactic sequence decreases, the responsibility of the pantomimist does not. Only when the outcome of his conflict has been clearly projected can he end his dramatic composition.

EXERCISES AND ASSIGNMENTS

1. There are three parts to this exercise.

   a. With a character and a situation of your own choosing, do an introduction and an inciting incident for the class. Stop there. Let the comment from the auditorium determine whether you have or have not established a logical basis and aroused sufficient interest for the body of the pantomime to follow.

   b. After you have received the class comment, continue your pantomime as planned, but with the understanding that the class is to stop you at the time of your climactic action. If you are halted at the right place, the members out front should be able to tell you what and where your crisis was.

   c. After completing your pantomime, check the logic of your conclusion against the reaction of the class.

2. To see how well you can bring off a whole pantomime, present one of moderate length on one of the following subjects:

   a. A student trying to crib on an examination.

   b. An athlete competing in one of these sports: bowling, fly casting, trapshooting, darts, archery, fencing. Do whatever research is necessary. There are problems of conflict, inciting incident, and crisis in this kind of pantomime that require special attention.

   c. A sick person trying to make or build something.

   d. An elevator operator in a malfunctioning elevator.

   e. An actor making up and dressing for performance.

Chapter 8

Center of Interest

So many and so varied are the human means of revealing thoughts and emotions that were one person to employ them all at once, he would be a chaos of expression. Indeed, in some degree this state occurs many times in life, and unfortunately on the stage as well. Hands, legs, shoulders, head, eyes, mouth—every part of the body is capable of moving in expressive ways.[10]

People, singly or in groups, are veritable information booths in motion. We all say many things about ourselves, say them simultaneously and say them continuously. In addition to the specifics of a special action or a definite utterance we give information as to size, weight, shape, approximate age, physical condition, state and style of clothes and hair, cleanliness of person, attitudes, what is being carried, and the purpose of our presence. If less obvious things were included, the list would grow appreciably. Knowing this, you must recognize that the number of items will in no way decrease when you step on stage.

THE DIRECTIVE

With so much information constantly being broadcast, even though each of us possesses an ability to screen and sort what he sees almost as soon as he sees it, it is obvious that control, in some measure, is necessary. The jumble of sounds that comes from a gathering of people all of whom are talking at once, makes it impossible to distinguish any one statement. If clear communication is desired from such a group, it is necessary that one person act as director.

When ideas and feelings are to be projected in a pantomime you, the pantomimist, must become the director of the activity. So that an audience will be able to follow you point by point, you issue the necessary instructions to yourself, planning your pantomime so that only one thing will be said by you at one time. This means that out of all the bits of

---

[10] For further discussion of "Center of Interest," see Part IV, Chapter 20.

information projected by you each moment, you determine which single item is the most important; you supply the directive.

CENTER OF INTEREST

Whenever our interest is engaged by anyone, we direct our attention to a specific point of focus. Obviously the point of focus will center on the most important position or action the person has assumed. This focal point is called the center of interest.

The principle of center of interest is based upon a physical fact: the human eye can focus on only one spot at a time. You can check this statement. Choose any word in this sentence and focus directly upon it. Holding the focus, try also to center on another word at the same time, even the next word in line. Now perform the same action on an object thirty or fifty feet away. Your experiments should demonstrate that the eye can focus upon only one spot, and that a small one, at any given moment.

Now let us illustrate how effectively this physical fact works to the advantage of the pantomimist. On stage and facing front, a young man sits before an imaginary table playing a game of solitaire. Even though hand and face are relatively close together, our pinpoint of focus, as we watch from our seats, will be first on one area and then on the other. We concentrate on a hand as it turns over a card; we look at the face, brows or mouth, for reaction; we watch the hand again to see how the card is played. If the tongue licks the lips before the card is turned, we focus on that movement; if the weight is shifted, we also note that. We watch a hand pull an ear, look at eyes scanning the table, focus on the foot that scratches an itch on the opposite leg. As a matter of fact, we will concentrate as directed on any area of the body, provided we are offered only one movement at a time.

With this gathered focus at his disposal, the pantomimist uses the concentration it contains to direct the audience step by step into the mounting tension of his action. But if, on the other hand, he dissipates that concentration by offering his viewers two or more competing movements at the same time, he weakens his whole effort.

ASSIGNMENT

Concentrating on center-of-interest movements only, perform a short pantomime of playing a game of solitaire or of making a cake or of repairing a carburetor, or any similar type of limited movement activity. Employ preliminary, arrested, and suspended movements as a part of the center-of-interest problem.

COMPLEMENTARY MOVEMENT

The ability to focus on one spot is not the only action of which the eye is capable. There is an old saying that we can see out of the corner of an eye, and like most such colloquialisms it holds some truth. Scientifically, we denote this as an action of our peripheral vision. When you look at a table—and it doesn't matter whether it is five or fifty-five feet away—you can see the whole table at one glance. Also, when you focus on one spot on the table you can still see, to the point of making an accurate description, the whole of the table and some of the area beyond. It is the use of your peripheral vision that enables you to do so.

Out of two such inseparable actions embracing both a focal point of attention and peripheral vision, comes the dramatic concept of a center of interest set within the framework of a specific background. It remains for the actor only to direct the focus and control the center of interest, making sure that the rest of the general picture is complementary to it, not in competition with it. Consequently, in pantomime we plan each bit of activity so that the position and movements of the general picture never contradict but always support the center of interest.

Complementary movement is the static or plastic activity of all parts of the body not included in the center of interest. Its purpose, with varying degrees of strength, is to point up, to reinforce, to add emphasis to the focus of attention. This can be done by the use of a direct line that runs into or points straight at the center of interest. The pantomimist has two such lines, which he employs continuously: the one established by the eye in the act of looking at something, and the line of the arm, hand, and fingers pointing toward or touching a target.

For example: A girl sits sewing a button on a dress. She looks down at her work. Her concentration causes us, the viewers, to do the same. If she looks up, so will we, directing our attention to the portion of her face that demands it—for instance, the smile, or the frown between the brows. Whatever part it is, it is the new center of interest. If she were to gaze across the room at a door or an object on the wall, we too would look there. Thus the direct line of her gaze became a complementary movement of the strongest sort.

Tracing back over her movements, we can see that her eye line changed its function several times. First it was complementary, then it became neutral when we looked to the mouth or the brows, then complementary again as she gazed across the room. From the effectiveness of her action we can derive an important principle: One of the basic functions of complementary movement is to direct the audience's attention to the center of interest.

No unit of the body does this better than the eye. Indeed, the act of looking, especially if it is sudden and vigorous, has an enormous effect upon others. Involuntarily they will repeat the action, trying to see what the looker saw. The effectiveness of this act for stage purposes can be demonstrated by sending one actor up front. Standing wherever he pleases, he is merely to look sharply from spot to spot within his area while the audience notes the response engendered.

By the same token it should be noted that anything that supports can also detract, unless it is properly controlled. Random eye activity, having the pull of a magnet, can disrupt the best-planned pantomime.

The second direct line employed by the pantomimist is that composed of the action of arm, hand, and fingers in pointing or touching. This action has much the same effect as the eye in directing audience attention and strengthening the center of interest; the act of pointing at an object is almost identical with the action of looking at it. In addition, because we generally hold in our hands the thing we work on, the sweep of the arm to the object forms another direct line. This was true in the case of the girl who was sewing on a button. Thus, if you wished to show an imaginary cut finger on stage, the line of the opposite arm would run directly to the center of interest when the other hand comes over to grasp the injured member. Add to that a direct look from the eye and a substantial increase of concentration has been applied to the focal point. Incidentally, if your eye were to look away and down and the complementary arm were to be dropped to the side, the cut finger could still hold the center of interest, provided it were given a prominent position. The degree of attention it would attract, however, would be radically lessened with the withdrawal of the complementary movement.

In coordinating the center of interest and its corollary, complementary movement with definite and economic movement, an obvious interplay of positions and actions will take place when the focal point of attention shifts here and there with the unfolding story. Each shift means that what was the center of interest becomes complementary movement when the shift takes place. To be in control of this process you must (1) know exactly where you are going to place the center of interest every moment of your pantomime, (2) know the sequential shift of the center of interest as you use first one part of the body and then another to carry the story forward, (3) never permit nervous movement, conscious or unconscious, to distract attention from the center of interest, and (4) so balance your complementary positions and movements that they will support and strengthen rather than compete with the focal point of attention.

To conclude this discussion let us conjure yet another image, this time from the point of view of the audience rather than from your point of view as an actor. As a result of all that has been said, can you now see, when you are on stage, how each member of the house will have a general impression of you from head to foot and will at the same time be able to focus sharply upon the one distinct point you designate as the center of interest? If you can imagine this, then you will understand how the viewers in the house will follow the development of your action, point by detailed point, without having to lose the frame of reference within which you act. You will further understand how the impact on the audience of the center of interest is increased when complementary movement is working for and not against it.

EXERCISES AND ASSIGNMENTS

Following are several sets of stage exercises, nondramatic in nature, whose purpose is to aid you to develop individual skills by varied practices in the creation and the sustaining of the center of interest.

1. *Sustaining the Center of Interest.* An imaginary prop is to be the center of interest. It is to hold the focus of attention throughout the pantomime. Using one of the suggestions below, you are to devise a series of actions, logical in the use of such an object, in which the imaginary prop is first handled, then moved, set down, picked up, and moved again. You are cautioned that a facial expression can easily steal the center of interest.

    a. Mold a small clay statue.
    b. Polish a pair of shoes.
    c. Display a lady's hat.
    d. Make and sail a paper airplane.
    e. Shape the hair of a costume wig.

2. *Moving the Center of Interest.* Repeat the pantomime you just did, but this time move the center of interest by a series of motivated actions from the prop to your face, to your hands, back to the prop, and so forth. Be sure the center of interest shifts cleanly and that the complementary movement aids rather than detracts.

3. *Checking the Center of Interest.* The purpose of this exercise is to run a spot check on the center of interest. As you perform a nondramatic pantomime from the list given below, a classmate will sit in the first row and call "Stop!" from time to time. At each call you are to halt your actions (do

not exaggerate the stop, or freeze) while the class checks the center of interest and the supporting movement. The group should note that the strength of the center of interest naturally varies throughout the pantomime.

a. Walk across the stage, see an object on the ground, turn it over with your foot, pick it up, react to what you see, trace its shape with your hands, dispose of it, and continue your walk.

b. Write a paper, frown in thought, look up a word, clean your glasses, drop your pencil, reread your work, write again.

c. Following the pattern of *a* and *b*, develop the exercise around the ironing of a dress, the painting of a stage flat, making up a preset on a bank of dimmers, arranging a costume on a clothing dummy.

4. *Giving and Taking the Center of Interest.* This is an exercise for two players. By handling an imaginary prop, passing it back and forth and reacting to it with facial expressions, let the center of interest be given and taken in equal amounts by each person in the pantomime. Do not work for length; a shorter period of time in which the center of interest is completely controlled is of greater benefit.

Chapter 9

Characterization

The addition of conflict to a series of actions makes those actions dramatic. The introduction of the element of characterization makes all such action more meaningful and important. Conflict supplies the dramatic component; characterization produces the human one.

A further development of this subject, in which well-known characters are created in the round, forms the content of Chapter 18. The concentration here is more limited: how to achieve the particular kind of movement that distinguished one character from another, causing all characters to appear as distinctly individual creations. The requirement is that your mind and body be flexible to the degree that you can increase the oneness of your acting self by the multiplicity of characters you will create.

THE BODY AS EXPRESSIVE INSTRUMENT

The varieties of communicative movements of which the body is capable are too numerous to classify. They are, however, not so many as to defy organization. Four points encompass the subject. They will be taken up two at a time.

The body either moves or it does not move. We are expressive when in action; we are equally expressive when at rest. We communicate with others by the movements we make; we do the same thing by the positions we take. Position and movement are two basic factors in the realization of expressive physical action.

The amount of expression we obtain through position and movement is in turn dependent upon two other elements: what we do and how we do it. What we do is the action we take in response to external or internal stimuli, actions that place us in contact with our environment. They make us known. For example, we walk for a purpose, we look for a purpose, we smile, reach, point, or perform any one of the thousands of movements with which the human being functions within his environment for a purpose.

In addition to what we do is the matter of how we do it, which, if properly used, increases by a major dimension the expressiveness of all movement. The manner of our movement reveals how we feel about what we do even as we do it, it signifies our personal reaction to our surroundings, it lets others see the nature of the core condition we contain. Thus, whether we (1) assume a position or (2) are in movement, (3) what we do, and (4) how we do it reveal us for what we are in any prevailing situation.

Direct Dramatic Action • We can supply terms for each of these last two points. What we do in a pantomime we simply call *direct dramatic action*. Less complex than the fourth point, it still is of major importance in interpretation. Because the action movements of our lives are usually commonplace we often miss their real significance. Yet what we do, the very act of choosing to do this in preference to doing that, tells as much about us as individuals as any other demonstration of our personality.

Granted, there are a multitude of activities all of us perform in common—eating, sleeping, writing, talking—actions that are part of our human condition, yet we ourselves regulate the doing of these actions. By our designation of when we do them, even by the simple choice of to do or not to do them at all, we signify our individuality. It will be a wise student who will not underestimate the value of the simple dramatic actions that often carry the work load in his pantomimes.

Type of Muscular Movement • In contrast to the above, the manner in which we perform dramatic actions involves considerations both more subtle and more complex. How we move can best be described as the *type of muscular movement* we employ. There are two convenient categories here. The first of these grows out of the fact that every human being varies greatly in the manner in which he moves, according to the stimulus that motivates the movement. As an individual you move one way in a moment of fear and quite another way at a time when you feel confident. You have one manner of eating when you are hungry and another when you are not. Therefore the variety of telling response within you, within each of us, is enormous.

Now we come to the first practical objective of the chapter: to develop each person's potential for expressiveness by increasing the range and the intensity of his own patterns of movement, thereby heightening his ability to express himself. To meet the requirements of this objective, here is a set of problems to be worked out on stage.

EXERCISES AND ASSIGNMENTS

1. *Correlation of Position and Movement.* Since position is simply static movement, movement in pause, there must be no contradiction between it

and the type of muscular movement employed. This exercise will demonstrate that strong, telling positions reinforce strong, telling movement, and vice versa.

Two students are to go on stage. One is to take a strong position, the other is to match it with a series of actions such as would logically follow. Three instances will suggest how the problem might be worked: sitting in a dentist's office, waiting; leaning on a yard fence on a hot summer's day; crouching against a wall on a dark night.

2. *Correlation of Position with Position.* To match one position with others without contradiction, create a situation for yourself in which you have to stand, sit, stoop, lean, and crouch.

3. *Variation of Type of Muscular Movement.* The purpose is to increase your range of expressiveness. You will do this by setting up a situation that motivates the use of one type of muscular movement. When it is established, you will introduce an incident that causes you to change your type of muscular movement markedly. The contrast is to be pronounced.

Illustrations: A feeling of confidence turns to one of uncertainty, laziness to apprehension, physical vitality to fatigue, well-being to injury, slackness to politeness, boredom to nervousness, caution to fear, cockiness to caution, respectfulness to superiority, liking to loathing, eagerness to contemplation.

CHARACTER MOVEMENT

A wide variety of types of muscular movement should have been exhibited in the above assignments, not only between individuals but in the contrasts developed by each of you. Still, varied as your range was, all the positions you took and all the movements you made were within the framework of action characteristic of you as an individual. Even though your movement varied according to circumstance, there was nevertheless a unique pattern of action noticeably your own, a recognizable manner that set you off as distinct from any other human being.

If good acting required you to play no other person but yourself, your whole dramatic development would lie in the perfecting of the variety of movements with which you respond to your environment, just as you did in the above assignment. In other words, you could always act yourself, but do it in the extraordinary manner required by acting rather than in the ordinary manner of life.

If you did only this, however, you would miss that great challenge to all players, the creating of a variety of distinctive characters in scene after scene and in play after play. Fortunately, actors instinctively respond to the stimulus of getting outside themselves, of stretching their oneness to accommodate yet another personality, until in a lifetime of playing they have increased their dramatic capacity to the point where they have played host to a multitude of characters.

The second practical objective of this chapter is that you develop the ability to achieve types of muscular movement not your own. If this can be done, the consequence will be that in addition to the ability to think the thoughts and to feel the emotions of characters not like you, you will be able also to portray convincingly to an audience what the new characters are like from the external view.

The first step is to discover what factors determine type of muscular movement. If you take yourself as a primary source, such physical attributes as size, shape, length or shortness of bone and muscle, state of health, rate of heartbeat and tempo of breathing are the principal determinants of your manner of movement. The same is true for all other persons, and be it noted, all characters.

But if these things cause your type of muscular movement, how are you going to create characters not like you, each of which will have its own movement determinants? Fortunately, the answer is simple: within yourself there is more than enough flexibility to encompass all your needs. As long as you have control over such basic elements as *tempo, energy, and shape of movement,* and by that control effect a breakaway from your own habit patterns, you will have the variety required to handle with distinction all the characters you will play.

EXERCISES AND ASSIGNMENTS

The basic intent is to see how distinctly and with what variety you can create positions and types of muscular movement *not your own.* The effort is to be limited to the handling of a problem rather than to the creation of a full pantomime.

1. Do this exercise twice, once with the positions and type of muscular movement that a friend of yours would use, one that you can observe closely, the second time as an imaginary character you will create. The emphasis is upon sensory alertness and physical response.

You are on one side of the stage. You must get to the shelter of a doorway on the other side by moving from a tree to a rock to a mound of earth to a low wall and finally to your objective without being seen by imaginary foes. Not once are we to see positions or movement typical of you.

2. Perform the short pantomime below twice, each time with the type of muscular movement you think any two of the four persons listed would employ: a math major who is an honor student, a physical education major taking a required course, a humanities student with minimum emotional restraints, and a music major with marked sensory responses.

It is night. A student sits in his or her own room attempting the completion of a math problem. The total from a set of figures on one sheet is compared with another total on a different sheet. They do not match. Pencil and papers are slammed on the desk; torso erect, hands cover the face or run

through the hair in exasperation. Then the body slumps; there is an awareness of stiff muscles from long sitting. Arms stretch. The subject rises and
moves away from the desk, loosening torso and shoulder muscles in the
process, then turns on a radio. First the legs and arms, then the head, respond
in movement to the beat. The action becomes energetic. But, in turning,
eyes light on the papers on the desk. An abrupt change occurs. The radio is
turned off, a cross is made back to the desk, where the student stands for a
moment, frowning in thought. Then, with renewed purpose, the subject sits
and takes up pencil and papers again.

3. A team of two pantomimists is needed for the next exercise. Note that a
marked contrast between the two will be necessary in the timing, energy
content, and shape of movements employed. One of the team is a sick person,
the other an efficient friend or nurse. The invalid is to move from a seat by
a window to a chair at the hearth, and wishes little aid. A slight change of
clothing might be made during the action.

4. The last exercise is a challenging one. In it you are to capture the
positions and types of muscular movement of one of the animals or birds
suggested below. Beyond choosing a situation typical of the subject's surroundings, do not attempt much in the way of dramatic involvement. Choose
from among a cat, chicken, peacock, squirrel, puppy, bear, deer, duck, caged
lion, or monkey.

SUGGESTED CHARACTER CLASSIFICATIONS

Now let us increase the scope of our practice by the addition of further information on characterization as it involves tempo, energy, and
shape in various types of muscular movement.

Although we recognize that the variety of character movement is so
vast as to defy complete cataloguing, we also know beyond question that
certain basic patterns are followed by human beings the world over and
have been since the beginning of man's time as a social animal. If, like
the scientist, we can first fit the character into a broad category, we can
then move to smaller classifications with more certainty.

There are three either/or classifications that, if not all inclusive, are
comprehensive in their coverage: the active/passive, the aggressive/
submissive, and the intelligent/unintelligent. These three categories are
useful yardsticks against which to measure both any primary source
being observed or any new part to be created. This is so because each
classification reveals its presence in a recognizable set of positions and
movements. Having employed such patterns innumerable times ourselves
and having seen them often, we have only to alert our memories and
to quicken our observations to increase manyfold our areas of usable
knowledge.

Active/Passive • This classification has to do with the presence or lack of health and energy in the body. Abundant vitality flowing to all portions of the body produces good muscle tonus. This reveals itself by the intensity of the positions and movements taken. A lack of vitality naturally produces the opposite effect. Vitality is manifest in those areas of the body most capable of activity. Conversely, passivity is characteristic of those spots where body action is minimal. Nowhere is this better illustrated than in the feet. If a person shifts his weight forward to the balls of his feet, he can, without moving any other portion of the body, bounce up and down. As heavy as the motionless body is, action manifestly is possible. Little wonder that this relatively small area is identified with so much that is active in human movement. To obtain a contrast, try this: Shift your weight all the way back on your heels and attempt to repeat the above action. No movement is possible, unless some other part of the body functions first to provide a lift. Obviously the heels are to be identified with passivity.

The more energy in the body the better able the body is to defy gravity. Therefore erect positions are expressive of the active element and slackness express the passive. Likewise, all movement that involves the bony hinges of the body, if infused with vitality, will move upward with ease against the constant pull downward of the earth force. At the same time, because gravity is relentless in demanding a constant output of strength to resist its tug, a measurable lack of energy will cause the human body to slump and to seek positions of rest. So the active/passive principle has to do with the degree of vitality in a person, a condition affecting every individual on earth every moment of his life.

Here, in opposite columns, is how these either/or conditions manifest themselves physically.

ACTIVE	PASSIVE
Good muscle tonus throughout.	Poor muscle tonus throughout.

Basic Patterns for All Positions

The weight is forward on the balls of the feet while standing, and erect or forward over the axis of the pelvis if seated. The base (distance between the feet) may be broad or narrow. The knees are generally straight, although the energy inherent in a crouch can be projected if they are bent. The abdomen is held in, the chest is slightly out with the shoulders held back. The head is erect and can be tilted to one side or another.

The weight is on the heels if standing and on the tail end of the spine when seated. The downward pull of gravity is effective, therefore the abdomen goes slack and protrudes and the shoulders slump forward. The head drops forward and down in proportion to the lack of energy in the neck muscles. In any and all positions the weight rests in that portion of the body where it best can lock itself in and avoid activity.

ACTIVE   PASSIVE
Basic Types of Muscular Activity

Active/passive movement operates harmoniously from the positions described above. There is no change in weight distribution nor in the erectness or slackness of posture.

In walking the emphasis is upon the balls of the feet. There is good articulation in all the joints. The arms swing freely from the shoulders. The muscles respond readily to impulses and control is apparent in the acts of getting up and sitting down, as they are in the handling of objects. All action reveals its above-average energy content.	In walking the weight is on the heel and the foot is moved forward rather than upward in the act of stepping. There is neither spring nor elasticity in the movements. While there need be no lack of articulation in the joints, the action is sluggish and there may be a tendency to use the gross muscles over the finer ones. Always the movements tend toward the minimal.

Aggressive/Submissive • This concept is identified with the individual's relationship to his environment. In the one case positions and movements are motivated by the actions of attack, in the other by those of defense. Although the aggressive element will always tend to identify itself with the active category and the submissive with the passive, it does not follow that each one must do so, therefore contradictions are possible. But note the basic characteristics of this category: aggressive movements and positions go out, expand, challenge; passive ones pull in, cover up, protect.

AGGRESSIVE   SUBMISSIVE
Basic Patterns for All Positions

Standing, the base is likely to be broad with the toes pointed out. The directional line of the body points straight toward its objective. The line of height will be erect or slightly forward. The hands, made into fists, are placed upon the hips. Elbows out are a major feature of the body pattern, as is a firmly set chin that seeks to lead the head. In bending or leaning, the above characteristics apply in accord with the requirements of balance. In sitting the weight is upright or forward and not too far back in the chair.	In standing the base is likely to be narrow. The toes may be turned in a little or a lot. The abdomen is pulled in and the shoulders hunched forward as though to protect a retracted chest. The elbows are tucked into the sides of the torso with the hands clasped over the abdomen. The chin is pulled in and back. Thus all vulnerable areas will be withdrawn and protected. Seated, the buttocks are either on the forward edge of the chair or pushed in to the back of it. Hands and elbows are as above. In the face horizontal lack-of-will lines are featured.

AGGRESSIVE   SUBMISSIVE

Types of Muscular Movement

There is purpose in all movements. The body goes toward, stands close to, or circles its target. Energy is required for aggressiveness, therefore movements are more intense than normal. A walk emphasizes the balls of the feet; the heels can be lifted off the ground in a teeter. Knees can easily be bent, ready for action. Arms go out to reach for things or to push at them. Hands rest on tables to support a forward leaning torso. The head turns sharply over the axis of the shoulders, looking at people or things. The tempo varies from deliberate to fast. The senses are alert.

The body pulls back or turns away from any greater force. It seeks to rest or hide in nondominant areas. The muscle tonus does not have to be poor, but it is never fully used, it is always held in check. The pigeon-toed feet are cautious in movement, the weight distributed between heel and ball. Arms go out tentatively, come back quickly. The hands go into pockets or are held behind the back, or work nervously against each other. The head turns quickly, alert for any sign of threat; the eyes repeat this action, and the muscles at the corners contract for a sharper than usual focus. The senses are alert, quick to respond to signs of danger; other than that, the tempo is not rushed.

Intelligent/Unintelligent • This category, which is not dependent on any kind of relationship to environment, has to do with the actual capacity of the brain and its ability to function. Barring injury or disease, there is a direct tie-up between the brain's ability to direct and to control and the movements a person makes in each of his life functions. The better the brain operates, the better the body responds in actions of all kinds and in all parts. The lesser the brain's capacity, the lesser the control of the body and the lesser the response. It follows that intelligence is expressed by well-regulated activity, even in the most finely drawn movement, while unintelligence is shown by grosser action. A simple illustration of the effects of intoxication demonstrates this.

Before liquor is consumed the intelligent person has good control of all his faculties, including his bodily balance. He can perform acts of minute delicacy, such as shifting his weight with ease, picking up small objects, letting his eyes move in all directions independently of his head position.

As drink detracts from the ability of the brain to function normally, however, gross muscular movement replaces all more finely drawn action. Control of balance becomes more and more difficult. To counteract the pull of gravity and to help the body remain upright the base must broaden. In response to the gravitational draw the muscles begin to sag in abdomen and shoulders. In a matching action the smaller actions of independent finger movement give way to the use of the hand as a whole; the arms have a tendency to swing as a unit. The head no longer turns as freely as it did but follows the line of the torso. The fine, delicate activity of the eye muscles is replaced by a gross action and difficulty is experienced in maintaining ordinary focus. This loosening action, representing loss of mental control, continues until, if enough liquor is consumed, the body becomes an inert mass incapable of any movement.

There is an old saying that states the principle being discussed in a different way: "The more brain used, the less brawn required." In a general way the occupations we follow bear this out, although here one can find many seeming contradictions, for instance, the farmer who has heavy muscles from doing heavy work but whose IQ is high, or in contrast, the football star whose physical coordination is remarkable but who must take woodworking classes to stay in school.

It should be noted in passing that the word emotional sometimes can be substituted for the term unintelligent. This is because certain feelings have the power to grip us so strongly we tend to lose control of ourselves and our movements. When this happens we temporarily become less intelligent than we normally are. "I was so angry I couldn't speak" is a common expression, and the implication is plain. Fear can cause the most intellectual of persons to act irrationally—consider what stage fright does to those of us in the acting profession—and it has been recorded that an excess of love makes some persons do strange things. While circumstances cannot change the amount of intelligence we possess, the degree to which we use what we have often changes. All of us perform stupid acts from time to time when such things as physical and mental fatigue, anxiety, and overeagerness, cut down the mind's capacity to function in a normal manner. And of course, all such changes are immediately shown in our positions and types of muscular movement.

Like the other two categories studied, the intelligent/unintelligent classification has its particular area of emphasis in the human body. We noted that the active/passive concept had much to do with the distribution of weight as well as the presence of good or poor muscle tonus, and the aggressive/submissive category emphasized such areas as the vulnerable abdomen and neck, in coordination with the protecting arms or the protruding elbows and chin. Now we find that the intelligent/unintelligent aspect quite naturally shifts the emphasis to the head, which is the housing for the brain, and to the face with its three divisions of mouth, eyes, and brow. For the first time these three portions of the anatomy will be emphasized in the descriptions to be given below, and for a very simple reason: as man's brainpower goes far beyond that of all other animals, so do the telling actions of his face. However, so used are we to this fact that it is usually only the actor who awakens to the miracle of expressiveness practiced daily on our countenances.

As you concentrate now upon this area in your study of primary sources note the basic conditions that obtain when positive mental activity occurs, as well as the results when such activity is of a negative nature. Raised brows, revealing horizontal lines, show a lack of will. Brows lowered into the vertical lines of a frown reveal an act of will. See how easily these actions verify themselves. Raise your brows quite high, look directly at another person and say, "I am thinking very hard." Was the statement accepted as truth? Now say the same thing while frowning and note the response. Check also what happens when the muscles around the eyes are pulled up and tightened in contrast to when the lids are allowed to go slack. Does not the energized action around the eye cause it to focus more sharply upon whatever it is observing, as though the mind insists on cautiously scrutinizing the eye's target? And when thinking hard do we not often tend to use the muscles in exactly the same way even when we are not focusing on any object?

How long ago was it that man developed the external actions of concentrated thought as an indissoluble corollary to the mental condition existing inside his head? And for that matter, how far distant was it in time that the action of elbows tucked in and hands held over the visceral region, positions which we as actors will now use in the characterization of a shy person, were originally employed in life and death situations? Does it not follow that the positions we take and the movements we make can be read and comprehended as primary symbols of the meaning of life actions simply because they are the basic expressions of life itself?

INTELLIGENT	UNINTELLIGENT
Basic Patterns for All Positions	
In all positions, standing, sitting, kneeling, and so forth, a narrow base is required. This applies to the knees as well as the feet. Vertical lines, not horizontal, are emphasized throughout the body. In any position the larger units· of the body, such as the leg, are segmentalized and the emphasis is placed upon the individual parts, such as the foot, the ankle, or	In all positions, standing, sitting, squatting, and so forth, a broad base is required. This is shifted to the knees when seated. Horizontal lines are emphasized, for example, the foreleg is held across the knee in sitting or the arms are extended along the back of a sofa at full length. Larger units of the body are emphasized, for example, the upper arm and forearm

INTELLIGENT   UNINTELLIGENT

Basic Patterns for All Positions

the foreleg; in the case of the hand, the fingers are emphasized over the thumb or the hand as a whole; the head is held in contrast to the directional line of the torso. The mouth is firm and closed. The forehead is of special importance. Here the vertical line of thought is expressed in the drawing together of the brows. The muscles of the eyes can be contracted slightly.

are held and swung as a unit, the eyes turn with the head, not independently of it. The thumb is employed in pointing rather than the forefinger. The hands rest as fists in the lap, and they cup or circle an object instead of holding it by pressure of fingers opposed to thumb. The mouth can be open and slack, the eyes open and staring. The forehead features the horizontal lines of wonderment.

Types of Muscular Movement

The narrow base is maintained in movement. There is good articulation at all joints, and the smaller units of the body move as separate agents, that is, the head turns in contrast to the shoulders, the eyes move independently of the head, the fingers enjoy individual distinction. Also the smaller muscles are emphasized over the gross ones, that is, the ankle is the point of contact when the legs are crossed, the forefinger is used for pointing, the arms do not swing as a whole when walking, the muscles around the eyes come into play. The tempo of movement varies greatly, the size of movement is small rather than large. Stiffness is unusual. Control is always apparent.

Variations of the broad base are employed throughout the body. There is good articulation at the joints, but the gross muscles are emphasized in the legs and the arms swing as a loose unit. Both thigh and shoulder are dominant. In walking the heel is employed more than the ball of the foot. The hand can be used as a whole; it often is an unbroken extension of the forearm. The torso turns with the hips more than it moves independently. The thumb becomes prominent. The head turns with the torso and the eyes with the head. The mouth is slack and can be opened and closed with the lower lip hanging. The eyes also open and close with slackness and have a tendency to stare. The eyebrows lift to show a lack of mental ability. Tempo tends to monotony, the size of movements to largeness.

Along with the study of these three categories of active, aggressive, and intelligent and their diametrically opposed extremes, there should be a matching study of the positions and movements of the persons who surround you in life. When you begin your observations the first thought to strike you will probably be that seldom do you see any of the extremes given above. But that does not mean that they are absent. It does mean that you must train yourself to see what is there.

If you were with a doctor in his office when a new patient came in, your eyes would see all that his eyes did, but because he knew what to look for he would immediately note outward signs of illness in the patient that would not be apparent to you. So it can be with you and your scrutiny of primary source objects. The extremes are easy to note, but the vastly greater number of close to normal movements, with their seeming and real contradictions are not. But if you train yourself to look from the general to the specific, from the larger to the smaller, by degrees you will learn to read positions and movements with great skill and clarity. Know in advance that any given person taken as a whole is a complex creature, but also know beforehand that the complex whole is made up of simple parts.

These three categories have been presented to you as basic points of departure, both for your analysis of character and for the effort of synthesis you must make to build your dramatic creations. The close to normal—the phrase is used in a general sense and we must realize that any psychologist at any moment can chill us with the question of what is normal—will always be the most difficult to see and to execute, but it is far from impossible to accomplish.

EXERCISES AND ASSIGNMENTS

1. Drawing upon what you know of the three either/or categories, select two of the suggestions below and create characters you think would fit. Work from observation and keep your thinking fresh so as to avoid the development of stock figures.

    a. A construction worker pouring cement.
    b. A construction worker reading blueprints.
    c. A policeman managing a crowd.
    d. A detective watching a suspect.
    e. A new student on registration day.
    f. An old student on registration day.
    g. A convalescent attempting to walk.
    h. An athlete warming up for a track event.
    i. A librarian checking books.
    j. A used car salesman working on a customer.

2. Create three different characters within one of the following situations. Only one of the characters may differ from you in age; all of them are to be at the same place and involved in the same event. For example, show us three different persons who might be at a college dance. The sequence for

each person should be no longer than is necessary to establish a solid characterization. Do not attempt a transition from one part to the next, but make a clean break, dropping the first before assuming the second, and so on.

    a. A school dance.

    b. The steps of the library.

    c. A dance class.

    d. A chemistry laboratory.

    e. A geology field trip.

3. Take your favorite character out of the play in which it exists and bring it to life in an episode that might have been written by the playwright but was not included in the play.

Part III

Voice

Chapter 10

The Voice

First the human organism felt. Then, because it felt, it moved, and the movement revealed what the feeling was. Such movement was the first form of human expression. On that primary basis the art of pantomime is established. As exceptional as that art is, it is not the only means man has to communicate to others what he thinks and how he feels.

By the use of certain parts of the body, not one of which originally was intended for such a purpose, man discovered and extemporized within himself the human voice. Thus human sound is a bonus attribute, a later testimonial to man's adaptive powers. Unknowledgeable in specific detail of what he was doing, only acutely aware of the immediate value of its use, man built human sounds into human speech.

In his long history man has developed many wonderful things. But then, by heaping a burden of untold repetitions upon what he has created, he so employs his creation that constant use dulls the bright awareness of his accomplishment. So we, the decendants of adaptive man, take his creations for granted. Possessing a unique instrument with an amazing capability for expression, we daily speak to each other as though vocal communication were the simplest and most commonplace of actions.

For most persons speech is a commonplace activity, but only because for them there is no pressing need to be mindful of the extraordinary action they are employing. For you it is otherwise. When you chose the art of acting as your area of concentration, you removed yourself from the ranks of the general. As a specialist in expression, you will be required to reveal the thoughts and feelings of many characters while at work in many plays in many different theatre buildings. Now you must ready yourself to use to maximum advantage the miracle of tone and the wonder of words.

THE ORIGIN OF SPEECH

In the beginning there was no vocal instrument in man. Then, out of the action of muscles originally designed to suck, bite, chew, swallow, protect, and breathe, a human tone was developed. Later, by adapting the movement of lips, jaws, tongue, and the muscles of the throat and chest to function in a subsidiary action, man produced speech.

When and why man made his first sound is not known, but enough has been learned to hazard a guess. It might have been a blow to the midriff or a muscular reaction to a sudden frightening sight that caused the first sound-producing action to occur, or it could have been the forced streaming of air through the throat caused by unusual exertion, or an impulse arising from the formation of some inchoate emotion that first initiated human vocal action. We do know that a sudden expulsion of air from the lungs, passing in sufficient strength through the throat, caused a muscle there to vibrate and so to form a sound wave. Grunt, yell, or the aspiration of heavy breathing, the sound was audible and noteworthy. Like motivated movement, it was produced for a reason, and the tone told what the reason was. It was so in the beginning; there has been no change since. The vocal instrument was developed for the specific purpose of increasing human expressiveness.

Once discovered and after successful trials were made, speech was developed in an evolving action over a long period of time. The process was complex, so involved that we still do not comprehend in full all we would know about the flood of messages and actions that work to produce tones that are soft or strong, high or low, fast or slow in a series of infinite combinations. But we do know a great deal, enough to form a solid foundation for the establishment of those basic vocal competences every actor must acquire before artistry is attained.

THE VOICE

The vocal instrument is a physiological complex of many parts. It is made up of muscles, cartilage, bones, and organs. These units are variously located in the torso, neck, and head areas. There they perform their several functions in a coordinated activity that first creates tone, then amplifies it, and finally shapes it into syllables.

The Making of Speech • The activity that produces speech is composed of four separate but related processes: *respiration, phonation, resonation* and *articulation*.[11]

Air drawn into the lungs by inhalation is forced out in exhalation. In its outward passage through the upper part of the throat it causes the twin muscles of the vocal folds to vibrate. The vibration produces the sound waves that are the basis for a human tone. The waves are amplified as they move upward through the resonating chambers of the throat,

[11] For a detailed development, see Appendix B, "The Processes of Speech."

mouth, and head. Now reinforced, the sound waves are altered into syllabic units by the chopping and shaping action of tongue, jaw, and lips.

Thus, related in reverse, the audible symbols of human speech are the result of an articulatory process that works upon a resonated series of sound waves produced in phonation by a respiratory action.

Tone and Words • The speech processes produce two expressive units: tone and words. To avoid ambiguity in the discussion of a term that has several meanings, it must be stated that *tone* is used in these pages in a phonetic rather than a musical sense: it is the sound of the human voice short of words, and it is the sound behind words. As two of the four tools the actor uses, tone and words complement or are complemented by the positions and movements of pantomime.

In the majority of instances in the work to come, the necessity to originate words as a portion of the creative process is not the responsibility of the actor. As a player your obligation is to comprehend in full the meaning, singly and in context, of the words provided for you by the playwright, and to guarantee their conveyance by mastery of articulation.

In contrast, the production of a dramatic tone *is* your responsibility. This means that you share the creative load with your author. In many instances, because tone sometimes is more expressive than words, you often will assume the greater burden.

Do not underestimate the expressive potential of your tone, even though everywhere today there seems to be a marked preoccupation with words as the main element of communication in our society. That a word is a remarkable invention of unreckonable importance is testified to by every book and every library in the land. But tribute paid to one of man's accomplishments need not obscure awareness of his excellence in another. Tone is also of human manufacture; it is created by as brilliant a technical process as anything else that man has made.

In the majority of instances, habit and unawareness impose restrictive limits on tonal performance. The result is that most persons make use of only a fraction of their expressive powers. This circumstance can be altered by a training program of exercises and problems designed to increase drastically both the performance potential of the vocal instrument and the creative perception of the performer.

In this respect, mind and tone function in mutual complement to each other. The more scope and depth the mind possesses, the more encouragement it gives to tone to match its accomplishments. Conversely, the more the tone is capable of in performance, the more apt the creative imagination is to discover new and deeper meanings in the material to be interpreted.

The Elements of Tone • Tone is made up of four elements: *quality, strength, time, and pitch.*

Although all four elements are present in each emission of tone, generally only one or two are emphasized at a time. Each emphasis is a conditioner of meaning. For example, if monotony of pitch is stressed, dullness, boredom, slackness of will or unintelligence is indicated. When softness dominates a tone, the caution of fear, or a quite different emotion, love, might be intended. An aspirate quality bespeaks, among other things, secrecy or awe, two states of being that have much in common. On the other hand, the pressure of time or the stress of an emergency would seldom be expressed by a slow tempo; instead, rapid delivery usually would be employed.

Each element has several parts. As with the parent element, each part can be emphasized in the making of a tone. The result is that the number of tonal combinations the voice can make are almost beyond reckoning. If restrictions are broken and the voice is thoroughly prepared, no passage in dramatic literature need remain unspoken for want of an interpretation of depth, power, and beauty.

AIMS

Concepts that contribute to the building of a creative imagination appear often enough as themes throughout this book to require no special emphasis here. Consequently concentration can focus on the improvement of the vocal instrument. To this end the following objectives are established: to improve quality, increase strength, acquire flexibility, achieve awareness, and institute control.

Quality • The objective is to develop the natural timbre of the voice so that a fully resonant tone results. Not all dramatic situations nor all characters require a pleasing tonal quality. On the other hand, a naturally poor quality seriously limits expression and tends to alienate audiences. If an unusual quality is called for, the actor with a trained instrument can produce it at will. When teachers and directors say that a good voice is one of the first requirements for acting, they actually mean that the quality of an actor's tone should be predominately *orotund.*

The orotund quality, produced by an emphasis upon the pharyngeal cavity during the resonating process,[12] is a pleasant tone at its worst and

---

[12] The large tube of the pharyngeal cavity is divided into three sections. In order of progression upward they are laryngopharynx, oropharynx and nasopharynx. Since the nasopharynx, which is directly behind the uvula, is closed off by that member during the production of an orotund quality, it is in the laryngopharynx and oropharynx that the desired resonation takes place.

a rich reverberative tone at its best. Some persons are endowed with such a tone by reason of physical structure. Others are not so fortunate, possessing voices that are less richly resonant. Unless a specific physical limitation is present, however, all can acquire a good orotund quality, first by understanding what the process entails, and secondly, by assiduous practice.

Strength • This objective places the player under two obligations. One is to acquire the requisite vocal strength to maintain full expression during long hours of rehearsal under production pressure. The other is to train his vocal mechanism so that it is capable of immediate response to each demand for increased or decreased volume. A soft tone that stays just above the projection line or limit of audibility and a full tone that seems to bulge the walls with the force of its intent are twin accomplishments of which an actor must be capable. The exercises of the next chapter concentrate on the achievement of these aims.

The dramatic process requires that each player not only have ready for use a full range of tonal strength but that he be capable of initiating and sustaining it without danger of injury to himself. Strength without strain is the aim. In *Fundamentals of Speech*, a book now out of print, C. H. Wolbert listed these conditioning phrases: ". . . in the diaphragm, power; in the throat, relaxation; in the mouth, flexibility." The first two lines succinctly indicate how strength with ease is obtained.

Flexibility • Again the objective is double. Muscular flexibility in the thoracic area of the body is required for proper breath control. If ribcage and shoulder muscles are sluggish in action and limited in scope, an actor's ability to make full use of the respiratory process is limited. As with strength, exercises dealing with this problem are listed in the next chapter.

Marked flexibility in the mouth area is essential for good articulation. Vocally, the first requirement of any actor is that he be heard (strength) and understood (articulation): without these prerequisites, even the finest interpretation is of little dramatic value. Proper articulation is a major aim. For this reason a special chapter in the Appendix is devoted to practice exercises.

Articulation is a matter of physical skill. Like the arm and hand movement of a fencer, the tongue and lip action of a player puts a premium upon swift and definite movement. Mastery is the purpose here. Overdone in practice sessions to an extent that seems excessive when contrasted with the slurred syllables of everyday speech, good articulation permits an actor to take pride in a skill so expertly performed it never calls attention to itself.

It must be recognized in all honesty that at present good articulation is not one of the outstanding attributes of the American actor. In comparison with his English and continental fellow artists he shows to lesser advantage. This condition need not exist for you. Your pride and your practice can guarantee that it does not.

The other aim of flexibility is in the use of tonal elements necessary for variety of expression. Monotony is a dread state in the theatre. Without constantly shifting emphasis upon the four elements of quality, strength, time, and pitch, it is certain to occur. This is especially true of pitch.

Few persons have an actual limitation of pitch range; when it occurs, mental or physical deficiencies generally are the cause. However, the range employed by the average voice engaged in routine conversation is surprisingly restricted. For you this fact should arouse both caution and concern. For all the set of habit and the negative result of disuse, the human voice still is capable of a remarkable stretch up and down the musical scale. Regardless of the particular register in which any one voice is placed, all require but thoughtful practice to make good use of a natural plasticity in pitch.

Awareness • First, a player must be conscious of the exact capabilities of his voice as it now functions. This means that he should have an exact appraisal of the nature of his vocal quality, the degree of strength he at present has and whether or not there is strain in moments of stress, how set or flexible he is in the matter of tempo, and exactly where his normal tone falls on the musical scale, in addition to how much variance there is in his pitch patterns. It also means that he should know how precise he is in the formation of syllables, and in addition whether he is one of that great mass of persons, actors and nonactors alike, who consistently fail to enunciate the final consonants of a word or the last words of a sentence. Further, it requires that he measure himself against standards of pronunciation so that common deficiencies or colloquialisms —for example, "git," "jist," "fer," "goin'"—do not mar his stage speech.

Second, he must have an awareness of what his voice can do as far as dramatic interpretation is concerned. A violinist who plays on a two-stringed instrument is usually limited to a two-stringed conception of music. An actor who is unaware of the vast number of strings he has in his own instrument is equally limited.

Third, he must know how he sounds to others. To achieve this awareness he must acquire an *audience ear*. An audience ear is to voice what an audience eye is to movement. The possessor is aware of exactly how he sounds at all times to all persons in each part of the house. An audience ear denotes an acquired skill. When set as a habit, it functions as a control unit upon all forms of vocal delivery, freeing the performer for a more spontaneous effort in expression.

Control • This vocal objective, when mastered, indicates ability to execute any action of which the voice is capable at the time such action is required. It includes the capability to laugh as well as cry whenever the script so indicates, to be tender as well as strong, to meet the articulation requirements of the most difficult passage, or to perform any of the multitude of other actions the dramatic experience demands.

Control is a mental attribute. Habituated by practice, it functions as a guidance system for the proper performance of all dramatic acts.

Meaningful Dramatic Tone

It is as possible to catch and hold the attention of an audience with a dramatic tone as with a dramatic movement. But, as was emphasized earlier in a discussion of the dramatic manner, the creation of a dramatic tone does not guarantee that the meaning of the spoken words will be clear to those listening, even though their attention is securely held. Actually, a discernible dramatic tone generally indicates that the user is more intent upon the single act of being dramatic than he is upon the act of expressing by dramatic means the various thoughts and emotions of his character. A good actor does not so limit himself.

Your tone announces your meaning. This has been true all your life. As a child, long before you knew words, you understood the meaning in tone. Whether it was in action or reaction, as an infant you put meaning in and took meaning out of all sounds. The faculty to endow tone with meaning or to recognize a meaning already there does not atrophy with the learning of language.

Ahead of you is a fertile field for exploration—or of reexploration, since in a very real sense you will rediscover what you already know—in which you will find out how exact in meaning your tone can be and, as a result, how much more variety and depth of meaning your tone can then accomplish.

Purpose

With the exception of singing, no other art or profession makes as many and as unique vocal demands upon its personnel as the art of acting makes upon a player. He is *one* who speaks in and through and for *many*, not as representative of but in identity with each role he plays.

Limited by the boundaries of his particular art form, he must practice a unique calling whose purpose is to be extraordinarily expressive of any character in any situation that can be put upon the stage.

To that end, the material of Part III includes physical exercises for voice development, explains the processes that produce speech, and considers the ways in which words and tones are made more dramatically expressive.

Chapter 11

Vocal Exercises

It is axiomatic that vocal exercise is essential to the acquisition and upkeep of a good voice. The following exercises, which deal in turn with respiration, phonation, articulation, and resonation, are designed for both individual and group work, the former to be performed in full or in part as a daily regimen, the latter as class activity at intervals consonant with the class program. (Group activity produces a unity, strength, and confidence not always possible of achievement by individual exercise alone.)

The following exercises are graded movements that stretch, loosen, and strengthen as they produce, resonate, and articulate sound.

SEQUENCE I: STRETCH, LOOSEN, STRENGTHEN. TORSO, THROAT

The first movements of any exercise should be slow and free from tension. The count is usually given in units of four for those calling cadence in group exercise.

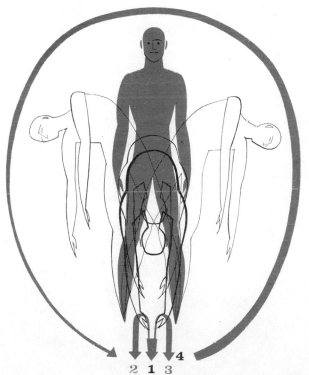

1. Bounce and stretch. Medium broad base; arms relaxed. (1) Bend torso at waist in full stretch forward and down; (2) bent over, bounce for stretch, hands hitting floor; (3) bounce; (4) on this count rotate the torso in a circle to the right, back, left, and front in a slow, full stretch. Repeat, going to the left. Do full exercise at least twice.

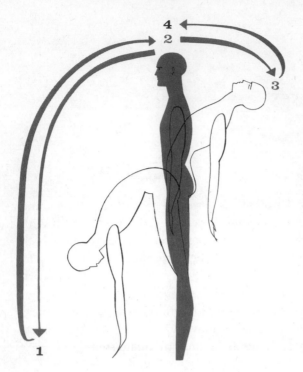

2. Front-back stretch. Medium broad base. (1) Bend torso at hips and touch fingers (or knuckles or palms) to floor; (2) straighten; (3) bend backward, stretching abdominal muscles; (4) straighten. Repeat multiple times at medium tempo. (Multiple times means from five to fifteen, depending upon time available.)

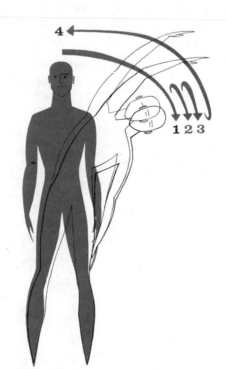

3. Side stretch. Medium broad base. (1) Raise left arm sideways up over the head, slide right arm down leg as far as possible, stretching torso muscles of left side; (2) bounce, using left arm for leverage; (3) bounce; (4) straighten. With same count and action go to the left, stretching right side of torso. Repeat multiple times at medium tempo.

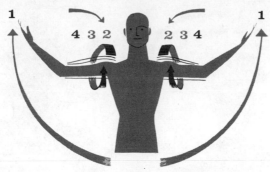

4. Shoulder circle. Extend arms to side at shoulder level, elbows bent one quarter. Relax facial muscles. (1) Make complete rotation of shoulders forward, down, back, and up; repeat on (2), (3), (4). Reverse action and repeat. Let the shoulders, not the arms, do the circling

5. Neck bounce and stretch. (1) Lower head forward; (2) bounce; (3) bounce; (4) full circle to right, back, left, and front again, and up. Reverse action to left. Repeat multiple times.

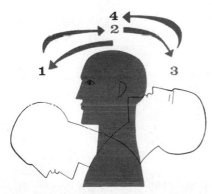

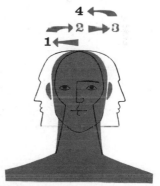

6. Front-back stretch. (1) Head forward and down; (2) erect; (3) up and back, chin extended; (4) erect. Repeat.

7. Profile stretch. (1) Twist head to right side, chin over shoulder; (2) front; (3) twist left; (4) front. Repeat.

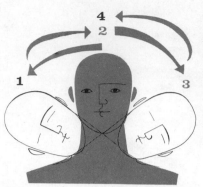

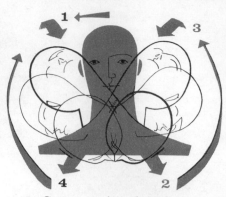

8. Side stretch. Face front during whole movement. (1) Stretch left neck muscles by trying to lay head on right shoulder (do not raise shoulder); (2) erect; (3) stretch to left; (4) erect. Repeat.

9. Crisscross. (1) Extend head on the bias up right, chin extended; (2) cross head diagonally down left; (3) roll and twist head up left, chin extended; (4) make diagonal cross down right. Repeat.

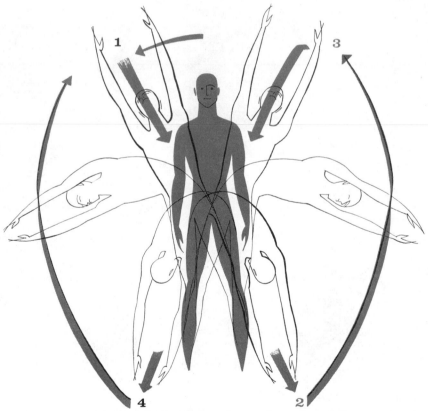

10. Crisscross for whole body. Repeat above exercise but with arms extended. (1) Reach up and off to the right, weight on right leg; (2) swing arms and torso diagonally down left, fingers touching floor outside left foot, if possible; (3) roll and twist torso and arms up left; (4) cross torso diagonally down right. On the count of (1) roll and twist up right and repeat whole exercise as physical condition permits.

Sequence 2: Breath Control.[13] Torso, Throat, and Mouth

As a rule, respiration is not consciously controlled, neither in the primary act of breathing to sustain life nor in the secondary use of the process for speech. To institute the kind of control necessary for his kind of speech, the actor consciously exerts his will on both inhalation and exhalation. The change he effects is an alteration of time and intensity. To meet dramatic needs as well as theatrical requirements, he breathes in more air than usual, holds it for a longer than normal period of time, and releases it with greater care—economy is essential during exhalation, or the inhaled supply will not answer his needs.

In ordinary speech no more than the middle and upper portion of lung space is engaged in breathing, leaving a deposit of residual air in the lower area. But the actor has need to make use of all the air storage space available. To do so he trains himself to breathe from the bottom up, filling the lower portion of the thoracic cavity first and the rest after. A visual check will reveal whether or not the action is being properly performed. If the lower ribcage expands before the upper part of the chest is elevated by the inflow of air, the breathing is being done from the bottom up, as it should be.

Breathiness. An impulse to use more air than necessary in syllable formation and to permit extra amounts of air to escape between words causes a waste of breath. This waste is often audible—and distracting.

In an opposite kind of action, breathiness is also manifest when an attempt is made to use too much of the air in the lungs before the next breath is taken. A certain amount of residual air must always remain in the lung sacs. An attempt to force out too much air leads to the practice of squeezing, in which final syllables are swallowed and final words dropped. To correct a tendency to squeeze, either initiate more breath breaks in the interpretive pattern or practice a greater economy on the amount of air held.

Any form of breathiness can become a dramatic affectation.

1. Inhalation and exhalation. Medium broad base. To check for proper action in the lower portion of the thoracic cavity, with fingers toward the center, place hands on the sides of the lower ribcage over the floating ribs. Breathe through the mouth, *not the nose.* Relax the throat muscles. Make as little sound as possible on both intake and outgo.

2. Continue above exercise, quickening tempo and decreasing count to (1) inhalation (still filling lung sacs from bottom up), (2) exhalation. Keep open, relaxed throat during entire count.

[13] For related subject, "Phrasing," see Appendix C, p. 407.

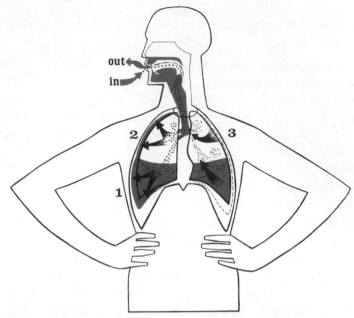

(1) Inhale, filling but not forcing the lung sacs at bottom of thoracic cavity; (2) inhale additional air to fill sacs in upper portion of thoracic cavity; (3) silently exhale, fully but without squeezing. Repeat. If dizzy, stop, recover, and continue less energetically.

3. During above exercise, halt action at irregular times immediately after inhalation; with lung sacs filled, hold breath; relax shoulder, neck, and hand muscles; move about in exercise station while holding breath for 15 to 35 count; exhale.

4. Without forcing, fill lung sacs to fullest capacity; moisten finger tip and hold six inches in front of mouth; purse lips in smallest, tightest circle possible; exhale in *steady* stream; gradually extend length of count from 12–15 to 30 plus. Do not squeeze. Note: In this exercise the small orifice formed by the lips is the control element.

5. Repeat the above with *open* mouth; hold the fingers in the opening to determine the steadiness with which the air stream is released. Do not squeeze. Gradually lengthen control from a count of 10–12 to 20–25. Note: control is now placed in the diaphragm and the intercostal muscles of the ribcage, where it is normally located for purposes of speech.

6. Again repeat the above, this time making the sound *ah*, as in *father*, as the count is given. Keeping the vowel low in pitch and soft in force, sustain the sound steadily and without irregularities of utterance. Gradually increase the ability to extend the count.

SEQUENCE 3: PHONATION. THROAT

1. With jaw dropped more than usual, but not forced down, and with relaxed throat, ejaculate the vowel sound *ah* (not *ha*) in short, clipped bursts; the force should be soft, the pitch low, and the tempo slow and regular in cadence. Let each sound be a vocal bullet—both now and later when tempo and strength increase, cleanly initiated, cleanly cut off.

2. Throat muscles still easy, with the pitch rising slightly in accomodation, steadily increase tempo and strength of the above exercise to full force, as physical conditioning permits, bouncing each *ah* off the opposite wall like a well-thrown ball.

3. Decrease the above to a soft force and slow tempo with three beats between ejaculations. Do not slur, keep the sound clean-cut. Rest muscles between sounds.

4. Repeat Number 2 above.

This exercise is the technical basis for a stage laugh, such as can be turned on and off at will.

SEQUENCE 4: ARTICULATION.[14] MOUTH

1. With jaws held together, purse the lips and circle them.

2. (1) Pucker the lips and extend them as far forward as possible; (2) pull them in and over the teeth; (3) applying pressure by means of the lower lip, pull and stretch the upper (the latter is usually the lazy member in articulation).

3. Expel air through relaxed lips, causing them to vibrate, alternate between sustained sound and short bursts.

4. Loosening the muscles that control the hinges of the jaw, slowly circle that member in a full swing, first to the right and then to the left. A tight jaw is detrimental to both full vowel sounds and proper consonant formation.

5. On the sound *ya*, freely drop the jaw downward. Gradually increase cadence from slow to fast; stop rapid action short of loss of muscular fluency.

6. Jaw lowered, say *la* with a precise tongue action; increase cadence from slow to fast.

7. In a sustained action alternated with short bursts, trill the tip of the tongue. (If difficulty is experienced, work from short bursts to sustained action.)[15]

[14] For further exercises, see Appendix D, p. 413.

[15] A slight trill of the back of the tongue is necessary to achieve a French or German dialect.

8. Softly at first and then with strength, and with exaggerated action, enunciate the plosive consonants *p–b* in the form of clean-cut vocal explosions; follow with *t–d*, and *k–g* (*ka–ga*).

9. Reading, exaggerate the enunciation of the word groups below; form the habit of placing an imperceptible stop at the end of all terminal syllables.

a. Old town, bank crew, cut down, wrinkled red ribbons, brand new, respiratory, murky mirror reflections, bread and butter, shrill scream, ice cream, I scream, crippled creek, rap tack, rap rack, vase safe, serves self, such sacks, felt lint, melt flint, lymph liquid, tried deed, hold down, sandwich, grade "A," switch casts.

b. Sea gull–sea eagle, mock all–mock call, think it–think kit, rapid rabbit–rapid rabid, tipped Tim–tipped Bob, safe for–save for, should not–shant not.

c. Rapid runner Ronald ran roughly 'round the route. Again the ghosts did clothe the posts with ghostly gaskets. Red rubber baby buggy bumper baskets. Peter Piper picked a peck of pickled peppers. How much wood would a woodchuck chuck if a woodchuck could chuck wood?

10. Catchall. In a medium to low pitch, with moderate tempo and with expert articulation, count from 1 to 20 on one breath, 20–40 on another, 40–60 on a third, 60–80 on a fourth, and 80–100 with a fifth.

Do not cheat by taking in air between words or syllables. Beware of breathiness and squeezing—it is better to breathe twice in a sequence than to squeeze. Strength should build from soft to strong as the count progresses. After stretching and loosening the torso and neck, repeat the exercise.

SEQUENCE 5: RESONATION.[16] THROAT, MOUTH, NASAL CHAMBER

Because of the vigor of the previous activity, it is well to be seated for this exercise. The purpose is to develop by practice the most pleasing quality in your tone. To do this the resonations of the pharyngeal cavity are to be supplemented by the reverberations of a larger than usual oral cavity and the sympathetic vibrations (through the roof of the mouth) arising in the nasal cavity. Certain sounds—the nasal consonants, serve our purpose better than others. As always, the throat is to be relaxed.

1. In a comfortable position, initiate a hum and sustain it very softly; be aware of the extent of vibration. Repeat several times.

---

[16] See *Resonation* in Appendix B, pp. 403-404, in "The Processes of Speech," and *Quality*, in Part III, Chapter 12, "The Elements of Tone," pp. 127-134.

2. Very softly, but as fully resonant as possible, say *no* three times, *mam* three times, and three times put them together. Do not slur.

3. Softly and resonantly say:

"O mistress mine, where are you roaming . . ."
"The king was groaning and moaning and roaming around the room."
"Roll on, thou dark and deep blue ocean, roll."
"How all occasions do inform against me . . ."

4. Repeat above using medium strength.
5. Group read, with medium strength:

JUNO: Honor, riches, marriage, blessing,
Long continuance and increasing,
Hourly joys, be still upon you,
Juno sings her blessings on you.

CERES: Earth's increase, foison plenty,
Barns and garners never empty,
Vines with clust'ring bunches growing,
Plants with goodly burthen bowing:
Spring come to you at the farthest
In the very end of harvest!
Scarcity and want shall shun you;
Ceres' blessing so is on you.

> The Tempest, Shakespeare, Act IV, Scene 1.

6. Group read, with strong, sustained force:

STEPHANO: The master, the swabber, the boatswain, and I,
The gunner and his mate
Lov'd Moll, Meg, and Marian, and Margery,
But none of us car'd for Kate.
For she had a tongue with a tang,
Would cry to a sailor, go hang!
She lov'd not the savor of tar nor of pitch,
Yet a tailor might scratch her wherere she did itch.
Then to sea, boys, and let her go hang!

> The Tempest, Shakespeare, Act II, Scene 2.

Chapter 12

The Elements of Tone

It is an unalterable fact that four separate elements are always present in every sound, and since the same physical laws apply, in every human tone as well.

Neither more nor less in number, and never represented by a substitute of any kind, the four elements of tone form one of the most elemental and most used means of communication between man and man. By his tone a person not only lets others know what he thinks, he reveals how he feels about what he thinks, what he does, and how he feels about what others think and do as well.

Each of the four elements—*quality, strength, time,* and *pitch*—has several parts. By a process of emphasis and de-emphasis upon the separate parts, elemental combinations of an infinite variety can be made. Individuals in all lands, innocent of any conscious training, make use of this fact to communicate an enormous number of facts and feelings each day. Without a thought in advance, one person will combine parts of the elements of tone in such a way that the single word *yes* may mean a slight, medium, or entire affirmation; and with no conscious analysis, a hearer will recognize the meaning intended. Nor does their language necessarily have to be the same; like movement, basic tonal meanings are international.

The elements of tone are present in everyone; an actor has no advantage over a nonactor. Yet he is under a specific obligation imposed by the communal nature of drama and his own position as master interpreter to be much more expressive tonally than those not of his calling. His only advantage is in becoming much more knowledgeable and practiced than the nonactor.

To that end we now concentrate on the composition of tone: its elements and their parts, how it is defined and produced, and exercises that identify tone with interpretation and lead to proficiency through practice.

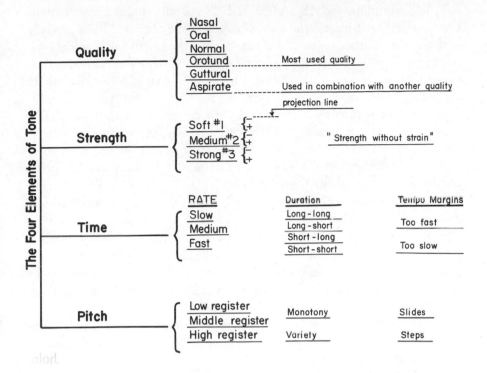

QUALITY (TIMBRE)

Definition · Quality is that element in any tone that distinguishes it from any other tone. If the middle C note on both a piano and a harpsichord were to be sounded with exactly the same degree of strength and for exactly the same amount of time, a listener could easily distinguish between the two tones. This is possible because of the difference in quality; the other three elements—strength, time, and pitch, were identical.

It is principally the element of quality or timbre that permits you to recognize the voices of your friends and allows them to recognize yours. Since individual distinction is so innately associated with a tonal personality, it follows that the element of quality is of first importance in the study and projection of a character.[17]

How Quality Is Produced • Quality is produced by the reverberation in a resonating chamber of the fundamental tone and overtones of a sound wave. Intimately associated with the physical act of resonation, the quality of a tone is determined by the size and shape of the resonating chambers through which the sound waves pass.[18]

[17] See Part IV, Chapter 18, "Characterization," pp. 258, 259.
[18] See Appendix B, "The Processes of Speech," p. 403.

It is a fortuitous fact that a marked degree of synchronization exists for most persons between the kind of sound wave the vocal folds produce and the size and shape of the resonating chambers through which the sound wave passes. It is upon the assumption of this physical coordination that the concept of what makes a normal voice is based. But there are some deviations.

If, because of physical structure, the pharyngeal, oral, and nasal resonating chambers are smaller than average in size, the quality of tone is likely to be flat and weak, even metallic. Conversely, if the resonating chambers are larger than average, a hollow, reverberatory quality probably will result. Both of these deviations can be improved or corrected by practice; if either is too pronounced, the advice of a speech pathologist should be sought.

It is an unfortunate fact that the average individual denies himself a more pleasing tone because he fails to make use of the flexibility of his lower jaw to increase the size of the oral cavity. The result is that vowels are partially rather than fully formed and resonation is less than it might be.

Knowing the benefit to be gained, you can improve your own quality by forming the habit of increasing, slightly and to the extent your physical structure permits, the downward swing of the lower jaw. As you do so the walls of the pharyngeal cavity will enlarge themselves in accommodation, and a sufficient change will result to cause a marked improvement of tonal quality.

Kinds of Quality[19] • Estimates of the number of different qualities the human voice produces vary among experts. Our concern will be with six of them. Although there is no such thing physically as tone placement, the concept lends a psychological aid to the achievement of the following qualities.

Orotund: produced by an emphasis upon the resonating capabilities of the pharyngeal resonating chamber, supported by a complementary resonating action from the oral cavity and sympathetic vibrations in the nasal resonating cavity. Orotund is heard as a rich, full, and pleasing sound. The orotund quality is used 90–95% of an actor's time.

Normal: results from an emphasis upon the resonations in the back part of the oral cavity and the upper portion or oropharynx of the pharyngeal cavity. Not unpleasant, this quality lacks both the distinction of the orotund quality and the extreme sounds of the other qualities. With practice an actor's normal quality changes into an orotund one.

[19] See Appendix B, "The Processes of Speech," pp. 403, 404.

When this occurs, the possession of a normal quality may be lost, but by then the loss will be of little concern to the actor.

Oral: produced by an emphasis upon the front and middle portion of the mouth area, with little discernable support from the pharyngeal and nasal cavities. This thin, flat, and relatively unpleasant quality derives from a simulated placement at the tip of the tongue and between the teeth and the lips. It is often associated with effeminacy.

Nasal: occasioned by the passage of sound waves directly into the nasal resonating chamber. This quality is often harsh to the point of offensiveness. On the other hand it can be merely a slight but disturbing quality mixed in with the normal or orotund. If a nasal quality is naturally predominant, the aid of expert treatment in a speech clinic should be solicited.

Guttural: results from an emphasis upon the lower portion of the pharyngeal cavity; sometimes impossible of production by a young female voice. The likelihood of strain is always present in the production of this quality, therefore special caution should be exercised. The sound of this quality can vary from an unpleasant rasp to a relatively pleasant type of orotund.

Aspirate: produced by causing a whisper. In a pure form an aspirate quality would be all air and no sound. Consequently, the aspirate is generally associated with another quality; in the theatre that quality usually is orotund. Unless an actor cautions himself in advance, projection can be a problem when this quality is employed.

The Uses of Quality • Partly because of the attractiveness of the sound, and more because of its ability to project a variety of thoughts and emotions, the orotund quality should be an actor's natural quality. The good voice most professionals list as one of the essentials of the art of acting is a voice of orotund quality. Overproduced, it can become an affectation.

With the exception of the normal, all other qualities are somewhat extreme. Consequently they are usually employed interpretively in acting extreme characters or in the delivery of extreme passages by more normal characters, as will be evident in the illustration and exercises that follow.

Jaques' speech, "All the World's a Stage," from Act II, Scene 7 of Shakespeare's *As You Like It,* has long been interpreted by actors in such a way as to form a model for the uses of the various tonal qualities.[20] Its study is as profitable for female as for male students.

---

[20] John Gielgud's recorded delivery of this speech is deservedly famous.

JAQUES: All the world's a stage,
  And all the men and woman merely
    players.
  They have their exits and their en-
    trances,
  And one man in his time plays
    many parts,
  His acts being seven ages. At first
    the infant,
  Mewling and puking in the nurse's
    arms.
  Then the whining schoolboy with
    his satchel
  And shining morning face, creep-
    ing like snail
  Unwillingly to school. And then
    the lover,
  Sighing like furnace, with a woeful
    ballad
  Made to his mistress' eyebrow.
    Then a soldier,
  Full of strange oaths and bearded
    like the pard,
  Jealous in honor, sudden and quick
    in quarrel,
  Seeking the bubble Reputation
  E'en in the cannon's mouth. And
    then the justice,
  In fair round belly with good capon
    lin'd,
  With eyes severe and beard of for-
    mal cut,
  Full of wise saws and modern in-
    stances;
  And so he plays his part. The sixth
    age shifts
  Into the lean and slipper'd panta-
    loon,

1 In explanation, surprised
They do not know —
normal — orotund

2 oral

3 nasal

4 forced orotund

5 aspirate-orotund

6 bombastic orotund

7 guttural

8 normal-orotund
9 oral-nasal

Notes

With spectacles on nose and pouch
  on side;

His youthful hose well sav'd, a
  world too wide

For his shrunk shank, and his big [10]
  manly voice,

Turning again toward childish [11]
  treble, pipes

And whistles in his sound. Last [12]
  scene of all,

That ends this strange eventful history,

Is second childishness and mere [13]
  oblivion—

Sans teeth, sans eyes, sans taste,
  sans everything. [14]

10 guttural-orotund

11 oral-nasal

12 normal-orotund

13 oral-nasal in
falsetto pitch

14 orotund

EXERCISES AND ASSIGNMENTS

Although the preponderance of your acting work will be performed in a normal-orotund quality, it is well to loosen up in practice on the other, more extreme qualities, discovering something of the flexibility you possess and building an awareness of expressive possibilities for the future.

1. The class, speaking in unison, is to count from one to sixty, changing quality on every multiple of ten in this order; nasal, oral, normal, orotund, guttural, aspirate.

2. Choosing any material immediately at hand, textbook, school newspaper, or other, read two sentences to the class in an orotund quality, then two in a nasal, two orotund, two oral, two orotund, two guttural, two orotund, two aspirate.

3. Practice your qualities on the following exercises.

Nasal

When dasies pied, and violets blue,
  And lady-smocks all silver-white,
And cuckoo-buds of yellow hue,
  Do paint the meadows with delight,
The cuckoo then, on every tree,
Mocks married men, for thus sings
  he—

It was a lover and his lass,
  With a hey, & a ho, & a hey nonino,
That o'er the green cornfield did pass
  In the springtime, the only pretty
    ring time,
  When birds do sing, hey ding a
    ding, ding:

Cuckoo;
Cuckoo, cuckoo: O word of fear,
Unpleasing to a married ear!

Sweet lovers love the spring.

Oral

When shepherds pipe on oaten
straws,
And merry larks are ploughmen's
clocks,
When turtles tread, and rooks and
daws,
And maidens bleach their summer
smocks;
The cuckoo then, on every tree,
Mocks married men, for thus sings
he—
Cuckoo; etc.

Between the acres of the rye,
With a hey, & a ho, & a hey nonino,
These pretty country folks would lie,
In the springtime, the only pretty
ring time,
When birds do sing, hey ding a
ding, ding:
Sweet lovers love the spring.

Guttural

When icicles hang by the wall,
And Dick the shepherd blows his
nail,
And Tom bears logs into the hall,
And milk comes frozen home in
pail,
When blood is nipp'd and ways be
foul,
Then nightly sings the staring owl—
Tu-who;
Tu-whit, tu-who—a merry note,
While greasy Joan doth keel the pot.

This carol they began that hour,
With a hey, & a ho, & a hey nonino,
How that a life was but a flower
In the springtime, the only pretty
ring time,
When birds do sing, hey ding a
ding, ding:
Sweet lovers love the spring.

Aspirate

When all aloud the wind doth blow,
And coughing drowns the parson's
saw,
And birds sit brooding in the snow,
And Marion's nose looks red and
raw,
When roasted crabs hiss in the bowl,
Then nightly sings the staring owl—
Tu-who; etc.

Song, *Love's Labour's Lost,*
Shakespeare

And therefore take the present time,
With a hey, & a ho, & a hey nonino,
For love is crowned with the prime
In the springtime, the only pretty
ring time,
When birds do sing, hey ding a
ding, ding:
Sweet lovers love the spring.

Song, *As You Like It,*
Shakespeare

4. Here are practice suggestions from roles in a wide range of plays, each of which might employ the vocal qualities indicated as a part of the characterization.

Nasal: Mrs. Soames, *Our Town*, Act II, the wedding speech. Mr. Kimber, *George Washington Slept Here*, Act I, Scene 2, the "gravel" speech.

Oral: Olga, *The Women*, Act I, Scene 2, the lines to Mary Haines. Witwould, The Way Of The World, any combination of his lines. (In Act III, Scene 3, his oral tone could be contrasted with a nasal tone by Petulant.)

Guttural: For a change from the usual crone tone, the actress could try a guttural tone on the First Witch in Act I, Scene 3, of *Macbeth*. Sir Antony Absolute in *The Rivals* is a good source for guttural. See Act III, Scene 1.

Aspirate: This quality generally arises out of situation rather than character. It is used to denote secrecy, awe, fear. Several sequences in the Balcony Scene in *Romeo and Juliet*, Act II, Scene 1, hold motivation for aspirate tone.

Orotund Tone • No player has ever suffered because of a good voice. An orotund tone is an actor's best quality, as pleasingly resonant as his physical makeup allows. This quality should not be forced, nor should it be emphasized to the point that it attracts attention to itself. Naturally developed to its full capacity, it will work to an actor's advantage in tryout and performance.

Antigone,[21] *Anouilh, Act I.* (It is dawn, gray and ashen, in a house asleep. *Antigone steals in from out-of-doors, carrying her sandals in her hand. The Nurse enters and asks, "Where have you been?")*

ANTIGONE: Nowhere. It was beautiful. The whole world was gray when I went out. And now—you wouldn't recognize it. It's like a post card: all pink, and green, and yellow. You'll have to get up earlier, Nurse, if you want to see a world without color. . . . The garden was lovely. It was still asleep. Have you ever thought how lovely a garden is when it is not yet thinking of men? . . . The fields were wet. They were waiting for something to happen. The whole world was breathless, waiting. I can't tell you what a roaring noise I seemed to make alone on the road. It bothered me that whatever was waiting wasn't waiting for me. I took off my sandals and slipped into a field. . . . Do you think that if a person got up every morning like this, it would be just as thrilling every morning to be the first girl out-of-doors?

Macbeth, Shakespeare, Act V, Scene 5. (*Macbeth, deserted by those who might have been his supporters, and at least partially aware of the distintegration of his physical and moral powers, in a quiet lull before the fury of the play's climax, has just been told, "The queen, my lord, is dead."*)

---

[21] From *Antigone*, by Jean Anouilh, adapted by Lewis Galantiere. Copyright 1946 by Random House, Inc. Reprinted by permission.

MACBETH: She should have died hereafter;
  There would have been a time for such a word.
  Tomorrow, and tomorrow, and tomorrow,
  Creeps in this petty pace from day to day,
  To the last syllable of recorded time;
  And all our yesterdays have lighted fools
  The way to dusty death. Out, out, brief candle!
  Life's but a walking shadow, a poor player
  That struts and frets his hour upon the stage,
  And then is heard no more. It is a tale
  Told by an idiot, full of sound and fury,
  Signifying nothing.

STRENGTH (FORCE, VOLUME)

Definition • It is usual to say that strength is the relative loudness or weakness of a tone, but these are not the best terms for use in a dramatic context. The sound of loudness is somewhat blatant and unattractive and, more importantly, often carries a connotation of weakness, even when volume is full. For our purposes the term loudness will give way to the word strength.

In like manner the word weakness should give way to the term softness. Even if weakness itself is the element to be stressed in a vocal interpretation, actual weakness will not do; dramatically speaking two negatives do not make one positive. It is better that our definition make a contrast between minimum and maximum volume. We can do this by using the words soft, medium, and strong.

The term relative was included in the first definition. It is an essential word. Strength is reckoned strong or soft only relatively. A voice that shouts in a room is much stronger than one that whispers, but the first is much less strong than the penetrating noise of a low-flying aircraft. What might be exceptional strength in a small theatre would only be medium strength in a larger place. Therefore strength must be recognized as a variable rather than a stable element of tone.

How It Is Produced • The element of strength is produced by the degree of arc of vibration effected in a vibrating body. The intensity of strength is determined by the force with which a column of air strikes the vocal folds; the amount of strength sustained in a tone is determined by the continuing force exerted by the column of air.[22]

The length and thickness of the vocal folds are important determinants of the volume a tone can attain. So also is the condition of muscular tonicity in the area surrounding the vocal folds. As a rule the

[22] See Appendix B, "The Processes of Speech," p. 401.

smaller vocal folds of the female cannot create as much strength as the larger muscles of the male. The same general observation holds between members of the same sex. However, there have been a large number of noteworthy exceptions to this statement. Of equal importance to all actors, male and female alike, is the fact that the good muscular tonicity that results from regular exercise is the single most effective guarantee of consistent vocal strength.

The power that initiates vocal force resides in the muscles of the diaphragm and the intercostals. The ability to sustain that power without strain depends upon the ease with which the muscles of the throat perform their functions. The thought of *strength without strain* should be an ingrained caution. But an accompanying thought must also be present: a fear of strain can produce the thing it fears; therefore freedom from fear is also essential.

Projection Line • A projection line is that extent of audibility below which a tone cannot be heard. The projection line may vary from voice to voice and from theatre to theatre. It is at once a caution and a guide to the actor.

The concept of a projection line applies to individual words as well as to the lines of a speech. When words or syllables are swallowed they fall below the projection line; when the lines of a speech are inaudible the same thing happens. In the theatre everything that is intended to be heard should be heard, from the slightest tone up to the strongest sound.[23]

In respect to the projection line, an actor's awareness is the functioning control element, his trained audience ear the measuring mechanism.

Stress • A long time ago our ancestors found that by adding extra vocal strength to a word, that word would take on an importance sufficient to give it a special meaning. By this very simple device enormous scope was added to man's ability to express himself. An illustration will demonstrate how effective this process is. Read the following sentence, each time giving stress where indicated:

I don't care what you say, I dón't care what you say, I don't cáre what you say, I don't care whát you say, I don't care what yóu say, I don't care what you sáy.

Obviously each statement gave a different and distinctive meaning to the basic thought.

More than anything else, a proper line reading depends upon stress. When, in rehearsal, a director asks you to give a different line reading, he really is indicating that you should change your stress—which, as you

[23] For discussion of dropping syllables and ends of sentences, see Appendix B, "The Processes of Speech," p. 405.

have just demonstrated above, is another way of saying that you should try a change of meaning on that line.

Stress, then, is of primary importance in projecting an interpretation. Note its determinate quality in the following lines. In the opening dialogue of Strindberg's *The Father*, the Captain has just been told that one of his men is waiting for orders in the kitchen.

> In the kitchen again, is he?
> CAPTAIN: In the kitchen again, is he?
> In the kitchen again, is he?

Later, in the next scene, Laura, the wife, asks the Captain:

> Am I to keep accounts now?
> LAURA: Am I to keep accounts now?
> Am I to keep accounts now?

So habitual is the use of stress that had any one of the above meanings been in your mind before you delivered your particular interpretation, you probably would have given the proper stress without thinking, for you, like most of us, are undoubtedly proficient in the practice of stressing words for meaning. Therefore your concentration should center upon making certain of your comprehension of a line or speech, and upon possessing the vocal flexibility that permits your voice to mirror your thought with exactness.

A caution must be made against pouncing. Extra stress, beyond actual need, causes attention to be called to the stress itself and so defeats its purpose. In this respect care should be taken in establishing the proper relationship between modifiers and the words they modify. As a general rule, do not stress an adjective over a noun (HAMLET: O what a rogue and peasant slave am I . . .) an adverb over the verb it conditions (she walked timidity), even when some accent is required, for if you do, you emphasize the lesser over the greater and disproportion results, both dramatically and in meaning.

Kinds of Strength • There are no established terms for the separate parts of this element other than the ones used to measure strength since time immemorial. They are good enough and apt enough for our purposes.

Soft. Softness is produced by a minimal action of the muscles that control the air stream, enough force being exerted on the vocal folds to keep all sounds above the projection line.

We term a soft strength a #1 force, using that numeral to represent a degree of volume such as is normal in the usual onstage conversation. A more precise gradation is added by the use of plus (+) and minus (−)

signs. A #1— would be a subdued tone, perhaps a whisper that stays just above the projection line, or a low, tender tone uttered as an endearment. A #1+ would represent a degree of emphasis slightly beyond normal, as when two voices are raised in argument or when a tone is required to carry the full length of a stage set.

Medium. This would be a #2 force. The muscles now exert enough pressure on the air stream to create an extra degree of volume, such as is necessary to make an emphatic statement, or for a shout or a call of medium proportions. The above-average intensity of a climax would often require a #2 force.

Strong. The #3 category is reserved for those relatively few occasions in which a character is forced to an extreme of tonal expression. Vocal sounds such as shouts of command, anger, or fear, or the utterance of a scream are included in this grouping.

Many plays, perhaps a majority of them, have little or no use for a #3 force. But when such strength is wanted, the play should not suffer for lack of an actor's ability to meet the requirement. The dramas of the Greeks, the plays of Shakespeare, and many romantic pieces, as well as farce comedies, often use the gradation of a #3 force to achieve desired results.

The Uses of Strength • The purpose of strength is to supply the energy quotient that projects a tone. On the stage the preponderance of energy expended is in the #1 and #2 groups, generally from a #1 to a #2—. This range includes all normal conversation, plus the increase necessary to give additional emphasis of an intermediate nature.

The use of force outside the normal range indicates that an exceptional emphasis is intended. Whether the softness of a #1— or the explosiveness of a #2+ is used, an extreme of interpretation is indicated. As a general rule, when other than normal strength is used the emotional content of what is said is high. We exhibit feelings when we utter subdued endearments or use the hushed tone of fear or, at the opposite extreme, explode in anger or assert aggressiveness or dominance. On the other hand, it is not normal to shout or to whisper ordinary thoughts. A review of your own experience in the use of the extreme categories of force will disclose the emotion-carrying potential of the tonal element of strength.

Strength and Intensity • Although dramatic intensity is produced in part by the other tonal elements, vocal strength is most closely associated with its use. The actor forever deals with emotional, physical, mental, and sensory intensities. To create them, he employs above-normal amounts of energy, even when a stage situation requires him to whisper in a #1— force. Even if intensity and strength are not interchangeable terms, their association, marked by the energy quotient they share, is so close we need not now make a point of their separation.

The climactic speech of Elizabeth in Anderson's *Elizabeth the Queen*,[24] Act III, presents a good example of the uses of vocal strength in dramatic interpretation. To increase concentration on this one element, the others of quality, time, and pitch, though operative, are not indicated.

Notes

ELIZABETH: No,[1] It's all I have.

1 1-, almost to herself

Why,[2] who am I
To stand here paltering with a rebel noble!

2 1+, awakening, startled and amazed

I[3] am Elizabeth, daughter of a king,

3 2-, Proudly erect

The queen of England, and[4] you are my subject!

4 1+, with something of scorn

Wh[5]at does this mean, you standing here eye to eye

5 2, strong again

With me, your liege? You[6] whom I made, and gave

6 1+

All that you have, you,[7] an upstart, defying
Me to grant pardon, lest you should sweep me from power

7 2-, energized by the thought

And take my place from me? I[8] tell you if Christ his blood
Ran streaming from the heavens for a sign

8 2+, indignation and anger in full flood

That I should stay my hand[9] you'd die for this,

9 1-, hissing

You[10] pretender to a throne upon which you have

10 2-, scornful

No claim,[11] you pretender to a heart, who have been
Hollow and heartless and faithless to the end!

11 1+, hurt, and moved by it.

[24] *Elizabeth the Queen* by Maxwell Anderson. Copyright 1930 by Longmans, Green & Co. Copyright renewed 1957 by Maxwell Anderson. All rights reserved. Reprinted by permission of Anderson House.

EXERCISES AND ASSIGNMENTS

Since many of the exercises given in Chapter 11 relate directly to the building of substantial vocal force, the following drills emphasize variety and awareness.

1. Practicing on any previously prepared speech, discover the limit of a #1— force for the room you are in. After that jump from it to a #1+ and back again. Repeat this drill several times. Face front at first if necessary, the better to judge the exact extent of the projection line. If you find difficulty, try tossing each word as though it were a penny or a pebble, causing it to strike the back wall with just enough force to carry.

2. As a group exercise, count from one to fifty, with one member calling off the numerical gradation on every group of five numbers. Follow this kind of pattern: 1—, 2—, 2, 1, 1+, 2+, 1—, and so on.

3. Using a #1— throughout, being careful to stay above the projection line, read, from the stage, the following lines from Duerrenmatt's *The Visit*,[25] Act III, the end of the forest scene between Schill and Claire. Claire, ruined by Anton Schill years before, has achieved such wealth, and the corrosive power that goes with it, that she can now return to her native village and, by promising financial aid and gifts, literally bribe the good people of the town to do away with Anton Schill. By a tacit acceptance of her offerings, but with no overt sign, they slowly weaken to her wish. By now the kindly Schill knows he is doomed. Deep in the forest, at a place known years ago, he is joined by Claire. In spite of the strangeness of their circumstance, a strong bond exists between them. Quietly they talk.

SCHILL: Here we are, Clara, sitting together in our forest for the last time. The town council meets tonight. They will condemn me to death, and one of them will kill me. I don't know who and I don't know where. Clara, I only know that in a little while a useless life will come to an end. (*He bows his head on her bosom. She takes him in her arms*)

CLAIRE: (*Tenderly*) I shall take you in your coffin to Capri. You will have your tomb in the park of my villa, where I can see you from my bedroom window. White marble and onyx in a grove of green cypress. With a beautiful view of the Mediterranean.

SCHILL: I've always wanted to see it.

CLAIRE: Your love for me died years ago, Anton. But my love for you would not die. It turned into something strong, like the hidden roots of the forest; something evil, like white mushrooms that grow unseen in the darkness. And slowly it reached out for your life. Now I have you. You are mine. Alone. At last, and forever, a peaceful ghost in a silent house. (*The music ends*)

[25] From *The Visit*, by Friedrich Duerrenmatt, adapted by Maurice Valency. Copyright 1958 by Maurice Valency. Reprinted by permission of Random House, Inc.

SCHILL: The song is over.
CLAIRE: Adieu, Anton.
SCHILL: Adieu.

4. Read the following from on stage. To place the concentration where it must be, read from stands, if possible, but do not permit the hands to grasp the stands for extra emphasis; like your vocal apparatus, let them be free but not tensed. If necessary, make the emotional content secondary to sustained strength at a #2 or #3– level.

The Glass Menagerie,[26] Williams, Act III, Scene 3. (*Tom, the son, is quarrelling with Amanda, the mother. A desperate frustration from unfilled desires impels them both.*)

TOM: What in Christ's name am I—
AMANDA: Don't you use that—
TOM: Supposed to do!
AMANDA: Expression! Not in my—
TOM: Ohhh!
AMANDA: Presence! Have you gone out of your senses?
TOM: I have, that's true, *driven* out!
AMANDA: What is the matter with you, you—big—idiot!
TOM: Look!—I've got *no thing*, no single thing—
AMANDA: Lower your voice!
TOM: In my life here that I can call my own! Everything is—
AMANDA: Stop that shouting!
TOM: Yesterday you confiscated my books! You had the nerve to—
AMANDA: I took that horrible novel back to the library—yes! That hideous book by that insane Mr. Lawrence. I cannot control the output of diseased minds or people who cater to them—BUT I WON'T ALLOW SUCH FILTH BROUGHT INTO MY HOUSE! No, no, no, no, no!
TOM: House, house! Who pays rent on it, who makes a slave of himself to—
AMANDA: Don't you DARE to—
TOM: No, no, *I* musn't say things! *I've* got to just—
AMANDA: Let me tell you—
TOM: I don't want to hear any more!
AMANDA: You *will* hear more, you—
TOM: No, I won't hear more, I'm going out!
AMANDA: You come right back in—
TOM: Out, out, out! Because I'm—
AMANDA: Come back here, Tom Wingfield! I'm not through talking to you!
TOM: Oh, go—
AMANDA: Tom! (*The scene continues for some time in the same vein*)

5. Prepare and present a short passage that requires a #3 force. The following characters at times use this degree of strength: Oedipus, Electra,

---

[26] From *The Glass Menagerie* by Tennessee Williams. Copyright 1945 by Tennessee Williams and Edwina D. Williams. Reprinted by permission of Random House, Inc.

Medea, Richard III, Lear, Macbeth and Lady Macbeth, Petruchio and Katherina in *The Taming of the Shrew*, Argan and Toinette in *The Imaginary Invalid*, Tony and Amy in *They Knew What They Wanted*, Eddie in *A View from the Bridge*.

TIME (TEMPO, PACE, RATE)

Definition • Time or tempo is the relative slowness or quickness with which we speak.

You will note that the word relative is again used, indicating that in drama time is as variable an element as strength, especially when contrasted with the stability of clock-made time.

Vocally a time unit is made up of two parts: duration of sound and duration of time between sounds. Interpretively each part is of equal importance, there being as much meaning in the length of a pause as there is in the hold or the lack of hold of a tone.[27]

How It Is Produced • Vocal time is produced by the action of the articulators when shaping sound waves into the vowels and consonants of syllables. Tempo is determined by the speed with which the articulators work; we speak slowly or rapidly according to the rate of movement of the tongue, jaw, and lips.

In all previous discussions of articulation the emphasis has been upon the precision with which the articulators moved. Now the speed of movement as an interpretive element is added to our considerations.

When an actor errs in the matter of pace it is generally because he speaks too rapidly; the pressure of playing seldom encourages slowness of delivery. It follows that at first an actor's principal concern with tempo should be to slow down, both in the speed with which he makes syllables and in the rate at which he issues one word after another. A rapid pace is more likely to reveal the nervous condition of an actor than it is to signify depth of meaning.

Kinds of Tempo • The tempo divisions of slow, medium, and fast are obvious enough to preclude discussion. More important is a consideration of time as duration.

The terms *long* and *short* can signify both length of time of duration of tone and length of duration between tones. Thus long-long would be a long duration of sound and a long duration of time between sounds. Short-short would be the opposite, while long-short would indicate long duration of tone followed by very short pauses between tones; short-long reverses the process.

[27] For a discussion of a dramatic pause, see Part IV, Chapter 21, "Tempo."

Practice on the divisions of long-long, long-short, short-long, and short-short can serve an exploratory purpose, giving an actor an opportunity to sense what variations of tempo signify. At the same time such practice will increase awareness and control.

Following the duration indicated by the lines under the phrase, try your vocal stretch as a technical accomplishment on the following:

Short-short: To be, or not to be . . .
Short-long: To   be,   or   not   to   be . . .
Long-short: T o b e o r n o t t o b e . . .
Long-long: T   o   b   e   o   r
               n   o   t   t   o   b   e . . .

Did you note that a long duration of time between sounds was perhaps the most difficult part of the exercise to accomplish? This fact can be directly related to the tendency of many actors to speak too rapidly, thus doing injury to fullness of meaning.

Tempo Margins • Extreme intensities of contrasting tempos must be kept within proper limits. It is as possible to speak too slowly as it is to speak too rapidly. Tempo margins inside a speed of too fast and too slow must be observed if an audience is to understand an actor and, at the opposite extreme, to maintain interest in what he says.

The Uses of Time • The rates of slow, medium, and fast are only interpretive reflections of the pressure of time. They are measurements of the need, or lack of need, to perform certain actions within a certain time limit. Both slow and rapid speech reflect this observation. On the other hand, a normal rate of delivery indicates that time is not a critical element in an interpretation.

The expression of some emotions demonstrate a reaction to the pressure of time. Nervousness indicates fear of an event. This feeling is accompanied by a wish to conclude the episode as rapidly as possible. The relatively slow speech of boredom expresses a lack of desire to perform any activity within a stated period of time. Conversely, we speak rapidly when we wish to reveal a thought before it escapes us or because of the excitement the thought generates.

Variety of tempo incites interest, monotony induces dullness. These facts indicate that an actor's concern must be with the thoughtful use of the first and a careful avoidance of the second.[28]

EXERCISES AND ASSIGNMENTS

1. A remedial action, capable of breaking the habit of too rapid speech, is

[28] Chekhov's play *The Three Sisters* is a case in point. It deals with the problem of dullness in country life. If the boredom of the characters were expressed by an emphasis upon a monotonous delivery, the play would soon lack both players and audience.

to pace a room while speaking in the tempo established by the walk. Enunciate only one syllable with each step. Later substitute words for syllables. This exercise is recommended for daily practice on whatever lines you are working on at the time.

2. The scene from Act III of *The Visit,* page 139, also provides a model for effective use of a (seemingly) slow tempo. The deliberate pace carries a quiet intensity of its own. Reread it now concentrating on the element of timing.

Lines from Act III of *Our Town,* in which the waiting dead speak, also offer good material on which to work for control of a sustained slow tempo.

3. For an illustration of rapid tempo, the scene from Act I, Scene 3 of *The Glass Menagerie*[29] is continued from page 140. In it the playwright attains sustained intensity, not only by means of vocal strength, but tempo as well. Note that the fast pace was made certain by a constant interruption of lines. Being careful of tempo margins, read the two passages together.

Tom: . . . I'm going out.

Amanda: You are going to listen to me, Tom Wingfield. I'm tired of your impudence.—And another thing—I'm right at the end of my patience!

Tom: What do you think I'm at the end of, Mother? Aren't I supposed to have any patience to reach the end of? I know, I know. It seems unimportant to you, what I'm *doing*—what I'm trying to do—having a difference between them! You don't think that.

Amanda: I think you're doing things that you're ashamed of, and that's why you act like this. I don't believe that you go every night to the movies. Nobody goes to the movies night after night. Nobody in their right minds goes to the movies as often as you pretend to. People don't go to the movies at nearly midnight and movies don't let out at two A.M. Come in stumbling, muttering to yourself like a maniac. You get three hours' sleep and then go to work. Oh, I can picture the way you're doing down there. Moping, doping, because you're in no condition.

Tom: That's true—that's very, very true. I'm in no condition.

Amanda: How dare you jeopardize your job? Jeopardize our security? How do you think we'd manage——?

Tom: Look, Mother, do you think I'm *crazy* about the *warehouse?* You think I'm in love with Continental Shoemakers? You think I want to spend fifty-five years of my life down there in that—*celotex interior!* with *fluorescent tubes?!* Honest to God, I'd rather somebody picked up a crow-bar and battered out my brains—than go back mornings! But I *go!* Sure, every time you come in yelling that bloody *Rise and Shine!* Rise and shine!! I think how lucky dead people are! But I get up. I *go!* For sixty-five dollars a month I give up all that I dream of doing and being *ever!* And you say that is all I think of, Oh, God! Why, Mother, if self is all I ever thought of, Mother,

[29] From *The Glass Menagerie* by Tennessee Williams. Copyright 1945 by Tennessee Williams and Edwina D. Williams. Reprinted by permission of Random House, Inc.

I'd be where *he* is—GONE! As far as the system of transportation reaches! Please don't grab at me, Mother!

AMANDA: I'm not grabbing at you. I want to know where you're going now.

TOM: I'm going to the movies.

AMANDA: I don't believe that lie!

TOM: No? Well, you're right. For once in your life you're right. I'm not going to the movies. I'm going to opium dens! Yes, Mother, opium dens, dens of vice and criminals' hang-outs, Mother. I've joined the Hogan gang. I'm a hired assassin, I carry a tommy-gun in a violin case! I run a string of cathouses in the valley! They call me Killer, Killer Wingfield, I'm really leading a double life. By day I'm a simple, honest warehouse worker, but at night I'm a dynamic czar of the underworld. Why, I go to gambling casinos and spin away a fortune on the roulette table! I wear a patch over one eye and a false moustache, sometimes I wear green whiskers! On those occasions they call me—El Diablo! Oh, I could tell you things to make you sleepless! My enemies plan to dynamite this place some night! Some night they're going to blow us all sky-high. And will I be glad! Will I be happy! And so will you be. You'll go up—up—over Blue Mountain on a broomstick! With seventeen gentlemen callers. You ugly babbling old witch!

4. An increase in tempo generally causes an increase of intensity. So does a contrast of tempos. Instances of both increase and contrast can be illustrated in the passage from *Elizabeth the Queen,* on p. 138. From a slow tempo, with duration of pause marked after the first word, "No,/ it's all I have," the pace, synchronized with vocal strength, builds to

1
I tell you if Christ his blood
Ran streaming from the heavens
  for a sign

2
That I should stay my hand /
3
  you'd die for this, . . .

1 #2+ force, fast tempo

2 arrested action, 3-5 beats

3 slow tempo, #1-force

Some actresses, of course, would not want to break after "hand," in which case the fast tempo would hold to the end of the phrase, where the thought content demands a short pause.

5. Excerpts suitable for stage presentation offering experience in the handling of a fast tempo can be found in many climactic spots, from the sustained narration of a messenger's speech in a Greek drama to the many such instances in *The Miracle Worker.*

PITCH

Definition • Pitch is that particular note struck on the musical scale by any tone. Although the pitch of a sung tone is more easily noted, every spoken sound has just as exact a pitch. If your ear is not aware of this fact, you can and should discover its validity by changing a spoken into a singing tone. Say the word *no* and hold the *o* as though singing; you will note that if the tone is steady there is an exact pitch. Deliberately raise a second *no* higher in pitch for a second check.

While it is important that an actor be aware of the fact that all tones have exact pitch, it is not necessary that he know what each specific pitch is, other than to recognize its approximate placement.

How It Is Produced • The tonal element of pitch is produced by the vibrations of the vocal folds. Pitch itself is determined by the number of vibrations per second of the vibrating body. The larger the number of vibrations the higher the pitch; the smaller the number, the lower the pitch.

Small thin bodies generally have the capacity to vibrate at a more rapid rate than larger, thicker bodies. The smaller vocal folds of the female produce a higher pitch than the larger muscles of the male. But all vocal folds have a natural elasticity that permits, within limits, a change of size and shape. For this reason the heavier, thicker cords of the male can alter the vibrating surface so that as much variety of pitch can be covered within his range as the female covers in hers. So flexible are the vocal folds in this respect that a span of three or four octaves is possible for most persons. To the actor this means that a remarkable variety of pitch inflection is his for the practice.

As was true in the use of the other elements, the average individual employs a limited range of pitch in normal communication. Although he uses enough to satisfy his ordinary needs, he denies himself an extra range of expression by lack of awareness and use. The actor dare not do the same. Of all the elements of tone, none is more closely associated with the revelation of thought than pitch.

Placement is the name given to the allocation of a tone to a note on the musical scale. Inflection is the term applied to variation of placement. By inflection—that is, by the movement of tone up and down the musical scale, meanings are expressed. By slides or by steps, by moving up or by moving down, or by moving both up and down, intelligence is conveyed from performer to auditor. Without conscious effort a speaker's tone will vary in pitch as a means of expressing his thought. With no more conscious awareness a hearer reads the tone he hears, taking from it the meaning intended.

Pitch and Strength • The number of vibrations per second (v.p.s.) the human ear can sense ranges from approximately 15 at the lower end of the scale to 15,000 20,000 v.p.s. at the upper. The general range of the human voice is from 80 to 853 v.p.s., representing a span from the lowest of male voices to the highest of female. But these facts are only of general interest to the actor. Of more importance is the relation between the two elements of strength and pitch.

As the strength of a tone increases the pitch rises. This is a natural tendency caused by the fact that when a strong force of air strikes the vocal folds it not only increases the amplitude of arc, it also makes the muscles respond with faster movement, thus raising the pitch. Therefore it is to be expected that when a player speaks with a stronger tone he may expect his pitch to rise proportionately. Unfortunately, the rise in pitch will also occasion a loss of depth or fullness of tone. Accordingly, the prospect of a gain in one direction could be offset by a loss in another. The act of control, however, is still in the actor's favor. It is possible for him to regulate the extent of the rise in pitch so that while he responds to a natural tendency and thus avoids the possibility of strain, he also makes sure that the new pitch level is not so marked as to cause a loss of quality. By this means, tones of command, sureness, dominance, and other like attributes are not sacrificed.

Kinds of Pitch • The terms low, medium, and high registers are in themselves appropriate definitions for the different divisions of pitch. Less than an octave in range, a register must be a variable measurement because of the natural differences in individual voices.

Since falsetto marks the top of range for all voices, and because falsetto can be spoken with clarity and some degree of expressiveness, it and the area immediately below would be included in your high register.

The middle register is not difficult to ascertain. Part of your normal conversational patterns fall within its range. These mark the lower section of this register. Exclamations of excitement or the stress of emphasized statements indicate the upper half. Unfortunately, many persons, actors included, confine most vocal communication to this register. Perhaps it is an unconscious response to social pressure that is the cause. Whatever the reason, the limitation marks a loss of expressiveness.

A low register is the one most suited to a player's purpose. Not that he will spend all of his vocal time there—far from it, for his expressiveness will range all over the scale. But his natural tone—that is, the tone that becomes natural to him as a result of his knowledge and practice—should be relatively low in register. The place on the musical scale and the range of this register varies greatly from player to player. A noticeable strain can manifest itself if the tone is forced too low, but common sense should keep this from happening. The upper part of this register probably will combine with the lower portion of the middle register to carry the bulk of an actor's communication.

The Uses of Pitch • There are two broad categories of expressiveness in pitch usage; monotony, which indicates unintelligence, boredom, the dullness of deep sorrow and other such negative attitudes, and variety, which conveys thoughts that are subtle as well as broad.

To indicate monotony it is not necessary to maintain a pitch on just one note; that limitation is seldom, if ever, heard. A range limit of approximately three notes, or five if the passage is long enough, will create the desired effect; a wider range, if joined by a monotony of tempo, can seem equally monotonous. Properly performed, this kind of limitation can be the basis for an interesting interpretation.

The limit on the amount of pitch variety a player can use is the limit of his own range. Ear awareness and a desire to use the full stretch of his physical capability can open to a player new concepts of interpretation not possible before. Close observation of primary sources will reveal that a truly expressive person continually uses all three registers in the course of ordinary communication, and does so without calling attention to the fact. It is incumbent upon an actor to better this performance, and to do so with equal unobtrusiveness. The greater the stretch of pitch and the more accustomed a player is to its use, the more readily will interpretive inspirations materialize.

Slides and Steps • A tone moves up and down the vocal scale in two ways: by slides and steps. So many and so diversified are the meanings that can be conveyed by these two actions, it is impossible to catalogue them all. Your own experimentation can be as revealing as a list.

The arrows indicate a pitch pattern. Read first with a narrow range of about three notes. Repeat, using approximately six. Begin with a continuous vocal slide:

I don't know.

Now break the slide with pauses as indicated:

I don't know.

Still sliding, pause still more:

I don't know.

Now substitute steps for slides:

I don't know.

Repeat the the drill using slide patterns on single words: *yes, well, never, oh, far, finished, exceptionally, consideration.* Next try the use of slides and steps on short phrases of your own composition.

From the rising inflection of a question to the falling, resting note of an assertion, the pitch patterns a person or a character uses grow directly out of his thought and feeling.

Nickles, Archibald MacLeish's representative of Satan in his verse play, *J. B.*,[30] requires as broad a play of pitch as any character in modern drama. To test what pitch can do, first read the passage below with a range limited to 3–5 notes, and then reread, letting your pitch patterns stretch to express the attitudes indicated. Nickles, it should be noted, has that extreme of malicious vitality that evil always seems to possess.

(*Nickles and his companion Mr. Zuss, who will later symbolize the force of good, or God, have just entered the empty ring of the circus where they work as peanut and balloon vendors. Surreptitiously, they intend to play out the story of Job. In response to Nickel's irony, Mr. Zuss exclaims——*)

Notes

MR. ZUSS: (*thundering*) What's so
    wrong with the world?
        1
NICKLES: Wrong with it!   1 Surprised amazement
        2
    Try to spin one on a dung-heap.   2 Challengingly contemptuous
        3   4
    I heard upon his dry dung-heap   3 aggressively positive, offered
        3   in proof that his attitudes
    That man cry out who cannot   are justified
        sleep.
        5   4 distastefully
    "If God is God He is not good,
    If God is good He is not God;   5 deliberately mocking
        6
    Take the even, take the odd,   6 shrugging
        7   8
    I would not sleep here if I could   7 bitterly
        9   8 arrested tone, slight pause
    Except for the little green leaves in
        the wood   9 smilingly simple
    And the wind on the water."
        10   10 shaking head in
MR. ZUSS: You are a bitter boy.   disapproval
        11
NICKLES: I taste of the world.   11 bitterly antagonistic
        12
    I've licked the stick that beat my 12 dryly sarcastic
        brains out—
    Stick that broke my father's bones.

30 *J. B.* by Archibald MacLeish. Copyright 1956, 1957, 1958 by Archibald MacLeish. Reprinted by permission of Houghton Mifflin Co.

EXERCISES AND ASSIGNMENTS

1. Flexibility, awareness, and control are the principal aims of these drills.

a. Determine the scope of your natural range. This can be done by working at a piano. If you have difficulty in matching a spoken pitch with a note on the instrument, hold the syllable long enough to fix it for comparison.

b. Establish the approximate location of each of your three registers by speaking in your low register on the count of one, the middle register on two, and the high register on three. As you continue the count, descend and ascend in order.

c. Using material from any source, read one paragraph in your lower register, first with monotony, then with variety. Within the limitation of one register sufficient variety can be obtained to make the reading interesting.

2. From observation of primary sources, select two short instances, one a demonstration of monotony of pitch in a usual life situation, the other an illustration of variety drawn from a different circumstance, and present both on stage so the audience hears a valid comparison.

3. Monotony invariably deals with negative attitudes. What limitation of pitch would you assign to the following?

a. Indifference: "I don't care. Do what you want, it is a matter of complete unconcern to me, now or any other time. Just let me alone."

b. Physical fatigue: "I'm tired—worn out. This heat is too much for me. Let the work go—dishes, beds, floors—let it all go. I've got to rest."

c. Defeat: Shylock, *The Merchant of Venice*, Act IV, Scene 1.
"I pray you give me leave to go from hence:
I am not well. Send the deed after me,
And I will sign it."

4. Variety of pitch is a live element in interpretation; it bespeaks physical, mental, or emotional vigor; it indicates active (but not always pleasing) attitudes.

The vocal stretch of pitch in the human voice is remarkable; it is equally remarkable how little of that stretch is used for expressive purposes, not only among unknowledgeable nonactors, but among players themselves. Early in his training each actor should work to achieve a breakthrough in his use of this element of tone, first by being conscious of the expressive possibilities increased stretch in pitch provides, and then by accomplishing the actual physical breakthrough itself. In your case, do not be deterred by the unusual sound that results from a free ranging up and down the pitch scale, but continue your practice until the use of the increased range becomes habitual.

What degree of variation of pitch would you use when reading one of the characters from the following excerpt from Act II of *She Stoops To Conquer*?[31] Hastings, left alone on stage, sees his sweetheart, Miss Neville, in

---

[31] This play, together with *Hamlet* and *The Imaginary Invalid*, because of the use made of each throughout the text, should be studied thoroughly to the extent that preknowledge aids in the many uses to which various excerpts are put.

this place he and his friend Marlow have mistaken for an inn. Delighted amazement mixes with marked affection as the two talk.

HASTINGS, *solus.*

HASTINGS: So I find this fellow's civilities begin to grow troublesome. But who can be angry at those assiduities which are meant to please him? Ha! what do I see? Miss Neville, by all that's happy!

Enter MISS NEVILLE.

MISS NEVILLE: My dear Hastings! To what unexpected good fortune, to what accident, am I to ascribe this happy meeting?

HASTINGS: Rather let me ask the same question, as I could never have hoped to meet my dearest Constance at an inn.

MISS NEVILLE: An inn! Sure you mistake! My aunt, my guardian, lives here. What could induce you to think this house an inn?

HASTINGS: My friend, Mr. Marlow, with whom I came down, and I, have been sent here as to an inn, I assure you. A young fellow whom we accidentally met at a house hard by directed us hither.

MISS NEVILLE: Certainly it must be one of my hopeful cousin's tricks, of whom you have heard me speak so often, ha! ha! ha! ha!

HASTINGS: He whom your aunt intends for you? He of whom I have such just apprehensions?

MISS NEVILLE: You have nothing to fear from him, I assure you. You'd adore him if you knew how heartily he despises me. My aunt knows it too, and has undertaken to court me for him, and actually begins to think she has made a conquest.

HASTINGS: Thou dear dissembler! You must know, my Constance, I have just seized this happy opportunity of my friend's visit here to get admittance into the family. The horses that carried us down are now fatigued with their journey, but they'll soon be refreshed; and then, if my dearest girl will trust in her faithful Hastings, we shall soon be landed in France, where even among slaves the laws of marriage are respected.

MISS NEVILLE: I have often told you, that though ready to obey you, I yet should leave my little fortune behind with reluctance. The greatest part of it was left me by my uncle, the India Director, and chiefly consists in jewels. I have been for some time persuading my aunt to let me wear them. I fancy I'm very near succeeding. The instant they are put into my possession you shall find me ready to make them and myself yours.

HASTINGS: Perish the baubles! Your person is all I desire. In the meantime, my friend Marlow must not be let into his mistake. I know the strange reserve of his temper is such that, if abruptly informed of it, he would instantly quit the house before our plan was ripe for execution.

MISS NEVILLE: But how shall we keep him in the deception? Miss Hardcastle is just returned from walking; what if we still continue to deceive him?—This, this way—

5. Certain characters make more vocal demands on an actor than others. The following suggestions for practice sum up the work of this chapter.

Women:

Ophelia, *Hamlet*, Shakespeare, Act IV, Scene 1. Madness is its own motivation; Ophelia's scene is a direct invitation to the actress to try her interpretive and performance powers.

Andromache, *The Trojan Women*, Euripides. A mother must say goodbye to her little son who is to be taken out and killed. See page 291, Chapter 19, Part IV, "Inner State of Being and Emotion."

Viola, *Twelfth Night*, Shapespeare, Act II, Scene 2. Masquerading as a boy, Viola is exhilarated by the occurrences her disguise causes; she adds an impish sense of fun and joy to the words she speaks after the departure of Malvolio.

Men:

Cyrano, *Cyrano de Bergerac*, Rostand, Act I, The famous nose speech challenges vocal variety.

Gratiano, in *The Merchant of Venice*, and Mercutio, in *Romeo and Juliet*, are Renaissance men, volatile, flamboyant, articulate, mockingly ironic, yet socially knowledgeable in what they say. Gratiano's "Let me play the fool" in Act I, Scene 1, and Mercutio's "Queen Mab" speech in Act 1, Scene 4 are recommended.

Chapter 13

The Expressive Word

A word is a symbol of an idea. We think, speak, and write ideas as words. The actor is immediately concerned with the first and second of these actions.

CREATIVE DYNAMIC

When a playwright shapes a word or sentence out of his thought and feeling, he invests it with a creative dynamic. When he puts that word or sentence down on paper, he makes his investment permanent. Words held in fixed patterns on flat pages are storage cells where intangible things from the spirit of the creator form quiet pools of power. The dynamic contained there is not lost, it is only at rest, held in suspension against the possibility of future release and use.

The time of rest for the artistic storage cell we call a play is indeterminate. Duration may be from yesterday or from twenty-five hundred years ago. Time is not critical; the creative dynamic rests, waiting to be tapped. The critical element is the manner and extent of release.

A reader releases the dynamic in words. Alone, in his own place of study, he effects a transfer of the investor's creative power to himself, sharing to the extent that he can the thoughts and feelings that were in the original work. The experience is internally exciting. Outwardly it is passive. The relationship is one to one; there it stops, fulfilled.

When an actor first becomes acquainted with a play, he is a reader. Bound by the one-to-one relationship between the creator and receiver, his reading is a complete experience. But he reads for preparation as well as completion. Like the reader, he taps the dynamic of his material. In him, however, it is not only to be contained, it is to be matched. An actor is as agressive a creator as a playwright.

The spoken word of the actor must contain as much creative dynamic for an audience as an author's written word does for a reader. This means that a player must match understanding with his playwright. It also means that his oral performance must be as clean-cut and clear as the written one.

Words are meaningful. So is tone. The playwright supplies the first, the actor the second. One must match the other. Since the actor's creativity follows that of the playwright and depends upon it, it is his responsibility to see to the matching.

Interestingly enough, when an author once invests a work with his creative dynamic, it thereafter becomes a source of supply without limit. Numberless connections can be made to an artistic storage cell. Spiritual laws, not physical, apply here. Five or five hundred or five thousand actors can tap the dramatic power and wisdom of "All the world's a stage," and each can draw to the extent of his capacity without draining or diminishing by one jot the dynamic of the original. This is an inheritance for all actors.

But the quiescent dramatic power contained in the lines of a part cannot transfer itself. No automatic process functions here. Each actor determines the extent of his own draw. He will pull off no more than he can handle, primarily because to him that is all there appears to be in the source. For example, consider two actors playing Hamlet; one may come close to matching the creative dynamic of the playwright while the other makes use of only a fraction of the potential contained in the play. Yet the supply is the same for both.

We know what a playwright's responsibility to his text is. He must have clarity of concept for what he wishes to say. He must choose the exact words that best express his concept. He must arrange them in the most meaningful context possible, so that his broad intent is conditioned by his subtle shadings, and both are capable of stimulating a desired response in a reader.

As far as an actor's responsibility to words is concerned, his task is to comprehend them, singly and in context, to memorize them with gain rather than loss of understanding in the process, and to deliver them with the intent and content as fully realized as possible.

Audible Thoughts

A word spoken is a thought revealed. It is an idea made audible.

Before ideas become audible they must be thought, energized with intellectual activity that has a focus. But because generalizations require less mental energy than disciplined thought, the tendency on the part of most of us is to let generalities prevail in our thinking. We imbue a definite pronoun with most indefinite antecedents: "*They* say it is so," or "*They* say it can't be done." Or we burden a catchall noun like *thing* with all manner of meanings: "So he's got this *thing* going for him." If an actor permits generalities to cloud his thinking, vagueness is sure to stigmatize his work. Furthermore, habit can cause him to believe that vagueness is definite.

As an instrument of expression, a word can be one of the sharpest of acting tools. It gains its edge by reason of the intellectual honing that precedes its use. A good playwright puts ideas down on paper with fullness and clarity for you to read and study. As he expands a basic thought, so must you. When he contracts his thought to give it the clarity of specificity, you are required to do the same. If a playwright goes beyond you by employing a new word or an involved phrase, your task is to put yourself on equal footing by looking up the word or by resolving the thought.

When an actor delivers an author's lines he makes a test of whether the words still belong to the playwright or whether he has also made them his own. In acting, joint ownership of the words that make up a role is essential to the creative process. Every playwright knows this and hopes for it as he writes his lines. Shakespeare, we may be sure, would be entirely willing to share title to even the famous "To be, or not to be," if he could be sure that the actor was willing to invest as much in the property as was already put in it.

Not all playwrights and not all plays require the same attention. The light, popular piece generally presents little or no problem, except that the player must be as clear and as exact as to meaning in a light farce and a slight phrase as in a more profound drama and an involved passage.

Other plays do present problems, especially those containing a subject content that is not a matter of widespread knowledge today, such as the historical references in Greek drama. This would also be true of pieces in which the words and word groupings differ from those to which we are accustomed. Shakespeare always requires special treatment in this respect. So do Ibsen, Strindberg, Chekhov, Pirandello, Beckett, Ionesco —all first-rate authors, as a matter of fact.

Paraphrasing

The simplest and most direct way to assure yourself of a precise and full comprehension of the thought content of your subject material is to tell yourself, in your own words, what each line of your script means. You paraphrase the author, not to substitute your words for his, but to arrive at a sharp and exact definition of his intent.[32]

[32] To those who fear that paraphrasing might cause a player to substitute his words for those of the playwright, the author can state that in thirty-plus years he has found this to be no problem, whether in Shakespeare or Arthur Miller. However, the actor who replaces a playwright's lines with his own expressions because his seem more natural and feel more "comfortable," or even adds "Look" at the beginning and "huh" at the ends of sentences, does create a problem—of a different sort.

Acting in our time suffers from the reason that too many players assume completeness of comprehension when only partial understanding is present. A glimmer of an idea is not good enough. Only when the player specifically tells himself what he means can he be sure that he knows what he is saying.

To illustrate, let us first deal with a single word, one of the simplest in the language. Suppose a person were to ask if you would return a book to the library on your way to class, and you were to answer, "Yes." Besides agreement, what will your answer mean? Do you intend it to say "I'd be glad to" or "All right, but I'd rather not"? Or should it mean "Of course, why do you ask?" or "O.K., but hurry up, I'm late"? When you decide exactly what that single word yes is going to mean and tell yourself so in unequivocal language, sureness will come into your work.

Restatement of Meaning • Many lines in plays say exactly what they mean. Therefore to paraphrase them is only to restate their intrinsic thoughts in your own words. Two sets of words for one thought results. At first glance the addition of actor-deduced phrases to the obviously expressed thoughts of a playwright may seem unnecessary and, in some cases, impudent or absurd. Such is not the case, at least to the player who seeks clarity of concept and exactness of statement. To him it is desirable to gain the sense of confidence that comes from a thorough understanding of each line of his part. For him a restatement, in clear, exact terms, of his concept of the meaning of lines is a desirable action.

Here is series of well-known quotations from *Hamlet* which, for our immediate purposes, can be taken to say what they mean. But what, exactly, is their meaning? Familiarity with well-known lines can produce the assumption that acquaintanceship assures comprehension. But that assumption is not always correct. You can make your comprehension more certain by concise statements of the interpretation you intend for the following lines.

HORATIO: . . . But, look, the morn, in russet mantle clad, . . . (I, 1)

HAMLET: O, that this too too solid flesh would melt,

Thaw and resolve itself into a dew! (I, 2)

POLONIUS: . . . This above all, to thine own self be true, . . . (I, 3)

HAMLET: . . . the play's the thing

Wherein I'll catch the conscience of the king. (II, 2)

HORATIO: Now cracks a noble heart. Good night, sweet prince;

And flights of angels sing thee to thy rest! (V, 2)

OPHELIA: O, what a noble mind is here o'erthrown! (III, 1)

OPHELIA: Could beauty, my lord, have better commerce than with honesty? (III, 1)

OPHELIA: Where is the beauteous majesty of Denmark? (IV, 5)

QUEEN: Come, come, you answer with an idle tongue. (III, 4)

QUEEN: There is a willow grows aslant a brook, . . . (IV, 7)

Commonplace Expressions • Always susceptible to a variety of interpretations, and much of the time no longer identified with original intent or meaning, is the series of commonplace expressions, especially greetings, that appear in everyday conversation and that are used in equal measure in our playscripts. Seldom does "How do you do?" really form the basis for an inquiry concerning health. Instead, in a life or a stage situation, it is a vocal vehicle for an extensive series of possible expressions: a polite acknowledgement of an introduction, a casual greeting, a murmured formalism, an eager utterance, a prefunctory expression, an overly polite effusion, and many, many others.

In this case memorization of a set of words is only part of an actor's responsibility. Equally essential to a good performance is the acquisition of specific knowledge of the meaning of even a commonplace expression. To counteract the effect of ambiguity, an actor again must make certain of the thought behind the line when he states that thought in words of his own choosing. And he becomes even more sure of his grasp of thought content when he writes it down, a practice recommended in all instances when uncertainty, obscurity, or complexity is associated with a speech. In the beginning it is a recommended practice for all interpretive work.

What five thoughts might properly be expressed by this one word?

Hello.   _____
_____
_____
_____
_____

And this sentence?

_____
_____
How are you?   _____
_____
_____

And this colloquialism?

_____
What do you say? _____
(Wha-dya-say)   _____
_____

The Single Word or Short Phrase • In addition to commonplace expressions, a short phrase or single word is also susceptible of superficial treatment in the matter of its comprehension. Yet the single word (in effect a sentence in itself) or the terse phrase has been selected by the author because conciseness or terseness is the specific expression he wishes to convey. Each such utterance should be as accurately studied and as clearly understood as its longer and more complex companions.

Earlier the word yes was used as an example of this point. Let us now take its opposite and, in a stated circumstance, assign it several specific meanings. For example, a suggestion is made by an influential group of friends that you assume the chairmanship of an important committee in student government. After careful consideration you give your answer— no. What five valid meanings might you be able to convey to them by this single word?

_____
_____
No.   _____
_____
_____

In Act I, Scene 2 of *Hamlet* a series of concise expressions occur. Often, in performance, these lines are delivered with little more concept than that the tempo of their utterance should be brisk. Interpretations of the meanings contained in this series may rightly differ, but just as rightly each interpretation should be clear and exact in the mind of each player.

In the scene before our excerpt begins, Hamlet has been apprised of the appearance of his father's ghost by the testimony of Horatio, whom he trusts, and Marcellus and Bernardo, who have twice seen the apparition. In an age when supernatural spirits were accorded the authenticity of common belief, this particular ghost's appearance has a marked effect on the young prince. Alert, disturbed, and cautious, he questions the others. He may do so as a prince to his subjects, as a military man to subordinates, or as a friend to friends, even as a companion to other companions. His first query is "Hold you the watch tonight?" to which Marcellus and Bernardo reply in unison, "We do, my lord."

Let us assume that these two speeches can be taken to mean what they obviously say. (We shall come back to them for further treatment in the next chapter.) Hamlet then asks, "Arm'd, say you?" Since only one thought can be in his mind, which of these three possible meanings would you choose, were you to utter these words?

	You will wear your usual weapons, I assume?
Arm'd, say you?	*I think a strong precaution is necessary.*
	I see you carry weapons, will you have them tonight?

And which of these three offered in reply?

	Of course, just as we usually do, my friend.
Arm'd, my lord.	*Indeed so, never fear, Sir!*
	These very weapons, honored sir.

The same terseness continues. Following the line of thought initiated above, how would you fill in each of the three possibilities?

From top to toe?	_____
	_____
My lord, from	_____
head to foot.	_____
	_____

Taking advantage of the space provided under *Notes*, continue your study for the rest of the excerpt.

Notes

HAM. Then saw you not his face?
HOR. O, yes, my lord; he wore his
  beaver up.
HAM. What, look'd he frowningly?
HOR. A countenance more in sorrow
  than in anger.

Notes

HAM. Pale or red?

HOR. Nay, very pale.

HAM. And fix'd his eyes upon you?

HOR. Most constantly.

HAM. I would I had been there.

HOR. It would have much amazed you.

HAM. Very like, very like. Stay'd it long?

HOR. While one with moderate haste might tell a hundred.

MAR.
BER. } Longer, longer.

HOR. Not when I saw it.

HAM. His beard was grizzled—no?

HOR. It was, as I have seen it in his life, a sable silver'd.

HAM. I will watch tonight; Perchance 'twill walk again.

HOR. I warrant it will.

In the Nunnery scene, Act III, Scene 1, of *Hamlet*, Ophelia has lines that can be treated this way. Turn to page 181 where the scene is presented in its entirety and apply your present study to the first eleven speeches.

Longer Sentences • Longer phrases and sentences, and the speeches that contain them, require as much as or more attention than the single word or short phrase. Context complicates ideas even as it expands them. To prevent ambiguity, the same specific paraphrasing is recommended. The process is demonstrated by two speeches from *She Stoops To Conquer*.

Young Marlow, as the text makes clear, is a well-balanced fellow. Of good upbringing and pleasing appearance, his assurance and boldness with such females as barmaids is balanced by a lack of confidence in himself and a painful shyness when in the presence of young ladies of his own social group. In the second sequence in Act II, he admits to both sides of his personality to his friend Hastings, first confessing his impudence "among females of another class," to which Hastings replies:

HASTINGS. But in the company of women of reputation I never saw such an ideot [sic], such a trembler; you look for all the world as if you wanted an opportunity of stealing out of the room.

Well, of course—you're right, couldn't be more so if
MARLOW.   Why, man, that's because I do want to steal out of
you tried. Damn it, time and again I've determined to turn things
the room. Faith, I have often formed a resolution to break the ice,
about, and just relax and let myself go. But don't you see, I
and rattle away at any rate.   But I don't know
can't make myself do it. Just one look, that's all it takes,
how,   a single glance from a pair of
from an attractive girl and I'm all gone in the knees. Oh,
fine eyes has totally overset my resolutions.   An impudent
I know that a really brash fellow can act modest when he wants,
fellow may counterfeit modesty, but I'll be hanged if a modest
but believe me, it can't be done the other way around.
man can ever counterfeit impudence.

Later in Act II, Marlow meets Miss Hardcastle for the first time and, in the scene that follows, demonstrates with painful clarity just how accurate his description of himself was. After much stammering and several attempts at escape from the trying situation, attempts she adroitly blocks, he finally is released and leaves. Alone, she gives vent to her feelings with a ringing laugh, and then speaks her thoughts.

What a crazy, wonderful joke! I can't believe
MISS HARDCASTLE.   Ha! Ha! ha!   Was there
it—he was so terribly, terribly serious. I'm amazed—why, he
ever such a sober, sentimental interview? I'm certain he
didn't even once see what I look like. But wait a minute, don't
scarce look'd in my face the whole time. Yet the fellow,
run him down too much. I do believe he was—well—rather attractive.
but for his unaccountable bashfulness, is pretty well too.
I'll grant he seemed to be fairly bright, but look out, that
He has good sense, but then so buried in his fears that it
painful shyness of his could be so tedious I'd prefer him to be
fatigues one more than ignorance.
less smart and better balanced. Now, let me think this out—yes,
                                        If
that's it—I just might be able to handle this situation so that
I could teach him a little more confidence, it would be doing
a certain somebody I know would be quite pleased. Should I play
somebody that I know of a piece of service.   But who is

a little game with myself? . . . As if I didn't know right now	
that somebody?	That, faith, is a question I
what I'm going to do!	
can scarce answer.	

The next meeting between Marlow and Kate Hardcastle, in Act III, is of an entirely different sort from their first. To apply this study to that material, turn to page 268 where the whole scene is presented. Choose a section for your concentration.

Double Meanings • Often a playwright sets down words that suggest an obvious meaning, but that, in the situation he has created, actually contain a different thought. To say mockingly "Oh, what a lovely morning," on a cold, gray day is a case in point. But even when the contradiction inherent in a sarcastic or ironic statement is not intended, a player will often rightly interpret an author's meaning to be other than the phrase or sentence seems to indicate.

A clear instance of this point is found in the fourth sequence in Act III of *She Stoops To Conquer*. Mrs. Hardcastle has just burst into the room after her discovery that Miss Neville's jewels are missing. Of course, there is no double meaning in her utterances, but Tony's lines call for expressions of a different sort, as you can see. For clarity's sake, write in what you think he actually is saying as he delivers each line.

Notes

MRS. HARDCASTLE: Confusion! thieves! robbers! We are cheated, plundered, broke open, undone!

TONY: What's the matter, what's the matter, mama? I hope nothing has happened to any of the good family!

MRS. HARDCASTLE: We are robbed. My bureau has been broken open, the jewels taken out, and I'm undone.

TONY: Oh! is that all? Ha! ha! ha! By the laws, I never saw it better acted in my life. Ecod, I thought you was ruin'd in earnest, ha, ha, ha!

MRS. HARDCASTLE: Why, boy, I *am* ruined in earnest. My bureau has been broke open, and all taken away.

Notes

TONY: Stick to that; ha, ha, ha! I'll
bear witness, you know, call me to
bear witness.

MRS. HARDCASTLE: I tell you, Tony,
by all that's precious, the jewels
are gone, and I shall be ruin'd for
ever.

TONY: Sure I know they're gone, and
I am to say so.

MRS. HARDCASTLE: My dearest Tony,
but hear me. They're gone, I say.

TONY: By the laws, mamma, you
make me for to laugh, ha! ha! ha! I
know who took them well enough,
ha! ha! ha!

Sometimes lines with a double meaning also have a double objective.
On occasion the obvious meaning is to be received and accepted by certain members of the cast while other characters are made aware of the
other, hidden meaning; it is with this latter group that the audience is
always included.

A scene in which two players can practice the projection of thoughts
not obviously intended by the written lines is found in *The Imaginary
Invalid*. Cleante, posing as a singing master, sings an impromptu duet
with Angelique in the presence of her father, Argan, Toinette, the maid,
and Argan's guests, M. Diafoirus and his son Thomas. Cleante's and
Angelique's words, sung or half spoken, mean one thing to Argan and
his guests, but quite another to each other and Toinette. The lines
Cleante now speaks must immediately do double duty.

Notes

CLÉANTE: (*To Argan*) The music for
the concert you have requested
your daughter and me to sing was
—er—composed for just such occasions as this. It is impromptu in the
the style of the Italian commedians.
But the speakers sing (*Angelique
reacts*), or the singers speak—a kind
of half and half performance. (*Ob-
liquely to Angelique*) But each sentiment is sincere, each singer—er—
speaker must utter what he truly
feels.

ARGAN: Utter—fiddlesticks. Sounds
terrible, but get on with it.

Cleante then explains that a young shepherd has fallen in love with a
beautiful shepherdess, but that she is threatened by her father with
marriage to another man—a dolt. Then, while both he and Angelique
pretend to be singing from parts, they speak or intone or sing their
feelings for each other.

Notes

CLÉANTE: Shepherdess, I'll wait no
longer,
Your true feeling I must know.
I can neither sleep nor slumber
'Till you answer—yes or no.
   (*She begins but he cuts her off.*)
Gently now, before you answer
By a smile, a word, a token,
Pray remember in my bosom
Beats a heart that can be broken.
     You can grant me joy or woe,
         Life or death,
       Tomb or breath,
        Yes or no.
ANGÉLIQUE: Shepherd, you need wait
no longer,
My true feeling you know.
I can neither sleep nor slumber
'Till I answer, yes—
CLÉANTE: Yes?
ANGÉLIQUE: Or no.
CLÉANTE: No?
ANGÉLIQUE: Or yes.
CLÉANTE: Yes!
ANGÉLIQUE: Yes, yes.
{ CLÉANTE: Oh, blessed word! } (*repeat*)
{ ANGÉLIQUE: Yes, yes—yes, yes. }
CLÉANTE: She answers yes!
ANGÉLIQUE: Yes, yes, yes, yes!
ARGAN: My, my, how remarkable.
Did you hear? That was my daugh-
ter—my daughter singing right off
like that. Remarkable!

CLÉANTE: Of course, monsieur, a most apt pupil, I told you so. But in this story she is betrothed to another man, a dolt, a—

ARGAN: Eh, so—but let her sing. That's what we want, let her sing.

CLÉANTE: Of course, monsieur, at once, monsieur. We all desire her to sing, so that we may learn what she intends to do about this dol— this other man. (*He sings again.*) Shepherdess, my love, my beauty, Dearest flower of my heart, If you do your filial duty, You and I and love must part. If you your father don't defy, Our love must die. And oh, sad day, If you obey Your father!

ANGÉLIQUE: (*speaking*) Bother father!

ARGAN: What?

ANGÉLIQUE: (*singing again*) When a father is a bother, When a father is a dunce, Who can help but bother father? If a daughter listened once To such a blockhead, his advice Would so confuse the world we live in, She would never listen twice.

ARGAN: (*splutters*)

CLÉANTE: You will defy?

ANGÉLIQUE: Yes, I—Yes, I Will run way.

CLÉANTE: You won't obey?

ANGÉLIQUE: I won't obey.

CLÉANTE: You won't obey your father?

ANGÉLIQUE: Bother! Bother father!

ARGAN: Stop, stop! You bother this father. Enough of this nonsense.

Special Phrasing • Words and word-grouping not in normal use today demand even more certainty of meaning, both for the actor who uses them and the auditor who hears them. It is possible that they also permit more flexibility of interpretation—certainly Shakespeare's lines do. In his plays, quality of performance is more important than complaisance with traditional standards. In Act II, Scene 1 of *The Taming of the Shrew*, Petruchio, ready to undertake his wooing of Katherina, the Shrew, begins a soliloquy with these lines: (*To Baptista and the others*) "I pray you do; I will attend her here, and woo her with some spirit when she comes." As before, let us suggest several possible meanings for each of the three phrases.

I pray you do; *I thank you for your courtesy;*
Yes! That's a good idea;
I suppose it is just as well to see her alone;

I will attend her here *Our meeting has turned out as simple as that.*
I'll stand, (looking around) right here.
Now, let me think about my plan of action.

And woo her with some spirit when she comes.
I'll be forthright and emphatic when I meet her.
I'm ready, and thus begins my venture.
I have it, I'll surprise her with aggressiveness.

Petruchio's next two lines read:

Say that she rail; why then I'll tell her plain
1.
2.
3.

She sings as sweetly as a nightingale
1.
2.
3.

What three possibilities of meaning would you offer?

Katherina enters at the end of Petruchio's speech and says:

Well have you heard, but something hard of hearing.
1.
2.
3.

They call me Katherina that do talk of me.
1.
2.
3.

The rest of the scene is filled with all manner of interpretive twists and turns, inviting a variety of line readings. Cut some of it to permit greater concentration when you work on one or the other of the two parts in the manner demonstrated above.

MEMORIZATION

Memorization of lines is an act of implanting word sequences in an actor's mind in such a way that they can be held for future recall without reference to the original source. Memorization of a line and comprehension of its basic meaning should be integral parts of the same process, with comprehension established as the first motivating step and line memorization following after.

An actor memorizes best by thinking of the idea the line represents instead of trying to reach the idea via blocks of words committed to memory. Proper memorization is a creative process rather than a mechanical effort. (There are exceptions to this—for example, memorization of technical passages with scientific terms, obscure material, and so forth.)

Each speech has an initiating thought motivated by the speech or action that precedes it. When that precedent action occurs or that precedent speech is given, the thought it prompts will spring readily to mind by reason of its logic. The following sentences of the speech, in a series of linked thoughts, should uncoil like a continuing length of rope, each one woven by association to the one before.

Memory work is most effective and most quickly accomplished when it is done as a whole effort. Several segments fit this concept: (1) a role is memorized in whole sequences or scenes or acts, continuity being the cohesive element that holds lines together; (2) lines must be synchronized with movement, therefore the whole action should be committed as a unit; (3) lines will be delivered within a set, while handling props and using furniture, and while performing in the presence of an audience in an auditorium of a known size, consequently an awareness of these elements should not be disregarded.

For most persons the memorization of passages made difficult by the presence of unusual words or involved contexts is easier and more permanent if a word association process is used. Word association was an action employed by actors and nonactors long before psychologists coined the term. In its practice, the memorizer arbitrarily links a word by reason of past experience or by mechanical or creative reasoning with the word or phrase he is to memorize. This process requires him to think of two closely connected ideas in one mental exercise. This causes a vigorous mental experience, one that makes a deep impress in the brain and that therefore can be more easily and clearly recalled.

EXERCISES AND ASSIGNMENTS

1. In your own words write out the meaning of one of the two speeches suggested below, read your intended meaning to the class, and then perform the speech. Both are from *Our Town* by Wilder. The first is in Act II, the second in Act III.

a. George explains his feelings to Emily when the two meet after their election to class offices.

b. Emily has been granted her wish to return to earth to relive one day of her life, her twelfth birthday, to find, if possible, the meaning it holds. The experience is more disturbing than she realized—too disturbing.

2. Certain outstanding works in the English language are so well known they are the common property of all and, with varying degrees of exactness, are commonly known by all. Unfortunately, such general sharing often erases the distinctiveness that is an inherent characteristic of these great works. Choose one of the selections listed below and deliver it with the simplicity its merit indicates, making an exact and meaningful statement on every phrase, one that is as fully expressed as it is clearly thought.

The Twenty-third Psalm; the Gettysburg Address; the Declaration of Independence; "Speak the speech, I pray you . . ."; "Friends, Romans, countrymen. . . ."

3. Take one of the speeches listed below, prepare it, and deliver it.

Men:

Twelfth Night, Shakespeare, Orsino, Act I, Scene 1.
"If music be the food of love, play on . . ."

King Henry IV, Part One, Shakespeare, Falstaff, Act V, Scene 1.
" 'Tis not due yet; I would be loath to pay him . . ."

Winterset, Anderson, Trock, Act I, Scene 1.
"You roost of punks and gulls!"

The Lady Is Not for Burning, Fry, Thomas, Act III.
"I also. I've been cast adrift on a raft of melancholy."

Blood Wedding, Lorca, Leonardo, Act III, Scene 1.
"What glass splinters are stuck in my tongue!"

Six Characters in Search of an Author, Pirandello, The Father, Act 1.
"But don't you see that the whole trouble lies here?"

The Chairs, Ionesco, Old Man.
"He was trying to get my goat."

Women:

King John, Shakespeare, Constance, Act III, Scene 4.
"Thou art not holy to belie me so . . ."

Romeo and Juliet, Shakespeare, Juliet, Act II, Scene 5.
"The clock struck nine when I did send the nurse . . ."

Anne of a Thousand Days, Anderson, Anne, Prologue.
"If I were to die now—"

The Lady Is Not for Burning, Fry, Jennet, Act III.
"I am interested in my feelings."

Blood Wedding, Lorca, Bride, Act III, Scene 1.
"Oh, how untrue! I want from you neither bed nor food."

The Beautiful People, Saroyan, Agnes, Act I, Scene 2.
(Do the series of speeches beginning with:)
"I'm not sure. The door's a big glass door . . ."

Six Characters in Search of an Author, Pirandello, The Stepdaughter,
Act I.
"Worse? Worse? Listen! Stage is drama for us . . ."

The Chairs, Ionesco, Old Woman.
"He said to me: 'You kill the birds!'"

Chapter 14

The Expressive Tone

We knew it all once—movement, tone, words; we held it in the conscious part of our minds the way a child holds a problem in mental suspension while he surrounds it with his reason and uses up its allocation of excitement. In that distant time the means of communication were integrally blended—words into tone and tone into movement.

At that time words, now our most refined form of communication, were still in direct contact, through tone, with the most elemental conveyer of messages, movement; all three were simply variations of one stem activity. Today it requires no more than simple recall to associate a basic tone with the three words, anger, anxiety, fear, and then to link the root meaning of the associated words and tones with the movement out of which the three words grew: a clutching at the throat.[33]

The actor needs to recognize overtly what now is only covert knowledge, that tone and words are vocalized movement, and that what is known in one field can be applied in another.[34] By scrutinizing what has become generalized and habitual, he can achieve a conscious awareness of the possibilities of his expressive tone.

VIABLE TONE

Tone is the vocal life of acting. It is produced by a physiological process that turns out sound much as a mechanical process turns out an item of hardware. But there is an element in tone that differentiates it from a manufactured product as decidedly as spirit differs from matter. Tone has its value in a communicative world because its mechanistic properties are personal, endowed with a power to express the unique state of being that is in each one of us.

RELEASE AND REVELATION

A tone does two things: it releases and it reveals. When speaking, each person discloses a part of himself, letting thoughts and feelings out

---

[33] See Skeat, *An Etymological Dictionary of the English Language.*

[34] Part IV, Chapter 16, "Synthesis and Synchronization," is devoted to the coordinated relationship between movement and voice.

into the air where, as sound waves, they move toward other, receptive bodies. What is released reveals either the exact core condition of the releaser or what the releaser wishes the receiver to believe the core condition is, which is in itself a revelation.

It is seldom that any one of us releases even a major portion of the thoughts and feelings that compose our inner state of being; to release all is impossible. But with varying degrees of freedom, depending upon our relationship to those around us, each of us daily reveals in quantity those things within that press for release.

THE MEANING OF TONE

How is it that tone is expressive?

The physiologist can tell of the areas of the brain involved in speech and describe the actions of nerves, muscles, and bones used in the vocal processes. The psychologist can explain impulses and motivations and the results of a desire-action drive. The physicist can diagram the various combinations possible among the elements of tone. And the man on the street exhibits elucidations of all of the above every time he says *yes* or *no*.

But neither singly nor together can any of the above explain how a human being, with split-second timing, selects one tonal pattern out of all the tonal patterns at his disposal and utters it as a relatively accurate expression of his meaning. He does it, and it is pragmatically effective.

The meanings we unconsciously but arbitrarily create probably evolved eons ago from an interaction between our body structure and our physical and social environment. Identified with individual or group desires and related to the successful accomplishment of life-fulfilling functions, the tonal patterns that first developed in a pre-speech time must have been labored and self-conscious. Responding to elemental motivations, they took on primary meanings in much the same way that movement did.

Basic meanings permeate our speech today. The tonal patterns that denote question, denial, appeal, enticement, demand, command, and so on are all in constant use. Deviations of meanings are also present. There is a positive as well as an uncertain denial, an insistent as well as a wavering demand, an imperious as well as a hesitant question, and a listener always knows which meaning is intended, even when he hears it in a language not his own.

The expressive process of speaking was effected with more and more sureness and with greater rapidity as time went on. Today, tones quickly and accurately release and reveal intended meanings, and ears receive and record them in the mutually satisfactory arrangement of human speech that exists between man and man.

Means and Ends • Tonal patterns and syllabic speech are the *means* of verbal communication. The successful transference from speaker to hearer of the content and intent of what is said are the *ends* of audible expression.

Because of centuries of practice the means of verbal communication are now habitual. The result is that our concentration focuses almost exclusively on the ends of that process. But an actor, more than ordinarily concerned with the expression of meanings, must be acutely aware of both. Without calling attention to the fact that he is now controlling a previously habitual action, he concentrates on the one as much as the other.

Primary Sources • You have already studied the nature of the four elements of tone. As a result you know how words are formed and how tones are made. This knowledge is the basis of your investigation of the meaning of human tone.

The first step is to acquire competence in the skill of hearing: one listens to his own tonal patterns and, as part of the same program, to the tonal patterns of others.

An actor with an experienced ear can detect, separate, and catalogue the elements that compose a tone as quickly and as surely as a trained musician can recognize and analyze the complex sounds of a symphony orchestra. The ability to isolate each element of tone and thus determine the degree of burden it carries in a vocal pattern is an essential part of ear training. By acute awareness developed through constant practice, the ability to take apart also becomes an ability to put together—and it is in the composition of a tone that meaning is contained.

Each tone reveals its motivation. When one particular tone, such as a cry of fear or an exclamation of pleasure, continually manifests itself in association with a certain situation, its universality is established. In this respect it is well to know that the eye is a friend to the ear, the former giving assurance to the latter that the tone heard is in exact correspondence with the situation that is seen.

For example, we know that an aspirate quality, a #1— force, a fast tempo, and the use of the middle register of pitch fit with a quick, stealthy walk. From experience we recognize that the sound of a laugh matches the action of laughing, and that a forceful vocal command is associated with a vigorous arm movement. Laboratory tests even prove that a smile can be heard, that is, it can be detected in a tone, as recorded voices have demonstrated.

To begin a research project of reading tonal patterns, it is good practice to progress from the general to the specific. As a botanist first notes the genera of plants for the sake of accuracy in his later detailed study, we can work from general categories to specific tonal traits.

In pantomime three basic categories were employed: *active-passive*, indicating a physical state of health; *intelligence-unintelligence*, denoting the extent to which mental faculties function as control units in all activities; and *aggressive-submissive*, relating an individual to his environment. They also apply to tone.

Active-Passive • As you analyze your own tones or the tonal patterns of others, note the degree of energy employed. Is a consistent vitality present or do extremes of weak or loud (soft or strong in our terms) manifest themselves? Does the voice alter itself noticeably with a change of circumstance, or does it steadily maintain a basic pattern? Can you detect good or poor muscle tonus, and if you note extremes of either, does physical or emotional vitality predominate? What degree of coloration does energy give to the tone? In which of the tonal elements does it manifest itself most?

With respect to this category, to what extent would vocal vitality be heard in these situations: a casual encounter between classes, a night patrol (recognize that a soft tone can be highly energized), a swimming pool party, a sick-room consultation, a lunch counter at rush hour, a funeral service, a deluxe hotel banquet, an afternoon at the race track, a climbing party at sunset time?

Intelligence-Unintelligence • As you listen with this category in mind, can you determine the amount of correlation between thought and tone in your own vocal patterns and in those of others? Is the voice made more than ordinarily expressive because of mental control, or do stock tonal patterns and expressions dominate? Can you detect shadings of meaning that add extra interest to what is being said? Are pitch and tempo regular to the point of monotony, or is variety present? What is the range of notes covered by most of those around you as they speak in ordinary conversation? What elements of tone are used to stimulate an intellectual interest in what is being said? Are you as aware of the functioning of quality and strength as you are of time and pitch? To what extent is the element of stress used to accentuate meaning?

What kind of tonal patterns do you think you might hear in these places: a graduate seminar, a Rescue Mission, a corporate board meeting, a town council, a farm grange meeting, an English I classroom, a guided tour in the United Nations building, a garage, a faculty staff room, a downtown street corner, a library counter?

Aggressive-Submissive • To what degree is there an emotional content in the tones you have been listening to? How often are the three representative emotions of love, fear, and anger exhibited? Is the tone controlled in most situations that surround you and are conversational points made with reasonableness during discussion or argument, or is there an unevenness in attack and reply? Can you tell when a voice seems to be in balance or out of balance with its surroundings? If so, can you analyze the tonal patterns on which you base your opinion? What elements of tone seem to receive the greatest emphasis during times of emotional stress? What makes a dominant tone, what a submissive one?

Using your sense memory when possible, recall the vocal patterns that would be heard in these areas: a playground, a traffic court, an exchange counter in a department store, a political platform during debate, ringside during a fight, a refugee camp, a football practice field, a shrine in a church, a company area at assembly time, a freshman orientation room during registration.

As you listen to a group of persons at any time and in any place, can you determine which individuals are most tonally active, which function under the greatest degree of habitual control, and which are the more assertive in their expressions? Noting the rise and fall of pitch, the stop and go of tempo, the off and on of volume, and the kind or kinds of quality used, do you not begin to understand how it is that you have been able in times past to read the meaning of the tonal patterns you have heard?

Do not fear that a detailed analysis of primary source material will make your own processes of dramatic speech laborious and conspicuous. There will be no lessening of the speed and ease with which your expressive means match the ends of your communicative needs. Improvement, not detraction, will mark your work as you gain additional clarity, exactness, variety, and power in all your tonal patterns.

ATTITUDE

In basic terms every tonal pattern reveals two things: what we think and how we feel; ideas and attitudes. This is a consistent rather than an occasional truth, and holds with equal force in acting as in life situations.

The content of a speech in a play is the thought of the speech, and generally is represented by the words employed. The previous chapter concentrated upon this aspect of dramatic communication.

Content is only half of any expressive load; it denotes what we wish to say. The other half tells what we think or how we feel about what is said. It is attitude. Attitudes relate us directly to our environment.

An attitude is the pervasive condition that exists in any individual at any given moment. It may represent physical or emotional, sensory or mental aspects of his core condition, or it may reveal combinations in varied patterns of all of these attributes. It may be directly and openly revealed, or restrained, or constrained, or hidden—but it will be there.

The same attitude may exist in varying degrees of intensity over a period of hours or days, or it may change completely several times each minute. It may prevail with such strength it involves the whole person, blocking out all normal acts of will, or it may be so slight as to be barely noticeable.

The Dramatic Attitude • To return to a previous point, it should be noted that there is a dramatic attitude. Properly handled, it never obviously manifests itself unless the situation or character indicates that it should. Instead, it channels its energies into the attitudes that denote a character's reaction to his situation. But if it is strong, as it often is, the dramatic attitude may permeate an actor's work to the degree that it dominates everything else, not only for the duration of a scene, but for the extent of an entire play. Unaware of its prevalence, an actor may think he is expressing many different attitudes when he is really exhibiting only one.

Character Attitudes • Every character in every play has an attitude every second he is onstage. Some attitudes are suggested by the playwright, others are not. Whatever the case, the actor should know the specific nature of each one, be aware of when it occurs, recognize how long it lasts, and know the precise moment of change. If there are combinations and overlaps, these should also be known.

You are already familiar with the act of detecting character attitudes. Every time you sensed a character's feelings you were, in effect, recognizing his attitudes. But the vague response that results from merely sensing something is not sufficient for our purposes. To achieve the exactness desired, comprehension must be matched with economy. Both can be represented by a single word or a terse phrase of precise meaning.

Note the positiveness that occurs when three different but specific words indicate the attitude to be held during line delivery. Note also how quickly the tonal pattern responds to a definite direction.

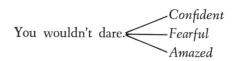

You wouldn't dare. ← Confident / Fearful / Amazed

The instructions are no less definite and precise when *one* attitude is expressed with varying modifications, a point that makes exactness of statement doubly imperative. A small miss is as bad as a miss of a mile.

You wouldn't dare.
Cockily confident
Composedly confident
Scornfully confident

Creative acting, in the matter of an expressive tone, derives first from sureness of understanding of the terms used, second from the ability to assume with spontaneity and conviction the attitude stated, and third from the possession of a voice flexible, responsive, and wide-ranging enough to carry with exactness the attitude or feeling intended.

For further illustration let us turn to the sequences from *Hamlet* that served our purpose when working on thought content. The first two speeches of the sequence, which before were given without paraphrase, now require our attention. Which of the three suggested attitudes would you choose? If you have a fourth of your own conception, what is it?

ATTITUDES

HAM. Hold you the watch tonight?
Businesslike
Decisively inspired
Determined

MAR. and BER. We do, my lord.
Impersonally military
Eager
Grim

Now we can complete the double purpose of vocal interpretation by adding suggested attitudes to match the paraphrased lines.

HAM. Arm'd, say you?

ATTITUDES

You will wear your usual weapons, I assume?   Matter-of-fact
I think a strong precaution is necessary.   Cautiously alert
I see you carry weapons, will you have them tonight?   Impersonally demanding

MAR. and BER. Arm'd, my lord.
Of course, just as we usually do, my friend.   Casually confident
Indeed so, never fear, Sir!   Eagerly cooperative
These very weapons, honored sir.   Assuringly positive

Now turn back to page 158 in the last chapter and add your selection of attitudes to the interpretations you have already given the lines. Women as well as men should work on this section.

The two speeches below serve as further examples and exercises in the selection and statement of attitudes.

In *The Taming of the Shrew*, Act V, Scene 2. Katherina, the shrew who has been tamed, perhaps not quite as thoroughly as her husband at present believes, has been ordered by Petruchio to tell the other wives present "what duty they do owe their lords and husbands." She does so with a delivery balanced between her previous aggressiveness and her newfound submissiveness, directing most of her speech toward the wives but some toward her husband. It is to be expected that she relishes the opportunity to speak strongly to the other women, and that she has confidence in her ability to perform the action well and forcefully.

       (Aggressively scornful)   *(Chidingly imperious)*
KATHERINA: Fie, fie! / unknit that threatening unkind brow, /
     (Cautionary command, with implied threat)
And dart not scornful glances from those eyes,
                (Remembered submissiveness)
To wound thy lord, / thy king, thy governor. /
        (Factually frank)
It blots thy beauty as frosts do bite the meads,
Confounds thy fame as whirlwinds shake fair buds,
And in no sense is meet or aimable. /
        (Sarcastically condescending)
A woman moved is like a fountain troubled,
      (Openly contemptuous, indicating plump widow)
Muddy, ill-seeming, / thick, bereft of beauty;
And while it is so, none so dry or thirsty
Will deign to sip or touch one drop of it. /
      (Forceful assertion, gradually blending
Thy husband is thy lord, thy life, thy keeper,
   into tender reasonableness)
Thy head, thy sovereign; one that cares for thee,
And for thy maintenance commits his body
To painful labor both by sea and land,
To watch the night in storms, the day in cold,
Whilst thou liest warm at home, secure and safe,
And craves no other tribute at thy hands
But love, fair looks, and true obedience; /
     (Righteously submissive, with faint
Too little payment for so great a debt.
   tongue in cheek)
Such duty as the subject owes the prince,
Even such a woman oweth to her husband; /

Continue the statement of attitudes for the rest of Katherina's speech.

And when she is froward, peevish, sullen, sour,

And not obedient to his honest will,

What is she but a foul contending rebel

And graceless traitor to her loving lord?

I am ashamed that women are so simple

To offer war where they should kneel for peace,

Or seek for rule, supremacy, and sway,

When they are bound to serve, love and obey.

Why are our bodies soft and weak and smooth,

Unapt to toil and trouble in the world,

But that our soft condition and our hearts

Should well agree with our external parts?

Come, come you froward and unable worms!

My mind hath been as big as one of yours,

My heart as great, my reason haply more,

To bandy word for word and frown for frown:

But now I see our lances are but straws,

Our strength as weak, our weakness past compare,

That seeming to be most which we indeed least are.

Then vail your stomachs, for it is no boot,

And place your hands below your husband's foot;

In token of which duty, if he please,

My hand is ready; may it do him ease.

In *Hamlet*, Act II, Scene 2, Hamlet has just watched the First Player of the visiting troupe perform an on-the-spot recitation of speeches from an old play in which the actor was visibly moved by the emotional content of his material. The young Prince sends all the others off stage. Alone, he identifies what he has just witnessed with his own situation.

(Bitter self-incrimination)

HAMLET: O, what a rogue and peasant slave am I! /
   (Ironic amazement)
Is it not monstrous that this player here,
But in a fiction, in a dream of passion,
Could force his soul so to his own conceit
That from her working all his visage wan'd,
Tears in his eyes, distraction in's aspect,
A broken voice, and his whole function suiting
      (Incongruous futility)
With forms to his conceit? / and all for nothing! /
 (Disparagingly)
For Hecuba! /
    (Aggressively argumentative
What's Hecuba to him, or he to Hecuba,
 and bewildered)   *(Wry*
That he should weep for her? / What would he do,
 self-incrimination)
Had he the motive and the cue for passion
     (Positively assertive)
That I have? / He would drown the stage with tears
And cleave the general ear with horrid speech,
Make mad the guilty and appal the free,
Confound the ignorant, and amaze indeed
The very faculties of eyes and ears. /
 (Bitter
Yet I,
 self-disgust)
A dull and muddy-mettled rascal, peak,
Like John-a-dreams, unpregnant of my cause, /
 (Admitted self-defeat) *(Hint of reverence)*
And can say nothing; / no, not for a king /
 (Sorrow, blending into anger)
Upon whose property and most dear life
      (Honest self-searching)
A damn'd defeat was made. / Am I a coward?
 (Challengingly, but subdued and intense)
Who calls me villain? breaks my pate across?
Plucks off my beard, and blows it in my face?
Tweaks me by the nose? gives me the lie i' the throat,
As deep as to the lungs? who does me this? / *(Turns to throne)*
 (Conviction)
Ha!

Continue from here. Set down the precise word or words that state the exact attitude you wish to indicate.

'Swounds, I should take it; for it cannot be

But I am pigeon-liver'd and lack gall

To make oppression bitter, or ere this

I should have fatted all the region kites

With this slave's offal. Bloody, bawdy villain!

Remorseless, treacherous, lecherous, kindless villain!

O, vengeance!

Why, what an ass am I! This is most brave,

That I, the son of a dear father murdered,

Prompted to my revenge by heaven and hell,

Must, like a whore, unpack my heart with words,

And fall a-cursing, like a very drab,

A scullion!

Fie upon't! foh! About my brain! I have heard

That guilty creatures sitting at a play

Have by the very cunning of the scene

Been struck so to the soul that presently

They have proclaimed their malefactions;

For murder, though it have no tongue, will speak

With most miraculous organ. I'll have these players

Play something like the murder of my father

Before mine uncle. I'll observe his looks;

I'll tent him to the quick; if he but blench,

I know my course. The spirit that I have seen

May be the devil; and the devil hath power

To assume a pleasing shape, yea, and perhaps

Out of my weakness and my melancholy,

As he is very potent with such spirits,

Abuses me to damn me. I'll have grounds

More relative than this; the play's the thing

Wherein I'll catch the conscience of the king.

DARKROOM REHEARSAL AND PERFORMANCE

Any one of the acting tools will receive greatest concentration when studied in isolation. Pantomime practice centers attention exclusively on movement. Voice work, dealing with either words or tone, receives the same emphasis when the body is held easily inactive during work periods. However, by the device of darkroom rehearsal and performance, even more than ordinary attention can be focused on vocal expression.

In classroom or in theatre, if all but minimal light is shut off, the ear of performer and listener alike achieves a degree of concentration not otherwise possible. In the quiet darkness the tonal expressiveness of an actor's voice reveals itself more exactly for what it is and what it can do than at any other time. Darkroom performances of every third assignment are suggested, as are periodic rehearsal sessions during play preparation time.

Mechanical recorders are fine devices for the scoring of a voice against a later playback; they afford an excellent opportunity for detached study of vocal performance. The use of such equipment is highly recommended.

EXERCISES AND ASSIGNMENTS

1. Select one of the following words and assign five distinct attitudes to its utterance: no, yes, stop, maybe, don't, never. State the changes of tonal pattern that occurred.

2. To isolate the problem of creation of attitudes, substitute counting numbers in sequence for dialogue in these situations for two persons: a shopkeeper and a tourist haggle over the price of a piece of pottery; a plainclothesman and a plainclotheswoman watch a station exit for a wanted suspect; a boy and a girl are on a high observation tower, and she is fearful of approaching the railing; a husband wants to sample a newly baked cake before a party dinner; strangers wait for a bus on a street corner.

This is not an exercise in improvisation. Plan your counting as carefully as you would dialogue and know the exact attitudes you are to assume.

3. The following scene from *Hamlet* has motivated multiple interpretations. Working with a partner, let your line readings indicate your choice. This is the Nunnery scene, Act III, Scene 1. Hamlet has just revealed the depth of his conflict in the "To be, or not to be" soliloquy. Now he sees

Ophelia approaching. She has been sent by her father, Polonius, to engage Hamlet in conversation so that he and the King secretly may observe if it actually is desperation of love that has caused Hamlet so radically to alter his behavior.

Notes

OPH: Good my lord,
   How does your honor for this many
      a day?
HAM: I humbly thank you; well,
   well, well.
OPH: My lord, I have remembrances
   of yours, that I have longed long to
   redeliver; I pray you now, receive
   them.
HAM: No, not I.
   I never gave you aught.
OPH: My honor'd lord, you know
   right well you did; and, with them,
   words of so sweet breath compos'd
   as made the things more rich. Their
   perfume lost, take these again, for
   to the noble mind rich gifts wax
   poor when givers prove unkind.
   There, my lord.
HAM: Ha, ha! are you honest?
OPH: My lord!
HAM: Are you fair?
OPH: What means your lordship.
HAM: That if you be honest and fair,
   your honesty should admit no dis-
   course to your beauty.
OPH: Could beauty, my lord, have
   better commerce than with honesty?
HAM: Ay, truly; for the power of
   beauty will sooner transform honesty from what it is to a bawd than
   the force of honesty can translate
   beauty into his likeness. This was
   sometime a paradox, but now the
   time gives it proof. I did love you
   once.

Oph: Indeed, my lord, you made me believe so.

Ham: You should not have believed me, for virtue cannot so inoculate our old stock but we shall relish of it. I loved you not.

Oph: I was the more deceived.

Ham: Get thee to a nunnery. Why wouldst thou be a breeder of sinners? I am myself indifferent honest, but yet I could accuse me of such things that it were better my mother had not borne me. I am very proud, revengeful, ambitious, with more offences at my beck than I have thoughts to put them in, imagination to give them shape, or time to act them in. What should such fellows as I do crawling between earth and heaven? We are arrant knaves all; believe none of us. Go thy ways to a nunnery.— Where's your father?

Oph: At home, my lord.

Ham: Let the doors be shut upon him, that he may play the fool nowhere but in 's own house. Farewell.

Oph: O help him, you sweet heavens!

Ham: If thou dost marry, I'll give thee this plague for thy dowry: be thou as chaste as ice, as pure as snow, thou shalt not escape calumny. Get thee to a nunnery. Go; farewell. Or if thou wilt needs marry, marry a fool; for wise men know well enough what monsters you make of them. To a nunnery, go, and quickly too. Farewell.

Oph: O heavenly powers, restore him!

Ham: I have heard of your paintings too, well enough. God hath given you one face, and you make yourselves another. You jig, you amble, and you lisp. You nickname God's creatures, and make your wantonness your ignorance. Go to, I'll no more on 't; it hath made me mad. I say, we will have no more marriages. Those that are married already, all but one, shall live; the rest shall keep as they are. To a nunnery, go.

(*Exit* Hamlet)

OPH: O what a noble mind is here o'erthrown! The courtier's, soldier's, scholar's eye, tongue, sword;

Th' expectancy and rose of the fair state,

The glass of fashion and the mould of form,

Th' observ'd of all observers, quite, quite down!

And I, of ladies most deject and wretched,

That suck'd the honey of his music vows,

Now see that noble and most sovereign reason,

Like sweet bells jangled, out of tune and harsh;

That unmatch'd form and feature of blown youth

Blasted with ecstasy. O woe is me,

T' have seen what I have seen, see what I see!

4. Select and read a speech from Beckett, Ionesco, Genet, or Albee.

5. In a darkroom assignment, present your interpretation of Katherina's or Hamlet's speech.

6. In another darkroom assignment, present a scene without movement. If it can be taken from a play that is to be presented publicly, so much the better.

Part IV

Acting

Chapter 15

The Acting Complex

Pantomime and vocal expression, each sacrificing a portion of its individuality, synthesize their separate disciplines to create the composite art of acting.

The Creative Dynamic

There is a reassuring thing about the art of acting. Your body, a visible and audible instrument of expression, is, like your mind, capable of infinite absorption and release. When it is put to use and is functioning fully, there is a feeling, known to every performer, that more can be done, that the creative dynamic has an unending stretch. With it the art of acting can be explored for limits; through it will come the discovery that there are none.

Your capacity to absorb, to embody within yourself an infinite number of factors useful in acting, is unlimited. The more you take into yourself, the more you can hold. And the more you contain, the greater will be your need to release what you have. When you do release it, a sense of strength, a belief in your capacity, will grow with each projection you accomplish, encouraging competence to enlarge itself into artistry.

THE CONVENTION OF ACTING

Long ago acting worked its way out of its associate role in primitive ritual to stand free and whole in one of mankind's favorite art forms. To do so it had to shake loose from the traditions of savage ceremonials, taking for itself, from the many diverse elements of the original, only those practices that suited its new purpose. By a process of selection and rejection the elements of secrecy, ritual, and religion were dropped and replaced by open communion, the dramatic form, and a spiritual sense that was enlarged to include beauty and laughter, and a deep concern for the way each man lived out his life.

In the process of change Thespis emerged, taking for himself the role to which you aspire today. The first actor known by name, he stands as prototype for all the players of the western world. It is fitting that he be so remembered, not because of the accident of his appearance in the chronology of theatrical time, but because of the importance of the position he assumed. As the old form gave way to the new and diffusion of function was replaced by specialization, the role of the actor stood out clearly. Beyond question, Thespis was the key figure in the dramatic process.

But if his role was to be featured in a way not allowed to any of his nonacting fellows, if he alone could appear in person to release his dramatic energies on waiting and receptive targets and alone take in person the flood of approbation that came at the end of his efforts, it had to be because he was willing to face and to accept an unique charge.

The most lifelike of all art forms, acting demands that the actor, in the midst of artificialities and himself distorting nature, move and speak in a manner as seemingly natural as possible. Working in an area that is not a living room or a garden or a battlement, but is instead a relatively small space separated from a larger one by a series of thin, painted flats or by folds of hung cloth, he must convincingly make believe that he is where he is not. Seldom expected to appear in person, he has to make the person in which he does appear seem to be the only person he is. Trained to create and to house within himself potent states of being, he is allowed to release such pent-up states only on condition that the dramatic explosion be part of a controlled process. Required to seem unaware of an audience, he yet has to make sure that all he does is projected to those seated before him.

Faced with such paradoxical conditions, our acting ancestors evolved a flexible kind of activity that successfully solved these particular dramatic problems. Their solution has stood the test of time. They have passed it on to us in the form of the convention of acting to be employed as our time and our needs demand.

THE ACT, THE PURPOSE, THE PLACE

The Act

Acting is the process whereby an inner state of being of extraordinary intensity, composed of emotions, thoughts, and sensations, is revealed in a dramatic manner to others by the external expressions of an actor.

All persons have inner states of being in various mixtures and in various strengths, and all persons release such states through normal channels of movement and speech, each release being a form of expression. But not all persons release their feelings well, or freely, or wholly, and when such releases come they are not always clearly revelatory of what is contained inside.

If the release is to be dramatic, performed with the quality the term presupposes, the execution will not only be free and full and clear, it will contrast most favorably in distinctiveness of manner and energy of execution when compared with other usual actions. But before this contrast can be effected, a significant degree of self-commitment is required of each aspiring actor.

Wholeness of self is the commitment you make to your art. All that you are and all that you have are to be at the service of your profession. Withholding any part, or inability to make any part function, will decrease to that extent your potential as an actor. Totality in offer and totality in release is the size of the commitment required. It is only from such fullness that the art of acting can draw its life and its strength.

The Purpose

The purpose of acting is to create a dramatic experience—a distinctive situation, at once intense, stimulating, and revelatory. The activation of the event is the responsibility of the players, but the involvement is to include all present. The subject material, whether light with fun or weighty with wisdom, should have the power to entice and hold in willing union everyone present.

The dramatic experience involves both the actor and the audience in proportionate measure to the contribution of each. Neither of the two participants is capable of creating this unusual state alone, but in combination each so complements the other that the resultant oneness is incomparably stronger than the physical sum of the two parts.

There are two circuits operating in the theatre during the time the play is on. One carries the full current of the dramatic experience created by the actors over the foots and out to the farthest reaches of the house. The other just as surely makes a return from the house to the stage with messages that tell of success or failure.

Quite possibly the audience will be the best teacher of acting you will ever know. The good people out front, unaware that they are performing any function other than sharing in the dramatic experience, tell those of you on stage in a hundred ways what should be done and what had better be left undone. At no other time, neither during the study nor the rehearsal period, can the dramatic experience truly come into being. It is when the play is on, in the presence of an evaluating audience, that the lessons of acting are most forcefully driven home.

Those who participate in the dramatic experience, on both sides of the proscenium arch, receive a reward out of proportion to the amount of time spent, taking information, stimulation, and beauty from the event, making it one of the most significant actions that can occur in the life of any society.

THE PLACE

The place for acting is in a theatre. Evolved to house the dramatic experience, the theatre began as a building but grew into an institution. As with most other human creations, it was subject to the vicissitudes of societal changes.

Treated with awe and reverence—and a sense of healthy utilitarianism —by the Greeks, it represented one aspect of the greatness of that memorable society. Lowered in function to provide entertainment for a sensuous and pleasure-loving people, the theatre of the Romans was debased morally and vitiated artistically. With the fall of Rome, there came a hiatus of several centuries. Then the churchmen of the Middle Ages, ignorant of what they were doing, seeking only the clearest and most emphatic way to project to their unlearned congregations the message of the Christian ethic, brought into existence again the institution their Councils condemned. Medieval acting, purposefully instructional in nature, gropingly found its way back into the dramatic forms, and ended by being as entertaining as it was devotional and more secular than religious.

Then came the Renaissance, and the actor found his true place in the theatre again, found it as splendidly and as greatly as he ever had before. Truly professional for the first time, the record he left behind showed his appreciation for the dignity of his newfound individuality. And the theatre, humanistic and nationalistic, vigorously investigative and ceaselessly creative, surpassed all previous theatres in range of development and depth of treatments. The dramatic activity of the *commedia dell'arte*, Marlow, Shakespeare, and Molière equalled the works of the Greeks; the *commedia erudita*, the literary drama of Italy; the court masques of the newly developed patron class; and the works of such lesser lights as de Vega, Jonson, and Corneille travelled an equally interesting if somewhat less high road.

The generations that followed narrowed the range of dramatic endeavor in both scope and quality, as demonstrated by the sententious style of the Restoration drama in England or the romantic splurge of the German theatre.

Then came the theatrical institution we know today, still idealistic and striving for greatness, still seeking to elevate the minds and spirits of its professionals and its public, but still subject to the tremendously leveling and very human activities of multitudes of persons, each of whom treats the institution as the thing he wants it to be. Whether it is to be merely a profit-making, profit-taking concern or a protean institution engaged in its ancient and proper activity of disclosing the problems and wonders of the human story is for you who would be its priests, practitioners, and custodians to determine.

PREPARATION-PRESENTATION PROCESS

In each of the previous parts of this book the preparation-presentation process of acting has been divided into three integrated and synchronized steps. Although all three constantly overlap each other in study and practice, a logical and well-defined order of development is clearly indicated. The three major steps are *comprehension, translation, and creation.* Here is a reiteration in terse form of what was stated at greater length in Part I, Chapter 4.

Comprehension involves the assimilation, organization, and understanding of the subject materials that form the basis for all dramatic effort. There are two divisions here: a comprehension of the nature and process of achieving the dramatic experience and a comprehension of the subject content of each specific acting project as it applies to characters and situations. *Translation* undertakes to change what is comprehended from ordinary source material into meaningful dramatic action. The extent of your ability (dramatic instinct) and your techniques (skills) will determine the quality of your work in this phase. *Creation* is a culminating activity in which what you have made meaningfully dramatic is projected from your work space, the stage, out across the foots to the last persons in your audience. Its acceptance by that body brings to fruition the whole process, and thus determines in good part the quality of the dramatic experience you create.

THE ACTING COMPLEX

Acting is made up of three diverse elements, each one of which acts as a conditioning agent upon the others. Together they make of acting a full and mature art form. With any element missing, however, or undeveloped, the fullness of the form is impossible of realization.

The Dramatic Element

Dramatic instinct is responsible for the first component of the acting complex. Simply stated, it is to be dramatic—just to be dramatic. Many regard this action as the most important of the three; some view it as making up almost the whole of acting.

It is a distinctive accomplishment. The dramatic manner is a unique way of moving and speaking, for which there is no substitute and of which there are no imitations. Capable of infinite variations, it still has a recognizable character. Anyone who can create it can be dramatic anywhere, at any time, and on any subject.

As a matter of fact, it is possible to be dramatic without a subject. A good actor, without benefit of a story, can be strongly dramatic in his action and satisfactorily gain and engagingly hold the attention of an audience—that is, be dramatic for the sake of being dramatic, a practice as old as drama itself.

A magnetic action of great power, the dramatic manner not only has a direct attraction for an audience, it is equally capable of capturing most or all of the concentration of its creator, obscuring ideas necessary for the scene's development because the act of being dramatic is the whole act—at once the content and the revelation, absorbing all in its singleness of purpose.

So stimulating and satisfying is this action that many actors pause here, content that in their execution of such a remarkable act they have achieved the main purpose of dramatic creation. So distinctive and engaging is this action to those on the receiving end that many audiences are equally content to accept it as the full expression of the dramatic experience. This condition has unquestionably been present in all times and places where drama has flourished.

Still, it is an incomplete action and produces a lesser immature art.

The Element of Meaning

Conditioned by knowledge acquired from observation of primary sources, the actor adds the element of meaning to the acting complex. He does so for a reason.

A drama is never a vehicle for itself—to be dramatic is never the whole intent of any major work. This does not mean that all plays have to be of a serious bent or loaded with message; it is merely that all plays intend something; otherwise they do not get on a stage or into print. Mood, message, or just plain nonsense, if a piece has merit, it has a character worthy of revelation.

The actor's effort should match that of the playwright. Slight or profound, the meaning inherent in a scene must be revealed by the player's action. Although an actor is always eager to attract and to keep an audience in his spell, his hold should not be merely mesmeric and momentary. More substance is needed to proportion the acting complex properly and give it the structural strength it requires: that substance is provided by the second component of the complex.

As two parts of a three-part process, the dramatic and the meaningful elements can be so fused into one indissoluable action that neither exists without the other, unless such is the specific intention of the player. When the oneness of these two elements is achieved, it is possible to be soundly and engagingly dramatic in a fully meaningful manner.

The Theatrical Element

A theatrical element is added to the acting complex because the activity takes place in a theatre, a particular area surrounded by particular conditions. Consequently, meaningful dramatic action has to be adapted to meet the spatial requirements of the physical plant.

Centuries ago this meant that in Athens, for example, in the theatre of Dionysus, the actor had to be dramatically effective to persons a few feet away and on a level with him as well as to others many yards off and much higher up on a hillside. Since the majority of our playhouses are modelled on the same basic pattern as those in Greece, the same requirements face us today. Therefore, the introduction of the theatrical element required that a set of acting expedients be developed and assimilated into the dramatic manner.

These new conditions were in no way detrimental to the dramatic action. Actually, they gave it definition by canalizing its activity, concentrating its effort, letting form support form and beauty complement beauty.

Technique is the name we give to the adaptation the physical theatre imposed upon the dramatic manner. The skills required have to do in large part with the manipulation of the acting instrument, the player's body and voice. The conditioning factors that operate are those of size, direction, and distance.

The theatre element can best be realized when the *theatre sense* of the player has been brought to a high pitch of development. At that time two sensibilities will be in active suspension within him: an awareness of gathered dramatic power and of the effect of its release, and a consciousness of the theatre space that surrounds him and of its capacity to contain the dramatic effort.

Dramatic creation is a shared thing. Dionysus represented the spirit of fertility and rebirth, in whom, as in you, the dynamic of creation was forever present. To that end, the acting complex you bring to life on stage should be as communal an experience as that enjoyed by the Greeks many centuries ago.

Chapter 16

Synthesis and Synchronization

Earlier, pantomime and voice were studied as entities in themselves. Now, in the fullest compass of all dramatic expression, the body and the voice are to be synthesized into one expressive unit. In the ordinary course of things this presents no physical or psychological problem: you have been correlating the actions of your body and voice ever since you were born, instinctively at first, habitually later.

SYNTHESIS IN ACTING

In a study of acting, however, with its necessary distortions, there is some danger that your usual coordination may be disturbed or lost. Not only must you accommodate your habitual synthesis to the requirements of being meaningfully dramatic in a theatre, you must do so for a variety of characters whose patterns of habit vary in differing degrees from your own.

Shakespeare, as actor and quite possibly as director, was aware of the problem. In "Speak the speech, I pray you . . ." (*Hamlet*, Act III, Scene 2) he first asked for the synthesis of body and vocal action that produces good articulation; and then he cautioned against the misuse of body and voice that produces both over- and underplaying. Later, by saying "Suit the action to the word," he gave the center of interest to vocal expression and made gesture complementary. But then he reversed the process, as all of us must do, by saying "the word to the action," indicating a variance of synthesis. In addition, by placing "action" before "word" and then "word" before "action," he also indicated that timing and sequence are factors to be considered in the coordinated working of an actor's body and voice.

Playing has not changed from Shakespeare's day to ours. The simple act of making a harmonious whole out of an actor's body is still the first requisite of the art. Your work in acting begins with a consideration of how best to synthesize and synchronize your two instruments of expression. If these agencies are out of harmony, few other things about acting are going to be right.

SYNCHRONIZATION

To the casual observer, the difference between the easy, unstudied gestures of everyday life and the same kind of action seen on stage in realistic acting may not seem very pronounced. To the expert the difference is obvious.

In ordinary use the great bulk of all hand, arm, facial, or body gesture, being subconsciously motivated, is unplanned. On the stage all movement is consciously created.[35] In daily life the average individual demonstrates an easy, fluent and functional correlation between his movements and his words, unconcerned with inadequacies or redundancies. The actor on stage must seem to be as easy, but dramatic needs make his job much more difficult.

In approaching the problems of synchronization, there are two areas on which to focus attention: *personal business*[36] or movement, which is a matter of individual gesture, and *stage business*,[36] which is movement from place to place within the confines of the set, exemplified by the stage cross.

PERSONAL BUSINESS

Personal business is character movement performed as an individual action of a personal nature. Its purpose is to reveal the personality traits of a character, making the revelation of distinctive mannerisms one of its key functions. It is gesture in which each part of the body is related to every other part, and all are synchronized with the character's vocal utterances. The synchronization can be performed in one of only three ways.

Either the gesture comes before the line, the line comes before the gesture, or both are done at the same time; in the latter case one must be selected as center of interest with the other functioning in support. Both the meaning and the strength of the statement are dependent upon the sequential development; therefore the order of action is important.

In Act I of Molière's *The Imaginary Invalid*, Toinette, the maid, on being summoned by her irascible master, pretends to strike her head

---

[35] This is true even though much stage movement is instinctual in origin.

[36] *Business:* "In a general sense, all action and movement on the stage apart from dialogue." *The Theatre Handbook,* Sobel, p. 119. Throughout the pages ahead, business, movement, gesture and action are often used as interchangeable terms. Employed thus in the professional theatre, there is no reason to set up restricted definitions here.

against a doorjamb. A mistress of counterattack, she does this to shift blame from herself to her accuser. In executing the action she lightly lays her head against the door frame, then raps the wood with her knuckles or kicks it with a foot, after which sound she exclaims:

TOINETTE: (*Straightening up*) Oh! ←———— *(Hands to head before sound,*
on the sound,
or after sound?)

Which synchronization will you choose? Why? There is a laugh contained in this business. Which action will best achieve it?

A more complicated instance is found in Act III, Scene 3, of *Hamlet*. King Claudius, with his back turned to the rest of the room, is kneeling in remorseful prayer when Hamlet enters behind him, unseen and unheard. Since Hamlet's purpose is to kill his stepfather, the King, in revenge for the murder of his own father, the present circumstance presents as fortunate an opportunity as he could ask for.

The problem for the actor playing Hamlet is that he must synchronize two separate actions with the three phrases of his first line. His first action is to draw his dagger, his second to step toward the kneeling king.

HAMLET: (*Does he draw before* | *or on* | *or after?*)
Now might I do it pat,
Now he is praying,

(*Step forward before* | *or on* | *or after?*)
And now I'll do it.

Dramatic tastes differ. The preference for a movement before, during, or after a line varies from actor to actor. In addition, the character's manner of expression is a strong conditioning factor. Unfortunately, no order of precedence can be set as a rule to be learned in advance of the need. Your judgement of what produces the most dramatically meaningful effect functions anew for every character and every situation.

No matter what the choice, all actions must be timed properly. Here again there is no overall rule to follow. The synchronization between gesture and speech is distinctively individual. It is something to be sensed, a condition to be developed out of a feeling of rightness that has been thoroughly tested in performance.

EXERCISES AND ASSIGNMENTS

1. Through simple exercises you can develop a sense of synchronized timing. Individually or as a group, perform the following business in the three

standard ways of correlation: movement before, during, or after the delivery of the line. Check your execution for both emphasis and meaning. Also note if the timing produces a sense of rightness in accord with your intent.

THE LINE	THE ACTION
No!	*Three shakes of the head.*
Let's shake hands on that.	*Hand thrust in offer of friendship.*
Come on, we'll be late.	*Beckon insistently—beckon shyly.*
Sorry, but I have to leave.	*Seated, rise reluctantly—rise eagerly—rise politely.*
Go—never darken my door again!	*Melodramatically point to door.*
Thank you very much.	*Smile.*
How do you do?	*Women nod, men raise a hat.*
Good afternoon, my lord.	*Women curtsey, men bow.*
Here.	*Offer a coin to a child.*

Observations about how movement and speech align themselves for meaning are in order and should be discussed on the basis of the information gained from the above exercise. Also to be considered is the size, duration, and intensity of a movement in relation to the nature and length of a line. Proportion and emphasis should be included as integral parts of the subject.

2. For the next exercise and those after, it is expected that the interpretive process, even when the concentration is on the problems of synchronization, will be based on knowledgeability of movement as derived from pantomime studies and the meaning of words and tones as learned in your vocal work.

The two speeches below are for individual performance. In neither case is the character required to be active in other than personal business, therefore emphasis can rightfully be placed on character movement. It must be remembered that personal gesture applies to all portions of the body, and that a turn of the head, an intake of breath, a shift of weight, a shrug of the shoulders, a smile, a frown are all actions to be correlated with line delivery.

In Act III, Scene 2 of *The Merchant of Venice*, Lord Bassiano has just chosen the right casket and so won the fair Portia. His joy is matched by hers as, with charm, poise, womanliness, shyness, demureness, eagerness— what the actress will—she commits herself and what is hers to his care and love.

Notes

PORTIA: You see me, Lord Bassanio,
    where I stand,
  Such as I am: though for myself
    alone
  I would not be ambitious in my
    wish,
  To wish myself much better; yet
    for you

I would be trebled twenty times
  myself;
A thousand times more fair, ten
  thousand times
More rich;
That only to stand high in your
  account
I might in virtues, beauties, livings,
  friends,
Exceed account: but the full sum
  of me
Is sum of nothing; which, to term
  in gross,
Is an unlesson'd girl, unschool'd,
  unpractic'd;
Happy in this, she is not yet so old
But she may learn; happier than
  this,
She is not bred so dull but she can
  learn;
Happiest of all is that her gentle
  spirit
Commits itself to yours to be di-
  rected,
As from her lord, her governor, her
  king.
Myself and what is mine to you
  and yours
Is now converted: but now I was
  the lord
Of this fair mansion, master of my
  servants,
Queen o'er myself; and even now,
  but now,
This house, these servants, and this
  same myself
Are yours, my lord. I give them
  with this ring;
Which when you part from, lose,
  or give away,
Let it presage the ruin of your love,
And be my vantage to exclaim on
  you.

In the first scene of *The Merchant of Venice*, that young man about town, Gratiano—flamboyant, satirical, brimming with life, at times sincere, always articulate—handles the center of interest with pleasure and ease as he tells of the part he has chosen to play in his society, even as he mocks the role of others. Almost as voluble with hands as with tongue, to what extent will he use gesture and how will he synchronize it with the following lines?

Notes

GRATIANO: Let me play the fool:
  With mirth and laughter let old
    wrinkles come,
  And let my liver rather heat with
    wine
  Than my heart cool with mortify-
    ing groans.
  Why should a man, whose blood
    is warm within,
  Sit like his grandsire cut in ala-
    baster?
  Sleep when he wakes, and creep
    into the jaundice
  By being peevish? I tell thee what,
    Antonio—
  I love thee, and it is my love that
    speaks—
  There are a sort of men whose
    visages
  Do cream and mantle like a stand-
    ing pond,
  And do a wilful stillness entertain,
  With purpose to be dress'd in an
    opinion
  Of wisdom, gravity, profound con-
    ceit;
  As who should say, "I am Sir
    Oracle,
  And when I ope my lips let no dog
    bark!"
  O, my Antonio, I do know of these,
  That therefore only are reputed
    wise
  For saying nothing; when, I am
    very sure,

If they should speak, would almost
damn those ears
Which, hearing them, would call
their brothers fools.
I'll tell thee more of this another
time:
But fish not, with this melancholy
bait,
For this fool-gudgeon, this opinion,
Come, good Lorenzo. Fare ye well
awhile:
I'll end my exhortation after dinner.

3. The excerpts from the two scenes below are taken from Oscar Wilde's *The Importance of Being Earnest*. To suit the purpose of this immediate assignment, furniture placement is the same for both excerpts, and in each case major stage action can be kept to a minimum, allowing the concentration to be placed on each character's personal business.

A table is at stage center. On it are the dishes and the food for afternoon tea. There are chairs at either side. It is suggested that all props be pantomimed.

In both scenes Wilde is flippantly and engagingly satirical. For all the lightness of his touch, however, there is substance rather than superciliousness in his lines. His characters are poised and handle themselves with an habitual grace. The costumes are 1900.

The first scene is in Algernon's London flat. It is the second sequence in Act I. Jack Worthing, who calls himself Earnest in town, has just been introduced.

ALGE. (*Handshake*) How are you, my dear Earnest? What brings you up to town?

JACK. Oh, pleasure, pleasure! What else should bring one anywhere? Eating as usual, I see, Algy!

ALGE. (*Stiffly*) I believe it is customary in good society to take some slight refreshment at five o'clock. Where have you been since last Thursday?

JACK. (*Sitting*) In the country.

ALGE. What on earth do you do there?

Notes

JACK. (*Pulling off gloves*) When one is in town one amuses oneself. When one is in the country one amuses other people. It is excessively boring.

ALGE. And who are the people you amuse?

JACK. (*Airily*) Oh, neighbours, neighbours.

ALGE. (*Sitting*) Got nice neighbours in your part of Shropshire?

JACK. Perfectly horrid! Never speak to one of them.

ALGE. How immensely you must amuse them! (*Takes sandwich*) By the way, Shropshire is your county, is it not?

JACK. Eh? Shropshire? Yes, of course. Hallo! Why all these cups? Why cucumber sandwiches? Why such reckless extravagance in one so young? Who is coming to tea?

ALGE. Oh, merely Aunt Augusta and Gwendolen.

JACK. How perfectly delightful!

ALGE. Yes, that is all very well; but I am afraid Aunt Augusta won't quite approve of your being here.

JACK. May I ask why?

ALGE. My dear fellow, the way you flirt with Gwendolen is perfectly disgraceful. It is almost as bad as the way Gwendolen flirts with you.

JACK. I am in love with Gwendolen. I have come up to town expressly to propose to her.

ALGE. I thought you had come up for pleasure? . . . I call that business.

JACK. How utterly unromantic you are!

ALGE. I really don't see anything romantic in proposing. It is very romantic to be in love. But there is nothing romantic about a definite proposal. Why, one may be accepted. One usually is, I believe. Then the excitement is all over. The very essence of romance is uncertainty. If ever I get married, I'll certainly try to forget the fact.

JACK. I have no doubt about that, dear Algy. The Divorce Court was specially invented for people whose memories are so curiously constituted.

ALGE. Oh! there is no use speculating on that subject. Divorces are made in Heaven—Please don't touch the cucumber sandwiches. They are ordered specially for Aunt Augusta. (*Takes one and eats it*)

JACK. Well, you have been eating them all the time.

ALGE. That is quite a different matter. She is my aunt. Have some bread and butter. The bread and butter is for Gwendolen. Gwendolen is devoted to bread and butter.

JACK. (*Helping himself*) And very good bread and butter it is too.

ALGE. Well, my dear fellow, you need not eat as if you were going to eat it all. You behave as if you were married to her already. You are not married to her already, and I don't think you ever will be.

JACK. Why on earth do you say that?

ALGE. Well, in the first place, girls never marry the men they flirt with. Girls don't think it right.

JACK. Oh, that is nonsense.

ALGE. It isn't. It is a great truth. It accounts for the extraordinary number of bachelors that one sees all over the place. In the second place, I don't give my consent.

JACK. Your consent!

In Act II, Gwendolen, the object of Jack's affections, has appeared at his country home, where she is introduced to his ward, Cecily. Cecily has fallen in love with Algy, who, like Jack in town, has called himself Earnest in the country. Thus the girls, after a most friendly meeting, have discovered that they both are in love with an Earnest, and this has caused a sudden chill between them. They are seated in chairs with the table between. Merriman, the butler, can be imagined.

Notes

GWEN. Are there many interesting walks in the vicinity, Miss Cardew?

CECI. Oh! yes! a great many. From the top of one of the hills quite close one can see five counties.

GWEN. Five counties! I don't think I should like that; I hate crowds.

CECI. (*Sweetly*) I suppose that is why you live in town?

GWEN. Quite a well-kept garden this is, Miss Cardew.

CECI. So glad you like it, Miss Fairfax.

GWEN. I had no idea there were so many flowers in the country.

CECI. Oh, flowers are as common here, Miss Fairfax, as people in London.

GWEN. Personally I cannot understand how anybody manages to exist in the country, if anybody who does is anybody. The country always bores me to death.

CECI. Ah! This is what the newspapers call agricultural depression, is it not? I believe the aristocracy are suffering very much from it just at present. It is almost an epidemic amongst them, I have been told. May I offer you some tea, Miss Fairfax?

GWEN. (*With elaborate politeness*) Thank you. (*Aside*) Detestable girl! But I require tea!

CECI. (*Sweetly*) Sugar?

GWEN. (*Superciliously*) No, thank

you. Sugar is not fashionable any
more. (*Cecily looks angrily at her,
takes up the tongs and puts four
lumps of sugar into the cup*)

CECI. (*Severely*) Cake or bread and
butter?

GWEN. (*Bored*) Bread and butter,
please. Cake is rarely seen at the
best houses nowadays.

CECI. (*Cuts a very large slice of cake
and puts it on the tray*) Hand that
to Miss Fairfax.

GWEN. (*Drinks the tea and makes a
grimace. Puts down cup and
reaches for the bread and butter,
but finds the cake. Rises*) You have
filled my tea with lumps of sugar,
and though I asked most distinctly
for bread and butter, you have
given me cake. I am known for the
gentleness of my disposition, and
the extraordinary sweetness of my
nature, but I warn you, Miss Cardew, you may go too far.

CECI. (*Rising*) To save my poor, innocent, trusting boy from the machinations of any other girl there are
no lengths to which I would not go.

GWEN. From the moment I saw you
I distrusted you. I felt that you were
false and deceitful. I am never deceived in such matters. My first impressions of people are invariably
right.

CECI. It seems to me, Miss Fairfax,
that I am trespassing on your valuable time. No doubt you have many
other calls of a similar nature to
make in the neighbourhood. (*Enter
Jack*)

For an alternate sequence to either of the above, see the excerpt from
The Time of Your Life on page 215.

Additional scenes that feature maximum personal movement with minimum stage business are found in (a) the drugstore sequence between George and Emily in Act II of *Our Town*; (b) the beach scene between Richard and Muriel in the last act of O'Neill's *Ah, Wilderness*; (c) the sequence with Anne and Peter in Act II, Scene 1, in *The Diary of Anne Frank*; (d) an excerpt from the scene between Laura and Jim, the candlelight scene, in *The Glass Menagerie*; (e) the two park bench scenes between Lorna and Joe in Act I, Scene 4, and Act II, Scene 2, from *Golden Boy*.

STAGE BUSINESS

The purpose of stage business is to reveal and to carry forward the meaning of a play. Although the director plans all stage business, its successful execution is the responsibility of the players. Entrances and exits, crosses and countercrosses, sitting down and rising are examples of stage business.

Stage business is a more difficult problem than personal business because it immediately relates the character to the whole set and all that is in it. Furniture, props, and other characters make the situation more complex. As soon as you move on to a set, the number and variety of reasons for your moving here and there, and how you are to do it, automatically grows. Motivations emerging from dramatic expediency appear, and adaptations to the interpretive requirements of other characters necessitate accommodation on your part.

In every play the director at some time or other is forced to say to one of his cast, "I'm sorry, but you've got to cross on that line," or "I know it's hard, but you've got to get all the way out on those words," and the actor must do just that. When this happens to you, as it will, it will put a premium on your ability to synchronize line and business to meet any contingency, even against a feeling of being mechanical rather than dramatically right.

The three possibilities for synchronization in personal business hold with equal force in the uses of stage business. Because of the greater complexity, two basic problems are added to the first three. In addition to learning how to coordinate a stage cross with a simultaneous line reading so that each fits the other like a hand and a glove, you must also learn how to stretch a short line over a long cross and how to contain a long line within a small action.

With these considerations pressing on you, you will have to answer such questions as, On what word will I stop in any given situation? On which one will I turn? How do I saunter all the way across the stage to the light switch when I have only a four-word line to carry me there?

How do I read my line so that when I reach my objective I do not have a good portion of it left over? These queries represent normal rather than isolated problems.

This much can be said for the above situation: no matter how forced or mechanical some of the business you are required to perform will be, you can always find a suitable motivation for it. By learning the use of a pause in delivery, or by the repetition of a word or a phrase for emphasis, a line can be stretched to cover quite a long cross. If a reverse situation prevails and a long speech is to be synchronized with a short movement, a reversal of the above action will be equally effective—that is, a pause or hesitation in movement while the line continues. In addition, mental states of concentration and intensity are of great aid in the support of necessary business.

In the assignments ahead some lines and some business will seem to flow together, achieving an aesthetically pleasing synchronization on their own, the action of a cross fitting the length of the line even to the point where the foot comes to rest after the final step as though it were a well-timed period placed at the end of the sentence—a subtle effect that, never calling attention to itself, you will achieve thousands of times. Such close harmony, though not with that exact effect, is to be tried for at all times, until the resultant smoothness truly carries out Shakespeare's admonition in such a way as to mark the effort as habitual.

But the necessities of stage business will often present you with difficult mechanical problems—hiding under a small table, putting on a heavy overcoat—that must be practiced until synchronization is achieved. In other instances, thoroughly motivated business can prove quite awkward due to the size of the action that must be taken—the kind that "hang over" in one direction or the other but, for all their disproportion, can become quite manageable with dextrous handling.

The conventions of acting are many, and many difficult problems of synthesis and synchronization will have to be faced along with those more easily solvable. In the hands of a practiced player the difficult ones look as easy as the easy ones actually are.

EXERCISES AND ASSIGNMENTS

The first two sets of exercises are for class demonstration and practice.

1.   *a.* Four players in rotation are to execute a full stage cross from R to L on the line, "That child never picks up anything."

b. Four more are to move the same distance on "How do you do," extending the arm for a handshake. (Note: the problem of sustaining an attitude is critical to the success of these exercises.)

c. Working in pairs and reversing the roles after the first series of efforts, one actor is to stand four or five steps away from an imaginary door while the other (as host) says, "Answer that ring for me, will you?" Replying, "Yes, I'd be glad to," the first turns and crosses to the door. Repeat the action with the first player at double the distance from the door.

d. Pantomiming such props as packages, suitcases, a needle and thread, a can and a canopener, and so on, have individual players cross from one stage area to another on a line such as "Please! Give me a hand with this—quick!" or "All right—don't rush me. I'll bring it over."

e. Experiment with ways in which the phrase "No, positively not!" sustains a cross from left center to stage right.

2. Where the short line on a long cross posed a problem in movement, the small action on a long line does the same thing for vocal delivery. Let several players try these exercises.

a. Seated at the breakfast table, you are only four paces from the shelf where the coffee pot rests. Your roommate asks you to pour another cup. Grumbling, you rise and cross as you say, "What's the matter, are you lame? Why don't you sit on this side of the table for a change? I don't see why I always have to be the one to jump up for the coffee. Every morning it's the same—you read the paper and I do the running, I—the pot's cold!"

b. Changing the liquid, try this delivery with the action suggested. "Here, give me your cup and let me pour you some tea. This is a special blend. We get it across town at the Farmers' Market. There is a little shop on your left just past the archway as you come from the parking lot. A man and his wife run it—specialize in nothing but tea—get shipments from all over the East. This came from Ceylon. We experimented with several and this seemed to be the best. Of course, it's all a matter of individual taste, but—here you are, try it."

3. Synchronize both personal and stage business in the scenes below. Although the emphasis is on the coordination of movement and lines, the basic competences of pantomime and voice must still serve as foundation for both your study and your practice.

Motivations for stage and personal business are contained within the subject content of each scene. Floor plan and furniture placement should be a matter of personal determination, deduced from a study of the material and influenced by personal intent. An illusion of costumes and props can work to your advantage.

a. Utilizing the gains from the accomplishments already achieved on the Nunnery scene from *Hamlet,* page 181, rehearse and present that scene as a problem in synthesis and synchronization.

b. An alternative, radically different from the above, is in *She Stoops To Conquer,* Goldsmith, Act II. Young Marlow, bold with a tavern wench, painfully shy with a genteel young lady, finds himself alone with Kate Hardcastle. That spirited and attractive girl, already informed of his reticence and now aware of the restraint that prevents him from facing toward or looking at her, takes full advantage of the circumstance to control the situation. Free to move, the better to observe her prospective suitor, she adroitly blocks his attempts at escape; her enjoyment is fully as strong as his discomfiture.

Notes

MISS HARDCASTLE: But you have not been wholly an observer, I presume, sir. The ladies, I should hope, have employed some part of your addresses.

MARLOW: Pardon me, madam, I—I—I—as yet have studied—only—to—deserve them.

MISS HARDCASTLE: And that, some say, is the very worst way to obtain them.

MARLOW: Perhaps so, madam. But I love to converse only with the more grave and sensible part of the sex—But I'm afraid I grow tiresome. (*Bows and makes for an exit*)

MISS HARDCASTLE: Not at all, sir; (*Quickly moves to block his attempt*) there is nothing I like so much as grave conversation myself: I could hear it for ever. Indeed, I have often been surprised how a man of *sentiment* could ever admire those light, airy pleasures, where nothing reaches the heart.

MARLOW: It's—a disease—of the mind, madam. In the variety of tastes there must be some who, wanting a relish for—um—a-um. (*Surreptitiously looking for another avenue of escape*)

MISS HARDCASTLE: I understand you, sir. There must be some, who, wanting a relish for refined pleasures, pretend to despire what they are incapable of tasting.

MARLOW: My meaning, madam, but infinitely better expressed. And I can't help observing—a—(*Making for another door*)

Miss HARDCASTLE: (*Aside, as she moves to prevent his exit*) Who could ever suppose this fellow impudent upon some occasions. (*Confronting him, smilingly, a fan partially covering her features*) You were going to observe, sir—

MARLOW: I was observing, madam— I protest, madam, I forget what I was going to observe.

Miss HARDCASTLE: (*Aside*) I vow and so do I. (*To him*) You were observing sir, that in this age of hypocrisy—something about hypocrisy, sir.

MARLOW: Yes, madam. In this age of hypocrisy, there are few who upon strict enquiry do not—a—a—a——

Miss HARDCASTLE: I understand you perfectly, sir.

MARLOW: (*Aside*) Egad, and that's more than I do myself!

Miss HARDCASTLE: You mean that in this hypocritical age there are few that do not condemn in public what they practise in private, and think they pay every debt to virtue when they praise it.

MARLOW: True, madam; those who have most virtue in their mouths have least of it in their bosoms. But I'm sure I tire you, madam. (*Again attempts escape*)

Miss HARDCASTLE: (*Again adroitly thwarts his purpose*) Not in the least, sir; there's something so agreeable and spirited in your manner, such life and force—pray, sir, go on.

MARLOW: Yes, madam. I was saying— that there are some occasions—(*Is she maneuvering him toward a chair or a corner?*)—when a total want of courage, madam, destroys all the—and puts us—upon—a—a—a——

MISS HARDCASTLE: I agree with you entirely: a want of courage upon some occasions assumes the appearance of ignorance, and betrays us when we most want to excel. I beg you'll proceed.

MARLOW: Yes, madam. Morally speaking, madam—but I see Miss Neville expecting us in the next room. I would not intrude for the world. (*Manages a partial escape*)

MISS HARDCASTLE: I protest, sir, I never was more agreeably entertained in all my life. Pray, go on.

MARLOW: Yes, madam. I was—but she beckons us to join her. (*Desperate with relief*) Madam, shall I do myself the honour to attend you?

MISS HARDCASTLE: Well, then, I'll follow.

MARLOW: (*Aside*) This pretty smooth dialogue has done for me. (*Quick exit*)

MISS HARDCASTLE: Ha! ha! ha! Was there ever such a sober, sentimental interview? I'm certain he scarce look'd in my face the whole time. Yet the fellow, but for his unaccountable bashfulness, is pretty well too. He has good sense, but then so buried in his fears that it fatigues one more than ignorance. If I could teach him a little confidence, it would be doing somebody that I know of a piece of service. But who is that somebody?—that, faith, is a question I can scarce answer. (*Exits*)

4. Two scenes, widely divergent in style, present similar opportunities for working out problems in synchronization. One begins just before the entrance of The Man in Act I of G. B. Shaw's *Arms and the Man*. The other is the "moving" scene from Act III, Scene 2 of Gibson's *Two for the Seesaw*.

CUES AND INTERRUPTED SPEECHES

The need for synchronization between movement and speech is nowhere more commonly yet critically demonstrated than in the matter of handling cues.

Three decades ago there was too much concentration in the training program on the technical process of picking up cues. Today there is too little. Then, the emphasis was upon tightness between speech and speech, or speech and movement; often the line following was snugged up to its cue in as close a fit as possible, giving, at times, an almost seamless effect to the flow of dialogue. Now, pauses occur while the actor accommodates the dramatic material to his personal responses. Good acting practice lies between these two extremes.

The needs and the nature of the dramatic experience decree that cues be picked up, but the handling must be flexible rather than rigid, the tempo and the intensity of the pickup being motivated by the dramatic requirements of the scene, never mechanically snug, never provokingly slow.

By itself a cue is a simple thing, but when hundreds of them are employed in the running of a single performance, they become very important to every one connected with a production.

Giving a Cue • A cue is a signal to begin an action. Generally, but not always, it comes at the end of a player's speech. There are cues for lines, for onstage actions, for entrances and exits, for light changes and sound effects, and for curtains. A cue can be physical as well as vocal.

If you are the player who gives a cue, you must know what that cue is and to whom it is given. Further, it is your responsibility to see that it is properly executed, whether it is a movement that signals the electrician for a change of lights, or a sound that brings another character on stage, or, as is most often the case, is simply the last words of a speech before another character picks up the center of interest.

Picking Up a Cue • If you are the player who is given a cue, you must know exactly what it is. In all cases you are to pick it up. That is another way of saying that you must not allow the progressive action of the scene to come to a halt by permitting a true pause to occur, there being a distinct difference between a true pause and a dramatic pause.

A cue is picked up in one of two ways, by a line or by a movement. Both are continuously employed in a scene's progression.

If the cue is picked up by a movement, the problem for the actor is minimal. Alertness of attention and cleanness and promptness of execution are the matters for his concern.

If the cue is picked up with a line, a slightly more involved technical process is required to execute the action successfully. It is an old, old practice.

If you are to pick up your cue vocally, while the cue is being given and not after it has been completed, you take the breath necessary to energize your coming line. Then, depending on the scene's tempo for the exact speed of your pickup, you come in clearly with the first words of your speech. The process is simple, requiring only concentrated practice now to acquire a mastery that will serve you for the rest of your acting life.

Do not be too slow. This will happen if you wait until after your cue is given to take a breath and deliver your line. Do not be too fast. If you are, you will "bite your cue," meaning that you began your movement or speech before the giver completed his signal.

The practice of cue pickup is integrally related to the principles of center of interest and to those of action and reaction. It is important for the two actors concerned to realize that the matter of audience attention is actually a physical part of the whole cue-giving, cue-pickup process. When you and the other actor are close together, and when there is no sudden shift in the thought content of the scene, there is no real problem involved. But if you and the other player are some distance apart, or if there is an abrupt or unexpected change of the scene's subject matter, then it may be a matter of a second or two before the audience can complete the physical action of shifting its focus of attention. In this case, slight though the time may be, the actor picking up his cue had better do so by the use of a preliminary movement or sound, thus giving the audience a signal that impels it to turn its attention to him. Then both he and the audience are ready to proceed with the main action or speech.

EXERCISES AND ASSIGNMENTS

Practice, inside the classroom and out, will establish cue pickup as a mastered technique.

1. Cue pickup for medium length speeches. *The Warrior's Husband*,[37] Thompson, Act III. Theseus, the leader of the Greek forces that have come

[37] *The Warrior's Husband* by Julian Thompson. Copyright 1931, 1932 by Julian Thompson. Copyright 1958, 1959 (in renewal), by Julian S. Thompson and Patricia T. Waterman. Reprinted by permission of Samuel French, Inc., New York.

to help Hercules capture the belt of the Amazon queen, now has as willing prisoner the Amazon warrior princess, Antiope. Whether they will be soldier comrades or more personal friends is yet to be determined. Excluding movement, read the speeches for technical practice in cue pickup.

ANTIOPE: I suppose I'm a perfect army mule for staying here with you.

THESEUS: You know you're not.

ANTIOPE: It's likely to cause each of us no end of trouble.

THESEUS: Let's worry about that when we have to. Come and sit down— soldier—and eat.

ANTIOPE: Oh, what the Hades! (*She sits*) I know what I—like about you.

THESEUS: What?

ANTIOPE: You have no beard. All our men have beards.

THESEUS: Well, that's no compliment—most of ours have none.

ANTIOPE: Why, that's true, isn't it? But why haven't you? Can't you grow them? Our men raise regular hedgerows.

THESEUS: Of course we can grow them. We shave them off.

ANTIOPE: Shave?

THESEUS: Yes—scrape the hair off every morning with a knife.

ANTIOPE: But why?

THESEUS: Why? Well! It's the custom, I suppose. It looks well.

ANTIOPE: Oh, no! I know! It's so you can look like women. You try to be warriors and look like us.

THESEUS: (*Laughing*) Don't be ridiculous!

ANTIOPE: That's it! You're so cute, with your little man-like face—trying to be so big, and warlike!

THESEUS: Any man would want to be as fine and brave as you are.

ANTIOPE: I? That's funny—when you are the only human being I've ever been afraid of.

THESEUS: Are you really afraid of me?

ANTIOPE: Yes—but I don't mind.

THESEUS: I'm glad you don't mind.

ANTIOPE: No. The amazing thing is I rather like it.

THESEUS: Perhaps what you think is fear is love.

ANTIOPE: Perhaps. (*She laughs*)

THESEUS: You know, I think you're the most beautiful girl I've ever seen.

ANTIOPE: I beautiful! How!

THESEUS: How! Why everything about you. Your face is lovely. Your arms are shafts of living ivory. The exquisite curves of your figure are enough to drive a man mad with longing.

ANTIOPE: The curves of my figure might do that?

THESEUS: Oh, but surely you realize that!

ANTIOPE: I realize they're enough to drive me mad! You haven't any idea how inconvenient they are when you're fighting.

THESEUS: Well, thank Zeus you have them. (*He puts his arms around her*).

ANTIOPE: Ah! This *is* nice, to be—fathered like this.

THESEUS: Fathered! Ye gods, young woman, you're not being fathered. You're being loved.

Medium-length speeches, with emphasis on cue pickup for multiple players, are found in Lorca's antirealistic play, *Blood Wedding*.[38] The Guests have come and are standing in the courtyard, calling their greetings to the Bride on her wedding day. Act II, Scene 1.

FIRST GIRL:
Awake, O Bride, awaken,
the morning you're to marry;
sing round and dance round;
balconies a wreath must carry.

VOICES:
Bride, awaken!

SERVANT:
Awake,
with the green bouquet
of love in flower.
Awake,
by the trunk and the
branch of the laurels!

SECOND GIRL:
Awake,
with her long hair,
snowy sleeping gown,
patent-leather boots with silver—
her forehead jasmines crown.

SERVANT:
Oh, shepherdess,
the moon begins to shine!

FIRST GIRL:
Oh, gallant,
leave your hat beneath the vine!

FIRST YOUNG MAN:
Bride, awaken,
for over the fields
the wedding draws nigh
with trays heaped with dahlias
and cakes piled high.

VOICES:
Bride, awaken!

SECOND GIRL:
The bride
has set her white wreath in place
and the groom
ties it on with a golden lace.

SERVANT:
By the orange tree,
sleepless the bride will be.

THIRD GIRL:
By the citron vine,
gifts from the groom will shine.

FIRST YOUTH:
Dove, awaken!
in the dawn
shadowy bells are shaken.

GUEST:
The bride, the white bride,
today a maiden,
tomorrow a wife.

FIRST GIRL:
Dark one, come down,
trailing the train of your silken
gown.

GUEST:
Little dark one, come down,
cold morning wears a dewy crown.

FIRST GUEST:
Awaken, wife, awake,
orange blossoms the breezes shake

---

[38] From *Three Tragedies* by Federico Garcia Lorca. Translated by James Graham-Lujan and Richard L. O'Connell. Copyright 1947 by New Directions. Reprinted by permission of the publishers, New Directions.

SERVANT:
A tree I would embroider her
with garnet sashes wound
And on each sash a cupid,
with "Long Live" all around.

VOICES:
Bride, awaken.

FIRST YOUTH:
The morning you're to marry!

GUEST:
The morning you're to marry
how elegant you'll seem;
worthy, mountain flower,
of a captain's dream.

FATHER:
A captain's wife
the groom will marry.
He comes with his oxen the
treasure to carry!

THIRD GIRL:
The groom
is like a flower of gold.

When he walks,
blossoms at his feet unfold.

SERVANT:
Oh, my lucky girl!

SECOND YOUTH:
Bride, awaken.

SERVANT:
Oh, elegant girl!

FIRST GIRL:
Through the windows
hear the wedding shout.

SECOND GIRL:
Let the bride come out.

FIRST GIRL:
Come out, come out!

SERVANT:
Let the bells
ring and ring out clear!
For here she comes!
For now she's near!

SERVANT:
Like a bull, the wedding
is arising here!

After practice and presentation of the above cue pickup exercise, it may be illuminating to make one or two run-throughs in which the actors *did not* take in breath until after the cue was completed.

2. Cue pickup for short speeches. Turn back to the excerpt from *Hamlet* on page 158 and use that material for practice purposes.

3. A scene that has no major stage business but requires that cues be picked up by personal movement as much as by the voice is found at the beginning of Act II of Saroyan's *The Time of Your Life*.[39] (*A man and woman sit at separate tables in Nick's bar. The man is Joe, a gentle, sensitive drinker, completely at home, and Mary, also a drinker and equally quiet about it. After a pause, Joe speaks.*)

JOE: Is it Madge Laubowitz?
MARY: Is what *what*?
JOE: Is the name Mabel Lepescu?
MARY: What name?
JOE: The name the initials M. L. stand for. The initials on your bag.
MARY: No.

[39] From *The Time of Your Life* by William Saroyan, copyright 1939, by Harcourt, Brace & World, Inc., and reprinted with their permission.

JOE: (*After a pause*) Margie Longworthy?
MARY: (*Very natural and sincere*) No.
JOE: Midge Laurie? (*She shakes her head*) My initials are J. T.
MARY: John?
JOE: No. (*Pause*) Martha Lancaster?
MARY: No. (*Pause*) Joseph?
JOE: Well, not exactly. That's my first name, but everybody calls me Joe. The last name is the tough one. I'll help you a little. I'm Irish. (*Pause*) Is it just plain Mary?
MARY: Yes, it is. I'm Irish, too. At least on my father's side. English on my mother's.

. . .

MARY: (*After a pause*) What do you do?
JOE: To tell you the truth, nothing.
MARY: Do you always drink a great deal?
JOE: Not *always*. Only when I'm awake. I sleep seven or eight hours every night, you know.
MARY: How nice. I mean to drink when you're awake.
JOE: (*Thoughtfully*) It's a privilege.
MARY: Do you really *like* to drink?
JOE: (*Positively*) As much as I like to *breathe*.
MARY: (*Beautifully*) Why?
JOE: (*Dramatically*) Why do I like to drink? (*Pause*) Because I don't like to be gypped. Because I don't like to be dead most of the time and just a little alive every once in a long while. (*Pause*) If I don't drink, I become fascinated by unimportant things—like everybody else. I get busy. Do things. All kinds of things, for all kinds of little stupid reasons. Proud, selfish, *ordinary* things. I've done them. Now I don't do anything. *I live all the time.* Then I go to sleep. (*Pause*)
MARY: Do you sleep well?
JOE: Of course.
MARY: (*Quietly, almost with tenderness*) What are your plans?
JOE: Plans? I haven't *got* any. *I just get up.*
MARY: (*Beginning to understand everything*) Oh, yes. Yes, of course.

Additional practice material on the combination of voice-movement cue pickup can be had by referring back to the excerpts from *The Importance of Being Earnest* and *She Stoops To Conquer*, in this chapter.

INTERRUPTED SPEECHES

An interrupted speech is one in which the thought of one character is not completed because another character breaks in on it, the second literally taking the center of interest away from the first. In the theatre as in life, interrupted speeches are quite common. The dramatic interruption, unlike the life action, is a controlled operation that follows a preset pattern. The two actors concerned, the interrupted and the interrupter, work together in the following manner.

The interrupted recognizes that the interrupted phrase is a specific cue and delivers it exactly as written; does not let the audience know that an interruption is expected; is prepared to stop speaking the second the interruption comes; if for any reason the interruption does not come, is prepared in advance to go on speaking in character to a normal finish for the line; releases the center of interest after the interruption.

The interrupter knows the exact cue and the exact moment of interruption; breathing controlled, cuts in at the right time on the interrupted speech, neither biting the cue nor being slow on the pickup; tops the other speech with the first word or two of the interruption to gain the center of interest; having topped the other, often takes a pause after the first or second word with a hesitation so slight it is hardly more than a suggestion, thus permitting the audience's attention to shift before continuing with the line. If the characters are quite close together, the need for a hesitation after the first one or two words of the interruption is almost nil, but if there is some distance between the two, there is a very definite reason for the slight pause. Many players sense this need and respond to it automatically, but it is not something that should be left to chance.

In the following example of interrupted speeches note the indication of the hesitation after the interruption:

FATHER: I don't care what plans you've made. You are going to stay home tonight, even if I have to—
SON: Dad—that's not fair. Yesterday you told me that I could—
FATHER: That—was yesterday. In the meantime you forgot your promise to clean out the garage. How do you expect me to keep my part of the bargain when you deliberately—
SON: But, Dad—you don't know what happened.

EXERCISES AND ASSIGNMENTS

In addition to the drill work below, further practice can be accomplished with the material from *The Glass Menagerie* in Part III, Chapter 12, p. 143, and that from *The Imaginary Invalid*, Part IV, Chapter 20, p. 316.

1. By converting the overlap of speeches intended by Molière into a succession of interrupted lines, we can use the excerpt from Act II of *The Imaginary Invalid* as drill work for this present assignment. Argan, the

imaginary invalid, greets and is greeted by his doctor, *M.* Diafoirus, in a *lazzi* (comic business) typical of the *commedia dell'arte* style.

ARGAN: Sir, with unbounded pleasure—
DIAFOIRUS: Sir, we are here—
ARGAN: I receive and accept—
DIAFOIRUS: My son, Thomas and I—
ARGAN: The honor you pay me—
DIAFOIRUS: To express to you—
ARGAN: Oh, if it were only possible—
DIAFOIRUS: Our great pleasure in—
ARGAN: That this poor body—
DIAFOIRUS: The courtesy you show—
ARGAN: Could have come to you—
DIAFOIRUS: In offering us—
ARGAN: But how well you gentlemen know—
DIAFOIRUS: The honor of an alliance—
ARGAN: That a poor, poor invalid—
DIAFOIRUS: Pray, accept my assurance—
ARGAN: Immured to his chair—
DIAFOIRUS: That in all things medical—
ARGAN: Can only assure you—
DIAFOIRUS: And, indeed, in all other matters—
ARGAN: That he is grateful for this opportunity—
DIAFOIRUS: We, father and son, are forever ready—
ARGAN: To express to you, gentlemen both—
DIAFOIRUS: To the best of our ability—
ARGAN: His humble desire—
DIAFOIRUS: To be at your service—
ARGAN: To be at your service—
DIAFOIRUS: Forward, Thomas, and make your compliments.

Chapter 17

Stage Business

Stage business or movement is all action, short of personal (character) movement, that takes place on stage during a scene or a play.

Ordinarily the setting of stage business is the function of a director. But for you, the actor, there will be many times when no director is available to block business for you. In addition, no player should deny himself the explorations and discoveries that come from creating the business for scene after scene in many different kinds of plays. From such activity you learn to block movement meaningfully and with expedition when you work alone, and coordinate your actions with those of others better when you are one of a group.

STAGE AND REHEARSAL TERMS

Stage and rehearsal terms, decidedly nonscientific, are a mixture of descriptive colloquialisms and practical words and phrases. There is no such thing as a standard set of terms; usage varies, not only between New York and Los Angeles, but between two adjacent rehearsal halls. Despite all this, it is seldom that a major problem arises, and communication of basic ideas and instructions generally progresses smoothly enough after initial accommodations.

STAGE GEOGRAPHY

The stage's geographical locations and their abbreviations are self-explanatory. The direction of *stage right* and *stage left* is determined by the actor's right or left as he faces the audience.

The designations *downstage* and *upstage* go a long way back in theatre history. When the element of perspective was introduced into stage decor in Italy at the time of the Renaissance, the stage floor was raked from the front to the back, sloping up in height as it got farther back from the apron, thus increasing the illusion of depth. The practice of so constructing stage floors continued until our own century, so that downstage literally meant down and upstage meant up.

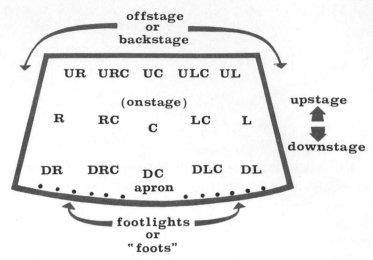

DR–down right; R–right; UR–up right; DRC–down right center; RC–right center; URC–up right center; DC–down center; C–center; UC–up center; DLC–down left center; LC–left center; ULC–up left center; DL–down left; L–left; UL–up left.

The term *stage level* has two meanings. One refers to any elevation above the stage floor through the use of risers or platforms; in this sense, a level is a technical term employed by the scenic designer and stage manager. As used by actors and directors, a level relates to the distance from the footlights of one or several stage characters. To play on a level with another actor is to be in a position equidistant from the footlights with that of the opposite person. This is the commonly accepted use of the term when applied to stage business.

Psychological Strength • By architectural design, onstage space is the dominant area in the theatre building. Within that area certain stage positions take on added psychological significance because of their juxtaposition to the audience. The most dominant areas are downstage and closest to the audience; the least dominant are upstage and farthest away—DC versus UR or UL. With the introduction of a set, however, concentration of light, furniture placement, or the use of elevations can alter the psychological significance of any geographical area. This is a fact of first importance in the achievement of meaning and intensity through stage movement.

Rehearsal Terms

A *stage cross* is any movement that takes a character from one place on stage to another. It can go in any direction; the distance is immaterial, anything more than a step or two being termed a cross. A countering action by a reacting character is a *countercross*.[40] For purposes of noting stage business, the cross can be abbreviated to X and the countercross to XX.

Here are other words and phrases as they may be heard in the context of rehearsal conversation. The first rehearsals of a play generally are *reading rehearsals*, at which time the play is read to or by the cast. They are followed by a *call* on the *callboard*, posted by the stage manager, for *blocking rehearsals*, when the director *sets the business* or *blocks the action* for a scene, meaning that he directs the actors in the major movements they are to perform. As a player you will be told to *take a X*, or *take a turn*, in or out. After you have done so, you will be expected to *take down* (write) your business in your *script*. On the other hand, switching verbs for no apparent reason, you are requested to *give your line* and *give your cue*; on occasions you might be asked to *throw a line* or *cue*. It is also said that you *deliver a line* or *deliver a speech*. An interpretation is sometimes called a *line reading*. You will be requested to *project* your voice if you speak too softly, or to *project* your movements if they drop off in vitality. And finally, you may have guessed that when anyone, in or out of the theatre, is told to mind his "P's and Q's," he really is being asked to look out for his props and cues.

Floor Plan • A floor plan is a blueprint of a stage set as seen from the point of view of anyone overhead looking directly down at the floor. It is a ground plan, traced in outline form, of the limits of a set. Although always drawn to scale by the designer, it is often roughly sketched in by or for the actor. Included in the floor plan is the onstage area and whatever furniture or set pieces it contains, which are indicated in skeletal form.

A *set piece* is a constructed bit of scenery, not attached to the set, which functions much as furniture does. Rocks, bushes, walls, and other such items, are set pieces.

An *elevation* is the technical term for a black-and-white or color sketch of a set, painted in perspective.

There are *interior* and *exterior* sets. A *multiple-set* play requires several different locations. These may be shown by totally different sets that require major *set changes*, or they may be part of a *unit set*, in which a number of basic pieces are used in differing combinations in each set.

An exterior set, not drawn to scale, with one piece of furniture and

---

[40] As a balancing action, the countercross is used much less frequently today than formerly, and rightly so, because concern for the nice appearance of the stage picture has decreased.

several set pieces, shows the floor plan for Act I, Scene 1 of *Liliom*, by Ferenc Molnar.

The author's description indicates a lonely place, somewhat hidden by shrubbery, in an amusement park on the outskirts of Budapest. A wooden bench is under an acacia tree next to one of the walks. It is sunset.

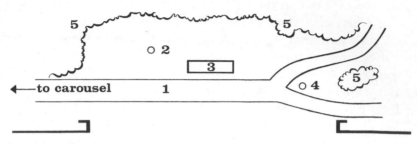

1. Walk.   2. Tree.   3. Park bench.   4. Lamp post.   5. Bushes.

RECORDING STAGE BUSINESS

Lacking any standard of notation, each player must of necessity devise his own system of recording his stage business in his script. But each will be well advised to observe certain conditioning factors:

1. Lack of adequate writing space, a major fault in printed playbooks, influences size and extent of notations. Abbreviations are almost mandatory—for example, X for cross, XX for countercross.

2. In contrast, the notation should be as extensive as time and space permits so that maximum information can be carried over to the next rehearsal.

3. The notation should be clear—today's scribble could be tomorrow's rehearsal puzzle.

4. The notation should be exact, noting precisely what is to be done and exactly when it is to occur.

5. Rehearsal time is always at a premium. Fast writing that does not sacrifice accuracy is a boon to actor and company alike.

6. Motivations remain clear when conditioning factors are succinctly set down. Statements of attitudes are helpful in this respect.

7. Sometimes a bit of personal business is as important as major stage business. It should be recorded.

8. A properly written stage direction is more reliable than the best memory.

The demonstration of recorded stage business below is to be identified with the floor plan for Act I, Scene 1 of *Liliom*.[41] Note that personal business is included along with stage business.

The conditioning factors for the demonstration are these: Liliom, barker and bouncer for a carousel, has just been discharged by Mrs. Muskat, owner of the merry-go-round, because he paid too much attention to Julie and her friend Marie; Julie, a servant girl, knows she will lose her position if she stays in the park with Liliom. Nevertheless, she does so.

Liliom, self-oriented, self-indulgent, rough and conceited, possesses an animal magnetism of such quality and strength that effort is no longer required to exercise it. His reputation, justly earned, is that he satisfies himself and his purse by affairs with servant girls who come to the amusement park. Julie, shy, lonely, capable of a complete commitment of self to anyone she loves, stands waiting for whatever action is to occur.

The intent of the full scene is to reveal that these two people, so different in personality and background, are drawn to each other to the degree that out of their meeting will come the dominant relationship of their lives. They are strangers at the beginning of the scene—Liliom alert but wary, Julie nervous but somehow sure—but at the end the bond between them, unvoiced but certain, is secure for their lives and beyond.

Marie has just taken an uncertain departure DL, leaving Julie standing at the crossroad in the walk. Liliom is on the grass above the walk slightly R of C. He is looking quizzically, and with a slight challenge, at Julie.

	Notes
R & C	1 She *looks at him, looks down, nods, looks at bench, x's, sits on R-end.*
LILIOM: / Now we're both discharged.[1]	
Have you had your supper?[2]	
JULIE: No. *eyes down*	
LILIOM: Want to[3] go eat something at the garden?	2 *Watch with interest*
JULIE: No.	
LILIOM: Anywhere else?	3 *Jerk head off R*
JULIE: No.	

[41] *Liliom* by Ferenc Molnar, translated by Benjamin F. Glazer. Copyright 1921 by United Plays, Inc. Copyright 1944 (Acting Edition) by Ferenc Molnar, Benjamin F. Glazer and Paramount Pictures, Inc. Copyright 1949 (in renewal) by Benjamin F. Glazer. Acknowledgement is also given to Lili Darvas Molnar, administratrix of the estate of Ferenc Molnar.

Notes

LILIOM: *shrug* / You don't come to this park very often, do you? [4] I've [5] only seen you three times. Been here oftener than that? *stop*

JULIE: Oh, yes.— *looks up*

LILIOM: Did you see me?

JULIE: / Yes. *looks down*

LILIOM: And did you know I was Liliom?

JULIE: They told me.

LILIOM: (*Satisfied, whistles softly*) [6] Have you got a sweetheart?

JULIE: No.

LILIOM: (*Stop, disbelief*) Don't lie to me.

JULIE: I haven't. [7] If I had, I'd tell you. I've never had one.

LILIOM: [8] What an awful liar you are. I've got a good mind to go away and leave you here.

JULIE: [9] I've never had one.

LILIOM: Tell that to someone else.

JULIE: (*Reproachfully*) [10] Why do you insist I have?

LILIOM: Because [11] you stayed here with me the first time I asked you to. You know your way around, you do.

JULIE: No, I don't Mister Liliom.

LILIOM: I [12] suppose you'll tell me you don't know why you're sitting here—like this, in the dark, alone with me [13]—You [14] wouldn't 'a' stayed so quick, if you hadn't done it before—with some soldier, maybe. This isn't the first time. You wouldn't have been so ready to stay if it was—what *did* you stay for, anyhow?

JULIE: So you wouldn't be left alone.

LILIOM: / Alone! God, [15] you're dumb! I don't need to be alone. I can have all the girls I want. Not only

4 Julie gives dubious shake

5 X to bench, on level with her

6 X up of bench to L end

7 Body turn to him

8 Head turn to her.

9 Look down, statement of fact.

10 Look up at him

11 He looks away as he swings R leg over back of bench

12 Leans elbow on knee.

13 Julie react, slight protest

14 attitude of knowing

straightening up

15 look at her

Notes

servant girls like you, but [16] cooks and governesses, even French girls. I could have twenty of them if I wanted to.

JULIE: I know, Mister Liliom.

LILIOM: What do you know?

JULIE: That all the girls are in love with you. But that's not why *I* stayed. (*Liliom reacts: "Oh?"*) I stayed because you've been so good to me.

LILIOM: Well,[17] then you can go home.

JULIE: I don't want to go home now.

LILIOM: And what if I go away and leave you sitting here?

JULIE: If you did, I wouldn't go home.

LILIOM: [18] Do you know what you remind me of? A sweetheart I once had—I'll tell you how I met her—One night, at closing time we had put out the lights in the carousel, and just as I was—(*He is interrupted by the entrance R of two policemen*)

16 *Leg off bench, still behind it*

17 *Amazement, X ing away 2-3 steps, on level with her*

18 *Looks in amazement, scratches or shakes head— arrested movement, sudden idea*

CREATING STAGE BUSINESS

Stage business, synchronized with line delivery, is the means whereby the meaning and feeling of a scene, put there by the playwright and augmented by the offices of director and actor, are made meaningfully clear to an audience.

In the enactment of your share of the expressive load, you will perforce rely on the knowledge of movement and tone gained from your study of pantomime and voice, and the basic competences developed in each.

Motivations • To discover what meanings are intended for projection in a scene, it is essential to determine the motivations that impel them. You will deal with several kinds of motivation.

1. *External motivations* are obvious causes prompted by external stimuli. Here are short examples: A is reading in a chair RC when the phone rings—he rises and Xs DL to answer it. B is a guest; when the

host invites her to sit down, she does so, Xing from a door R to a chair LC. C drops a pencil and stoops to pick it up; D Xs the stage to close a window.

2. *Internal motivations* derive from those mental, emotional, sensory, or physical impulses that prompt actions. Here are more examples. D is a student studying. A hard-to-solve problem causes him to throw down his pencil and lean his head on his arms. E is another student. She becomes thirsty while writing at the kitchen table. With her mind still on the lesson's problem she Xs to the faucet. F is a woman on a jury. During deliberations she is asked a question. Troubled for an answer, she leaves her place at the conference table and Xs to window UC, thinking of her reply.

The term motivation should be intimately associated in your mind with the word desire. Each character in a play, no matter on which side of the conflict, desires one thing or another, his desires ranging as far as there are human wants unfulfilled. The desire drive, canalizing energy and action into the conflict, is the prime mover in the forward pacing of a play. In every acting assignment, now and later, one of the first targets of your study should be the motivational desire of your character and the action it brings into play.[42] Of subsequent interest is the sympathetic or antagonistic motivational drives of the other characters in the scene.

3. Always, because so many people and so much equipment must be brought into working harmony, there are *obligatory motivations* for you to handle. Sight lines, set changes, furniture placement, size of playing area, needs of other characters, reaction assignments—all require that you perform business that strict fidelity to truth would not sanction. Nevertheless, the constraints of the form and the needs of a scene oblige you to respond with actions that might seem forced or out of character and dramatically untruthful. Few scenes are so well written, directed, and acted that the players never have to comply with an obligatory motivation. The understanding of why such a need exists and a willingness to respond to it for the good of the whole are marks of competence in acting.

Motivations, which wrap the *why* and *what* of stage action in such a tight dramatic package, grow out of the relationships every character has with his environment and all the persons in it.[43]

[42] In the discovery, dissecting, and shaping of motivations, it would be well for every player to scrutinize his own external and internal drives. It may be revealing to discover how much of an interpretation is the expression of an actor's own drives and how much is the expression of the character's drives.

[43] For a full discussion see Part I, Chapter 4, p. 35.

Relationships • Meaning is revealed by context. You as an individual, or you as a character in a play, are a relating person; you take on dimensions, acquire traits, think thoughts, feel emotions, act physically, and react sensuously as one of the constituents in a life pattern. Invisible lines of desire, need, likes and dislikes, compulsions, habits, and instincts tie you to everything in your environment. We who know you, read who and what you are as you move and talk in the context of your surroundings. Each of us plays off the persons and objects around him, and each is played off in turn, in a never-ceasing revelation that shows us for what we are and shows life for what it is.

Altered to fit the needs of the dramatic form, relationship is the cornerstone on which all meanings are built. The interconnection of persons and things can be shown in many different ways:

1. By the positions a character takes, the kind and manner of movement he makes, the things he says and how he says them;

2. By a character's *closeness to* or *distance away* from other persons or objects (desires), his *turns toward* or *away from* them (likes and dislikes);

3. By the manner of his touch, the nature of his look, the choice of words used to talk about objects, places, or persons, and the tone behind the words;

4. By the amount of energy and the degree of intensity in the character's commitment to a relationship.

EXERCISE

Remembering the natural harmony existing between an inner state of being and its outward manifestation in movement and tone, how would you block the business for the last part of the scene between Liliom and Julie? What is the thought content of the lines, and what, in exact words, are the attitudes of the characters to the place, the time, and each other? With movement that is neither static nor busy, that is not only dramatic but meaningfully so, that plays to and with the other character rather than to the audience, how will you project the thoughts and feelings of your character to an audience?

In the excerpt from *Liliom*[44] already given, the scene was stopped with the entrance of the two policemen. Now, those two worthies have exited, after warning Julie of the dangers inherent in an association with the notorious Liliom. For purposes of brevity, the sequence has some internal cuts.

[44] See page 223 for copyright statement.

JULIE: (*After a brief pause*) Well, and what then?

LILIOM: (*Not understanding*) Huh?

JULIE: You were beginning to tell me a story.

LILIOM: Me?

JULIE: Yes, about a sweetheart. . . .

LILIOM: Oh, yes, yes, . . . Say—tell me—ain't you—that is, ain't you at all—afraid of me? The officer told you what kind of a fellow I am—and that I'd take your money away from you—

JULIE: You couldn't take it away—I haven't got any. But if I had—I'd give it all to you.

LILIOM: You would?

JULIE: If you asked me for it.

LILIOM: Have you ever had a fellow you gave money to?

JULIE: No.

LILIOM: Haven't you ever had a sweetheart?

JULIE: No.

LILIOM: Some one you used to go walking with. You've had one like that?

JULIE: Yes.

LILIOM: A soldier?

JULIE: He came from the same village I did.

LILIOM: That's what all the soldiers say. . . . Where did you walk?

JULIE: In the park.

LILIOM: And your virtue? Where did you lose that?

JULIE: I haven't got any virtue.

LILIOM: Well, you had once.

JULIE: No, I never had. I'm a respectable girl.

LILIOM: Yes, but you gave the soldier something. . . .

JULIE: You have to. But I didn't love him.

Notes

LILIOM: Do you love me?

JULIE: No, Mister Liliom.

LILIOM: Then why do you stay here with me?

JULIE: Um—nothing.

LILIOM: (*A pause, music is heard*) Want to dance?

JULIE: No. I have to be very careful.

LILIOM: Of what?

JULIE: My—character.

LILIOM: Why?

JULIE: Because I'm never going to marry. If I was going to marry, it would be different. Then I wouldn't need to worry so much about my character. It doesn't make any difference if you're married. . . .

LILIOM: Suppose I were to say to you —I'll marry you.

JULIE: You?

LILIOM: That frightens you, doesn't it? You're thinking of what the officer said and you're afraid.

JULIE: No, I'm not, Mister Liliom. I don't pay any attention to what he said.

LILIOM: But you wouldn't dare marry anyone like me, would you?

JULIE: I know that—that—if I loved anyone—it wouldn't make any difference to me what he—even if I died for it.

LILIOM: But you wouldn't marry a rough guy like me—that is—eh—if you loved me—

JULIE: Yes, I would—if I loved you, Mister Liliom. . . .

LILIOM: (*A pause*) Suppose—you had some money—and I took it from you?

JULIE: Then you could take it, that's all.

LILIOM: (*Another brief silence*) All I have to do—is go back to her—that

Muskat woman—she'll be glad to
get me back—then I'd be earning
my wages again.

JULIE: (*She is silent. The twilight
folds darker about them. Softly*)
Don't go back—to her—

LILIOM: There are a lot of acacia
trees around here.

JULIE: (*Pause*) Don't go back to
her—

LILIOM: (*Pause*) She'd take me back
the minute I asked her. I know
why—she knows, too—

JULIE: (*Pause*) I can smell them, too
—acacia blossoms—
(*Some blossoms drift down from
the tree to the bench. Liliom
catches one and smells it*)

LILIOM: White acacias!

JULIE: (*After a brief pause*) The
wind keeps bringing them down.
(*They are silent*)
                Curtain

Playing Areas • When a scene or a play has been chosen for presentation and assigned to the stage for rehearsal, each onstage area alters its character and becomes a new place, one with an individuality all its own. Outlined by the walls of an imaginary set, the space takes on a composite character, made up of the related areas within its confines. RC is still where it was, but now it is a particular kind of RC.

A room is an entity in itself; it also contains entities, subdivisions of the whole. It has a specific purpose, contrasting with the purposes of other rooms. Within that purpose, lesser uses exist, each a subdivision deriving its character from its function. In a set these smaller spaces become playing areas. By the way characters move into and out of them, and by what is done there, their purpose is made clear.

Thornton Wilder creates playing areas in a wonderfully imaginative way in *Our Town*. Beginning with a bare space, he has his Stage Manager select one geographical area after another throughout the play, assigning a scene or scenes to each, thus giving it the distinctiveness that comes from use. Some of the areas are small, but several occupy the whole stage. In this last circumstance the entire area takes on the character of the latest assignment, nor is there any detraction because it was used differently before. In several instances a new playing area will overlap the space of two previous ones. In a more restricted way, *Death of a Salesman* utilizes multiple playing areas, some fluid, some static.

Traffic and Parking Areas • Every set, indoors or out, living room, office, or garden, can be separated into *traffic* or *parking areas*. There is a meaning in the movement that uses these spaces; there is just as much meaning when the basic use is contradicted—for example, a boy and girl sit on steps oblivious to the flow of traffic around them. One meaning or several is attached to a space by what is placed there, who uses it, and what is done there. It is easy to identify playing areas when they are associated with such words as work or rest, play or food. Some areas are characterized by warmth—for instance, around a fireplace, or by coldness—by an open window; some are rendered distinctive by light or darkness, freedom or constriction, elevation or depth. The geographical spaces of the stage and the associations connected with playing areas offer themselves as motivational devices for the planning of stage movement.

Sequence and Playing Areas • The length of a sequence within a scene is determined by its content. As a general rule each sequence has one subject. When the subject changes a new sequence comes into being. Also as a general rule, the new sequence requires a new playing area, not for the sake of variety, which is only a fortunate by-product, but because it is the meaningful thing to do. For example, if you will check the demonstration from *Liliom*, you will find that each of Liliom's X's mark the beginning of a new sequence. The most creative stage business is business that is placed in the correct playing area and makes the best use of the objects located there.

Playing Within the Illusion • To achieve the full possibilities of the meaningful relationship inherent in the use of playing areas, it is necessary that as little distortion as possible be made in the action patterns of a character. It is not good acting to break or warp that relationship by aiming lines and movement straight out, or slanted out, to the audience. More meaning can be projected by movement that plays within the illusion, achieving depth as well as width, than can be revealed by the notion that as much movement as possible must be given directly to the audience.

Details • The cumulative effect of a scene may attract you when reading a script; it may manifest itself when you are at work in rehearsal. But no strong effort is ever achieved in one grand, inspired sweep of action; it is built by adding each small, complete detail to the next small complete detail. As a composer breaks his total creative effort into bars of music filled with notes and rests, so you break the wholeness of scene or sequence into the dramatic details of single movements and single tones.

In the main, it is in the performance of details that your acting ability will be manifest. As a fine pianist goes over in endless repetition the detailed fingering for every portion of his concert number, so the fine actor repeats his execution of the details of his action. In proper proportions, the more nearly perfect a scene is in details, the better the scene will be. The practice of details demands more time than any other single element in play preparation. Individual practice between rehearsals is the ideal time for the accomplishment of this phase of acting.

ADDITIONAL POINTERS

Here are additional points of importance to the setting and execution of stage business.

1. *Doors* • Single doors swing one way; exterior doors swing on stage, but interior doors generally are hinged upstage and swing off. Double doors can cause ungainly movement if not properly handled; as a general rule, open the door farthest from you, thus you do not have to swing up and out of the nearest door's arc before entering or leaving the stage.

2. Looking directly down at the stage floor so that the eyelids curtain the eyes is a negative movement of some strength. You will do well to discover the difference between actually looking down and seeming to do so.

3. As a rule, do not back into place, into either a standing or a sitting position. Such a movement is awkward, unless properly motivated. If awkwardness is desired, that is a different matter.

4. Going up or coming down steps, either in costume or in modern dress, is a matter for concern, especially if the movement is to be performed with dignity and poise. To look down at the steps, either in ascending or descending, detracts from the dignity of the movement. Enough of a view of the steps can be obtained from peripheral vision to give confidence that where your foot falls, there a step will be.

For the actress who must move up steps in a long-skirted costume, the natural expedient of grasping the front of the gown with either one or both hands—using forefinger against thumb, not clutching the material as though it were wet wash—so that the skirt is raised just enough to clear the next step, is all that need be done.

5. A similar problem confronts the actress wearing a long dress or the actor with a flowing cape when the action calls for a kneeling or a low sitting position. The going down is easy. It is the tendency to step on the skirt or cape when rising that renders caution necessary. To handle the

garments properly, place the material where you want it with a hand movement as you go down and, with your foot, make sure of free footing before rising.

6. Stage exits that involve several actors often require attention. There is a natural tendency for anyone making an exit to stop offstage as soon as he or she is out of sight of the audience. But if the first actors off keep going, their companions should have no difficulty in properly effecting the completion of the movement.

7. *Ad lib* is a stage direction to fill in with movement or words as you think fit. It means *as one wishes.* When applied to stage work, however, the term must be more rigorously conditioned: *a.* It should be given in keeping with the character portrayed and with the mood of the play. *b.* The movement and the words used should not be left to chance utterance, nor should they vary from performance to performance. *c.* It is not permissible to be cute or clever, inserting phrases intended only for the ears of fellow performers; such juvenilities have a way of getting out into the house in a most unexpected manner. *d.* The ad lib should be in exact proportion to its motivation.

8. Curtain calls are a necessary adjunct to the play. After watching the players express themselves for some time, the audience also wishes to express itself. It is recommended that: *a.* All calls be rehearsed as a part of the dress rehearsal regimen. *b.* The call does not tease the audience into stronger demands than the situation merits. *c.* It does not do damage to the illusion the actors have labored to create and maintain.

EXERCISES AND ASSIGNMENTS

1. Each student is to use his classmates to demonstrate how *closeness to* and *distance from* and *turns toward* and *turns away* reveal the identity of a unit group he has observed while on campus, or at work, or in transit. The class is to name the group and distinguish the elements that gave it its identity.

2. Each student is to use three pairs of his classmates to demonstrate revealing groupings such as gather around a campus bench or on the library steps or around a classroom door. The pairs should have separate interests at first, and then be motivated into a common interest. The class is to identify the relationships shown.

3. By chalk-talking on a blackboard, demonstrate the uses to which playing areas in these or similar locations might be put: the lounge in a student union, the seats and aisles of a railroad car, one side of the area around a swimming pool, a promenade deck on a ship, the lobby of a theatre, a living room.

4. Create a floor plan and the business for one of the scenes below and present your work to the class.

a. A Midsummer Night's Dream, Shakespeare, Act I, Scene 2. Lysander and Hermia, enjoying a forbidden love, meet outside Athens to make their way to a place beyond the power of both father and Duke where they can be married. The play is lighthearted, a mixture of realism and fantasy, of high and low comedy. The two enter.

Notes

LYS: Fair love, you faint with wan-
    dering in the wood;
  And to speak troth, I have forgot
    our way:
  We'll rest us, Hermia, if you think
    it good,
  And tarry for the comfort of the
    day.
HER: Be it so, Lysander; find you out
    a bed,
  For I upon this bank will rest my
    head.
LYS: One turf shall serve as pillow
    for us both:
  One heart, one bed, two bosoms,
    and one troth.
HER: Nay, good Lysander; for my
    sake, my dear,
  Lie further off yet, do not lie so
    near.
LYS: O! take the sense, sweet, of my
    innocence,
  Love takes the meaning in love's
    conference.
  I mean that my heart unto yours
    is knit,
  So that but one heart we can make
    of it;
  Two bosoms interchained with an
    oath;
  So then two bosoms and a single
    troth.
  Then by your side no bed-room me
    deny,
  For, lying so, Hermia, I do not lie.
HER: Lysander riddles very prettily:
  Now much beshrew my manners
    and my pride,

Notes

If Hermia meant to say Lysander
  lied.
But, gentle friend, for love and
  courtesy
Lie further off; in human modesty,
Such separation as may well be
  said
Becomes a virtuous bachelor and
  a maid,
So far be distant; and, goodnight,
  sweet friend.
Thy love ne'er alter till thy sweet
  life end.
Lys: Amen, amen, to that fair prayer,
  say I;
And then end life when I end
  loyalty!
    (*Retires a little distance*)
Her: With half that wish the wish-
  er's eyes be press'd!
    (*They sleep*)

h. Miss Julie,[45] Strindberg, Act I. In a time of great playwrights, Strindberg stands out as one of the greatest. In a troubled time he was one of the most troubled. Perhaps that is the reason the sharp bite of conflict is so marked in all of his plays. Foremost among the tensions he generates is the struggle between male and female, between man and wife, between lovers— even when the relationship is that of superior to inferior, of mistress to servant.

The action of the play takes place in the kitchen of the Count's manor house on Midsummer Eve in Sweden in the 1880's. Miss Julie has come into the kitchen from the dancing outside and now has demanded that Jean, her father's valet, return to dance with her. In the doorway Jean stops with a cry, his hand cupped over one eye.

Notes

Miss Julie: You've caught some-
  thing in your eye. Let me see.
Jean: It's nothing. Just a bit of dust.
  It'll go away.
Miss Julie: The sleeve of my dress

[45] From *Miss Julie* by August Strindberg, translated by E. M. Sprinchorn, Published by Chandler Publishing Company, San Francisco. Copyright 1961, by Chandler Publishing Company. Reprinted by permission.

must have grazed your eye. Sit down and I'll help you. (*She leads him to a chair. With a corner of her handkerchief she probes for the bit of dust.*) Now sit still, absolutely still. (*She slaps his hand*) Do as you're told. Why, I believe you're trembling—a big, strong man like you. (*She feels his arm*) With such big arms!

JEAN: (*Warning*) Miss Julie!

MISS JULIE: Yes, *Monsieur Jean?*

JEAN: *Attention! Je ne suis qu'un homme!*

MISS JULIE: Sit still, I tell you! . . . There now! It's out. Kiss my hand and thank me!

JEAN: (*Rising*) Listen to me, Miss Julie!—Christine has gone to bed!—Listen to me, I tell you!

MISS JULIE: Kiss my hand first!

JEAN: Listen to me!

MISS JULIE: Kiss my hand first!

JEAN: All right. But you'll have no one to blame but yourself.

MISS JULIE: For what?

JEAN: For what! Are you twenty-five years old and still a child? Don't you know it's dangerous to play with fire?

MISS JULIE: Not for me. I'm insured!

JEAN: (*Boldly*) Oh, no you're not! And even if you were, there's inflammable stuff next door.

MISS JULIE: Meaning you?

JEAN: Yes. Not just because it's me, but because I'm a young man——

MISS JULIE: And irresistibly handsome? What incredible conceit! A Don Juan, maybe! Or a Joseph? Yes, bless my soul, that's it: you're a Joseph!

JEAN: You think so?

MISS JULIE: I'm almost afraid so! (*Jean steps boldly up to her, grabs her around the waist, kisses her. She slaps his face*) None of that!

JEAN: Are you still playing games or are you serious?

MISS JULIE: I'm serious.

JEAN: Then you must have been serious just a moment ago, too! You take your games too seriously and that's dangerous. Well, I'm tired of your games, and if you'll excuse me, I'll return to my work. The Count will be wanting his boots on time, and it's long past midnight.

MISS JULIE: Put those boots down.

JEAN: No! This is my job. It's what I'm here for. But I never undertook to be a playmate for you. That's something I could never be. I consider myself too good for that.

MISS JULIE: You are proud.

JEAN: In some ways. Not in others.

MISS JULIE: Have you ever been in love?

JEAN: We don't use that word around here. But I've been interested in a lot of girls, if that's what you mean. . . . I even got sick once because I couldn't have the one I wanted—really sick, like the princes in the Arabian Nights—who couldn't eat or drink for love.

MISS JULIE: Who was the girl? (*He does not reply*) Who was she?

JEAN: You can't make me tell you that.

MISS JULIE: Even if I ask you as an equal—ask you—as a friend? . . . Who was she?

JEAN: You.

3. *Pygmalion*,[46] Shaw, Act II. This excerpt, from a scene for four, features multiple relationships in a room that holds work and traffic and parking areas. Professor Higgins, specialist in phonetics, has been explaining his procedures and his instruments to his guest, Colonel Pickering, expert in Indian dialects, when Mrs. Pearce brings Liza Doolittle into the room. Both attitudes and actions are indicated in the script.

Notes

HIGGINS: (*Recognizing Liza*) Why, this is the girl I jotted down last night. She's no use: I've got all the records I want of the Lisson Grove lingo; and I'm not going to waste another cylinder on it. (*To Liza*) Be off with you: I don't want you.

LIZA: Don't you be so saucy. You aint heard what I come for yet. (*To Mrs. Pearce*) Did you tell him I come in a taxi?

MRS. PEARCE: Nonsense, girl! what do you think a gentleman like Mr. Higgins cares what you came in?

LIZA: Oh, we are proud! He aint above giving lessons, not him: I heard him say so. Well, I aint come here to ask for any compliment; and if my money's not good enough I can go elsewhere.

HIGGINS: Good enough for what?

LIZA: Good enough for you. Now you know, dont you? I've come to have lessons, I am. And to pay for 'em too: make no mistake.

HIGGINS: Well!!! (*Recovering*) What do you expect me to say to you?

LIZA: Well, if you was a gentleman, you might ask me to sit down, I think. Dont I tell you I'm bringing you business?

HIGGINS: Pickering: shall we ask this baggage to sit down, or shall we throw her out the window?

[46] *Pygmalion* by George Bernard Shaw. Reprinted by permission of The Public Trustee and The Society of Authors, 84 Drayton Gardens, London, England.

LIZA: (*Running behind furniture*) Ah-ah-oh-ow-ow-ow-oo! (*Wounded and whimpering*) I wont be called a baggage when Ive offered to pay like any lady.
(*Motionless, the two men stare at her from the other side of the room, amazed*)

PICKERING: (*Gently*) But what do you want?

LIZA: I want to be a lady in a flower shop stead of sellin at the corner of Tottenham Court Road. But they wont take me unless I can talk more genteel. He said he could teach me. Well, here I am ready to pay him—not asking any favor—and he treats me zif I was dirt.

MRS. PEARCE: How can you be such a foolish ignorant girl as to think you could afford to pay Mr. Higgins?

LIZA: Why shouldnt I? I know what lessons cost as well as you do, and I'm ready to pay.

HIGGINS: How much?

LIZA: (*Back to him, triumphant*) Now youre talking! I thought youd come off it when you saw a chance of getting back a bit of what you chucked at me last night. (*Confidentially*) Youd had a drop in, hadnt you?

HIGGINS: (*Peremptorily*) Sit down.

LIZA: Oh, if youre going to make a compliment of it——

HIGGINS: (*Thundering*) Sit down.

MRS. PEARCE: Sit down, girl. Do as youre told.

LIZA: Ah-ah-ah-ow-ow-oo!

PICKERING: (*Courteously*) Wont you sit down? (*He places a chair for her*)

LIZA: (*Coyly*) Dont mind if I do.

HIGGINS: What is your name?

LIZA: Liza Doolittle.

HIGGINS: (*Declaiming gravely*) Eliza, Elizabeth, Betsy and Bess,
  They went to the woods to get a bird's nes':

PICKERING: They found a nest with four eggs in it:

HIGGINS: They took one apiece, and left three in it. (*They laugh*)

LIZA: Oh, dont be silly.

MRS. PEARCE: You mustnt speak to the gentleman like that.

LIZA: Well, why wont he speak sensible to me?

HIGGINS: Come back to business. How much do you propose to pay me for the lessons?

LIZA: Oh, I know whats right. A lady friend of mine gets French lessons for eighteenpence an hour from a real French gentleman. Well, you wouldnt have the face to ask me the same for teaching me my own language as you would for French; so I wont give more than a shilling. Take it or leave it.

HIGGINS: You know, Pickering, if you consider a shilling, not as a simple shilling, but as a percentage of this girl's income, it works out as fully equivalent to sixty or seventy guineas from a millionaire.

PICKERING: How so?

HIGGINS: Figure it out. A millionaire has about £150 a day. She earns about half-a-crown.

LIZA: (*Haughtily*) Who told you I only—

HIGGINS: (*Continuing*) She offers me two-fifths of her day's income for a lesson. Two-fifths of a millionaire's income for a day would be somewhere about £60. It's handsome. By George, it's enormous! it's the biggest offer I ever had.

LIZA: (*Rising, terrified*) Sixty pounds! What are you talking about? I never offered you sixty pounds. Where would I get—

HIGGINS: Hold your tongue.

LIZA: But I aint got sixty pounds. Oh—

MRS. PEARCE: Dont cry, you silly girl. Sit down. Nobody is going to touch your money.

HIGGINS: Somebody is going to touch you, with a broomstick, if you dont stop snivelling. Sit down.

LIZA: (*Obeying*) Ah-ah-ah-ow-oo-o! One would think you was my father.

HIGGINS: If I decide to teach you, I'll be worse than two fathers to you. Here. (*Offering handkerchief*)

LIZA: Whats this for?

HIGGINS: To wipe your eyes. To wipe any part of your face that feels moist. Remember: thats your handkerchief; and thats your sleeve. Dont mistake the one for the other if you wish to become a lady in a shop.

Chapter 18

Characterization

Character is the humanizing element in all drama, the focal point of man's interest in man, the link between the particular and the universal.

Characterization is the process whereby you, as an actor, create an illusion of a distinct stage personality, not your own, which you reveal during a public performance for acceptance by an audience.[47] The quality of your creation is determined in the main by four factors: the truth of your creation, the wholeness of it, the distinctiveness of it, and the acceptance of it. The successful achievement of these factors is dependent upon the range and depth of your knowledge and understanding, upon your sympathy and belief, your ability and skill.

The roles to which you apply the process of characterization may be close to you in age and situation, in personality and physical attributes. Or they may be radically different from you in any or all the above respects.

To encompass the work of this chapter, let us select as models two characters, one female, one male, from two well-known plays and study the roles from inception to completion through the processes of comprehension, translation, and creation. But first we must establish an attitude to the work ahead.

ARTISTIC OBJECTIVITY

As a creative actor your sympathy and comprehension must take you beyond the limitations of such past habits of thought and action as put a restriction upon the way you think and feel about the roles you play. No dichotomy of good or bad should guide your appraisal. You may not sit in judgment and say of any character that this one is right or that one wrong. You simply say, this character *is*, and what he is I must know, and knowing, play.

Artistic integrity does not permit likes and dislikes to stand between an actor and the role he is to create. We err often in this respect. It would

[47] Characterization from the point of view of pantomime is treated in Part II, Chapter 9.

be good to see an actress play the part of Mrs. Phelps in *The Silver Cord*, who did not say in effect to the audience, "I know this woman for what she is, and I dislike her every bit as much as you do."

No one is a hypocrite to himself. It is granted that Mrs. Phelps performs acts hurtful to herself and to those around her. But she does not do them because she has said to herself, "I know the difference between right and wrong, and I deliberately choose the wrong." She does those acts because she is as she is. If she tries to mold her son into a husband-lover image, she does so out of need, not hypocrisy. The actress who misses sincerity by refusing identity with Mrs. Phelps pushes truth from the stage and destroys the intent of the play.

Belief: Identification with your role, based on comprehension and sympathetic understanding, must be a willing action on your part before it can function as a performance fact. You have little chance of persuading an audience to accept the integrity of your creation if you yourself are not first persuaded. To obtain identity, you cannot reserve yourself in whole or in part, but must release yourself mentally, physically, and emotionally; you must make your whole self available for such uses as your character demands.

COMPREHENSION OF THE CHARACTER

Our discussion of character creation follows a series of logical investigations.[48] Two characters will be chosen as prototypes to illustrate how the process works.

Roles fairly removed from the personalities of average players are best for our purpose. Such parts always seem easier to conceive and to create than straight parts.

Comedies both, Molière's *The Imaginary Invalid* and Oliver Goldsmith's *She Stoops To Conquer* are plays theatre people have always kept on the active and available list. Each piece contains a character admirable for our purpose: Toinette in *The Imaginary Invalid* and Tony Lumpkin in *She Stoops To Conquer*. Even though one of the roles will not be yours to enact, it is requested that you study both plays as the first assignment of the chapter.

The Playwright and His Play • The part of Toinette in *The Imaginary Invalid* has a discernible line of theatrical descent. Her immediate

[48] Not all character study, now or later, permits or even requires as full and detailed a coverage of the subject as will be offered in the pages ahead. But both the coverage and the activity it motivates are essential actions to be encompassed in your study now. Fortunately, the effort that now extends from hours into days later will shrink from days into hours as experience grows.

progenitor was one of the female zanies of the *commedia dell'arte*, *Colombina* by name. Molière, as a dramatic author, made his intent obvious in each of his plays. Through satirical comedy and broad farce he exposed the foibles of the bourgeois and upper-class society that surrounded him. True to the traditions of the *commedia*, he was not afraid of bringing exaggeration into the theatre, nor was he in the least timid about making strong demands on the actor or actress who would play one of his roles.

Goldsmith's *She Stoops To Conquer*; or, *The Mistakes of a Night*, is a delightfully improbable play. From a realistic point of view much of the critical action may seem to strain credulity—a point of relative unimportance, because the intent of the author was not realism. In his day he was the leading proponent of what he called *laughing comedy* as opposed to what he termed the *sentimental comedy* of the preceding generation. His intent was to produce a dramatic piece that would offer two hours of hearty fun in the theatre. He did just that, as thousands of performances from his day to ours can testify. The piece is one of the theatre's great comedies.

Relating the Role to the Play • A character must be related to the play that gives it life. This is necessary at the beginning of a project, when objectivity is possible. Later, multiplicity of details may blur the earlier clarity.

The relationship of a role to the play can be determined on the basis of the answers received to the following questions:

1. Is the role the protagonist or antagonist? If it is neither, on which side of the conflict does it stand?

2. What is the extent of its contribution to the conflict? What is the extent of its participation? This is a more important question than one that asks the number of lines in the part and the length of time on stage.

3. The next query is a composite one and evolves out of the last one asked; the answer will apply with equal force to both. What is the basic *want* of the character, the *desire* motivating the actions taken, the *source* of the character's energy drive?

4. How does the basic desire relate the role to the other parts in the piece? Does it act upon them more forcibly than it is acted upon? Or is there a variation, as is most likely, one way and then another, according to the basic desire drives of the others?

5. How is the role related to the major business of the play? Does it force the action and help to set the pace, or does it respond more by reacting to the active part of others?

Toinette: Ladies first—and if it is protested that Toinette is no lady, we can immediately retort that though she is not, she probably could perform one better than most of those who were to the station born.

Toinette is not the protagonist of *Invalid*. That function is fulfilled by her master, Argan, who, interestingly enough, because he is in some ways his own worst enemy, also acts as antagonist from time to time. In the subplot, it is Angélique, Toinette's mistress, who is protagonist. But in both the main and the minor actions, Toinette is as close to the protagonists as a character can be; often she assumes that function for them. In both cases, time after time, she conceives the stratagems that send the protagonists into action to achieve their desires, time after time she supplies the energy drive that increases the intensity of the conflict and moves the play forward. It is a strange situation, because, for all her activity, Toinette's desires are only secondhand, she wants what her master and mistress want. Yet it is she who generates the dynamic that gives their wants life—a point that Molière and the unknown scenarists of the *commedia dell'arte* made over and over again—that is, that the leisure class, to which Argan and his *ménage* belong, has reached a state in which they are no longer capable of solving their own problems.

Always Toinette is in or close to the center of action of the play. Always she acts more forcefully on it than it on her; never is she merely acted upon. She is the pacemaker of the piece, and those who play her must be aware of her responsibility in this respect. Remembering that hers is a role related by direct theatrical bloodlines to the most vital, lusty, and farcical roles the western theatre has ever seen, the character types of the *commedia dell'arte*, you who play her will do well to put her in her proper setting, which is not the temperate comedy of a modern drawing room piece. She requires room, mentally and physically, and freedom from restraint to work her will upon the other characters and her magic upon the audience.

Tony: Tony Lumpkin also requires scope, but in his case it is as much to effect his machinations as it is for him to be of aid and comfort to others in the play. For Tony is in the somewhat unique situation of being on both sides of the play's conflict. Out of sheer deviltry he is on the side of the antagonist at the beginning of the piece: it is his advice to Marlow and Hastings that generates the first momentum in the play's conflict. Later, he is of definite help in resolving the problems of the young people who form the protagonist group. But in both instances, his motivations remain true. All his action arises out of his basic desire to satisfy his own wants. In this respect his role is major in the play, even if he is on for less time than some of the others.

Tony's contribution to the forwarding action is always vigorous and sizeable. Like Toinette, he is a pacemaker and an *agent provocateur*, and bears a responsibility to the production of first importance: the initiation of much of the critical action depends on his vigor of attack. Unlike Toinette, everything he does is to gratify selfish desires.

Life History • Each character to be portrayed represents an illusory human being who has lived a certain length of time, generally under ascertainable circumstances, and is a physical and psychological entity at the time the play begins, before the progression and dramatic conflict have worked their way upon him or her.

If the character to be created is a historical one of sufficient importance to rate space in the pages of history, the life story can be had from that source. If the part is historical but fictional, the background material may be available about a similar person who actually lived. If the character lives in the present time, the life story of a close acquaintance may serve. Or perhaps, as is so often the case, you will have to take bits and pieces—some from your background of general knowledge, some from your own experiences, some from the experiences of others, to fill out the whole story for the stage personality you are going to create.

Occasionally the playwright has performed this function for you. When he so favors his actors, you have the most reliable kind of material to work on. Liza Doolittle in Shaw's *Pygmalion*, Willie and Biff Loman in Miller's *Death of a Salesman*, and Tom in William's *The Glass Menagerie* are a few examples that demonstrate how wonderful an aid a well-conceived life history is to the player.

It must be said that Goldsmith has done better for us than Molière. The facts of Tony Lumpkin's life history, most of which come to us through the biased observations of his mother, are sufficient to allow the actor a sense of assurance in filling out the remainder. We are familiar with Toinette's theatrical history, but there is not the slightest clue to her life story in the play. In this not unusual circumstance it becomes the responsibility of those who would play her to turn amateur historian and do the job.

Toinette's Life History: In a society of many strata, Toinette's family was located on one of the lower levels. In medieval times they were bondsmen, but the humanizing effect of the Renaissance filtered down to even the lowest classes and made servants of those who had been serfs. Freed from the restrictions of feudalism but now responsible for itself, each family employed the talents of its members to maintain what little place it had in the emerging capitalistic society of the mid-1600's.

For Toinette and all like her, there was no hope of any kind of formal education. Whatever learning they had came from the in-service training of those fortunate enough to obtain a place for themselves where they would be accepted into a family on a servant basis, exchanging labor and loyalty for food, lodging, and clothes.

Toinette was among the fortunate ones. As a child she was placed in a substantial family where material comforts were plentiful and where more love and affection was exchanged than the conflict of the play would have us believe. But, if we know our subject at all, the girl was not the only fortunate party. Toinette, we are persuaded, never left the household short of anything guaranteed in her part of the contract—Argan being French, you may be sure there was a contract, legally written, duly notorized and filed in the appropriate archive—but gave more than she received. Mentally and physically she had the ability to do this.

Tried by the trials of plague and famine, tested by the vicissitudes of a society that placed minimal value on the survival of those of the lowest classes, her family bred qualities of physical stamina and mental alertness into its successive generations. Toinette is a credit to her line, possessing more capability and distinction than any other member of the cast. Her education was pragmatic—she learned what was expedient for her to know and more besides, becoming capable of service in every matter of consequence to the family.

Her age is indefinite. She is old enough to know the facts of life from many angles and young enough to relish the observations and the experiences of those facts. Unmarried, she lacks no men in her life. Could we but see her in her kitchen or on the street, we would be assured of her youthful attractiveness and womanly accomplishments.

She is as proud of her adopted family as any member of it, a not unusual circumstance for one who gained her relation by adoption rather than by birth. For some years, if the truth were known, she has been the pivotal force within it. Familial well-being is her main concern, and the maintenance of that condition, from her point of view, is her basic desire. This is her position at the play's opening.

Tony Lumpkin's Life History: Tony Lumpkin was born in rural England in the latter part of the eighteenth century, in a period of relative social, economic, and political stability. Growing into young manhood when we in America were preparing for our Revolutionary War, he was ignorant of the event and untouched by it, his range of interest being bounded by the area to be covered in a good fox chase. His father, a substantial country squire, died when Tony was quite young. His mother married again and married well, for herself and her son.

A healthy boy, Tony grew up a member of a county family, dominant socially and economically in that limited community. As squire's son he performed none of the onerous labors of farm life, enjoying instead all the vigorous privileges of his position. Well cared for, he learned early that a greater gratification of his wants could be had from his doting mother than from his better balanced stepfather. The fact that an inheritance was due him when he came of age added, even while he was young, to an attitude of independence. His mother, his money, his position, and his health were the principal environmental factors in his life.

His childhood activities were normal in kind and intensity for his station. His own natural vigor of body and his favored position made him a leader among his companions. The revolution in education, only slightly behind the growing Industrial Revolution, had no effect on his life. Formal studies required too much discipline and imposed too much restraint, therefore his knowledge of letters and figures was at a minimum. On the other hand, a natural interest in animal husbandry and plant life, in an area of vigorous climate, encouraged great physical activity. Therefore Tony's occupational knowledge and accomplishments were at a maximum.

If the conditions of life are satisfactory and expectations are founded on basic desires, any threat of change is regarded with suspicion and distrust. Tony could not help but be standoffish with strangers and wary of any plans, especially marital ones, that did not coincide with his particular wants. Self-centered for all of his twenty-one years, limited in range of interests but completely involved within those limits, secure under a parental roof, free from responsibility and not required to labor, Tony has lived his life vigorously and in a manner most acceptable to himself.

Personal Attributes at Curtain Rise

A physical and psychological entity at the time the play begins, the character you are to portray has personal attributes that should be known to you in detail; it is at this point an actor's creation begins.

To obtain a clear and objective view of a role, the simplest procedure is to ask a series of questions about the character. When organized into an interrogatory pattern that can be directed toward all roles, the list can be gone through efficiently and with some ease and the queries that are not critical for any particular character can be easily sloughed off.

The sources from which you derive answers are the playwright's physical and psychological description of the part; what the character says about himself, linked with the comments other characters make about him; and what the character has done or refrained from doing.

Physical Attributes • From the answers to the following questions, can you form a fairly complete visual image of the part, seeing it in both position and movement?

1. Is the character short or tall, lean or heavy, strong or weak, healthy or sickly, malformed or normal?

2. Are the character's movements fluent and graceful or jerky and awkward?

3. Are the face and figure of a pleasing aspect—and if so, to what extent—or is the reverse true?

4. Is muscular tonicity at a high or low level?

5. Is a specific physical appearance demanded—Richard III, the Dauphin in the St. Joan plays, Tony in *They Knew What They Wanted*—or is a general adaptability to the role all that is necessary?

6. Among the four elements of tone—quality, force, time, and pitch—is any one (or two) emphasized?

7. Is there a tendency to variety or monotony, especially in pitch and tempo?

8. Does any one particular quality—nasal, gutteral, orotund, and so on—give distinction to the tone?

9. Is there affectation in the speech patterns?

10. Is colloquialism predominant and are there many common mispronunciations, or has the speech been trained?

Psychological Attributes • In the inner state of each character lie the elements that motivate external actions.

1. Is the character emotionally mature or immature, capable of experiencing strong emotional responses, or limited in this respect?

2. Are certain emotions stronger than others, and if so, which ones are they?

3. Are there any areas of emotional sterility?

4. Is the character aware of emotional strengths and weaknesses, and does this awareness have any bearing upon his emotional stability?

5. Is the role intelligent or unintelligent, fast or deliberate or slow in thought, retentive or nonretentive of ideas?

6. Is the mind both factually and imaginatively active, or does one of these attributes seem to preclude the other?

7. Is the character purposeful and alert, or does a state of aimlessness and slackness prevail?

8. Is there a good mind in the character with but little mental inclination to make use of it, or is the mental capacity limited but employed as fully as possible?

9. Is the character aware of his mental condition, and does he feel strongly about it one way or another?

10. Is there any aberration apparent?

Personality Traits and Attitudes • A complete concept of a role cannot be formed until the vital area of relationships has been explored.

In previous instances in which we related a character to its environment, you were made familiar with the directional words *toward, away, against.* The use of these terms was postulated on the idea that there are three principal ways individuals act on and respond to the active forces in an environment: some go toward life, some withdraw from it, others fight against it. We will apply the test of these three words to Toinette and Tony. But this is not all we must do in the matter of relationship. It is necessary to inquire if the character has been successful in the posture it has taken toward life.

Societal demands have from the beginning required that each individual conform in some measure to group life. If one conforms well he in the broadest terms is a success, if badly he is a failure, if not at all he is an outcast. Of course we are complex enough to register differently in various areas: we may get along very well in one aspect of our community life but fail in another; somewhere or other there probably is a minister who is also a consistent traffic violator.

To grasp in full the personality traits of a character, there are two questions to be asked: (1) Is the character's attitude toward society as a whole aggressive, submissive, or defiant? (2) Is the character in balance or out of balance with his group? These questions, directly asked, will point to direct answers, but it must be recognized that a certain number of combination interrogations are also possible. For example, aggressive in balance or out of balance, submissive in balance or out of balance, and so forth.

When in balance, the aggressive quality reveals itself in positive leadership, as in the case of the class president, the director of a play, the head of a large corporation. When out of balance, the aggressive element may manifest itself in the actions of a political dictator or a criminal, or swing its possessor from the *toward* to the *against* group.

When a submissive person is in balance with his community life a quiet, retiring individual is sure to be found, one of those who always remain in the background, a follower who is content that others lead. But an out-of-balance member of the away-from group would be one who truly seeks withdrawal, as in the case of the painfully shy person, or the more extreme instance of the alcoholic or the drug addict, representing those who attempt a full break from reality by liquor or the "fix."

When the in- or out-of-balance criterion is applied to the defiant group, interesting results occur. The in-balance but against-conditions-as-they-exist individuals generally make leaders of minority groups and militant causes. Eugene Debs, Norman Thomas, Martin Luther King, Jr., as well as the founders of quite a few religious movements, come under this heading. Members of racial and national groups—Negroes, Mexicans, Jews—are often forced by society into the *against* category. If they are in balance, they lead lawful movements seeking redress of grievances, but when out of balance they break into open revolt. Unfortunately, the instances of this last statement are legion throughout the world today.

The defiant individual who is also out of balance is a marked person. He is the juvenile delinquent or the older criminal; of him our society is all too painfully aware.

The placement of the character in the proper social level is another matter of which you must take cognizance. Stratification by classes is much less marked in the United States than it is elsewhere in the world. Yet we, too, have our groupings, most of which are determined on an economic and social basis, as is expected in a capitalistic and republican society. Success in monetary affairs generally means elevation in society; there are very few highly placed persons or families who are poor or indigent. But there is great flux in our society, represented by our constantly changing status symbols and the avidity with which we attempt the possession of them.

Of course, the characters you will portray will not be limited to those born and living in the United States. Recognition that societal groupings elsewhere differ radically from ours is necessary. Research is your means of learning how to make proper social placement for the foreign roles you will perform.

Change and Growth • Each character, at the beginning of a play, possesses a totality of being that is the result of all the living experienced up to that time. But in every play there is a planned progression in which the character participates in some manner. It follows that you must be cognizant of the change and growth that occurs within your character as the piece moves forward. As you know your role at the beginning of the play, so must you know what it is in full at the play's end. Only in this way can you comprehend the totality of the character you are to create at each stage of its progress.

To obtain change-and-growth information, another series of questions can be asked.

1. Is the character's growth primarily concerned with external, materialistic advances—the achievement of wealth or position?

2. If the answer to the above query is affirmative, your questions need to focus upon situational elements: how does the character do what is done, and when and why?

3. If the growth is internal, and the more substantial the character the more likely it is to be so, your questions must concentrate on the personality traits of the role. Does the character grow in dignity or in power, in wisdom or in cunning?

4. Is there progress toward a more moral being? Have recognizable qualities of a spiritual nature manifested themselves by the end of the play?

5. Is maturity of mind or body the goal the author has set for the character?

6. Or is a degeneracy of will or desire apparent? Is the growth of a reverse kind, leading to a less moral being or a less pleasing personality?

7. What is the result of the growth or the deterioration? Does it produce materialistic gain or loss? Is personal happiness or unhappiness achieved?

8. When and how does the growth manifest itself?

9. Does the change affect in any way the basic desire of the character? If so, how?

10. And always the last question: why?

The Whole Character • Every role, like every person, has an amazing number of facets to the personality. You have only to check yourself to grasp the truth of the statement. What are your dominant character traits in a variety of situations: in an acting class, in a history class, when called into the dean's office for correction, when with your closest friends, when with strangers, when on a date?

How many facets are there to your personality? How many to your role? It is almost impossible to reach a limit in either case. However, out of the possible hundred and one aspects of a character, only a limited number can be touched upon by the playwright and by you in the limited playing time at your disposal. But the half-dozen or dozen you select are of prime importance.

To be sure of adequate coverage in a desire to achieve wholeness of character, you can do no better than to tabulate your findings. As your comprehension of the role grows and the principal facets of the character begin to appear with certainty, you will do well to list them, consulting both dictionary and thesaurus if necessary, for exact meanings. Single words, or words conditioned by a modifier, will serve.

Now that we have touched upon the life history, the physical and psychological attributes, the change-and-growth characteristics and the necessary wholeness of a role, let us turn again to our two models, Toinette and Tony and, as the last act of the comprehension section, sum them up as to the points covered.

Toinette: Physically Toinette is a fountain of vitality. Her energies flood every situation in which she appears. But she is also lazy, with little enthusiasm for routine activity. She is extremely agile and has excellent muscular control. She can be either delicate or coarse in movement, sometimes is both within the same scene.

She is emotionally healthy, experiencing feelings fully and without any pronounced lacks or excesses. Delightfully uninhibited, the release of emotion is spontaneous and free. Her range of feeling is wide, but her love is stronger than her hate, her anger more potent than her fear, her pity and scorn prominent but no more so than her tenderness and affection.

Mentally Toinette comes close to brilliance. Her intuition, or perhaps prescience, permits her an understanding of the other characters and of the play's situations more clear, more penetrating by far than that of any other member of the cast. She is the alter ego of the playwright. She is agile-witted, never lacking a device to aid master or mistress when either is in need of help. She reasons well. She replies quickly and her answers are witted with the sting of satire.

In her relationships with her society she is aggressive and in balance. Her personality traits are marked. She is quite patently impudent but impartially so, for she exhibits her impudence to those she likes as well as those she dislikes. She is optimistic—there is always a solution for every difficulty. Behind her front of impudence she is sentimental, loving, and sympathetic. In contrast she can be cruel, for she is no more hesitant in voicing penetrating mental digs than she is in administering seemingly painful injuries such as pinches, slaps, bites, and blows. For her superiors, especially her young mistress or master, she has a definitely moral attitude. If she were to be shown with a lover of her own, we feel quite certain she would be just as definitely amoral.

Her basic desire is to sustain the well-being of her family, even if she must be somewhat rough when doing it. But by play's end she should be quite satisfied, for all her wants are realized: her master is shaken out of his hypochondria, her mistress has her young man, and the two threats to family security are dissipated with the discomfiture of the stepmother and the banishment of the medical corps.

Toinette is one of those rare leading figures who undergoes no change or growth during the play. Her personality alters neither one way nor the other, but remains steadily purposeful from beginning to end. Her actions affect alteration and growth in others, protagonist and antagonist alike, but she is always as she was.

So Toinette's word list would include brilliant, agile-witted, satirical, vital, lazy, physically flexible, impudent, optimistic, sentimental, loving, sympathetic, cruel, moral, and acceptably amoral.

Tony: Physically Tony, like Toinette, abounds with vitality. He is strong and agile. His mind controls his movement, therefore he is not awkward. But his actions are coarse, with large muscles emphasized over the smaller ones, and he expresses himself grossly. There may be an inclination to visualize him as stout, but this is not a necessary characteristic of the role, and if one were influenced by such an image, it could be to the detriment of both part and player. An external and unessential characteristic should not be given precedence over a necessary one.

Emotionally he is given to strengths and weaknesses. He would experience strongly the harder, larger, fuller emotions like anger, excitement, fear, gratification, hunger, coarse humor of the kind that leads to a guffaw rather than a laugh. Hate is too negative an emotion for him; it requires that the owner pour something of himself out for another person, and Tony does little of that. He is emotionally weak only in that he lacks balance. Certain areas, such as those involved in tenderness and pity, seem bleak in him.

Tony does not possess a mind of brilliance, but he is not mentally retarded. The important point is that he makes excellent use, for his purposes, of the brains he has. His mental faculties are well organized; within the scope of his thinking he is quick-witted. In a formal sense he has little or no education, but he has occupational knowledge in some abundance. He can be sly and cunning, but he would much rather act than think about it. The stimulants to his mental processes are limited to the exact bounds of his spheres of interest.

His personality is a combination of aggressive-defiant elements. The defiant attitude is most clearly marked in his first scenes in the play. Later, as he sees opportunities for gratification of his wants, he becomes a shade more compliant and aggressively aids the protagonists. In balance with his surroundings, he is honest according to the mores of his rustic environment. He is blunt in his assertions, given to either/or opinions. He has a deep love of mischief.

As already noted, there is a change in Tony, a slight softening, which, we must agree, is a favorable growth, at least for those who must be around the boy. Mulish and standoffish at first, he even consents later to perform a little make-believe with Miss Neville. At the last, his keen enjoyment of the mischief he works on his mother breeds a strong empathy in the audience.

So Tony's word list would include, youthful, of average intelligence, quick-witted, occupationally educated, vital, strong, agile, coarse, aggressive, honest, opinionated, mischievous.

Key Words • Quite obviously all the character traits selected for either Tony Lumpkin or Toinette cannot be given equal emphasis within the scope of each play. The time element alone would not permit it, to say nothing of the confusion likely to arise in the mind of both actor and audience over the plethora of information.

One of the basic acts of creation is selection. Selection is motivated by intent. From the full list of attributes allotted a character you, the player, should select the one, two, three, or at the most, four traits that will best project your intent to the audience. You place your emphasis on these, letting them dominate in your choice of patterns of movement when you are in the translation stage of your activity. The others are used as complementary attributes to round out your creation.

From the longer list the shorter one is made. Variance can be expected when and as each individual player goes to work. From what has been listed so far, the following can serve as working examples:

Tony	*Toinette*
quick-witted	agile-witted
coarsely agile	physically flexible
aggressive	*impudent
*mischievous	optimistic

The starred words designate the one most emphatic trait for each role. These are the key words that must be translated into meaningfully dramatic movement and tone.

TRANSLATION

After a beginning has been made on the comprehension of a character, but before the process is completed, you initiate the activity of translation.

Translation is the process whereby what is comprehended is given overt form in meaningfully dramatic expression. The act of translation is the principal activity of the preparatory period, requiring more time and a greater variety of effort than any other phase in the entire creative process. Translation time is rehearsal time, and it is in this area of activity that you will spend the major part of your working life.

In the translation period you function in diverse but complementary ways. In a general but overlapping order of progression, you are first a receptive, then a responding, and finally a releasing agent. If you are wise, you strive to achieve your ends by a two-directional approach, working from the inside out and the outside in.[49] By this means you bring an inner state of being into harmony with the external expression of that state.

In rehearsal, with your key words as guides, you attempt to catch the spirit, the personality of the role, so that as time progresses you think the thoughts of your character more and more, as he would think them, at his tempo, his intensity, with his range and point of view; experiencing his emotions, feeling, as much as possible, his kind of anger or longing, liking or fear; trying to see with his eyes, shaping objects and persons as you believe they would appear to him, and hearing sounds as you think he might hear them. And then, that there be correspondence between the internal and external, you attempt to stand and to move as the character would, taking his positions and type of muscular movement rather than your own, and creating, as much as possible, his tonal patterns instead of those dramatically usual to you.

Patterns • Your character concepts, when translated into action, will be revealed to the audience by positions and movements and tones. Each of these three media, when organized and correlated with each other, form patterns—that is position patterns, movement patterns, tonal patterns, and each or all are effective means of communication in direct ratio to your knowledge and proper use of each.

This time, as we again employ our two models for demonstration purposes, the opportunity will be given you to choose the position and movement patterns you believe proper for the role you are interested in. With the key words for your character in mind, create your patterns as you answer the following questions, visualizing as much of the role as possible while it grows.

Position and Movement

1. In both position and movement is the weight generally forward on the balls of the feet, or is it over the middle or on the heels?

2. Is the base broad or narrow, or are both positions employed as circumstances alter?

[49] See Part II, Chapter 5, "The Expressive Body."

3. How do the heels strike the ground when walking? Is there a bounce or a drag in the step?

4. Is the character either splayfooted or pigeon-toed?

5. When seated, how does he or she cross the legs—at the ankles or knees, and how broad is the base?

6. Does the abdomen protrude—if so, is it because of weight or personality—or is it pulled in, or in the position required by naturally good posture?

7. Within the limitations of the character's physical makeup, is there good posture? If not, are the shoulders habitually hunched forward or stiffly held back?

8. Are the elbows aggressively thrust out or timidly tucked in? Might there be a middle or normal position between the two extremes? Is it likely that the character would employ more than one elbow position or movement?

9. Do the arms and hands swing and move as units, or is there great flexibility at the joints?

10. Is the hand often used as a whole unit, as when it is formed into a fist placed on the hips, or is there flexible action between fingers and thumb?

11. Is the chin aggressively extended or shyly pulled in?

12. The head, does it thrust toward objects and persons or withdraw from them? Does it ever turn away from things in distrust or disgust, or tilt from one side to another in a display of interest? Does it droop from muscular slackness or is it held erect?

13. Which is habitual, an emphasis upon the horizontal or the vertical lines of the forehead? Is marked flexibility in this respect proper for one of our characters?

14. Do the eyes squint? If so, is it because of poor eyesight or because of an habitual attitude of distrust? Or are the lids opened wide in amazement or innocence? Would your character run the gamut of all of the above actions?

15. Is the mouth held slackly open or does an attitude of determination cause tenseness in the jaw and lip muscles? Are the corners of the mouth more often pulled up in good humor than pulled down in bad?

Type of Muscular Movement

1. What is the state of the character's muscle tonus?

2. How much vitality will be expended in movement?

3. How much variety of movement will there be?

4. Is the movement more gross than refined? If there is variance, as there is for most characters, what is its extent?

5. What is the size of the character's movements—how large a stride, how much extension for a hand wave, what the extent of a nod of the head, how large or small the smile?

6. What is the basic tempo of the character's movements, what the intensity?

7. Is there a tightness or looseness in the moving muscles?

8. Will the character tend to use many or few actions when handling or describing an object?

9. Are the hands habitually in contact with some portion of the character's clothing, such as a pocket, a belt, the pleats of a skirt, a lapel, a handkerchief or a handbag?

10. Is the type of muscular activity aggressive, withdrawn, or defiant?

11. Is there good control and coordination of the muscles or is the opposite true?

Tonal Patterns • The initiation of the character's tonal pattern follows the same procedure outlined for position and movement.

Toinette's key words were agile-witted, physically flexible, impudent, optimistic. Flexibility in the use of all four tonal elements is a certainty with her. She is one of those extraordinary characters who runs a wonderfully wide gamut of tonal patterns as situation varies with situation, and her relationships, unlike Tony's, vary according to the person she is with and the situation in which she is immediately involved.

Quality: Basically orotund, but at some time or other she would use all the others. She employs aspirate when she whispers, guttural when she counterfeits the doctor, nasal and oral when she mocks.

Force: Soft to strong. At one time she moves her lips but makes no sound at all, on other occasions she yells. Her excellent muscle tonus requires basic strength throughout.

Tempo: Slow to fast. She dawdles, she rushes. She has a quick start-and-stop delivery.

Pitch: Basically the low register, but here again she would move all over the scale, employing both steps and slides.

Tony's key words were quick-witted, agilely coarse, aggressive and mischievous. The coarseness and aggressiveness can be obtained by emphasis on quality and force; the other two attributes projected by a like emphasis on tempo and pitch. Here is a suggested tonal pattern for him:

Quality: Orotund, with some guttural, and a little nasal. He dominates his companions in his rustic environment. He swears roundly. He also grumbles. He might mimic.

Force: Medium to strong. He is not a quiet one. He bawls his orders. He is outspoken, he does not care who hears him. He can talk down his mother.

Tempo: Medium fast, except when bored. He blurts his speech. He likes action, dislikes restraint.

Pitch: Mainly low register, with variety obtained by swinging into the middle and upper registers. He growls, but he also howls. He slides his pitch when he wishes, but when eager will use steps to put a mischievous idea into words.

Relationships • Let us further relate Toinette and Tony to their environments, organizing the approach in the categories of costumes, props, furniture, and persons.

How does the character wear his costume, and what use can you make of his manner? For answers to these questions the word list made up for each character must be consulted. Suppose pride were one of the key words for a certain role. The character's financial circumstances may determine the quality and the cut of suit or dress, but pride would influence the manner in which the character wears his clothes. A beggar without pride would wear his clothes in one way, a beggar with pride in another. The same difference would exist between two wealthy citizens.

In addition to the basic purpose of wearing clothes, does the character use them for any other purpose? As a mark of social standing, for example, or as a means to attract attention? Is there any subconscious motivation, such as a release for nervous tension? Are the pockets in constant use? Will the character continuously fuss at a crease in the pants or with the length of a sleeve, or if female, with stockings or straps or the twist of a skirt? Such key words as nervousness, habitual or momentary, or impatience would motivate a characteristic fussiness. The words calmness or assurance would indicate an opposite type of movement. There is a variation of the above: What does the character think of his clothes? Tony Lumpkin would have no hesitancy about wiping greasy fingers on trousers or waistcoat. Toinette might or might not do the same, depending on whom she is with, and whether she is in the kitchen or in the drawing room.

Tight-fitting or voluminously extensive, the costume should be an extension of the character. As such it can be an aid rather than a hindrance to character creation.

Toinette: Even though she is a servant, Toinette is an intimate of M. Argan's household, therefore the material and fashion of her dress would be better than those of an ordinary maid; still, her costume would bear evidence of her servant status. In her attitude toward many things she is quite flexible, almost mercurial, and so there are times when she would be most mindful of her clothes, taking care and pride in them, and other instances in which she might let them become stained and rumpled. But in the play we see her almost entirely in a front-parlor relationship, therefore the first condition pertains. As a self-assured person she does not fuss with her dress. Aware of the complement to her person from any attractive costume, she would wear hers with a becoming manner.[50]

As far as props and furniture are concerned it must be remembered that Toinette, as a servant, has few possessions, nor can she expect to have many more; therefore no sense of personal ownership relates her to the objects of the household. Furthermore, the care of cups, glasses, decorative objects, and furniture is within her list of duties; when we labor without possession, we generally feel no great fondness or sense of care for the objects handled. Accordingly, Toinette would seek to conceal a broken glass rather than regret its loss. With no financial stake in the furnishings, she would, without thought, rest her feet on a sofa or stand on a brocaded chair to reach a candle sconce on the wall. In the desperation of a chase, pursued by her master, she would walk on, jump over, or hide under furniture. On the other hand, as a member of the family, she would not permit such liberties to anyone else. In the performance of her regular duties she may not care if the chairs are well dusted or not, but after an unwelcome visitor rose from one—any of the antagonists could fit that category—she would take great pains to wipe it clean.

In her relationship with people she favors proximity; she would be close to those she loved and, being aggressive, she would stand close to those she dislikes, especially if there were any kind of an argument involved—all of which indicates that she loves and she fights in a positive manner. Her impudence indicates familiarity. She would show this in the amount and the manner of personal contact. Of all the persons in the play she alone would feel free to touch friend, master, mistress, or foe, with a caress or a blow—there should be plenty of each—and this in spite of the fact that intimacy in contact was socially unacceptable according to the manners of the time. It is also necessary that she show indifference in many instances; therefore she would stand off or turn away from others, pretending interest in a fingernail or in a thread on a sleeve while another was speaking. Signs of boredom, if boredom were experienced,

[50] It is conceivable that Toinette could be created as a slatternly character; in the hands of some actresses such a characterization might be brought off with brilliance.

would be exhibited with little attempt at concealment. By the same token she would press forward with eagerness toward each event or person who interested her.

Tony: Tony, as a rural young man, would wear wools, tweeds, heavy cottons—serviceable clothes, no city fashions for him, but as squire's son his dress would be of the local best. If he were to strive for show in his clothing, he would favor brightness, and it would be strength of color, not its harmony, that would attract him. His interest and his care of clothes are almost nil. Mud, food, or the signs of animal husbandry, after a casual brushing-off, would cause him little concern. He would favor worn over new clothes, and a good pair of boots would mean more to him than a fancy waistcoat. A riding whip is more important and used more by him than a handkerchief. He would have no appreciation for good taste exhibited in the dress of others.

This young man would have a high regard for a good horse, a fine ram, a good gun, and a few sporting and drinking companions. But for the furniture and the furnishings he must use in the play he has no regard whatsoever. Aside from the contents, a piece of fine china would mean no more to him than a coarse mug, and he would handle both in a like manner. He would as soon put his boots on his mother's furniture as on the tables and chairs at the Three Pigeons. He would never stop to admire a fine picture or a bit of excellent embroidery, and he could walk around a new piece of furniture without seeing it—if he did not kick it out of his way.

With persons, he is familiar with those he knows and likes. With all others, unconcern or distrust would cause him to keep his distance. When his interest is aroused, his directional line is head on, but when the opposite is true, he turns away or moves off entirely. He voices his opinions directly, with no attempt at subtlety and no care for how they are received. Driven by his basic desire, which is to service his personal wants as soon and as satisfactorily as possible, his course of action is always as direct as can be. Unless change would benefit him, he wants none of it; already he is to be counted in the conservative class.

For all of the above, we somehow feel that once the boorishness of boyhood is past and he has attained some of the things he desires, there will be a softening in Tony Lumpkin, as demonstrated in the latter half of the play. Perhaps it is because an audience is safe from his machinations that its members have always been quite fond of the young man.

Distinctive Character Movement • A composer of music employs an excellent device to bring continuity, consistency, and distinctiveness into his work. It is called a theme. All art forms have a theme, of course, but its use in a musical composition offers a particularly apt illustration for our purposes.

A theme is a creator's basic statement, in succinct terms, of his fundamental intent. It is expressed in the very beginning of his work. Thereafter, like a good thread in a fine cloth, it is woven in at certain intervals, either as first enunciated or embellished with variations. Beethoven's *Fifth Symphony* is an excellent and well-known example. In this composition the main theme is so simply and so strongly stated at the beginning of the first movement the auditor cannot miss it. As the performance progresses the theme is anticipated, recognized, and enjoyed by the listener whenever it reappears. This is a good thing to have happen in any art form.

The device can produce just as fine a result when employed in character creation. From one to four distinctive character movements, revealing any one of the role's most important personality traits, can be woven into movement or position or tonal patterns as they extend throughout the play.

Motivations for distinctive character movements are found in the uniquely personal habits of all individuals. Here are some examples:

1. A farmer, one of whose key words is masochistic, picks with his thumb and forefinger at the calluses in the palm of his other hand. This is his basic movement. The motivating impulse for this and the following variations is subconscious. In the proper situations the exact movement might be repeated three times throughout the play. But on several other occasions he rubs the calluses over the knuckles of his hand, or raises the hand to his mouth and uses his teeth on the ridged skin.

2. The president of a women's cultural club has the word imperious to denote one of her character traits. A basic head movement is indicated. Whenever her mental state becomes imperious her head rises high and straight up, with the chin tucked in a little. Variation number one would be to turn her head quickly from side to side, sweeping the room with her glance to see or to silence any contradiction from among her followers. Variation number two could be a short, quick nod of the head to give emphatic assent to another's statement; conversely, a quick, short shake from side to side would denote emphatic denial. A third variation occurs when she uses her head to reinforce emphatic statements in a speech; it is as if she would tap or hammer her points home.

3. Not all habitual character movements are subconsciously motivated. As a demonstration of consciously motivated character movement that would also have distinctiveness, an eighteenth-century fop—*ego hunger* is one of his key phrases—takes snuff from his ornamental box

with a display of overgraceful hand and arm movement. Thumb and forefinger daintily pinch a small quantity of the powder, the wrist then flirts the hand, the arm sweeps up to the nostril, two quick sniffs are taken and the arm comes down, the lid of the box is closed with the forefinger, tapped once into place, and the receptacle is returned to the pocket.

4. A student, demonstratively vain, has an unusually resonant voice, low in pitch and orotund in quality. To make others aware of his splendid natural endowments, he consciously watches for those spots in conversation into which he can throw vocal interjections, a *yes*, a *no*, or a *hum*. In his own conversation he lingers slightly over those vowel sounds he favors. He bridges his phrases and sentences with elongated *a-a-ahs*.

What distinctive character movements will you create for Toinette or Tony?

EXERCISES AND ASSIGNMENTS

1. Using the delineations given earlier, or substituting such other key motivating words as you deem justifiable, put Toinette or Tony Lumpkin on stage in each of the projects listed below.

a. Working outside the context of the play, present on stage the position, movement, and tonal patterns for the character.

b. Give illustrations of distinctive character movement.

c. Demonstrate the character's relationship to costume, properties, and furniture.

d. It is beneficial to create situations as suitable for the character as those the playwright has chosen. For Toinette, invent a scene around the circumstance of her trying on a dress belonging to her mistress, probably the latter's latest and finest acquisition. Do the same exercises for Tony in the situation in which he steals the casket of jewels from his mother's room.

e. Put each character on stage in a scene or scenes from the play.

2. The roles of George Gibbs and Emily Webb in *Our Town* offer an excellent contrast to the character delineations of Toinette and Tony. Perform them in the five steps given above.

3. Two other roles, both of which are reckoned among the world's greatest, should come next. Prince Hamlet, in *Hamlet*, will offer a challenge to the actor. Joan of Arc, in the Shaw play, will do the same for the actress. Treat them as completely as the others.

4. A study and practice should be made of parts that fall in the nonyouthful category. Here are some suggestions: *Private Lives*, Noel Coward—Elyot and Amanda; *The Father*, August Strindberg—the Captain and Laura; *Elizabeth the Queen*, Maxwell Anderson—Elizabeth and Essex; *Reunion in Vienna*, Robert E. Sherwood—Rudolf and Elena; *Ah, Wilderness*, Eugene

O'Neill—Nat and Mrs. Miller; *Candida*, G. B. Shaw—Morell and Candida; *The Little Foxes*, Lillian Hellman—Regina and Horace; *The Guardsman*, Ferenc Molnar—the Actor and the Actress; *What Every Woman Knows*, James M. Barrie—James and Maggie; *The Crucible*, Arthur Miller—Proctor and Elizabeth; *Juno and the Paycock*, Sean O'Casey—Captain Boyle and Juno.

5. Caricature has been practiced and enjoyed in the theatre since the days of the Greeks. Its stringent economy, its balanced exaggeration, its stark tellingness provide excellent subject material for a problem in characterization. In introducing it here the purpose is not to poke fun at, to deride, or to be cruel (as some of its famous practitioners have been) to the subjects chosen— the purpose is to cause the doer to pare down to the barest essentials, to create in a few bold, revealing positions, movements, and tones the very essence of the person portrayed. Choose a subject person, not necessarily an exaggerated personality, from a source that offers adequate opportunity for study, and caricature that person onstage in an original situation.

Chapter 19

Inner State of Being and Emotion

The creation and maintenance of an inner state of being and of one of its components, emotion, are subjects of sufficient importance to warrant treatment in a separate chapter, even though both matters are an integral part of characterization. A separate discussion is the more necessary because in the portion of the subject that deals with emotion we are concerned with one of the most controversial aspects of acting, both in the training and professional phases.

INNER STATE OF BEING

THE PERSONAL INNER STATE

An actor's ability to create and sustain various inner states of being for his roles is conditioned by his capacity to do the same thing within himself. Here individual limitation asserts itself; weaknesses balance strengths in nearly all players.

Around a theatre it is commonplace to hear comment that A is warm but B is cold onstage, that C is an intellectual player and D emotional, and it could well be that each opinion is correct. The point of concern to us is that the comment is usually made as if there were a standard, a fixed condition of perfection to which all should adhere; we create and project an idealized image, which few if any can achieve, and then criticize those who were born and shaped by environment in a different pattern.

But we know in fact that unlikeness is an unavoidable condition among players and therefore a proper state. History teaches us that fine actors are of many orientations. Each player begins with what he is and adds to this, increasing his capacity in as many ways and with as much depth as possible, to end infinitely more capable, but still just as individual as ever.

That you may do so, it is necessary that you observe yourself and others with all the perspicacity at your command. Thus it is incumbent upon you to make good use of your innate and developed ability to read movement and tone; the life around you is your text. If your scrutiny is keen and your judgement sound, you will learn more, much more, than even the psychologists suspect. Watch positions, observe types of muscular movement, hear and record tones so that you may refer to them afterwards for a clearer understanding of their meaning. And be aware of relationships, always be conscious of relationships.

THE INNER STATE COMPLEX

What is an inner state of being? To answer that question with certainty one would have to possess more knowledge than anyone now has. It has been termed a spirit, a personality, a soul, an organic mass, a psychological entity; it is in part chemistry and electricity and physiology.

Being neither psychologists, physiologists, chemists, or physicists, we approach the subject from a somewhat limited point of view, seeking to ascertain as much as is applicable to our needs. Our attitude is pragmatic. We are not experts; we learn as much as we can of those operations pertinent to the creation of a dramatic experience.

Made up of many parts, the inner state of being generally maintains a condition of equilibrium among its elements under normal conditions. But when, in response to some internal or external motivation, the state of being increases in intensity, one or several of the component parts function more actively than others, thus giving a discernable character to the state at that time.

Nature, Intensity, and Duration • A core condition may be one in which a mental, physical, sensory, or emotional condition is dominant, or in which a combination of two or more of these elements is pronounced. It may be a weak, a medium, or a strong state, and it may last for only a second or it may extend itself as the prevailing condition in the body for hours, days, or weeks.

An example shows how the kind, the strength, and the length of an inner state complex may vary within one series of action blocks: you are a college student, it is night, and you are alone and engrossed in study. (As you read, note the intensity and duration of each inner state.)

A scraping sound, harsh, sudden, and unpleasant, comes from outside your window. Startled (emotional), you sit up and listen intently (sensory). The sound comes again. Uncontrolled, the sensation you associate with fear (emotion) seems to flood your midsection. Unthinking (non-intellectual, non-sensory, but highly emotional), an impulse sends you to the window to pull down the blind (physical). Tense and fearful (physical and emotional), you listen (sensory). Again the sound comes, but after it there is an unmistakable sound of a choked-off laugh. Past experience indicates that friends have used you as the butt of a joke. Resentful that you were both fooled and frightened, you respond with a momentary feeling of anger (emotion). Seeking revenge, anticipating the fun of getting even (emotion), you stand in thought (mental). A garden hose is connected to the outside wall near a side entrance to your building; the throw of water will reach your window. Alert (sensory), you walk back to the table and slide your chair into place as though settling for study again (physical). As silently as possible (sensory, physical) but with a feeling of excitement (emotional), you cross to the door, exit, and speed down the hall. Quietly you let yourself out the side door (the last states still pertain), and feel in the darkness for the hose (sensory, physical, emotional). Finding the nozzle, you turn it toward the space under your window. With your left hand you locate the faucet. A vigorous turn sends the water arching through the air. Startled exclamations clearly indicate that you are on target. Two figures escape in headlong flight. You laugh (emotional), turn off the water, and return to your room (emotional, physical). Any sequel to this incident you can fill out from your own experience.

Likely responses were suggested to you in this prankish action. But what would have been the states and actions if a stage character, two of whose key phrases were *gentle shyness* and *naivete*, were to perform a like sequence in your place? Can you reconstruct the incident from this point of view? Or suppose a figure very like either Toinette or Tony were to enact the scene; what, then, would be the nature, intensity, and duration of the inner states?

Attitudes[51] • Much has already been said and some practice performed on this subject. To identify it more intimately with the inner state of being it represents, let us apply the subject to a scene, using an exact word or word combinations as explicit directives to the players. The excerpt, from Act I, Scene 1 of *She Stoops To Conquer*, shows Tony in his first appearance in the play. The stage business is set in brackets, the attitudes in parentheses. Note that some stated attitude must be in existence every moment of the character's time onstage. (In no case is any attitude a dramatic one, yet the scene will be dramatic.)

[*Mr. and Mrs. Hardcastle are on. Tony enters, crossing the stage*]

MRS. HARDCASTLE: (*With exaggerated affection*) Tony, where are you going, my charmer? Won't you give papa and I a little of your company, lovee?

[51] Part III, Chapter 14, "The Expressive Tone," contains material pertinent to this subject. It would be well to review it in conjunction with the present study.

TONY: (*Impatient and unresponsive*) I'm in haste, mother, I cannot stay.

MRS. HARDCASTLE: (*Maternally authoritative*) You shan't venture out this raw evening, my dear: (*with unfounded concern*) you look most shockingly. [*She has stopped him, or he pauses to put on gloves or a cloak or to seek a riding crop.*]

TONY: (*Impatient and slightly annoyed*) I can't stay, I tell you. (*With pleasurable anticipation*) The Three Pigeons expects me down every moment. There's some fun going forward.

HARDCASTLE: (*With set opinion and disapproving*) Ay; the ale-house, the old place: I thought so.

MRS. HARDCASTLE: (*In scorn and disapproval*) A low, paltry set of fellows.

TONY: (*Offended and a little astounded*) Not so low, neither. There's Dick Muggins, the exciseman; Jack Slang, the horse doctor; Little Aminadab, that grinds the music box; and Tom Twist, that spins the pewter platter.

MRS. HARDCASTLE: (*Wheedling and coquettish*) Pray, my dear, disappoint them for one night, at least.

TONY: (*Matter of fact and unconcerned*) As for disappointing *them*, I should not so much mind; (*with dry humor*) but I can't abide to disappoint myself.

MRS. HARDCASTLE: [*Detaining him*] (*Conclusively determined*) You shan't go.

TONY: (*Determined and unconcerned*) I will, I tell you.

MRS. HARDCASTLE: I say you shan't.

TONY: (*With roguish humor and physically bullish*) We'll see which is stronger, you or I.

[Exit, hawling her out.]

EXERCISES

That you may determine the attitudes that represent inner states, two practice projects follow.

1. *She Stoops To Conquer*, Goldsmith, Act III. This scene is the reverse companion of the one between Marlow and Kate Hardcastle studied earlier, page 208. This time Marlow is the aggressor, bold enough to cause Kate, posing as a barmaid, to protect herself from more than a kiss.

Notes

MARLOW: What a bawling in every part of the house; I have scarce a moment's repose. If I go to the best room, there I find my host and his story. If I fly to the gallery, there we have my hostess with her curtesy down to the ground. I have at last got a moment to myself, and now for recollection. (*Walks and muses*)

Notes

MISS HARDCASTLE: (*Entering*) Did you call, sir? Did your honour call?

MARLOW: As for Miss Hardcastle, she's too grave and sentimental for me.

MISS HARDCASTLE: Did your honour call?

MARLOW: No, child! Besides, from the glimpse I had of her, I think she squints. (*She reacts and recovers*)

MISS HARDCASTLE: I'm sure, sir, I heard the bell ring.

MARLOW: No, no! . . . (*Looks full in her face*) Yes, child, I think I did call. I wanted—I wanted—I vow, child, you are vastly handsome!

MISS HARDCASTLE: O la, sir, you'll make one asham'd.

MARLOW: Never saw a more sprightly, malicious eye. Yes, yes, my dear, I did call. Have you got any of your—a—what d'ye call it in the house?

MISS HARDCASTLE: No, sir, we have been out of that these ten days.

MARLOW: One may call in this house, I find, to very little purpose. Suppose I should call for a taste, just by way of trial, of the nectar of your lips; perhaps I might be disappointed in that, too?

MISS HARDCASTLE: Nectar? nectar? that's a liquor there's no call for in these parts. French, I suppose. We keep no French wines here, sir.

MARLOW: Of true English growth, I assure you.

MISS HARDCASTLE: Then it's odd I should not know it. We brew all sorts of wines in this house, and I have lived here these eighteen years.

MARLOW: Eighteen years! Why one would think, child, you kept the bar before you were born. How old are you?

MISS HARDCASTLE: O! sir, I must not tell my age. They say women and music should never be dated.

MARLOW: To guess at this distance, you can't be much above forty. Yet nearer, I don't think so much. By coming close to some women, they look younger still; but when we come very close indeed—(*Attempts a kiss*)

MISS HARDCASTLE: Pray, sir, keep your distance. One would think you wanted to know one's age as they do horses, by mark of mouth.

MARLOW: I protest, child, you use me extremely ill. If you keep me at this distance, how is it possible you and I can ever be acquainted?

MISS HARDCASTLE: And who wants to be acquainted with you? I want no such acquaintance, not I. I'm sure you did not treat Miss Hardcastle that was here a while ago in this obstropalous manner. I'll warrant me, before her you look'd dash'd, and kept bowing to the ground, and talk'd, for all the world, as if you was before a justice of peace.

MARLOW: (*Aside*) Egad! she has hit it, sure enough. (*To her*) In awe of her, child? Ha! ha! ha! A mere awkward, squinting thing! No, no! I find you don't know me. I laugh'd, and rallied her a little; but I was unwilling to be too severe. No, I could not be too severe, curse me!

MISS HARDCASTLE: O! then, sir, you

are a favourite, I find, among the
ladies?

MARLOW: Yes, my dear, a great favourite. And yet, hang me, I don't
see what they find in me to follow.
At the Ladies Club in town I'm
called their agreeable Rattle. Rattle,
child, is not my real name, but one
I'm known by. My name is Solomons. Mr. Solomons, my dear, at
your service. (*Offers to salute her*)

MISS HARDCASTLE: Hold, sir; you
were introducing me to your club,
not to yourself. And you're so great
a favourite there you say?

MARLOW: Yes, my dear. There's Mrs.
Mantrap, Lady Betty Blackleg, the
Countess of Sligo, Mrs. Longhorns,
old Miss Biddy Buckskin, and your
humble servant, keep up the spirit
of the place.

MISS HARDCASTLE: Then it's a very
merry place, I suppose.

MARLOW: Yes, as merry as cards, sup-
pers, wine, and old women can
make us.

MISS HARDCASTLE: And their agreeable Rattle, ha! ha! ha!

MARLOW: (*Aside*) Egad! I don't quite
like this chit. She looks knowing,
methinks. You laugh, child?

MISS HARDCASTLE: I can't but laugh
to think what time they all have
for minding their work or their
family.

MARLOW: (*Aside*) All's well, she
don't laugh at me. Do *you* ever
work, child?

MISS HARDCASTLE: Ay, sure. There's
not a screen or a quilt in the whole
house but what can bear witness to
that.

MARLOW: Odso! Then you must shew

Notes

me your embroidery. . . . (*Taking her hand. Enter Hardcastle*)

MISS HARDCASTLE: Ay, but the colours don't look well by candle light. You shall see all in the morning. (*Struggling*)

MARLOW: And why not now, my angel? Such beauty fires beyond the power of resistance.—Pshaw! the father here! My old luck: I never nick'd seven that I did not throw ames-ace three times following. (*Exits*)

2. *The Crucible*,[52] Miller, Act II, Scene 1. A wood. Night. It is in the 1690's, the time of the Salem Witchcraft Trials. Proctor, whose wife, Elizabeth, has been accused of witchcraft and who is now in jail, meets with Abigail, one of Elizabeth's accusers. Proctor and Abigail have previously had illicit relations. Proctor enters, holding a lantern for the girl. She has a wrap over her nightgown. There is a log on stage.

He is physically strong, mentally sharp, though presently troubled, and emotionally robust, a man of power and conviction, but now alone against mass hysteria. Abigail, intuitively quick, cunning in gaining her desires, also physically and emotionally strong, now has a heady sense of power from the prominent role she plays as one of the bewitched girls.

Notes

PROCTOR: I must speak with you, Abigail. (*She does not move, staring at him*) Will you sit?

ABIGAIL: How do you come?

PROCTOR: Friendly.

ABIGAIL: (*Glancing around*) I don't like the woods at night. Pray you, stand closer. (*He does so*) I knew it must be you. When I heard the pebbles on the window, before I opened up my eyes I knew. I thought you would come a good time sooner.

PROCTOR: I had thought to come many times.

ABIGAIL: Why didn't you? I am so alone in the world now.

PROCTOR: (*As a fact. Not bitterly*) Are you! I've heard that people ride a hundred mile to see your face these days.

ABIGAIL: Aye, my face. Can you see my face?

PROCTOR: (*Holds lantern up*) Then you're troubled?

ABIGAIL: Have you come to mock me?

PROCTOR: (*Sets lantern down*) No, no, but I hear only that you go to the tavern every night, and play shovelboard with the Deputy Governor, and they give you cider.

ABIGAIL: I have once or twice played the shovelboard. But I have no joy in it.

PROCTOR: This is a surprise, Abby. I'd thought to find you gayer than this. I'm told a troop of boys go step for step with you wherever you walk these days.

ABIGAIL: Aye, they do. But I have only lewd looks from the boys.

PROCTOR: And you like that not?

ABIGAIL: I cannot bear lewd looks no more, John. My spirit's changed entirely. I ought be given Godly looks when I suffer for them as I do.

PROCTOR: Oh? How do you suffer, Abby?

ABIGAIL: (*Pulls up dress*) Why, look at my leg. I'm holes all over from their damned needles and pins. (*Touching her stomach*) The jab your wife gave me's not healed yet, y'know.

PROCTOR: (*Seeing her madness now*) Oh, it isn't.

ABIGAIL: I think sometimes she pricks it open again while I sleep.

PROCTOR: Ah?

ABIGAIL: And George Jacobs—(*Sliding up her sleeve*) he comes again and again and raps me with his stick—the same spot every night all this week. Look at the lump I have.

PROCTOR: Abby—George Jacobs is in the jail all this month.

ABIGAIL: Thank God he is, and bless the day he hangs and lets me sleep in peace again! Oh, John, the world's so full of hypocrites! (*Astonished, outraged*) They pray in jail! I'm told they all pray in jail!

PROCTOR: They may not pray?

ABIGAIL: And torture me in my bed while sacred words are comin' from their mouths? Oh, it will need God Himself to cleanse this town properly!

PROCTOR: Abby—you mean to cry out still others?

ABIGAIL: If I live, if I am not murdered, I surely will, until the last hypocrite is dead.

THE DOMINANT STATE

There are instances in life and in plays in which one prevailing state of being of marked intensity exists for some time. For example, when death comes to one who is close and dear, those affected live for some days under a pall of grief and a persistent sense of loss. Singular and pervasive, this core condition dominates all other states and actions. But during the time of its extent other responses intrude, momentarily influencing and even altering the first condition, but never eradicating it entirely.

Many playwrights have made extensive use, with most telling effect, of the dominant, prolonged, and intense state. A large number of great characters are given one basic response to maintain most of the time they are on: Oedipus, Electra, Medea, Antigone, Hamlet, Othello, Hedda Gabbler, many of Chekhov's characters, Willie Loman, Blanche Dubois, and Laura in *Glass Menagerie*—the list could be continued for some length. Not all such attitudes are negative.

THE LIABILITY OF FOREKNOWLEDGE

Change is the keynote of all drama. From the opening situation in Act I, a play and the characters in it enact a progression through to the concluding circumstances at the end of the last act. This progression will not take place if the actor's rather than the character's point of view prevails.

Very much aware of the more intense responses of a character in Acts II or III (or IV or V), a player tends to superimpose those states on the role in Act I. This is especially true if a play has a light beginning and a tragic ending. But remember that an actor always has a foreknowledge of the role and its development, but a character never has. You know the tragic ending of *Romeo and Juliet*, but Romeo and Juliet do not. For them hope and happiness are the keynotes of their existence until Tybalt is killed, and on those notes the earlier scenes should be played.

Three sequences in *Romeo and Juliet* are nicely spaced to give you an opportunity to try this principle. Do not let the poetic diction of Shakespeare subdue your delivery any more than you let the tragic end dominate a joyous beginning.

In the first scene strive to show in movement and tone those actions embodying the sweep of excitement and hope that makes the moment a most happy one for the two youthful lovers, even against the smilingly restrained demeanor of Friar Lawrence. In spite of the odds against them, all three are confident of success.

Act II, Scene 5 (Scene 6 in some editions). Friar Lawrence's cell. Enter Friar and Romeo.

Notes

FRIAR: So smile the Heav'ns upon
    this holy act
  That after-hours with sorrow chide
    us not!
ROMEO: Amen, amen. But come what
    sorrow can,
  It cannot countervail th' exchange
    of joy
  That one·short minute gives me in
    her sight.
  Do thou but close our hands with
    holy words,

Then love-devouring Death do
    what he dare—
It is enough I may but call her
    mine.
FRIAR: These violent delights have
    violent ends,
And in their triumph die like fire
    and powder,
Which as they kiss consume. The
    sweetest honey
Is loathsome in his own delicious-
    ness
And in the taste confounds the
    appetite.
Therefore love moderately, long
    love doth so,
Too swift arrives as tardy as too
    slow.
(*Enter Juliet*)
Here comes the lady. Or, so light a
    foot
Will ne'er wear out the everlasting
    flint.
A lover may bestride the gossamers
That idles in the wanton summer
    air,
And yet not fall, so light is Vanity.
JULIET: Good even to my ghostly
    confessor.
FRIAR: Romeo shall thank thee,
    daughter, for us both.
JULIET: As much to him, else is his
    thanks too much.
ROMEO: Ah Juliet, if the measure of
    thy joy
Be heap'd like mine, and that thy
    skill be more
To blazon it, then sweeten with
    thy breath
This neighbor air and let rich
    music's tongue
Unfold th' imagined happiness that
    both

Receive in either by this dear encounter.

JULIET: Conceit, more rich in matter
than in words,

Brags of his substance, not of orna-
ment.

They are but beggars that can
count their worth,

But my true love is grown to such
excess

I cannot sum up sum of half my
wealth.

FRIAR: Come, come with me, and we
will make short work,

For by your leaves you shall not
stay alone

Til Holy Church incorporate two
in one. (*Exeunt*)

Act III, Scene 5 presents a contrast. Mercutio and Tybalt are dead,
Romeo banished. The happiness of Act II is gravely threatened—but
hope is not dead. What both Romeo and Juliet will now do is motivated
by the expectation that all will yet come right; they live in a time of
quick changes and long chances. After all, Romeo has just spent a night
in what is for him the most dangerous place in all Verona.

This is a middle scene, halfway between the joy of the beginning of
the play and the tragedy of the end. The place is Juliet's bedroom or on
her balcony. It is dawn. The married couple have had their first, secret
time together; the wonder and delight of their intimacy is still new.
Teasing and jest are very much a part of their relationship[53]; in contrast,
dawn can be very awe-inspiring, especially when one is with one's husband or wife. But separation is necessary, and in that there is no joy.

JULIET: Wilt thou be gone? It is not
yet near day,

It was the nightingale and not the
lark

That pierc'd the fearful hollow of
thine ear;

---

[53] Traditionalists may disagree with this; they would be even more shocked at a little
bawdy humor in some of the movement and mock heroics on some of the lines, yet
these are meaningful actions with newlyweds, and have an endearing as well as a
truthful quality.

Nightly she sings on yond pome-
granate tree.

Believe me, love, it was the nightingale.

ROMEO: It was the lark, the herald
of the morn,

No nightingale. Look love, what
envious streaks

Do lace the sev'ring clouds in yon-
der East—

Night's candles are burnt out and
jocund Day

Stands tiptoe on the misty mountain tops.

I must be gone and live or stay and
die.

JULIET: Yond light is not daylight,
I know it, I.

It is some meteor that the sun
exhal'd

To be to thee this night a torch-
bearer

And light thee on thy way to
Mantua.

Therefore stay yet, thou need'st not
to be gone.

ROMEO: Let me be tane, let me be
put to death,

I am content, so thou wilt have it
so.

I'll say yon grey is not the Morning's eye—

'Tis but the pale reflex of Cynthia's
brow;

Nor that is not the lark whose notes
do beat

The vaulty heav'n so high above
our heads.

I have more care to stay than will
to go.

Come death, and welcome! Juliet
wills it so.

How is't, my soul, let's talk, it is
not day.

JULIET: It is, it is! hie hence, be gone
 away.
 It is the lark that sings so out of
  tune,
 Straining harsh discords and unpleasing sharps.
 Some say the lark and loathed toad
  chang'd eyes,
 O now I would they had chang'd
  voices too,
 Since arm from arm that voice doth
  us affray,
 Hunting thee from hence with
  hunt's-up to the day.
 O now be gone, more light and
  light it grows.
ROMEO: More light and light—more
 dark and dark our woes.
 (*Enter Nurse*)

In Act V, Scene 3 the contrast with the situation at the opening of
the play is developed in full. The passage of events forecast by the
Chorus in the Prologue (for the audience, not for the characters) is
ready for consummation. Now attitudes of complete despair and defeat
are truly motivated—attitudes only mitigated by the beauty and distinction of the lines.

Romeo, believing Juliet dead, has come at night to her tomb, there to
take his own life by poison. Unexpectedly encountering Paris, he kills
that young man in a sudden, swift duel. Then he is alone.

              Notes

ROMEO: . . . Let me peruse this face.
 Mercutio's kinsman, noble County
  Paris!
 What said my man when my be-
  tossed soul
 Did not attend him as we rode? I
  think
 He told me Paris should have
  marry'd Juliet.
 Said he not so? or did I dream it so?
 Or am I mad, hearing him talk of
  Juliet,
 To think it was so? O give me thy
  hand,

One writ with me in sour Misfor-
tune's book.
I'll bury thee in a triumphant
grave.
A grave? O no, a lanthorn, slaugh-
ter'd youth,
For here lies Juliet, and her beauty
makes
This vault a feasting presence full
of light.
Death, lie thou there, by a dead
man interr'd.
How oft when men are at the point
of death
Have they been merry—which their
keepers call
A lightning before death. O how
may I
Call this a lightning? O my love,
my wife!
Death that hath suck'd the honey
of thy breath
Hath had no power yet upon thy
beauty.
Thou are not conquer'd—Beauty's
ensign yet
Is crimson in thy lips and in thy
cheeks,
And Death's pale flag is not ad-
vanced there.
Tybalt, ly'st thou there in thy
bloody sheet?
O what more favor can I do to thee
Than with that hand that cut thy
youth in twain
To sunder his that was thine
enemy?
Forgive me, cousin. Ah, dear Juliet,
Why art thou yet so fair? shall I
believe
That unsubstantial Death is amor-
ous
And that the lean abhorred monster
keeps

Thee here in dark to be his para-
  mour?
For fear of that I still will stay with
  thee
And never from this pallet of dim
  Night
Depart again: here, here will I re-
  main
With worms that are thy chamber-
  maids, O here
Will I set up my everlasting rest
And shake the yoke of inauspicious
  stars
From this world-weary'd flesh. Eyes
  look your last,
Arms take your last embrace, and
  lips (O you
The doors of breath) seal with a
  righteous kiss
A dateless bargain to engrossing
  Death!
Come bitter conduct, come unsav'ry
  guide,
Thou desp'rate pilot, now at once
  run on
The dashing rocks thy seasick
  weary bark.
Here's to my love! O true apothe-
  cary,
Thy drugs are quick. Thus with a
  kiss I die.

Immediately after Romeo's death, Friar Lawrence enters, come to awaken and rescue Juliet. He discovers Romeo's dead body.

FRIAR: Romeo!
  Alack, alack, what blood is this
    which stains
  The stony entrance of this sepul-
    cher?
  What mean these masterless and
    gory swords

To lie discolor'd by this place of
  peace?

Romeo, O pale! Who else? what!
  Paris too?

And steep'd in blood? Ah what an
  unkind hour

Is guilty of this lamentable chance.
The lady stirs. (*Juliet rises*)

JULIET: O comfortable Friar, where
  is my lord?

I do remember well where I should
  be

And there I am, where is my
  Romeo?

FRIAR: I hear some noise. Lady, come
  from that nest

Of death, contagion and unnatural
  sleep.

A greater power than we can contradict

Hath thwarted our intents, come,
  come away.

Thy husband in thy bosom there
  lies dead,

And Paris too. Come, I'll dispose of
  thee

Among a sisterhood of holy nuns.
Stay not to question, for the watch
  is coming.

Come go, good Juliet, I dare no
  longer stay. (*Exit*)

JULIET: Go get thee hence, for I will
  not away.

What's here? a cup clos'd in my
  true love's hand!

Poison I see hath been his timeless
  end.

O churl, drunk all and left no
  friendly drop

To help me after? I will kiss thy
  lips,

Haply some poison yet doth hang
  on them

Notes

To make me die with a restorative.
Thy lips are warm.
WATCHMAN: (*Off*) Lead, boy, which
    way?
JULIET: Yea, noise? then I'll be brief.
    O happy dagger,
This is thy sheath—there rust and
    let me die.
(*She stabs herself and falls*)

EMOTION

Fine acting is like fine surgery or an exceptionally good athletic contest. Restricted by the place of performance to a limited kind of action, further restricted by those laws of nature or man that apply to the activity, each performer, working under great physical, mental, and emotional pressure, is required to perform to the maximal level of his ability within a limited amount of time. These natural and contrived conditions constitute challenges to the abilities and skills of an actor, a surgeon, or an athlete. In each case, the core of the challenge lies in the fact that the work is intense, the stakes significant, and the hope of rewards high. In each case, the period of performance is crucial, a time of success or failure.

Because emotion is one of the ingredients in most instances of intense human endeavor, and because the dramatic experience is an intense occurrence in itself, the relation of emotion to dramatic expression has an importance sufficient to warrant consideration in a separate section. Our interest centers on the fact that this distinctly human condition exists as an exciting potential for dramatic exploitation.

You, as a player, required by the nature of acting to perform at above-average intensity at all times, must also be prepared to meet the challenge of those often-repeated moments when exertion goes beyond the usual high level of endeavor. Sometimes, of course, the emotional discharge is slight, easy of creation and release. Other times, it is intense, filled with the passionate energy of a human need crying for expression, or surging out from an inner exuberance of joy or love to envelop all within its contact. Disciplined explosions, we may term these last, controlled abandonments, which permit fullest release with greatest security, so that the emotional experience achieves maximum intensity at the same time as the creator is most certain of its effectiveness.

EMOTIONAL EXTREMES

In its most fervid moments offstage and, unfortunately, many times onstage, emotion is sometimes wildly released, exceeding the limits of control. Under the same circumstances, emotion can be, and often is, a constrained feeling, an excitement held in, repressed, denied free and full expression. In fine acting, neither of these conditions can pertain. The extremes of not enough or too much control are twin threats to a superior performance. Our need is for fullest feeling freely achieved and freely released within the disciplines of the dramatic experience.[54]

EMPATHY AND ANTAGONISM

In a life situation, an emotional experience grows to fullness and completion within the context of the immediate situation, involving only those directly concerned. In a dramatic experience, the life situation is translated into dramatic action in order that many persons may witness and share the feelings expressed.

For emotions to be witnessed, they must be made manifest in external action. Actors, themselves cloaked with anonymity through characterization, are required to reveal the feelings they create, even if a prototype would seek to restrain the expression of such feelings in real life.

Emotional releases are of many kinds, each one of which can motivate a response in a perceiver. As a general rule the responsive feelings are either pleasant or unpleasant. Witnesses to pleasant feelings respond with receptive attitudes based on a feeling of sympathy. This is an *empathic* response. Empathy is created when the feelings of the characters, projected from the stage to the audience, are matched with a response in kind by the people out front, which is in turn projected back to the stage. Sympathy breeds sympathy and produces empathy, a condition stronger than the sum of its parts.

When an empathic state exists, the spiritual duality of audience and actors disappears in a shared experience in which the persons out front, by spontaneous identification, enjoy in full strength the emotions created by the characters onstage. Emphatic response requires participation that, if properly engendered, gives pleasure in experiencing all emotions, even those shunned in daily life, such as sorrow, anger, and hatred.

But if there is anything unpleasant about the manner of release of an emotion, antagonism, empathy's opposite attitude, will characterize the audience's response. Set in opposition to the projections from the stage, the people out front react adversely to the emotions expressed. This re-

[54] At this point, collateral reading on "The Nature of Emotion," p. 423 in Appendix E, is suggested.

sponse can also be felt by the players. A feeling of empathy is essential to the creation of a dramatic experience; antagonism negates the whole process.

All emotions, if they hold the possibility of a pleasurable experience or offer the enticement of a safe emotional release, have the capacity to produce an empathic reaction. The nature of an emotion, per se, presents no bar to audience participation. Therefore, the sharing of feelings is predicated on the manner of the emotional release.

We regard with antagonism anything that embarrasses or threatens us. When such a situation arises, we protect ourselves by withdrawing from the experience emotionally. Reference to your past experiences will illustrate the point.

Can you recall having been eager to share a smile or a laugh, only to have your response slacken or disappear because someone else smiled too much, or laughed too long or too loudly? Have you been embarrassed when a demonstration of affection or love became too personal, too revealing? Have tears ever disconcerted you? Has anger you might have shared alienated you because of the threat it posed? How does weakness, revealed in public, affect you? And can you see how members of an audience, seeking participation, could be forced into an emotional withdrawal because of an unfortunate manner of emotional release onstage?

THE CREATION OF EMOTION

Emotion comes into being in highly individualistic ways. Five actresses might portray the character of St. Joan in the Shavian play of the same name. All five will read the author's explicit directions; all five might give excellent interpretations. In each creation, however, there will be broad or subtle variations in every emotive passage. This is the rule for all parts and all players. A conclusion is simply stated: there is no preset emotional pattern into which each actor must compress his feelings.

How does the actor create emotion? This question and its companion —how and with what reality does the player experience the feelings he creates?—are as important as they are polemic, and they at once plunge us into what is probably the oldest and most violent of all dramatic debates.

In old essays and dramatic criticisms, in theatre history books or in yesterday's rehearsal conversations, when the subject of emotion in acting comes up, partisanship is usually apparent and the remarks often heated. It is natural that this is so. The subject is provocative, intimate, and one in which everyone has had some experience. Therefore, everyone knows something about it, and many have expert feelings on the subject.

The Creation of Emotion a Deliberate Act • Unless abnormality is present, there is no drastic problem in the creation of emotion in daily life. As a part of the vital process of living, individuals, when motivated, generate emotional responses of different kinds and of varying intensities many times each day. Emotion waits upon impulse and comes into being only as a reaction.

In acting, a radical change occurs. Feeling cannot, as in life, await the chance of motivation to achieve spontaneity. If you are the actor, when your script indicates that you are to laugh, at that precise moment you must effect the act, and if you are a good actor, your response will be spontaneous. In rehearsal and later in performance, you must effect an unnatural act as though it were a normal one—which it will be when you have mastered the process. It is in the proper manner of doing so that dispute rages.

Probably the greatest divergence among actors lies in that some players, as a result of past conditioning—past learning, the psychologist would term it—have developed tendencies of a repressive nature and now must find ways to break through these restrictive barriers. Others begin their training enjoying relatively quick and free emotional responses. One circumstance applies to both types: the emotional experience is so intimate and so constantly in play that most persons are quite aware of their capabilities or their lacks in this area of human conduct. Such awareness can be a help in the work ahead.

Emotion and the Fictional Imagination • Members of both groups are subject to a common danger. The concept of how emotion is to be created may be the result of fictional imagination, formed in earlier years but still operative as a strongly entrenched habit when more serious study begins. If this is so, a distorted emotional response usually results. Forced, breathy and tensed, such an action may best be described as acting at acting. Unaware himself and unchecked by others, the player who gears his reaction to a fictionalized concept can go to the extreme of believing he is playing with telling passion when he actually is simply taking an emotional bath onstage. In a mature institution, immaturity of concept or practice stands out in painful clarity.

The Exercise of Emotion • For the actor who has a facility in emotional expression, growth to meet the needs ahead is a matter of practice. This entails the translation of personal and observed experiences into meaningful dramatic action. It does not mean that freely felt and freely released offstage anger or sorrow or affection is immediately suitable for onstage use. Personal experience is the basis for departure in the creative process, not the desired end. It is not enough that the player feel right himself, his creation must also be right dramatically and theatrically.

If you are one of those who enjoy ease in emotional release, to begin your practice you should explore your own potential to discover your range. It may be that you are volatile in the initiation of emotion in some areas and phlegmatic in others. You may find laughter difficult and sorrow easy, fright hard to generate but compassion easy.

First, test yourself in your own room, using a mirror from time to time to serve as an audience eye, thus keeping ever present the ultimate aim of your practice. For material, recall and enact again the various emotions you experienced in the last few hours, remembering that the bulk of feelings you will be called upon to create onstage will be those most commonly present, while those involving any great depth of passion appear only at rarer intervals—*Camille* plays, but not every night.[55]

After a survey of your most frequently used emotions, increase your range to include those less frequently experienced. Do not attempt strong intensities at first; emotional strength will be more nearly sure if not forced. Later, add those feelings associated with the more unusual events in your life.

After close observation, attempt to enact the emotional experiences of others. The laughter of your friends, their taunts, worries, condolences, angers, and joys can supply you with unlimited source material. Retain each individual's point of view as best you can as you store audio and visual images for later recall in your rehearsal period.

If you experience difficulty in bringing an emotion into existence, remember that external positions, movements, and tones are but extensions of an inner state of being, and that though they are ordinarily the result of the promptings of an internal state, they can also become the cause. Take the positions, execute the movements and tones you have observed in yourself and others, and let the race-old association of the outer and inner terminals function for your benefit.

You may conclude, after an appraisal of your past emotional responses, that you tend to repress rather than express your feelings. In no sense will your findings indicate that you have a less than normal capacity to experience emotions. In you, as in those who enjoy a freer response, the reaction to stimuli is identical.

Emotion is a learned reaction. Environmental forces teach each of us

[55] In the generation of emotion some persons advocate that the actor allocate as much time as is necessary to recapture in detail the inciting incident that prompted an emotional impulse, the better to guarantee spontaneity of response. Others suggest the remembrance of childhood experiences, especially those that were traumatic in nature—the loss of a loved doll, the fright of a darkened room—the better to make the acting experience more personal by transferring a similar emotion from one event to the other, the years between notwithstanding. Such practices go the long way around, making more of preparation for work than of the work itself. In normal cases, nature does her best to make the emotional experience a facile phenomenon; health lies that way. A beginning based on familiar acts encourages understanding at the same time as it facilitates practice.

to answer the request of that first impulse to emotional action in slightly or vastly different ways. In some the attitude is permissive, indicating that experience has taught them to believe it is desirable to respond freely to the initial impulse. Others have learned lessons that tell them permissiveness is not desirable, therefore they have the habit of placing a check of some kind upon the emotional action that would follow the impulse.

If you tend to repress your emotions, your problem is to find a way to counteract the lessons of your particular environmental classroom. To remove the psychological blocks that now restrict your emotional responses, you must change your attitude toward the value and the need and the use of the emotional experience. To achieve adequate feeling and release, the permissive petcock of your mind must be turned from *Off* to *On*.

Strongly in your favor is the fact that you sought a type of activity that not only demands but enjoys emotional release. The desire that caused you to turn to acting in the first place is as firm as any tendency you have toward restricting emotional expression. Indeed, it is quite likely that a desire to break from former restrictive habits was the prime mover in your decision to undertake dramatic work; it is as good a motivation as most. Nowhere could you find circumstances more favorable to your purpose.

EXERCISES

1. This exercise is designed to explore your ability to respond to emotion-stirring stimuli. Some form of physical contact is to be the motivation for your emotional response. Develop a short sequence such as would naturally follow from the initial contact.

   a. The Pleasure Orientation. Tenderness, affection, love, sorrow, and their associated feelings are to be engendered by the holding of hands, by a hand touching a face, by an embrace, by a kiss. In addition to the man-woman relationship, create others on a friendship or a young-elderly basis.

   b. The Fear Orientation. In this exercise it is necessary for one of each pair alternately to assume the aggressive role. Fear, fright, anxiety, alarm, dismay, dread, or terror (be specific) is to be created as a result of a handshake that is too strong, or of a twisting of an arm, a grasping of the hair, a push, a blow, or any other kind of action aggressive enough to warrant a strong emotional response.

   c. The Anger Orientation. Employing the same kind of physical contact as in the exercise above, change the emotional response to one of pique, bitterness, malice, anger, hate, and similar reactions.

2. This exercise is designed to produce contrasting emotional responses in the two persons in the scene. Using the expedient of counting in sequence

rather than making up lines, let tone and movement be the means of projecting feelings to the audience. Enact one of the following suggestions, or originate a sequence of your own.

  a. A sergeant instructs a private on the drill ground.

  b. Two student nurses await their first experience in surgery.

  c. A husband comes home to find that his wife has rearranged the living room furniture.

  d. An engaged couple apply for a marriage license.

  e. Two dancers rehearse a dance step.

  f. A director and an actor work on a scene.

3. Three players, choosing a situation that represents them as office workers, travellers in a bus terminal, students on campus or in class, or others, watch an imaginary occurrence that causes them to respond with smiles that grow into laughter. The short incident over and the laughter finished, each turns to individual concerns, performing some sort of activity routine to the situation. But whenever eye contact is made in the course of the activity, the smiles and the laughter return. (Do not force the laughter by squeezing it out; laugh only to an extent that is manageable.) Count in sequence rather than creating dialogue.

The Management of Emotion

Short or long in duration, slight or strong in intensity, when an impulse to emotional action manifests itself, the emotional state is in being. It is marked by a feeling of which the owner is internally aware, and may be shown by some kind of external action. In a life situation, the question of whether emotion is managed or mismanaged is determined by societal regulation. In the theatre the successful or unsuccessful government of this viable element is conditioned by the dramatic disciplines.

How the actor manages or does not manage the emotional state is the second of the two questions raised some pages back. Several ideas will be advanced on the subject, but of one thing we may be sure: uniformity of practice will not be among them.

Proportion • Cause and effect are so interrelated in the lives of all of us, it is common knowledge that a slight or a strong motivation is matched by a slight or strong response. The proper proportion between the two is ingrained in our sensibilities, so much so that any imbalance between the two is immediately noted. As a little push should not cause a great fall, so a slight stimulus should not be followed by an overdone effect. Conversely, an inciting incident of some force should not be negated by a failure to realize fully the potential of the response. Therefore, in the study of a scene, you must be alert to the equilibrium our sensibilities demand.

The Power of Suggestion • The use of the power of suggestion increases the potential of emotion as an intensifier of the dramatic experience. You demonstrate both skill and creative ability when you let the audience do some of your work for you. Not only must emotion be a shared experience, but there are many times when the people out front can and should carry the bulk of the emotional load. The actor who laughs too much at his own jokes cuts off the laughter of others; the actress who weeps too copiously denies tears to her audience; anger can alienate; physical love can embarrass. Where suggestion rather than actuality promises the greater response, it should be used.

Feeling the Part • As important as any aspect of emotional experience, and certainly the most controversial, is a discussion of the extent to which emotion is personalized on stage or, in theatre parlance, of how much the actor should feel his part. But before examination of that polemic subject, you should know something of the degree to which this question has caused division within the theatre.

The Paradox of Acting • Boldly and with marked partisanship, the French essayist and encyclopedist, Denis Diderot (1713–1784) gave his answer to how personal emotion should be and how intensely it should be felt by the actor onstage. In *The Paradox of Acting*, 1770, he supported the cause of antiemotionalism against that of its opposite in acting. Predicating his thesis on a belief that the intellectual rather than intuitive approach to a role was the better method, his postulate held that mental control assured accurate observation of primary sources, objective translation of material into dramatic form, and guaranteed sustained and consistent quality in each performance. Naturally he felt that an intuitive approach did not produce such desirable results, that emotionalism was more apt to control than be controlled, and that an uneven and an unfaithful performance would derive from such a practice.[56]

In Diderot's time, the polarity of the problem was demonstrated in full scale by the work of two rival actresses in the *Comédie Française*. *Mlle.* Hyppolite Clairon was the delight of Diderot and his friends. Meticulous in her preparation for a role, she sought realization of her idealized image—the characters she portrayed were of heroic proportions—by a discipline of mind and body that insured control of each segment of her work. *Mlle.* Marie-François Dumesnil provided an excellent contrast. Of

---

[56] For all actors who would ground themselves soundly in the historical background of their subject, *The Paradox of Acting* is standard reading. But no matter what the reader's alignment, pro or con, the brochure should be studied within the context of the terminology and the philosophy of its day. Diderot's work provoked many answers, William Archer's *Masks or Faces* being one of the most notable, even though it came over a hundred years later. (A Dramabook edition contains both *Paradox of Acting* and *Masks or Faces*, with an excellent Introduction by Lee Strasberg.)

a volatile temperament, her intuitive approach made her a follower of her feelings rather than the master of them. Inconsistent in quality and steadiness, still she achieved moments of greatness unequalled by her rival.

Diderot sustained his cause with energy, but with what total effect we do not know. Apparently it did not occur to him or his friends that neither of the two, Clairon or Dumesnil, would have been successful in following the work patterns of the other. This points up the fact, so often overlooked in debate, that what one player has found acceptable in theory and profitable in practice may or may not be of like benefit to another. But it is human nature to want one's own beliefs to prevail. It is for that reason that the tall lean player is inclined to say to the short stout one, "get into my costume, it is just the thing for you."

On the basis of the discussion above it is obvious that an answer cannot be given to the question of how fully an actor should feel the emotion he is to express. Instead, the answer must be discovered, and the discovery will be individual.

Whatever the findings, the actions involved are these: first the actor generates emotion in his way and to the extent he can, next he controls the feelings he has generated so that they increase rather than decrease the effectiveness of his effort, then he releases the emotion so that it can be felt in such a way that there is some form of sharing between him and his audience. How to do these things is the target for your discovery.

EXERCISES AND ASSIGNMENTS

1. Solo speeches for practice and performance.

a. The Trojan Women,[57] Euripides, translated by Gilbert Murray. Andromache, wife of the slain Trojan hero, Hector, and now herself a captive of the Greeks, says goodbye to her little son. He will be taken from his mother's arms by the Greek soldiers and thrown to his death from the ruined walls of Troy.

Notes

ANDROMACHE: Go, die, my best-be-
    loved, my cherished one,
In fierce men's hands, leaving me
    here alone.
Thy father was too valiant; that is
    why

[57] *The Trojan Women* by Euripides, translated by Gilbert Murray. Reprinted by permission of George Allen & Unwin, Ltd., 40 Museum St., London, England.

They slay thee! . . . Weepest thou?
Nay, why, my little one? Thou
    canst not know.
And Father will not come; he will
    not come;
Not once, the great spear flashing,
    and the tomb
Riven to set thee free! . . .
(*To a Grecian soldier*)
How shall it be? One horrible
    plunge, deep, deep down?
And thy neck—Ah, God, so cometh
    sleep!
And none to pity thee! Thou little
    thing,
That curlest in my arms, what
    sweet scents cling
All round thy neck! Beloved; can
    it be
All nothing, that this bosom cradled
    thee
And fostered; all the weary nights,
    wherethrough
I watched upon thy sickness, til I
    grew
Wasted with watching? Kiss me.
    This one time;
Not ever again. Put up thine arms,
    and climb
About my neck: now, kiss me, lips
    to lips . . .
O, ye have found an anguish that
    outstrips
All tortures of the East, ye gentle
    Greeks! . . .
Quick! take him: drag him: cast
    him from the wall,
If cast ye will! Tear him, ye beasts,
    be swift!
God hath undone me, and I cannot
    lift
One hand, one hand, to save my
    child from death.

b. Macbeth, Shakepeare, Act I, Scene 5. Lady Macbeth has just had news of King Duncan's imminent visit, making his assassination possible. Avid for power and position, she is exhilarated as she makes a compact with the forces of evil to sell her soul for the crown. Her manner is demonic. (Her belief in the presence of spirits, not yours, must operate.)

Notes

LADY MACBETH: The raven himself
    is hoarse
  That croaks the fatal entrance of
    Duncan
  Under my battlements. Come, you
    spirits
  That tend on mortal thoughts, un-
    sex me here,
  And fill me from the crown to the
    toe top-full
  Of direst cruelty! Make thick my
    blood,
  Stop up th' access and passage to
    remorse,
  That no compunctious visitings of
    nature
  Shake my fell purpose, nor keep
    peace between
Th' effect and it! Come to my
    woman's breasts,
  And take my milk for gall, you
    murth'ring ministers,
  Wherever in your sightless sub-
    stances
  You wait on nature's mischief!
    Come, thick Night,
  And pall thee in the dunnest smoke
    of hell,
  That my keen knife see not the
    wound it makes,
  Nor Heaven peep through the
    blanket of the dark,
  To cry 'Hold, hold!'

c. She Stoops To Conquer, Goldsmith, Act V, Scene 2. Tony has subjected his mother to the roughest ride possible in their neighborhood. Bruised and befuddled, and believing that she is miles from home, Mrs. Hardcastle is set down from her coach at the back of her own garden.

MRS. HARDCASTLE: Oh, Tony, I'm killed. Shook. Battered to death. I shall never survive it. . . . (*She collapses against him*)

TONY: Alack, mama, . . . you would be for running away by night, . . .

MRS. HARDCASTLE: (*Piteously*) I wish we were at home again. I never met so many accidents in so short a journey. Drench'd in the mud, overturn'd in a ditch, stuck fast in a slough, jolted to a jelly, and at last to lose our way! Whereabouts do you think we are, Tony?

TONY: By my guess we should be upon Crackskull Common; . . .

MRS. HARDCASTLE: O lud! O lud! the most notorious spot in all the country. . . .

TONY: Don't be afraid, mama, . . . Two of the five that kept here are hanged, and the other three may not find us. . . . Is that a man galloping behind us? . . .

MRS. HARDCASTLE: (*She yelps*) The fright will certainly kill me.

TONY: Do you see any thing like a black hat moving behind the thicket?

MRS. HARDCASTLE: Oh death! (*Mr. Hardcastle appears, recognized by Tony*)

TONY: . . . (*Low and intense*) Ah, it's a highwayman, with pistils as long as my arm. A damn'd ill-looking fellow.

MRS. HARDCASTLE: Good Heaven defend us! . . . O lud, he'll murder my poor boy, my darling. (*Blindly throwing herself at Mr. Hardcastle's feet*) Here, good gentleman, whet your rage upon me. Take my money, my life, but spare that

young gentleman, spare my child,
if you have any mercy.

MR. HARDCASTLE: My wife, as I'm a
Christian! . . .

MRS. HARDCASTLE: (*In an agony of
fright*) Take compassion on us,
good Mr. Highwayman. Take our
money, our watches, all we have,
but spare our lives. We will never
bring you to justice, indeed we
won't, good Mr. Highwayman.

MR. HARDCASTLE: . . . What, Doro-
thy, don't you know *me*?

MRS. HARDCASTLE: Mr. Hardcastle,
as I'm alive! My fears blinded me.
But who, my dear, could have expected to meet you here, in this
frightful place, so far from
home. . . .

MR. HARDCASTLE: . . . So far from
home? . . . you are within forty
yards of your own door! . . . don't
you remember the horsepond, my
dear?

MRS. HARDCASTLE: (*Comprehend-
ing, with a full change of feelings*)
Yes, I shall remember the horsepond as long as I live; I have
caught my death in it. (*With a
gleam in her eye, rounding on
Tony*) And is it to you, you graceless varlet, I owe all this? I'll teach
you to abuse your mother, I will.

TONY: Ecod, mother, . . . (*Beginning
a retreat*)

MRS. HARDCASTLE: (*Taking after
him, going off*) I'll spoil you, I will.
(*Exits*)

d. *Death of a Salesman*,[58] Miller, Requiem. Linda, wife of Willy Loman,
stands by his grave for a last farewell to the man she loved with such tenderness and compassion.

[58] From *Death of a Salesman* by Arthur Miller. Copyright 1949 by Arthur Miller.
Reprinted by permission of The Viking Press, Inc., New York.

LINDA: Forgive me, dear. I can't cry.
I don't know what it is, but I can't
cry. I don't understand it. Why did
you ever do that? Help me, Willy,
I can't cry. It seems to me that
you're just on another trip. I keep
expecting you. Willy, dear. I can't
cry. Why did you do it? I search
and search and I search, and I can't
understand it, Willy. I made the
last payment on the house today.
Today, dear. And there'll be nobody home. (*A sob rises in her
throat*) We're free and clear. (*Sob-
bing more fully, released*) We're
free. We're free . . . We're free . . .

e. *Henry IV*, Part I, Shakespeare, Act I, Scene 3. Young Harry Percy,
called Hotspur, volatile of temper and violent in manner, defies the command
of the King that he turn over the prisoners he has captured in a recent revolt.

HOTSPUR: (*Calling after the exiting
King*) And if the devil come and
roar for them
I will not send them. I will after
straight
And tell him so, for I will ease my
heart,
Albeit I make a hazard of my
head. . . .
Speak of Mortimer?
Zounds, I will speak of him! and
let my soul
Want mercy if I do not join with
him.
Yea, on his part I'll empty all these
veins,
And shed my dear blood, drop by
drop in the dust,
But I will lift the down-trod Mor-
timer

Notes

As high in the air as this unthank-
 ful king,
As this ingrate and canker'd Boling-
 broke.

 f. A Marriage Proposal, Chekhov. In this classic comedy of Russian
country life, Lomov comes to the house of his neighbor to ask the hand of
the daughter. Somewhat nervous, he awaits her appearance.

Notes

Lomov: I'm cold. My—my entire
 body is shaking, just like when I
 took examinations. There now, settle down. Be decisive, that's the
 thing. I mustn't think so much, or
 hesitate, not—not even talk about
 it. No use waiting for an ideal love,
 it never comes. So, that takes care
 of that. Now, be calm. (*He stands
 still, relaxes, smiles. But then his
 body begins to shake again, a leg
 first, then the torso.*) It's cold! (*He
 moves.*) Now, let me just look at
 this. Natalia is a first-class housekeeper, a fine—well, not bad looking, and she can read and write—
 (*he laughs a little*)—what more
 could I ask? (*He groans.*) I'm so
 ner-ner-nervous there's a roaring in
 my ears. I'm—I'm hot. (*He mum-
 bles.*) Water—water (*he pours and
 drinks*). Ahhh. Now, let's see—
 where was I? To marry, or not to
 marry, that's the question. Well,
 I'm thirty-five, that's critical—much
 longer and I'll not—. I need to lead
 a regular life—that's the thing, especially since I have a weak heart.
 (*Feels his pulse.*) Hmmmm, palpi-
 tations. My sensitive nature, that's
 what keeps me ex-excited. Even
 my—my—my—my (*slaps hands over
 his mouth, pauses, then speaks*

through the narrow opening) my lips tremble. (*One hand goes to a temple.*) My temple throbs. And I can't sleep. I just start to doze and the muscles on my left side jump. Then I itch, right in the middle of my back, or I get a twitch in my hand. My heart thumps and my head pounds. I go crazy if I don't get up. I have to walk up and down, up and down, to calm myself. Then, when I lie down and am just ready to close my eyes in sleep, I get a cramp in my leg. That's the way it goes, night after night after— (*Natalia enters*)—Oh!

g. *A View from the Bridge*,[59] Miller, the last sequence in the play. Eddie, jealous because his niece Catherine is in love with an illegal immigrant, Rodolpho, has reported Rodolpho and his brother Marco to the authorities. Rodolpho can escape deportation by marrying Catherine, but there is no hope for Marco. Despised by Catherine and now threatened by Marco who earlier spat in his face, Eddie, beyond control of his actions, faces Marco in the presence of neighbors.

Notes

EDDIE: Maybe he come to apologize to me. Heh, Marco? For what you said about me in front of the neighborhood? (*He is incensing himself and little bits of laughter even escape him as his eyes are murderous and he cracks his knuckles in his hands with a strange sort of relaxation*) He knows that ain't right. To do like that? To a man? Which I put my roof over their head and my food in their mouth? Like in the Bible? Strangers I never seen in my whole life? To come out of the water and grab a girl for a pass-

[59] From *A View from the Bridge* by Arthur Miller. Copyright 1955 by Arthur Miller. All rights reserved. Reprinted by permission of The Viking Press, Inc., New York.

port? To go and take from your own family like from the stable—and never a word to me? And now accusations in the bargain? (*Directly to Marco*) Wipin' the neighborhood with my name like a dirty rag! I want my name, Marco. (*He is moving now, carefully, toward Marco*) Now gimme my name and we go together to the wedding. . . . Marco knows what's right from wrong. Tell the people, Marco, tell them what a liar you are! (*He has his arms spread out and Marco is spreading his*) Come on, liar, you know what you done!

2. An exercise for reading. *Lazarus Laughed*,[60] O'Neill, Act I, Scene 1. The scene is Lazarus' home. He has been raised from the dead for three days and is now surrounded by his family and guests. (The physical basis for stage laughter that can be created and sustained without strain is to be found in the Third Sequence—"Ah, ah, ah"—of the Vocal Exercises in Chapter II, Part III.)

(*The company is seated, comprising Lazarus' Father and Mother, his sisters, Martha and Mary, and his wife Miriam. There is a chorus of Old Men. Wine is poured and all raise their goblets toward Lazarus—then suddenly they stop, and an awed and frightened stillness prevails, for Lazarus is a strange, majestic figure whose understanding smile seems terrible and enigmatic to them.*)

FATHER: (*Pathetically uneasy*) You frighten us, my son. You are strange—standing there—(*In the midst of a silence more awkward than before he rises to his feet, goblet in hand—forcing his voice, falteringly*) A toast, neighbors!
CHORUS: (*In a forced echo*) A toast!
ALL: (*Echoing them*) A toast!
FATHER: To my son, Lazarus, whom a blessed miracle has brought back from death!
LAZARUS: (*Suddenly laughing softly out of his vision, as if to himself, and speaking with a strange unearthly calm in a voice that is like a loving whisper of hope and confidence*) No! There is no death!

60 From *Lazarus Laughed* by Eugene O'Neill. Copyright 1926, 1927 and renewed by Eugene O'Neill and Carlotta Monterey O'Neill. Reprinted by permission of Random House, Inc., and Jonathan Cape Limited, London.

(*A moment's pause. The people remain with goblets uplifted, staring at him. Then all repeat after him questioningly and frightenedly*)

ALL: There—is—no—death!

SIXTH GUEST: (*Suddenly blurts out the question which is in the minds of all*) What did you find beyond there, Lazarus? (*A pause of silence*)

LAZARUS: (*Smiles gently and speaks as if to a group of inquisitive children*) O Curious Greedy Ones, is not one world in which you know not how to live enough for you?

SIXTH GUEST: (*Emboldened*) Why did you say yes, Lazarus?

FOURTH GUEST: Why did you laugh?

ALL: (*With insistent curiosity but in low awed tones*) What is beyond there, Lazarus?

CHORUS: (*In a low murmur*) What is beyond there? What is beyond?

CROWD: (*Carrying the question falteringly back into silence*) What is beyond?

LAZARUS: (*Suddenly again—now in a voice of loving exaltation*) There is only life! I heard the heart of Jesus laughing in my heart; "There is Eternal Life in No," it said, "and there is the same Eternal Life in Yes! Death is the fear between!" And my heart reborn to love of life cried "Yes." and I laughed in the laughter of God! (*He begins to laugh, softly at first—a laugh full of a complete acceptance of life. The crowd in the room are caught by it.*)

CROWD: (*In a chanting manner*) Lazarus laughs!
Our hearts grow happy!
Laughter like music!
The wind laughs!
The sea laughs!
Spring laughs from the earth!
Summer laughs in the air!
Lazarus laughs!

LAZARUS: (*On a final note of compelling exultation*)
Laugh! Laugh with me! Death is dead! Fear is no more!
There is only life! There is only laughter!

CHORUS: (*Chanting exultingly now*) Laugh! Laugh!
Laugh with Lazarus!
Fear is no more!
There is no death!
(*Repeating the lines, the laughter builds and builds and builds*)

3. *The Crucible*,[61] Miller, Act II, Scene 1. This is a continuation of the sequence practiced earlier, p. 272. Now the material is more intense. Abigail, having justified herself as accuser of others, turns directly to Proctor.

[61] See p. 272 for copyright statement.

ABIGAIL: . . . Oh, John, I will make you such a wife when the world is white again! (*She kisses his hand*) You will be amazed to see me every day, a light of heaven in your house, a—(*He backs away, amazed*) Why are you cold?

PROCTOR: My wife goes to trial in the morning, Abigail.

ABIGAIL: (*Distantly*) Your wife?

PROCTOR: Surely you knew of it?

ABIGAIL: I do remember it now. How —how—Is she well?

PROCTOR: As well as she may be, thirty-six days in that place.

ABIGAIL: You said you came friendly.

PROCTOR: She will not be condemned, Abby.

ABIGAIL: You brought me from my bed to speak of her?

PROCTOR: I come to tell you, Abby, what I will do tomorrow in court. I would not take you by surprise, but give you all good time to think on what to do to save yourself.

ABIGAIL: Save myself!

PROCTOR: If you do not free my wife tomorrow, I am set and bound to ruin you, Abby.

ABIGAIL: (*Her voice small——astonished*) How—ruin me?

PROCTOR: I have rocky proof in documents that you knew that poppet were none of my wife's; and that you yourself bade Mary Warren stab that needle into it.

ABIGAIL: (*A wildness stirs in her, a child is standing here who is unutterably frustrated, denied her wish, but she is still grasping for her wits*) I bade Mary Warren——?

PROCTOR: You know what you do, you are not so mad!

ABIGAIL: Oh, hypocrites! Have you won him, too? John, why do you let them send you?

PROCTOR: I warn you, Abby!

ABIGAIL: They send you! They steal your honesty and—

PROCTOR: I have found my honesty!

ABIGAIL: No, this is your wife pleading, your snivelling, envious wife! This is Rebecca's voice, Martha Corey's voice. You were no hypocrite!

PROCTOR: I will prove you for the fraud you are!

ABIGAIL: And if they ask you why Abigail would ever do so murderous a deed, what will you tell them?

PROCTOR: I will tell them why.

ABIGAIL: What will you tell? You will confess to fornication? In the court?

PROCTOR: If you will have it so, so I will tell it! (*She utters a disbelieving laugh*) I say I will. (*She laughs louder. He shakes her*) If you can still hear, hear this! Can you hear! (*She is trembling, staring up at him as though he were out of his mind.*) You will tell the court you are blind to spirits; you cannot see them any more, and you will never cry witchery again, or I will make you famous for the whore you are!

ABIGAIL: (*Grabs him*) Never in this world! I know you, John—you are this moment singing secret Hallelujahs that your wife will hang!

PROCTOR: (*Throws her down*) You mad, you murderous bitch!

ABIGAIL: Oh, how hard it is when pretense falls! But it falls, it falls! (*She wraps herself up as though*

Notes

to go) You have done your duty by
her. I hope it is your last hypocrisy.
I pray you will come again with
sweeter news for me. I know you
will—now that your duty's done.
Good night, John. (*Backing away*)
Fear naught. I will save you tomorrow. From yourself I will save
you. (*Goes. Proctor is left alone,
amazed and in terror*)

4. Additional scenes for study and practice, in which the emotional content
is of many kinds, from the laughter of *What Every Woman Knows* to the
frantic action of *The Lesson*.

The Children's Hour, Lillian Hellman—Karen and Martha, Act III.
  "No, you won't. Never, darling."
Of Mice and Men, John Steinbeck—George and Lennie, Act III, Scene 2.
  "Where's them guys goin'?"
Anna Christie, Eugene O'Neill—Burke and Anna, Act IV.
  "Let you not be hiding from me."
Pygmalion, G. B. Shaw—Eliza and Higgins, Act V.
  "Put out the lights, Eliza . . ."
What Every Woman Knows, J. M. Barrie John and Maggie, Act IV.
  The last short scene.
Ghosts, Henrik Ibsen—Oswald and Mrs. Alving, Act III.
  The last scene.
The Gentle People, Irwin Shaw—Philip, Jonah, and Goff, Act III, Scene 3.
  The whole scene.
All My Sons, Arthur Miller—Chris and Keller, Act II.
  The last scene.
The Barrets of Wimpole Street, Rudolph Besier—Barret and Elizabeth,
  Act V.
  "Do you know why I am back so early?"
The Waltz of the Toreadors, Jean Anouilh—General and General's Wife,
  Act II, Scene 2.
  "We must thrash this matter out, Madam . . ."
The Lesson, Eugene Ionesco—Professor and Pupil, near end of act.
  "Here's one, Mademoiselle, here's a knife!"

Chapter 20

Action and Reaction

Acting, as Shakespeare says, holds a mirror up to nature, albeit one distorted by the magnification, intensification, and beauty of art. In like manner reaction mirrors action, holding up in turn a responsive glass that shows the creator of an action how his effort has been received. Expression addressed to no one or that, if addressed, receives no response, is of one dimension only. But expression that finds a responsive target is two-dimensional and doubly effective, the cause being measured and given additional meaning by the response to the effect. Action without reaction is like a missile without a mark.

Action and reaction is a cyclical process, old as social life. As constant as social activity, it is the form of all communication. It also is the parent pattern for the procedure of that name we follow in acting.

One person expresses a thought or releases an emotion. By sight or sound the expression is projected to another person. Received by that other one as an effect, a response immediately is generated. The activity that caused the effect is called an *action*, the response a *reaction*.

When a reaction has been assimilated, the receiver then creates an action response of his own, which is projected back to the originator. Whenever people work or play together, action causes reaction; reaction is followed by recovery and in its turn motivates action. This is the continuous cycle of the communicative process.

Reaction, as a discernible element in acting, is employed too seldom in present-day acting practice. Apparently content with the inner feeling of a reaction, many players fail to make that response manifest, either to the actors with whom they work or to those who witness the activity. Yet demonstrated reaction is as beneficial an element in acting as any the player has to deal with.

THE REASON FOR REACTION

One man can lift a mass of material to a certain height. Two men can lift the same mass to a greater height. Add the energy potential of still

304

more men and the possibilities of achievement of men against mass increase in direct ratio to the energy quotient brought into play.

A scene is a mass of dramatic material that is to be sustained for a certain length of time and raised to a certain height. When two, or four, or six actors work together, the possibilities of more sustained carrying power and a higher lift are predicated on a conditioning phrase: *if they work together*. That they might do so, the joint effort of action and reaction was taken long ago from its primary-source context and adapted as one of the basic practices of acting. The resultant act of coordination contains a potential that can noticeably increase the effectiveness of any scene in which it is used.

CONTROL OF THE CENTER OF INTEREST

The center of interest has been defined and discussed in other sections of this book.[62] Because of its importance to the present subject further development is required, especially since the center of interest is, so to speak, now on the move.

The center of interest is seldom stationary for any length of time. Actors give and take it in a variety of ways. Each shift can be so managed that the transfer is sure and clear. Here are a series of considerations that pertain to the center of interest.

1. Each actor must know where the center of interest is at all times.
2. Much of the time the center of interest moves so easily from one character to another, there is no problem involved in its movement. For example:

    a. One person ends his speech by asking a question of another. A normal interest in the reply causes attention to move to the one who is to answer.

    b. As one character finishes his line he looks toward the character who is next to take the center of interest. The focus of attention follows his look. (The actor who does this, however, must not fall into the common error of directing his look toward the other character simply because he knows who next is to take the center of interest. He may not anticipate with his actor's knowledge what his character must not seem to know.)

    c. When two characters are engaged in easy conversation and sit or stand relatively close together, the normal flow of dialogue directs the focus of attention as the center of interest moves from one to the other.

---

[62] See Part II, Chapter 8, "Center of Interest."

3. The actor who relinquishes the center of interest should not continue with an action or a sound that would cause attention to remain on him. For illustration, if character A ends a speech but continues to stare out over the heads of the audience, the strength of his stare will demand the attention that should then move elsewhere. If the actor who gives the center of interest cannot himself direct his attention to the one who is to take it, he should decrease the attractiveness of what he is doing to the extent that no competition for the center of interest ensues.

4. The most common means the actor has for taking the center of interest is the employment of a preliminary movement or sound. Here are a few of the most common.

a. An intake of breath.

b. A look at an object, person, or location before speaking or moving in that direction.

c. The utterance of an introductory word in a sentence, when such a word has been supplied by the playwright. For example, "There—do you see what I mean?" Note that where the author would place a comma the player interposes a pause so that the center of interest has time to shift its focus.[63]

d. The utterance of the first word of a line before the line is given in full, as: "Now—now, what do you mean by that remark?"

e. The raising of a hand for attention.

f. The slapping of hands together, or of hands on legs, or of hands on the arms of a chair.

g. The performance of a small action such as putting down a glass or a book, or of returning a cup to its saucer, or of picking up an object.

h. The performance of a larger action such as rising from a chair or opening a door.

It is your responsibility to know where the center of interest is and to be skillful in giving and taking it. In all cases it should not be evident to the audience as a contrived effort; it must seem to be a natural direction of interest that moves easily from one character to another or from one place to another.

---

[63] As legitimate and as helpful as the use of a preliminary sound is, a strong caution must be expressed. Of recent times two words have been overemployed to such an extent their use now indicates a malpractice in acting. One is *well* and the other its colloquial companion *look.* "Well, I'm fine," or "Look, what are you doing tonight?" and "Look, I've got to study." There may be nothing intrinsically wrong with the use of either of these two words in usual or colloquial speech, but there is a great deal wrong when one or the other is heedlessly overemployed as a crutch to what purports to be naturalistic delivery.

EXERCISE

Present any scene that has been performed previously and concentrate upon the giving and taking of the center of interest.

Peripheral Vision • All that is seen by the eye outside or beyond a point of direct focus is peripheral vision. This physical faculty permits you to form conceptions of a fairly large scene rather than of just a portion of it. For example, if you are playing a game in which you must throw a ball over the heads of opposing players to someone on your side, you can see your opponents out of the corner of your eye even though you focus your attention directly upon your fellow player. In a more serious sense, if human beings did not possess peripheral vision, present-day automobile traffic would be impossible.

In a way, reaction is what the audience sees out of the corner of the eye. An experiment will demonstrate this. Place one player onstage at RC, another UC, a third DLC, and a fourth at L. Let the actor at RC raise his right hand, palm toward the audience. Have the audience focus directly on the center of the palm. Then, one at a time, let each of the other players make both small and large movements. Begin the action with the player closest to the center of interest.

From this experiment two facts should be apparent, both of which are important in the practice of reaction. The first is that positions and movements outside the point of immediate focus are sufficiently discernible to be used as aids in support of the center of interest. The second fact is that the farther away a reaction character is, the stronger or the more exaggerated his movement must be. In other words, the size of the reaction movement is in direct ratio to its distance from the focus of attention. Thus, if there were seven actors onstage at a time when the center-of-interest character made an important announcement, in the stir of excitement caused by the statement the reacting players farthest away from the center of interest should make the largest movements.[64]

DESIGN

The element of design has as much applicability to acting as it does to decor. Actors make as effective patterns with meaningful dramatic

[64] Distortion is antifactual—but so is all art. Art forms distort to some degree or they are not art forms—acting certainly not the least among them. Moreover, distortion is one of the elements of truth in art. Artistic truth is one thing, sociological truth another. Both are valid within their respective regimens, but only untruth results if they are confused with each other. The action of a player, placed under an obligation to make his action expressive to the persons seated in the last row in the house, is truthful to his circumstance, and to that truth he must be willing to commit himself even when he is required to make a gesture of more size than he might think fitting.

action as a scenic designer does with set and lights. When the element of design is working as it should, the eyes of the viewers are put under effective control. All reaction positions and movements are so manipulated that they continually insist that the audience concentrate nowhere but on the center of interest.

Mass, line, and *color* are the elements of design that function as reactive agents. Each has its separate task to perform in support of the center of interest.[65]

Mass • The person of one player standing onstage represents a certain mass. Add the person of another player and the mass is doubled. An animate mass is attractive to the eyes of a spectator. Let two animate masses be close together in the persons of two actors and the attraction of each to the spectator is halved. But the viewer, because of limitations of eyesight, cannot halve his focus, he must concentrate on only one of the players before him. Since the players are not to contest but to aid each other, this is exactly what they desire. The following illustration demonstrates the point.

One actor stands at stage C. Two others stand at RC and LC respectively, each facing toward and looking at the actor between. The player at C automatically becomes a stronger and more important mass than he would be if he stood alone. If the mass of figures around him is increased, the degree of his importance rises correspondingly. In addition, the actors have put into operation their own system of control of attention. As long as the supporting players continue to look at the center of interest, they effectively direct any wavering glance back to that place. By this simple device, which is capable of infinite variations, mass in reaction can both strengthen the center of interest and control the attention of the audience.

Since the center of interest, sometimes stationary, sometimes mobile, is always known, the distribution and arrangement of reaction characters in relation to it becomes a matter of importance to you as an individual actor, if for no other reason than that you will be so employed for the greater portion of your time onstage. For example, if there are three actors onstage and the center of interest is equally divided among them, each one will spend two thirds of his time as a reaction character.

When you are one of a group of reaction characters of a *mise en scène,* knowledge of a few simple practices will help you to be a contributing rather than a detracting factor in the scene's development.

---

[65] All three of these elements are brought into play by the technical aids to illusion that surround the player—that is, set, lights, sound, furniture, costumes, and properties, but these are more properly production considerations and are not pertinent, beyond noting, to the discussion that follows.

1. The arrangement of complementary masses should not be exactly symmetrical; each group should be a little off-center in balance.

2. The distribution of mass should not be static. One of the most intriguing problems of reaction lies in the fluidity of groups that shift at the same time they support the constant changes of the center of interest.

3. Except in chorus work, straight lines are to be avoided by players grouped in mass.

4. Duplication of foot or arm positions by two players in the same group is not good practice.

5. Depth gives strength and solidity to a mass; in groups of three or more players, some should be located upstage of others and partially covered by them.

6. The size of the mass is directly related to the size of the surrounding playing area. At times the mass needs to be spread out, at others it should be compact—this is from a consideration of proportion.

7. No member of a group should stand or sit so that he seems to be in isolation and unrelated to the others, unless there is a specific motivation for such placement. Groups can be knit together by connecting hand and arm movements.

8. The size and strength of supporting masses can vary with telling effect as individual actors leave one group to join another.

Line • Masses of players, even though they display strength in form and distinctiveness in arrangement, cannot be permitted to float without anchor about the stage. If they do so, they will detract from the strength of the scene as much as they might otherwise add. The known and established center of interest invariably is the point of focus. The element of line in design, like a rope that secures one mass to another, is the holding force between the center of interest and reaction individuals or groups.

The greatest degree of supporting strength from a complementary mass to the center of interest is obtained when a direct line connects the two. Touching, pointing, and looking are direct lines. For example, one actor sits at a desk RC, facing toward C, signing a document. Three other players stand in a group UC watching him. There is greater size and more strength, potentially, in the mass of three than in the lone figure at the desk. But the three players do not develop that potential; they do not even retain it, but pass it on by the simple act of looking at the seated person. The latter is in a stronger and more important position because of their action. Thus mass in reaction transmits its energy potential from itself to the center of interest. In this case the transmittal was accomplished by one of the simplest of all movements, looking.

The situation in the above illustration can be reversed. Suppose the three players standing UC were facing the other way and looking at a piece of furniture located LC. The direction of their look creates a direct line from them to the object of their regard, and at the same time renders negligible the importance of the man behind them. Further suppose that one of the three were kneeling by the piece of furniture, a chair, with his hand on the chair arm, while one of the other two was pointing directly at it. The importance of the man behind the desk would be decreased even more.

Sometimes, when it is not feasible to supply support from complementary sources to the center of interest by a direct line, variety can be obtained by the use of an indirect line. Listening is one such. So is a body position that faces directly toward the center of interest but does not have the direct connection offered by looking. A third indirect line is established when one character looks at or touches the person of a second who is pointed toward or looking directly at the center of interest. This last action is of much use in arranging groups of players who stand or sit in a supporting mass, for quite obviously not every member of a complementary group faces or looks directly at the focal point of attention.

To obtain variety and to demonstrate the use of both the direct and indirect line, the first illustration can be used again. A man is seated at the desk RC. This time he is reading a document. Supporting player Number 1 is seated on the upper corner of the desk, his back partially to the audience, turned just enough to look directly at the reader. Complementary player Number 2 is seated in a chair L of C facing straight on to the man at the desk, but is not looking at him; instead, Number 2's head is resting on the back of the chair, his face tilted up, his eyes closed, with the length of his body stretched out in a straight line pointing toward the reader. Number 3 is standing a little to the L of UC, face to the audience, but with his head down and his hands in his pockets. He is listening intently to the reading.

This picture presents a mixture of direct and indirect lines. The man at the desk presents a stronger focal point of attention than if he sat alone in the room. But if one of the supporting players unintentionally begins an independent action, the effect is marred, and the audience is left in uncertainty as to where to place its attention.

Line, like mass, may be both static and fluid. In the illustration above only positions were given. Mobility is possible as soon as any character executes a movement, in which case the use of line becomes fluid. The illustration can be continued.

As the reading by the center-of-interest character progresses, Number

1 ceases to look directly at the reader, but continues to project the fact that he is listening. At a certain predetermined spot, he will stand up, and a little later turn his head partially toward the center of interest. As Number 1 rises, Number 2 will open his eyes and look directly at the reader. Later he will lean forward in his chair and gaze more intently at the man behind the desk. For purposes of variety as well as for emphasis, he might lower his head and let his eyes idly rest on the floor as he listens to the reading. Then, as the scene builds, he looks up again, or rises in emphatic reaction to a point made. Further, he can heighten the scene by a reaction movement that carries him to the desk, or, if opposition were needed, that moves him farther away from the center of interest. Number 3 looks at the reader—he had only been listening— at the same time as Number 1 changes from looking to listening. Then when Number 2 assumes the strong position of leaning forward in his chair, he, Number 3, turns and looks at him instead of at the center of interest. When Number 2 lets his gaze go down to the floor, Number 3 again looks at the man behind the desk. When Number 2 Xs to the desk, Number 3 adds strength and emphasis of both line and mass by dropping down to stand somewhat behind and close to the other.

If the center of interest in the above illustration were to be moved, it could be taken over by any of the supporting players. In this case the direct and indirect lines of the reaction characters would have to adjust to the new situation. By actions of giving and taking, the focus of attention also could move with ease from one to another of those players who had at first been only reaction characters, in a circle, before being returned to the original point of focus at the desk.

EXERCISE

1. With the reader counting numbers rather than reading sentence-structured material, work out for onstage performance the above or similar uses of direct and indirect lines in reaction. Do not predetermine the attitudes of the characters, but let them grow in rehearsal.

2. Perform a like exercise employing five or six reaction characters. One student should be assigned as director. Keep the reaction movements definite and in proper proportion and the timing precise. Be sure the center of interest character is aware of his power to motivate reaction, and that he paces his delivery in coordination with it.

Color • The use of color as an element of design is limited to the color of costume and flesh and hair. Under such restrictions color is perhaps not as important a factor in reaction as mass and line, but it is not so unimportant that it can be disregarded.

The color of the costume to be worn by you generally is determined by the costume designer. Your responsibility lies in employing the colors you have at your disposal correctly. Following is a list of points that can aid you in the use of color as a reactive agent.

1. Bright values are more attractive to the eye of the spectator than somber or dark tones.

2. Light costumes, light skin, blond hair, especially when any of these is placed in a strongly lighted area, can detract from the center of interest, if care is not taken in their employment.

3. Minor characters who wear colors that might attract attention are best employed in the depth positions in mass groupings.

4. Color strength can be used to establish the direct line that ties a group of reaction characters to the center of interest.

5. A flash of color can give emphasis to something done or something said by the center-of-interest character.

6. The flesh tones of arms, shoulders, and faces have just enough color strength to function as reactive agents within the peripheral vision range of the audience. Turning heads and moving arms can serve to punctuate the actions or the statements of the center of interest.

EXERCISE

This exercise poses problems in the use of design as a reaction element. Dialogue is not important in this assignment. If used, it should be in terse sentence form; the exercise can be done in pantomime. Each group should have a director.

The scene is to represent a casual assembly of students divided into four distinct groups, two to five in a group. The setting could be a campus lawn, the corridor of a classroom building, the lounge of a student union, or the foyer of a theatre between acts of a play.

Keeping each group separate, shift the center of interest in a normal fashion from one group to another, until some individual in each has handled it. Then bring on an actor who will carry the news that the school's well-liked student body president has been accused of stealing and is about to be expelled. The carrier of the news goes to one group first, gives his information to them, and proceeds to a second group. After that his function is taken over by one or two others. The groups change in size and position as the news spreads.

RECOGNITION POINT

When words are put in sentence form, as in this very instance, the meaning of the sentence does not reveal itself to you until a certain point in its structure is reached. In demonstration, read this well-known quotation from *Hamlet*: "The play's the thing wherein I'll catch the conscience of the king." The meaning of the sentence, the point of recognition, is not realized in full by reader or listener until the last word is read or heard.

A recognition point most often is found near or at an expression's end. The reason is that the first words in a sentence's structure usually are preparatory terms that function as mental conditioners. They ready the mind for the instant flash of comprehension that occurs at the crucial moment when the sentence suddenly makes sense.

It follows that the recognition point contains the cue for any reaction to be given. This appears to simplify your problem as far as reaction timing is concerned, and indeed it does—except for the fact that theatrical conditions insist that not you but the audience establish the position of the recognition point. This is because you, through familiarity with the script, often move the recognition point forward, sometimes to the place where you have the full thought even as the first words of a line are uttered. But when you are listening to a line for the thirtieth or fiftieth time, your audience is hearing it for the first time. Stage tempo is based on the unified speed with which actors and audience participate in the dramatic experience; thus the recognition point is determined by the unprepared auditors rather than by the prepared player.

EXERCISES

1. Have one actor, with back to audience, read the following speech by M. Diafoirus from *The Imaginary Invalid* while the reaction characters of Thomas Diafoirus, Argan, Toinette, Angelique, and Cleante time their diverse reactions to each recognition point in the sequence. Be sure the reader paces his delivery in coordination with the reaction responses. One student should be assigned to direct each group.

DIAFOIRUS: (*Talking about his son Thomas*) I have cause to be both pleased and satisfied, Monsieur, but not just because I am his father. His imagination has never been active, nor has he ever had as much wit as others. Instead, he has been sober and taciturn—and that has given me pride, because it shows he has rare judgment, and that is a necessity in our profession. He was always slow. His teachers had a devil of a time teaching him to read—he was nine before he learned! Since trees that grow slowly bear the best fruit, I was inordinately pleased with the rate of his progress. He found college difficult, but he doggedly perservered, and occasionally his instructors praised his good intentions. But always, as I can say without boasting, he was vigorously and noisily disputatious, participating in all college debates. He let no notion pass without arguing it to the finish, always on the negative side of the question! But what pleases me most in my son is that he follows my example with exactitude in practicing with no deviation whatsoever the precepts of the ancients. I am proud to say that he does not comprehend any of the modern teachings, nor does he recognize as valid any of the recent discoveries in our profession.

2. Three scenes from Archibald MacLeish's verse play, *J. B.*, also offer opportunities for practice in the handling of the recognition point. They are in Act I: the Soldiers', Reporters', and Policemen scenes.

3. Tetzel's speech from Act II, Scene 1 of Osborne's *Luther* provides another choice for this exercise.

REACTION AS AN AGENT OF INTERPRETATION

One of the functions of reaction is to indicate to an audience how to interpret a stage action. For example, when the boss, bending over, is mistakenly kicked by an employee, it is his reaction that indicates how the audience is to respond. The expression on his face can cause a feeling of apprehension or it can trigger a laugh.

In Noel Coward's one-act play, *Fumed Oak*, Henry, the protagonist, must slap the face of his mother-in-law. Since the action of a younger man striking an older woman is normally unacceptable, the reaction response of the mother-in-law must signify how the action is to be interpreted. If she were to indicate that the slap had given her serious hurt, then in that moment the roles of protagonist and antagonist would be reversed and the comedy of the situation lost. But if her reaction is one of startled incredulity that a meek son-in-law would dare to do such a thing, and that it is only her inflated ego that is hurt, then the audience is told, in effect, that laughter is the proper response.

In another example, Argan, the hypochondriac in Molière's *The Imaginary Invalid*, has on the table beside his chair a strange assortment of medicine bottles. The first potion he is to swallow comes from his favorite bottle. He sniffs at the spoon held before him by Toinette. Smacking his lips in anticipation, he gulps the stuff. If this were the complete action, the audience would be left with the belief that the medicine was wonderfully tasty. But as he swallows, Toinette makes a gagging grimace, and the audience knows just how bad the potion is.

EXERCISES

Reaction as an interpretive element can be emphasized in such original exercises as the following.

1. One actor performs a pantomime of shaving, using straight action movements. Then, with another player on stage as a reaction character, the pantomime is repeated. This time the reaction player tells the audience how to interpret the main action by demonstrating a strong attitude toward it. Such states as impatience, anxiety, or amused toleration are suggested. The reaction character could be a wife, parent, friend, or younger brother.

2. The stump speech of a campus politician draws mixed reactions from a listening student group.

3. A controversial subject is the basis for a classroom lecture. (The difference in relationship of student to student in Exercise 2 and student to professor in Exercise 3 should be reflected in the nature and intensity of reaction movements and sounds.)

REACTION AS AN AGENT OF INTENSITY

It should be clear by now that the development of reaction lies almost entirely within the actor's province. No playwright, even if he so desired, could write into his script the myriad reactions each sequence demands; even the one-act play would be drawn to impossible lengths. But the playwright does indicate the intensity potential of his scenes. It is then your responsibility as a player to achieve that intensity. Reaction is one of your prime means of doing so, for reaction not only measures the force of an effect, it also functions either as a stimulator or a goad to the action that creates the effect. Each reaction movement and sound can be one of a series of steps designed to intensify a scene's progress. By agreement or by disagreement, the steps are formed. Each of these attitudes is of equal value.

Agreement • If there is little or no tension present, an agreement between two or more persons can be an easy, unintensified action. But agreement, containing as it does consent to a word or an act, has a dramatic utility. Inherent in an attitude of agreement are qualities of enthusiasm and excitement, each of which denotes states of more than usual intensity.

A reference to your own experience can make the matter clear. At a student meeting the leader of the group proposes a course of action that obtains immediate approval. Enthusiastic responses and contributing ideas come from all directions. If the leader is to maintain dominance over the gathering, he must top in force each response while he permits the favorable reaction to grow. Thus each successive reaction is, in effect, a step whereby the intensity of the scene is increased.

An example of intensification through agreement is found in Act I of *The Imaginary Invalid*, in the scene between Angélique and Toinette.

Your knowledge of the play and the characters precludes further explanation.

(*Toinette, back to doorway, is busy with a feather duster. Angélique enters, looks around, then speaks in a sharp whisper*)

Notes

ANGÉLIQUE: Toinette!

TOINETTE: (*Startled*) Angélique! Your father—

ANGÉLIQUE: (*Twirling into the room, radiant with her own thoughts*) Look at me!

TOINETTE: (*Dryly*) I am—what else do you think—

ANGÉLIQUE: Oh, Toinette!

TOINETTE: Yes, my—

ANGÉLIQUE: Do you know what I'm thinking, what I feel?

TOINETTE: (*Again dryly*) Our new lover, yes? Dreams and talk, nothing else for six days—

ANGÉLIQUE: Yes, oh, yes! (*Breaks her attitude to look sharply at Toinette*) Well, aren't you going to ask me about him? Please, say something—talk to me about him.

TOINETTE: No chance, my—

ANGÉLIQUE: (*Not waiting for the reply*) I love to hear you speak about him. Talk, keep talking. (*Toinette attempts a word*) I eagerly await each moment when I can reveal how my heart feels. Toinette, oh, Toinette, do you condemn my thoughts?

TOINETTE: (*Stoutly*) Never, Angéli—

ANGÉLIQUE: (*Interrupting*) Is it wrong of me to cherish such sweet (*she lingers on the word*) feelings?

TOINETTE: (*In sympathy*) Of course not—

ANGÉLIQUE: Must I not respond to his tender words of love?

Notes

TOINETTE: (*Making a quick attempt*) Heaven for—

ANGÉLIQUE: Tell me, Toinette, was it not Fate that brought about our chance meeting?

TOINETTE: It could have—

ANGÉLIQUE: Was he not chivalrous to defend me, especially since we had never seen each other before?

TOINETTE: Indee—

ANGÉLIQUE: He was so gallant.

TOINETTE: Certainly he—

ANGÉLIQUE: He was gracefulness itself.

TOINETTE: That's right.

ANGELIQUE: And oh, Toinette, isn't he a superb figure of a man?

TOINETTE: Yes, but—

ANGÉLIQUE: And handsome?

TOINETTE: Beyond quest—

ANGÉLIQUE: And noble in everything?

TOINETTE: True, very—

ANGÉLIQUE: And isn't it annoying that I am so restrained with no chance to enjoy our mutual love?

TOINETTE: Yes, it—

So the scene goes, with Toinette's interrupted attempts at agreement forming dramatic steps whereby Angélique increases the intensity of the scene.

Not all instances of intensification through agreement are as broad as the above illustration suggests, but if the possibilities of creating intensities by this means are broken down into subtle as well as obvious responses, some idea can be gained of the full use that can be made of reaction in this respect. Movement, sound, and words can be employed.

EXERCISE

In actress pairs, prepare and perform the above scene, or enact a similar one, such as that between Juliet and the Nurse in Act II, Scene 5 of *Romeo and Juliet*.

Disagreement • The opportunities for building tension by disagreement are even more apparent than they are when minds meet in agreement. The dramatic constant of conflict is seldom better fed than when opposition flows from reaction characters to challenge the strength of a center-of-interest thought or action.

An example of intensification by disagreement is found in Act I, Scene 2 of *King Henry IV*, Part 1. In the sequence quoted below, the King and Hotspur address each other in a clash of wills and temper. A direct look, a turn to or away from, an exclamation of protest, surprise, or contempt, a snort, laugh, sardonic or mocking smile, a deprecatory hand movement, the repetition of an offending word just uttered by the speaker—all these are honest and viable means of showing disagreement in reaction. In the speeches given below, a check marks the place where a reaction might occur.

Notes

KING: Why yet he doth deny his
    prisoners,✓
But with proviso and exception,
That we at our own charge shall
    ransom straight
His brother-in-law, the foolish Mor-
    timer,✓
Who, on my soul, hath willfully
    betray'd
The lives of those that he did lead
    to fight
Against that great magician,
    damn'd Glendower,✓
Whose daughter, as we hear, that
    Earl of March
Hath lately married. Shall our cof-
    fers then
Be emptied, to redeem a traitor
    home?✓
Shall we buy treason, and indent
    with fears,
When they have lost and forfeited
    themselves?
No, on the barren mountains let
    him starve;✓
For I shall never hold that man my
    friend,
Whose tongue shall ask me for one
    penny cost

To ransom home revolted Mor-
timer.
HOTSPUR: Revolted Mortimer!
He never did fall off, my sovereign
liege,
But by the chance of war.✓ To
prove that true
Needs no more but one tongue for
all those wounds,
Those mouthed wounds which vali-
antly he took,
When on the gentle Severn's sedgy
bank,
In single opposition hand to hand,
He did confound the best part of
an hour
In changing hardiment with great
Glendower.✓
Three times they breath'd and
three times did they drink,
Upon agreement, of swift Severn's
flood,
Who then affrighted with their
bloody looks,
Ran fearfully among the trembling
reeds,
And hid his crisp head in the hol-
low bank,
Blood-stained with these valiant
combatants.✓
Never did base and rotten policy
Color her working with such
deadly wounds,
Nor never could the noble Mor-
timer
Receive so many, and all willingly.
Then let not him be slander'd with
revolt.
KING: Thou dost belie him, Percy,
thou dost belie him.
He never did encounter with Glen-
dower.✓
I tell thee,

Notes

He durst as well have met the devil
　　alone
As Owen Glendower for an enemy.
Art thou not asham'd?✓ But sir-
　　rah, henceforth
Let me not hear you speak of Mor-
　　timer.
Send me your prisoners with the
　　speediest means,✓
Or you shall hear in such a kind
　　from me
As will displease you. My Lord
　　Northumberland,
We license your departure with
　　your son.✓
Send us your prisoners, or you will
　　hear of it. (*Exit King*)✓

EXERCISE

In male pairs, rehearse and perform this or a like scene.

It will be noted, in the above scenes, that each reaction commands the focus of attention for a short moment. However, the reaction movement or sound still should be classed, in your planning, as a response rather than an action.

In some scenes both agreement and disagreement can be exploited to advantage. A stage struggle, waged in the presence of others, presents such an opportunity. The principal intensity of the scene is motivated by the struggle of the two combatants, but each fighter has his proponents, and much of the scene's intensification can be effected by the sounds and movements that pour in from all sides as part of a planned development.

Summation

Setting the changing reaction patterns during rehearsal requires time and patience on the part of both director and actors. On many occasions as much effort is necessary for the establishment of reaction business as is used for blocking the play's main action. Nor is there any escape from this fact; discernible reactions, by agreement or by disagreement, make meanings clearer and involvement more certain than if the scene lacks this invaluable dramatic ingredient.

Each reaction movement, position, and sound should be as precisely set as the movements, positions, and lines of the center-of-interest char-acter. It is to be expected that as your study and practice progresses, constant application of your faculties will cause tentative efforts to grow into mastered skills. When that occurs, your facility in reaction will become an habitual action, and you will bring into rehearsal and performance a proven ability as bonus for yourself and those with whom you play.

ASSIGNMENTS

1. The following scenes offer opportunities for the use of reaction as an agent of intensity and interpretation, as well as other points explained in this chapter. Select scenes from them for class performance.

Electra, Euripides, the Gilbert Murray translation. MESSENGER: "Forth of this hut we set our faces clear . . ." Use Electra and about six others for Chorus. Some portions of the speech can be cut.

Mary of Scotland, Maxwell Anderson—Mary and Elizabeth. The final scene in the play.

Ah, Winderness, Eugene O'Neill—Nat and Richard, Act III, Scene 3. Nat tells Richard about the facts of life.

The Cradle Song, Martinez Sierra—Sister Joanna and Theresa. The scene is in the second act.

The Silver Cord, Sidney Howard—Mrs. Phelps, David, and Christina. The last scene among the three.

The Glass Menagerie, Tennessee Williams—Amanda, Tom and Laura. "We can't say grace until you come to the table." Act I.

The Zoo Story, Edward Albee—Peter and Jerry.

2. The total effect of scenes where the principal characters are surrounded by numbers of other persons often depends for success upon the elements of design and intensification and interpretation as manifested in crowd reactions. In few other instances is the discipline of a fine production more noticeable than in the manner in which groups of reaction characters carry out their important function. Exactness of position, preciseness of timing, sureness of attitude, and awareness of intensities are the major factors with which the players must deal—and concentration, always concentration during every moment of the scene's progress. Several scenes are suggested for group work; in them, without weakening the roles of the principal characters, place special emphasis upon reaction functions.

King Henry IV, Part I, William Shakespeare—Prince Hal, Falstaff, Poins, Bardolph, et al.—many male and female characters can be added to this scene from Act II, Scene 4. FALSTAFF: "Well, thou wilt be horribly chid tomorrow when thou comest to thy father."

Cyrano de Bergerac, Edmond Rostand, translated by Brian Hooker, Cyrano, Valvert, and the Crowd. CYRANO: "Take notice, all who find this feature of my countenance a theme for comedy." Act I. Or the *duel-ballade* sequence from the same act and in the same setting.

Six Characters in Search of an Author, Luigi Pirandello—the Family, the Manager, and the Actors. Begin with the entrance of the Family in Act I.

Other plays with scenes or sequences applicable to the present study: *The Crucible, The Diary of Anne Frank, The* Caine *Mutiny Court Martial, The Hasty Heart, You Can't Take It with You, The Man Who Came to Dinner, My Sister Eileen, Stalag 17, The Teahouse of the August Moon, Three Men on a Horse, Waiting for Godot, Look Back in Anger.*

Chapter 21

Tempo and Climax

TEMPO

Tempo, in acting, is primarily an interpretive element. Certain desire drives motivate rapidity of action, certain others do not. We know that hesitancy prompts an uneven pace, and that steadiness of purpose is shown by regularity of rate. Such meanings are revealed quite simply by the speed with which we move or talk in daily life, and we can expect that the same meanings will obtain when we adapt the same tempos to the stage.

THE ADAPTIVE PROCESS

Of major importance is the difference between the tempos you as a person have established in the habitual pace of your everyday living and the tempo patterns you are now to create in your acting. In this respect you continually face the question of whether you will limit the roles you play to your personal pace patterns, or whether you will accommodate yourself to the varied tempo needs of the characters you create.

Of equal concern is the need to handle tempo as a deliberate rather than a purely responsive action—which means that you as a player are responsible for initiating the various speeds of your action, instead of permitting your rate of movement to be determined by the chance pressures that operate around you.

TEMPO MARGINS

Tempo is a relative term. It is determined by the duration of time of action and the duration of time between actions; consequently it is also a variable term. Further, it is a limited term, the limitations being imposed by both the dramatic and the theatrical form, a matter of which you are well aware by now. As a result, you are bound by certain margins you cannot disregard without danger to the effectiveness of your playing. The margins are the boundaries of the two extremes, slow and fast.

The motivation for the specific tempo to be employed in any scene is drawn from the intent of the creators. When you work alone or with one or two other players in preparation for an assignment, the responsibility for the pace of the scene is yours, your determination being based upon the author's indications and your purpose in doing that particular scene.

The difference between one scene and the next suggests that few scenes in series should be played at exactly the same tempo. When monotony of tempo exists in sequence after sequence—the illusion of monotony as a planned effect is an altogether different matter—the effectiveness of tempo as an interpretive agent is lost.

The Too Slow Margin • Dramatic slowness is not a margin in itself. The margin is touched only when the word *too* is added. Whenever this condition occurs, it indicates that the players, in execution of movement or in cue pickup or line delivery, are failing to match the content and intensity of a sequence with a proper pace. There are several quite common reasons for the existence of this condition.

1. The initiatory work on a play, in study and rehearsal, is, of necessity, slowly paced: the study of a piece and its background requires time for research, contemplation, and discussion; the setting of business, with the noting of directions, is a relatively slow process; and the often ragged transition from a script-in-hand to a line-in-head condition plays havoc with a scene's proper tempo. The result is that improper tempo habits can be established at the same time as other elements are being welded into proper shape. For this reason determination of the overall tempo patterns for a play should be made at the beginning of the rehearsal period. These should then be balanced by the variance of individual scenes.

2. A too personal involvement of the player in his part, especially when emotions of deep sorrow, love, or like feelings are involved, can cause serious loss of perspective, leading the actor to believe that inner fullness of feeling is matched by a like outward showing when, in fact, it is not. A too slow tempo is a usual result of such a state.

3. Whenever, in farce or tragedy, the audience moves ahead of the actors in thought or feeling, a too slow pace is indicated. Often such a condition occurs when players attempt to inject more meaning into a script than it can rightfully hold. In an age more aware of social conditions and environmental pressures than any other, we might tend to read in more meaning than was intended or could possibly be contained there.

To correct a tendency toward a too slow tempo margin, your awareness, sense of perspective, and deliberate initiation of control is necessary. Because you became used to one pace when other elements were being shaped in the early rehearsal periods, it does not follow that what seems right through repetition is right. Stage tempo is a composite thing, resulting from several contributing sources: playwright, director, actor, and audience.

The Too Fast Margin • Much that has been said in the section above also applies to the too fast tempo margin. In addition, three new considerations are to be noted.

1. No portion of the dramatic piece, no matter what the personal inclination of the player or the action of a primary source might be, may move at a pace too rapid for the audience to follow. This is as true of movement as it is of line delivery.

Rehearsal familiarity can create the assumption that the people out front will see and hear all that transpires on stage as clearly and with as much rapidity as those who have lived with the dramatic creation so closely and for so long. As a consequence a tempo that seems quite right to an actor can be quite wrong for an audience.

2. A too fast tempo is the enemy of good articulation, causing both slurring and dropping of syllables The too rapid pace takes sharpness and distinction away from movements, requiring the audience to be content with general impressions rather than distinct knowledge. It can cause error in the handling of stage props; in the case of a stage struggle, it will expose the actor to serious injury.

3. A condition of nervousness permeates all public appearances. Fear of failure and hope of success are two opposite streams that feed the same pool of feeling. A state of nervousness is never more insistently present than in the persons of players preparing for or performing a role. But its presence must be a trade secret of the profession, one shared only with fellow workers. The personal emotional condition of the player—and the director can be included in this statement—is not the proper determinant for the tempo patterns of a scene or play.

Tempo as an Agent of Interpretation

Varieties of tempo can make telling points in interpretation. In demonstration, read the sequence below with regularity of utterance (and fullness of tone), as though the characters were performing a usual action in a usual way.

Hamlet, Shakespeare, Act I, Scene 1. Francisco is the guard on duty at one of the regular sentry stations on the walls of the castle at Elsinore. He is relieved by Bernardo.

BER. Who's there?

FRAN. Nay, answer me: stand, and unfold yourself.

BER. (*As though it were the password*) Long live the king!

FRAN. Bernardo?

BER. He.

FRAN. You come most carefully upon your hour.

BER. 'Tis now struck twelve; get thee to bed, Francisco.

FRAN. For this relief much thanks: 'tis bitter cold,
    And I am sick at heart.

BER. Have you had quiet guard?

FRAN. Not a mouse stirring.

BER. Well, good-night.
    If you do meet Horatio and Marcellus,
    The rivals of my watch, bid them make haste.

FRAN. I think I hear them.—Stand, ho! Who is there?

Now read the passage a second time, but with the motivation of two soldiers performing an oft-repeated and dull routine of duty. Remember tempo margins.

Again read the passage, but this time as though these conditions pertained: it is late, and cold; a single torch makes a solitary pool of light, but there is deep darkness in the shadows of pillars and walls; the sentry post is an important one and, with a threat of war from the north, there is potential danger in every unexpected sound and movement. Alert, neither soldier will take any chances, he will kill first and question later.

The Tempo of the Role • Each character in a scene has a tempo potential all his own. According to the needs of the scene he may or may not be called upon to display it.

Continue reading the above scene after the entrance of Marcellus and Horatio. For our purposes suppose the last set of conditions still apply. In addition, Bernardo and Marcellus have previously seen the ghost; Horatio has not. Consequently, they are both excited and apprehensive; he is tolerantly skeptical. The scene picks up where we left off earlier.

FRAN. . . . Who is there?

HOR. Friends to this ground.

MAR. And liegemen to the Dane.

FRAN. (*Saluting*) Give you good-night.

MAR. O, farewell, honest soldier: who hath reliev'd you?

FRAN. (*Stops momentarily*) Bernardo has my place. Give you good-night.
    (*Exits*)

MAR. Holla! Bernardo!

BER. Ssssh! What, is Horatio there?

HOR. (*Dryly, drawing his cloak more tightly about him*) A piece of him.

BER. (*With eager excitement*) Welcome, Horatio: —welcome, good Marcellus.

MAR. (*Responding in kind*) What, has this thing appear'd again tonight?

BER. I have seen nothing.

MAR. Horatio says 'tis but our fantasy, (*Horatio nods and smiles*)
 And will not let belief take hold of him
 Touching this dreaded sight, *twice* seen of us:
 Therefore I have entreated him along
 With us to watch the minutes of this night;
 That, if again this apparition come
 He may approve our eyes and speak to it.

HOR. (*Disparagingly*) Tush, tush, 'twill not appear.

BER. (*Insistently and grimly*) Sit down awhile,
 And let us once again assail your ears,
 That are so fortified against our story,
 What we two nights have seen.

HOR. (*Tolerantly*) We-e-ll, sit we down,
 And let us hear Bernardo speak of this.

BER. (*Looking around and crouching before he speaks*)
 Last night of all,
 When yon same star that's westward from the pole
 Had made his course to illume that part of heaven
 Where now it burns, Marcellus and myself,
 The bell then beating one,—

MAR. (*With a cry of fear*) Peace, break thee off; look where it comes again!
 (*Enter Ghost, armed*)

(What Horatio's tempo would be for the rest of the scene may be imagined.)

The above readings should have demonstrated that variations of meaning in both character and situation can be projected by variations of
tempo. Consequently you should know the motivation that determines
the tempo of your scene, whether it comes from the effect of an idea
working on a group of people, or from the personality of a character, or
from the sweep of an action or an emotion.

THE COMPOSITE TEMPO

There is no one constant tempo to a play. The pace of any dramatic
piece is like the body of a river, sometimes running swiftly, sometimes
gliding slowly, but always moving. Each river has a characteristic pace,
one peculiar to it alone, which is a composite of all its variations. In a
fundamental way it is the same with a play, but with this additional
consideration.

The mass of audience is one of the composites out of which a play's tempo pattern evolves. The pace of any scene is determined by the rate at which the players can play and yet maintain contact and continuity with the audience. The tempo of a play, therefore, is determined by the nature of the materials presented, by the requirements of the characters and the situations, and by the ability of the audience to move forward in step with the action.

THE DRAMATIC PAUSE

There is a difference between a true pause and a dramatic pause. A true pause is one in which all activity ceases; it is as abhorrent in the theatre as the vacuum is said to be abhorrent in nature. The dramatic pause is another matter.

A dramatic pause occurs when a situation has been created onstage that is pregnant with internal growth, a situation that increases and builds best when left alone. Imbued with the power of suggestion, the pause contains a chain reaction of thought or emotion that requires time for expansion and fulfillment; in it each person present takes upon himself the task of completing the thought or emotion in his own way and to his own satisfaction.

For demonstration of a dramatic pause, let us turn again to *Hamlet*, Act III, Scene 1. Feeling very much alone and harassed on every side by unsympathetic attitudes, Hamlet, now a "have-not" in a castle and kingdom where he was a "have," turns on Ophelia in the "Get thee to a nunnery" scene to vent his frustration and anger. Yet at one moment he arrests his flow of dialogue to say, softly and with regret-tinged tenderness—

HAM. . . . I did love you once.
OPH. (*Quickly looks up at him, and then down. Very Softly*) Indeed, my lord, you made me believe so. (*Pause. She looks up again, and their eyes hold the look*)
HAM. (*After some time, abruptly turning away*) You should not have believed me; . . .

Later, in Act V, Scene 2, Hamlet, dying from a thrust of the envenomed point of Laertes' sword, begs Horatio to live and tell the truth of all that has occurred. Then he dies.

HAM. . . . The rest is silence. (*Dies*)
HOR. (*Kneeling, holding the Prince in his arms*) Now cracks a noble heart—
(*Tenderly, he lays the body down. Softly, compassionately and with love*)
Good-night, sweet prince,
And flights of angels sing thee to thy rest!

(Almost cutting the last syllable because of a surge of emotion, he bows his head and turns his face away upstage. He holds thus for several moments. Then, startled, he briskly asks)
Why does the drum come hither?

THE TEMPO OF COMEDY AND TRAGEDY

There is a thought around the theatre that all comic timing is fast and that all tragic timing is slow. It is a wrong concept. As with tempo itself, all comic and all tragic timing is derived from the composite tempo of the individual piece. Every tragedy has scenes of fast-moving action—for example:

Hamlet: The Ghost appears; Hamlet discovers the guilt of the King; he kills Polonius; Laertes threatens the King; Laertes and Hamlet fight in the graveyard, they fight in the castle.

Every tragedy has slow-moving action—for example:

Hamlet: Polonius is reluctant to say goodbye to his son; Hamlet muses in soliloquy form (and uses a wide variety of tempo within the soliloquy); the Queen tells of Ophelia's death; the King meditates before he prays; the dead Hamlet is borne off the stage at the end of the play.

In reference to comedy the illustrations can be varied. *The Imaginary Invalid:* The character of Argan has a slow tempo potential; Toinette's tempo potential is essentially fast. *You Can't Take It With You:* Leisurely living is the key to tempo in the Vandenhoff-Sycamore family, yet fire works explode in the basement, and the house is raided by the police. *Harvey:* Elwood P. Dowd is a calm, serene individual, but the sanatorium staff becomes frantic in its search for him.

The only statement that can be made about the variation of tempo between tragedy and comedy is that the former may have a tendency to be a little slower, or at least to seem so, and the latter a little faster. This is based on the fact that a profound idea requires more time to prepare and to project than does a slight one. But the profound idea is not limited to tragedy; comedy also has its significant moments.

CONTRAST

For sheer effectiveness few other dramatic practices equal the result obtained by the use of the element of contrast in tempo. The pattern is known to nearly every player who possesses a strong dramatic instinct: the delivery of lines or the execution of business begins at a moderate pace but quickens as the scene builds until an illusion of speed is accomplished. Then there is a sudden stop, followed by a pause and a continuation of the line or business at a much slower tempo. This pattern has been used by actors from the earliest times up to the present moment.

Note how naturally it develops in these lines from *Hamlet*, Act II, Scene 2, in which two instances occur in short order within the "O, what a rogue and peasant slave am I!" soliloquy:

HAM. . . . Am I a coward?
Who calls me villain? breaks my pate across?
Plucks off my beard and blows it in my face?
Tweaks me by the nose? gives me the lie i' the throat,
As deep as to the lungs? who does me this, ha?
(*Arrested action, pause, then continuance with slower tempo*)
'Swounds, I should take it: for it cannot be
But I am pigeon-liver'd, and lack gall
To make oppression bitter; or ere this
I should have fatted all the region kites
With this slave's offal:—(*another build begins*) bloody, baudy villain!
Remorseless, treacherous, lecherous, kindless villain!
O, vengeance! (*Again arrested action, pause, and pickup in slower tempo*)
Why, what an ass am I. . . .

Equally effective at times is the opposite practice: the employment of a slow tempo that, after a pause, picks up again with increased pace. Ophelia uses it, motivated by meaning as well as madness, when, in Act IV, Scene 5 of *Hamlet*, she says, in the plaintive tones of one who has retreated from reality,

OPH. I hope all will be well. (*With a sigh and slowly*)
We must be patient: but I cannot choose but weep, to think they should lay him i' the cold ground. (*Pause, then fiercely and with a rush*) My brother shall know of it: (*another pause, with a return to the former slow tempo and childlike utterance*) and so I thank you; for your good counsel.—Come, my coach! Good-night, ladies; good-night, sweet ladies; good-night, good-night. (*Exit*)

The use of contrast can be in good or poor dramatic taste in direct ratio to the honesty of its motivation. If the player who employs it does so only because of a wish to be dramatically effective and brings it into play on every possible occasion regardless of motivation, then he is open to the charge of being affected.[66] But when the same player limits his use of contrast to those instances in which it has an honest motivation, it can be said of him that he is a truly creative actor.

[66] Closely akin to this fault is another. See "The Run-on Line" in *Phrasing* in the Appendix C, p. 407.

ASSIGNMENTS

1. Prepare an original exercise for three or four persons, using the device of counting rather than prepared dialogue, in which the tempo of the scene has at least three marked changes.

Example: Several persons sit in a living room with little to do (slow and/or monotonous timing); an invitation by telephone rouses them to excited activity (fast but nonregular timing); an incident of some sort prevents their leaving (erratic timing).

2. To demonstrate the potential of tempo as an interpretive element, select one sequence from each of these one-act plays and read or present it onstage. *Riders To the Sea*, John Millington Synge; *The Sandbox*, Edward Albee; *The Red Peppers*, Noel Coward. Which will be slow, which medium, and which fast?

3. For a study in contrasts, select one sequence from the beginning, one from the middle, and a third from the end of *The Lesson* by Eugene Ionesco, and read or perform each onstage in close succession.

4. One-act plays are an excellent source for studies in tempo. Here are several titles for your consideration: *The Twelve-pound Look*, James Mathew Barrie; *Anatol*, Arthur Schnitzler (any one of the episodes); *The No 'Count Boy*, Paul Green; *Aria da Capo*, Edna St. Vincent Millay; *Six Who Pass While the Lentils Boil*, Stuart Walker; *The Marriage Proposal*, Anton Chekhov; *The Moon of the Carribees*, Eugene O'Neill; *This Property Is Condemned*, Tennessee Williams, *The Caretaker*, Harold Pinter; *Krapp's Last Tape*, Samuel Beckett.

CLIMAX

A climax is a peak, a high point to which actors as characters climb in excitement and hope in some plays, or labor in indecision and distress in others. But always it is a goal, a place to strive toward, where gratification or disappointment, solution or absolution, terror or peace is granted or achieved.

Climax is the logical and natural result of conflict—that lead string that pulls—or goad that drives—the players on and up. Without a conflict-generated climax, drama could not exist; without the achievement of a play's natural high point, actors would not want to act; without involvement in a conflict, with its struggle toward resolution in a climax, audiences would not frequent the theatre. Human desire, as well as natural form, demands culmination. In few other places is it as well realized as it is in a dramatic climax.

DEFINITION

Containing the generic concept of an episodic graduation toward a point of culmination, a dramatic climax is an action in which the opposing forces of protagonism and antagonism commit themselves to a final struggle, from which a decision, one way or the other, derives.

A climax is contained in a special scene and is known by that special title. Although it is always more intense in one way or another than the body of material that surrounds it, it still is intimately related to the surrounding material and can never be divorced from it. Therefore an actor's and an audience's heightened reaction to a climax is only a reaction to the most intensified portion of what is and must be one continuous whole. Its relationship to dramatic structure is demonstrated both by its position, strategically located in a natural culmination point about four fifths of the way through, and by its energy, an accumulation of the powers gathered throughout the play.

A climax may be achieved in many different ways: through a clash of wills, as in *Mourning Becomes Electra* or *Death of a Salesman*, or through the conflict of ideas as in *Right You Are, If You Think You Are*, or the competition of emotions as in *The Emperor Jones*. It may contain the piece's heartiest laugh, its most satisfying flow of tears, its greatest surge of excitement, its most provocative thought.

Crisis • A dramatic action of a special kind, termed a *crisis*, is an integral part of the climax. It is the specific word or action that precipitates the decisive struggle that culminates the conflict. It is the incitement that makes the climax inevitable, a preliminary movement for what is to follow.

The reason for a crisis is that, on the stage as in life, people in conflict do not, upon meeting, fling themselves full tilt into a verbal or physical contest. They maneuver, they test each other by acts of opposition. Somewhere in the maneuvering something is said or done that triggers one or both of the characters into the overt clash of the climax. That something said or done is the crisis.

MINOR AND MAJOR CLIMAXES

In the same play no two points of climax are exactly alike either in motivation or achievement, or in importance or meaning. The differences between them indicate a simple method by which they can be graded: minor and major.

The terms minor and major are relative. Each one depends for its particular title and its degree of importance upon the intent of its creators. With each change of intent there will probably be a change of climactic emphasis, so that what was formerly a minor climax could conceivably become a major one.[67]

There is only one major climax to a play. When the whole piece is broken down into sections, each section will have a minor climax. It is the actor's responsibility to recognize and to comprehend the relationship that exists between the minor climaxes and the major climax in a play.

In this respect, you would do well to emulate the planning of the military strategist by having each minor climax represent a skirmish between the forces of the protagonists and the antagonists. Each skirmish is planned to test the strengths and weaknesses of the opponent and is executed on the basis of achieving a limited objective; one skirmish is followed at intervals by the next one, until the opposing forces lock in the final and decisive struggle that is the contest's major climax. At that time there is no limited objective, for each side commits itself wholly to the struggle, to gain a victory or to suffer a defeat.

You and your director perform the cognitive action of allocating the emphasis each climax requires, and you do so in order that there may be coherence and proportion in your work. In this respect a climax chart can be a helpful aid.

The Form of Climax

A climax is shaped like an upwardly inclined arrowhead, thus: The points of separation at the left suggest the distance between the opposing forces of the conflict at the beginning of the scene, while the point of contact at the right denotes the fusion of the forces in the final struggle. The resolution, of course follows a single line: .

Not all climaxes observe the clear-cut lines of the above illustration. Some are amorphous in form and difficult to detect. The fine examples of *Othello, Candida, A View from the Bridge,* and *A Streetcar Named Desire* are not mirrored in all dramatic work, and comedy may tend to be less well supplied with discernible climaxes than tragedy.

Conflict • The subject of conflict has been discussed at enough length to permit an assumption that a definition is not required here. Suffice it to say that conflict is the cause of climax, or, in reverse, climax marks the culmination of conflict. Each is a natural extension of the other.

---

[67] It is not unusual for people in the theatre to squabble over the placement of a climax, or to assign different values to the same one. For the reason given above it is possible that both sides are right, the error being that each has in mind a separate intent, of which each is ignorant because neither has thought to formulate it, or which, if known, is not stated to the other.

A series of statements follow that are pertinent to your understanding of conflict.

1. You must discover the basis on which it exists. This can be done by the simple expedient of working out the plot line of the story. It can also be determined by a translation of the stated theme in terms of a clash of forces.[68]

Of direct use to the actor is a statement of conflict evolved out of the desire drives of protagonist and antagonist.

2. You should know the extent of separation between the opposing forces at the beginning of a play. For example, a very wide gap separates the desires of Professor Higgins and those of Eliza Doolittle in the first scene of *Pygmalion*—as a matter of fact, a connection exists only for those familiar with the play. In sharp contrast, the two sides of the conflict in *King Henry IV*, Part I, are so close together, they are in direct and heated contact in the opening scenes. Of course, it is understood that all lines of the main conflict meet in the climactic scene, but it is beneficial to know how far the two sides have to progress toward the ultimate contact, and how long and with what intensity they must sustain themselves.

Two examples will demonstrate that it is easy to overstretch or over-intensify a minor climax at the beginning of a play, leaving later climaxes barren of expected builds. When Argan chases Toinette at the end of Act I of *The Imaginary Invalid*, the action could be conducted with such vigor it would remain the most energetically effective climax in the whole play, as it did in one production with which the author was associated; in MacLeish's *J. B.* it is easy for Nickles to be at his satanic best in sprightliness of action and vehemence of utterance in the first minor climaxes of the play—there is encouragement in the script for this —with consequent loss of strength later as the conflict builds to the major climax.

3. That conflict may be translated into meaningful dramatic action, you need to be aware of the specific intent embodied in the conflict. As the specific intent changes, the specific positions, movements, and tones of the actor must alter in like manner.

CHARTS

With the caution in mind that it is easy and sometimes detrimental to overload a production with too much discussion and too little doing, or with more time spent on the drawing of graphs than in the setting of

[68] With increasing frequency we tend to state themes and conflicts in academic phrases, more often conceived in the study than the rehearsal hall. This can have a stultifying effect on creative action.

business, the following chart is offered as a picturization of relationships between the two sides of a conflict.

The play is *The Imaginary Invalid,* and the statement of conflict runs like this: Argan, a hypochondriac and his own worst enemy, continues to give himself into the hands of the antagonists—his wife, who is after his wealth, and the doctors, who are after his health. Toinette, standing in her master's stead, takes his interests as her own, even acts for him against himself. By this means she protects the faithful members of his family and exposes the unfaithful. This statement is broad enough to include all subplots of the play as part of the main one, assuming that Argan, in his right mind, would desire the detection of falseness in his wife, the granting of happiness in love to his daughter, as well as the cure for himself.

The graph shows the distance separating the opposing forces at the play's beginning, it depicts the relation of the minor climaxes to each other and to the major climax, it indicates whether the attack comes from the protagonist or the antagonist group and the degree of impact. Lest any chart prove a burden rather than an aid to a production, it may be more beneficial to sketch a picturization roughly rather than set one down in as precise detail as the following figure shows.

CLIMAX CHART: *The Imaginary Invalid*[69]

Protagonists: Toinette, Angélique, Cléante, Béralde, Louise (?).
Antagonists: Argan, Béline, Bonnefoi, M. Diafoirus, Thomas Diafoirus, Fleurante, Purgon.

Sequences: The sequences, Act I through Act III, are numbered so that a ready reference may be made from the description to the figure. The characters in the scene are listed in parentheses.

Act I

1. Argan establishes his hypochondria (Argan, Toinette)
2. Angélique establishes her lover (Angélique, Toinette)
3. Argan outlines the marriage plans—*first minor climax* (Argan, Angélique, Toinette)
4. Toinette states the side of reason—*second minor climax* (Argan, Toinette)
5. The wife, Béline, begins her machinations; the pillow scene (Argan, Béline, Toinette)
6. The purpose of the wife and notary is revealed: Toinette thwarts the signing of the will by running off with the pen; she is being chased by Argan at curtain—*third minor climax.* (Argan, Béline, Bonnefoi, Toinette)

[69] Three act divisions supplant the five in the original.

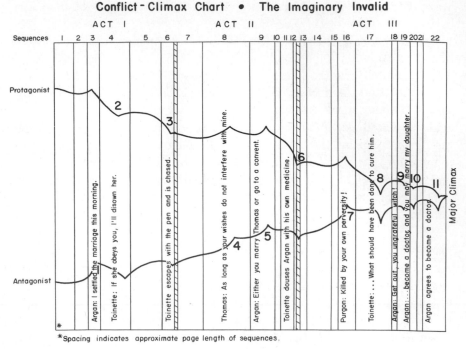

Conflict - Climax Chart • The Imaginary Invalid

Protagonist aggressor in minor climax 2, 3, 6, 8, 9, 10, 11
Antagonist aggressor in minor climax 1, 4, 5, 7

*Spacing indicates approximate page length of sequences.

Act II

7. Cléante presents himself in the disguise of a musician (Cléante, Toinette, then Argan and Angélique)

8. The future son-in-law, T. Diafoirus, is presented; the lovers practice a duet; Cléante is dismissed—*fourth minor climax.* (Argan, Toinette, Angélique, Cléante, M. Diafoirus, Thomas Diafoirus)

9. Argan attempts to set the marriage contract; Angélique and Béline quarrel—*fifth minor climax.* (Argan, Toinette, Angélique, Béline, M. Diafoirus, Thomas Diafoirus)

10. The medical examination (Argan, M. Diafoirus, Thomas Diafoirus)

11. Cléante's disguise is exposed (Argan, Louise)

12. Béralde, Argan's brother, is introduced. A climax is needed here at the end of Act II. The ballet is possible, and it could be offered in lieu of a climactic action; a climax in which Toinette thwarts the taking of medicine by Argan would do—*sixth minor climax* (Argan, Toinette, Béralde)

Act III

13. Toinette plans impersonation (Toinette, Béralde)

14. Argument over doctors and medicines (Argan, Béralde, Fleurante)

15. Béralde blocks Fleurante's treatment (Argan, Béralde)

16. Argan is damned, medically—*seventh minor climax*; *crisis* for major climax (Argan, Toinette, Béralde, Purgon)

17. Toinette impersonates a doctor—*eighth minor climax* (Argan, Toinette, Béralde)

18. A trap is set for Béline (Argan, Toinette, Béralde)

19. Béline betrays herself—*ninth minor climax* (Argan, Toinette, Béralde, Béline)

20. Angélique proves her love—*tenth minor climax* (Argan, Toinette, Béralde, Angélique)

21. Angélique is promised to Cléante (Argan, Toinette, Béralde, Angélique, Cléante)

22. Argan is persuaded to become a doctor himself—*major climax* (Argan, Toinette, Béralde, Angélique, Cléante)

Intensity • If the climax takes its form from the nature of the conflict, it gains its force from the intensity of the struggle; its energy is in direct proportion to the strength of the opposing desire drives of protagonist and antagonist when they meet in a minor or major climactic scene.

Intensity has many shapes and many degrees of strength. It may be on the light side, its shape and energy formed by laughter. This is the case in the last minor as well as the major climax in *She Stoops To Conquer*: the former is the bottom-of-the-garden scene and the latter marks Kate's final conquest. In contrast, intensity may wear the shape of violence, as in the climactic swordplay of *Hamlet*, or the strangulation of Desdemona in *Othello*. It may be piquant and tenderly touching as in the plays of J. M. Barrie, or distressing, as it so often is in the works of Tennessee Williams. Whatever its nature, the selection of the kind of intensity is primarily the playwright's problem. Your task is to give life and force to it.

You can be aided in the playing of a climax by the skillful manner in which the author builds his scene, by the technical director's management of light and sound, or by the stage director's manipulation of the players, but in the final analysis it is the intensity that you generate at the moment of enactment that determines the success or failure of the scene.

The intensity of a climax can also be charted on a graph. Its picturization is probably the best known of all such visualizations. Unfortunately, the image most usually drawn is not really a correct one. No play begins its dramatic progress at a certain level of intensity and then sweeps forward and upward in a gradual curve until it reaches its highest point. Represented on a chart such progress would show thus:

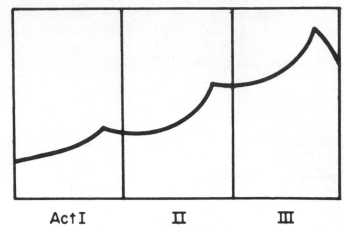

Act I   II   III

A good play moves forward in a much more interesting and varied manner. A series of high points followed by dips on the chart more clearly represents the forward progress of a dramatic piece.

A graph showing the intensity of the various minor and the one major climax is a simpler affair than the conflict-climax chart on page 336. For that reason it may be the more practical of the two. On it necessary relationships are made clear. The forward progress of the play is shown, sequence by sequence, by the horizontal movement across the chart. The intensity of each climax, in ratio to the others, is demonstrated in the degree of upthrust of the vertical line.

It is not difficult to execute such a graph. In many cases a sketch will serve as well as a precisely defined chart. Once the graph has been put on paper the sheet can be carried into rehearsal where it is available for easy reference.

She Stoops To Conquer is not the happiest choice to serve as model in this instance. It is easier to lay out the form for this particular kind of graph for a play like *The Crucible* or *Mourning Becomes Electra* or *Tiger at the Gates*, for the simple reason that the more clear the line of conflict the more definitely located are the high points of interest. It is when a conflict is generalized or tends to be ambiguous that difficulty develops.

Such is the case with *She Stoops To Conquer*. Yet it is a tight piece, solidly constructed and well balanced in characterization and incident. It is just that Goldsmith was not aware that a play should be written to fit a form. He wrote to produce a piece that would bring hearty laughter back into the theatre, to replace the sentimental snickers that had long been heard there—and he accomplished his aim.

The statement of conflict for *She Stoops To Conquer* must be a general one, although the intensities will be specific: to gain happiness, through an appropriate matching of mates by the five young people of the cast, is the aim of this particular dramatic experience. The statement is broad enough to include the main action and the subplot of the piece. Two principal obstacles shape the conflict and lend energy to it.

The first is the matter of Marlow's reserve, which is responsible for the main line of conflict. The second is Mrs. Hardcastle's determination to match Constance Neville with her darling Tony, which forms the secondary plot of the story. These two actions run parallel and almost separate courses, there being but an occasional overlap between them.

It is obvious that the major climactic scene at the end of the play shortly and conveniently resolves all problems. Less obvious and less noteworthy are the twin crises that swing each separate line of conflict into the culmination of the climax: the appearance of Hardcastle and the elder Marlow from behind the screen is one and the reappearance of Hastings and Neville the other. In neither case can it be felt that the crisis functions with its usual force, a matter that, in this case, means little one way or the other to the enjoyment of the play.

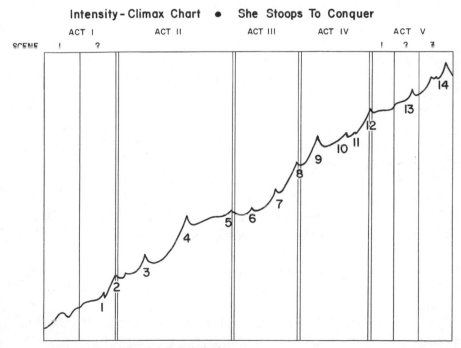

Intensity - Climax Chart • She Stoops To Conquer

Main story line: 1,2,3,4,6,8,9,10,12,14
Subplot action: 5,7,11,12,13,14

CLIMAX CHART: *She Stoops To Conquer*

Here is a list of the climactic sequences in the play. All are minor except the last. The numbers below correspond to those on the chart on page 339. The distance between scenes on the chart is in proportion to the running time of the scene.

1. *The inciting incident:* Marlow's and Hastings' attitude toward Tony, summed up in Marlow's line ". . . the son, an awkward booby, reared up and spoiled at his mother's apron strings." This incident applies with more force to the main action than to the subplot. Act I, Scene 2.

2. Tony persuades Marlow and Hastings to travel on to the Hardcastle "inn." The end of Act I, Scene 2. Main story line.

3. Marlow insists upon examining the bill of fare. End of third sequence, Act II. Main story line.

4. Marlow flounders: "This pretty smooth dialogue has done for me." End of first scene with Miss Hardcastle, Act II. Main story line.

5. Tony and Hastings form forces to thwart Mrs. Hardcastle, gain the jewels for Miss Neville, and free Tony. Last sequence, Act II. Subplot action.

6. Hardcastle and Miss Hardcastle agree to reject Marlow, but only "on conditions." First sequence, Act III. Main story line.

7. Tony provokes his mother by his insistent agreement that the jewels have been stolen. Mrs. Hardcastle: "Do you insult me, monster? I'll teach you to vex your mother, I will!" Middle sequence of Act III. Subplot action.

8. Hardcastle threatens to turn Marlow out immediately. Miss Hardcastle postpones the action by an hour. End of Act III. Main story line.

9. Hardcastle and Marlow quarrel violently over Marlow's behavior. Third sequence of Act IV. Main story line.

10. Marlow admits his attraction for Kate, the barmaid; she privately decides to have him, if at all possible. Middle of Act IV. Main story line.

11. Mrs. Hardcastle reads Hastings' letter and resolves to whip Miss Neville off to old Aunt Pedigree. Second sequence from end of Act IV. Subplot action.

12. Three-way quarrel among Tony, Hastings, and Marlow over how matters have fallen out. End of Act IV. Main story line and subplot action.

13. Mrs. Hardcastle berates Tony for the trick of the journey he played on her. "I'll teach you to abuse your mother, I will." End of Act V, Sc. 2. Subplot action.

14. Double crisis and major climax: Marlow and Miss Hardcastle, Hastings and Miss Neville are united, and Tony is freed. End of play.

SUMMATION

To what dramatic heights can a play go? How intense can some of its moments become? The answer is found in what can be done with the period of climax. In many plays the limiting element is the actors' abilities and skills, for both plays and audiences manifest almost unlimited possibilities for great heights and intensities in the dramatic experience.

The moment of climax in any fine drama is the moment of greatest challenge. Down through the centuries it has brought forth the greatest acting the world has known.

ASSIGNMENTS

1. Select two minor climactic scenes from either *The Imaginary Invalid* or *She Stoops To Conquer* and relate them to the major climax by performing the three together.

2. Select a play with a strong line of conflict; several are suggested below. After a thorough study state the nature of the play's conflict in concise terms. Then prepare a climax chart for the play, denoting minor and major climaxes.

3. Demonstrate the working of the chart by the presentation of some of the scenes involved.

4. Select a climactic scene of major proportions from another play and present it with all possible strength. Suggested plays follow.

Othello, William Shakespeare; *Volpone*, Ben Jonson; *The School for Scandal*, Richard B. Sheridan; *The Father*, August Strindberg; *The Cherry Orchard*, Anton Chekhov; *Candida*, G. B. Shaw; *The Play's the Thing*, Ferenc Molnar; *Long Day's Journey into Night*, Eugene O'Neill; *A View from the Bridge*, Arthur Miller; *A Raisin in the Sun*, Lorraine Hansberry; *Picnic*, William Inge; *The Country Girl*, Clifford Odetts; *Look Back in Anger*, John Osborne; *The Bald Soprano*, Eugene Ionesco.

Chapter 22

Styles of Acting

A style is a special way of writing, moving, or speaking that is selected because of its fitness to demonstrate an artist's particular point of view. It derives its character from the attitude its creator holds toward his society and, in a more limited way, because of his feeling for a certain form of artistic expression.

A style is born because an artist—he is more likely to be a writer, painter, or musician than an actor—finds current forms of expression insufficient or wrong for his purposes. Whether what he wishes to say is a restatement of old ideas or a broadcast of new ones, his quarrel is with inherited means of expression. If his creative imagination is as rich in inventiveness of form as it is in the formulation of valid concepts, he generally ends up both a pioneer and a leader in the establishment of a new style.

Since style derives from attitude, in acting a style embodies a state of mind. If a style is presented with conviction, it is because the state has become an integral part of the actor's core condition in rehearsal and performance, along with the other constitutents that grow out of a development of character and situation.[70]

Before the modern era, each period had its own distinctive style, from which its adherents never varied. In contrast, one of the distinguishing characteristics of our theatre is its receptivity to all styles, embodying an eclecticism that permits us an increase of scope in expression never possible before. That we make full use of this fortunate fact is evidenced weekly in the offerings of both our educational and professional theatres.

Of the many varieties of style, certain ones are standard. Each came into being as a condition of its time, motivated by its environment and given form by sedulous search for a distinctive utterance by the people engaged in the activity. Leading into the modern era, there was Neoclassicism, against which Romanticism rebelled. Then the Naturalistic-

[70] For a full discussion of dramatic styles and the names and activities of the persons associated with their genesis and practice, reference should be made to texts dealing with the history of the theatre, and to works that embody dramaturgical concepts.

Realistic genre was shaped in protest against Romanticism. After that came the antirealistic movements—Impressionism, Expressionism, Symbolism,—which were opposed to the naturalistic-realistic school. We shall deal with most of these; we have already dealt with one of them—our attention to Realism has been almost a preoccupation.

Realism holds a dominant position in our theatre because it has the least distortion, is separated by the narrowest gap from the movements and tones of the drama's primary sources; it communicates its messages from the level closest to life situations, thus permitting the quickest association of thoughts and feelings and the most facile transfer of ideas from primary sources to the dramatic form and from the dramatic form back again to life experiences.

We will consider each style in the order of its evolvement on the modern European-American scene.

NEOCLASSICAL

Neoclassical acting is not practiced in America today. That fact, however, must not preclude a discussion of the subject, because knowledge of the genre is necessary to a discussion of the movements that follow.

Neoclassical is a historical term, used to describe the dramatic activity of part of the European stage, mostly French, in the eighteenth and the first part of the nineteenth centuries. The word *neo* means new; the term classical refers to the activity of the great fifth century in Greece, when the mighty dramas of Aeschylus, Sophocles, and Euripides were being played. Neoclassical means that the dramatic activity being enacted is like in kind to that of antiquity. The rub, as far as acting is concerned, is that no one knows for sure just how the Greek players played. We know how the playwrights wrote plays, and a little of how they staged them, but we can only conjecture about the manners of dramatic movement and delivery.

We assume, although we must make it clear that it is assumption and not fact, that the stateliness and the magnitude we feel in the plays were mirrored in the acting. If this were so, then the movements of the action must have been more measured than ours, must have been deliberate rather than flexible, and limited in scope. It follows that positions and postures would be emphasized, and that the sweep of an arm, made larger by the flow of lines in a costume, would have been used often instead of the modern stage cross.

In any case, the writers and actors in Renaissance France, reading Aristotle, made such an assumption, for the plays of Corneille and

Racine in the seventeenth century specifically demand a somewhat static but stately manner. We strongly suspect that through the years this treatment was generously mixed with romanticism, but to give neoclassical acting its due, we must note that, were it the sole style employed, there would be minimal emphasis on movement of the kind we use today and maximal emphasis on such items as ordered and cadenced delivery of lines, beauty of diction and nobility of passion. Aristotle's phrase, "of a certain magnitude," describes something of the lofty sentiment contained in these pieces. We may be sure that the movement employed did not contradict the attitudes and the passions contained therein.

Physical Characteristics • In neoclassic acting, an upright carriage, tending toward severity of line in neck, shoulders, and arms, but never toward stiffness, is maintained over a narrow or but slightly broad base. The weight, resting on a heel or over an instep, is evenly distributed on either side of the kind of perpendicular line that emphasizes height. Neither knees, abdomen, nor shoulders sag, but, exhibiting the restrained vitality that is always present, respond to an inner discipline that emanates from the spirit of the character.

Arms may hang in formal lines, or one hand, elbow out, may rest on a hip. In addition, one hand may extend part way across the abdomen in a poised, restful manner, and may also come up to grasp the lapel of a coat or the curving lines of a toga. In moments of obstinacy both arms may be folded across the chest or, in contrast, be locked behind the back.

The head sits well over the shoulders, neither tilted forward nor back. When it turns to right or left, the actor should feel a sense of contrast between it and the shoulder. There is firmness in all areas of the face, in the line of the mouth, around the eyes and in the muscles of the brows.

In neoclassic styled movement there is always a sense of disciplined vitality. The pace is measured, seldom hurried, and moderate in tempo, unless emotional excitement prevails. There is freedom of articulation in all the joints, but few of them are forced into extreme angles; a sense of line precludes that kind of action.

Fullness without stretch and moderate stateliness characterize arm movements. The limb may sweep into a full extension when pointing a direction or giving a command, or when fully raised above the head in prayer to a god. Restrained in the number of movements employed, the arms tend to stay longer in one position than is usual in most styles.

More emphasis is placed upon the resonant voice—that is, the orotund quality, and on a strong tone than in any other genre. But flexibility is essential, too, made necessary by the length of speeches and the variety of their contents. Often as noble as it is impassioned, the material of a neoclassic play makes strong demands on the vocal competence of an actor. Unusual phrases and unusual phrasing put a premium on both mastery of articulation and breath control.

Statuesque and declamatory, performed with dignity and conscious grace, this style of acting was practiced in France and copied elsewhere to some extent until the advent of the modern period, when Romanticism, Naturalism, and Realism came in as movements of protest against the formal, rule-bound playing of previous periods. Neoclassical acting, however, did not disappear. Modified, it is practiced in the great national houses of France that still keep the treasured cadences and lofty sentiments of Corneille and Racine on the boards, and by the modern Greek actors who revive on the original stages the work of their great ancestors. But in the English-speaking world, with the disappearance from the stage of such pieces as Dryden's *All for Love*, Addison's *Cato*, and the advent of more melodramatic and romantic plays, nearly all evidences of what may be termed neoclassical acting disappeared.

Whether the stately, sentimental, and powerful acting of such greats as the Kembles in England and Thomas Abthorpe Cooper in America will come to our stages again is unforeseeable. If it does, it will be because some persons, turning from the realistic, psychologically meaningful dramas of today, seek escape in a drama that attempts to rise above the level of things men do into the realm of things they might and ought to do.

Examples • 1. *Phaedra*,[71] Racine, translated by R. B. Boswell, Act II. As well known and as representative as any, this play has held the stage as a major masterpiece of the French theatre for nearly three hundred years. Elevation of thought and passion and purity of diction have appealed afresh to each generation of French playgoers; the play and the theatre that holds it have come to epitomize something of the grandeur of the nation.

Phaedra, struggling in vain against an illicit passion, at last confesses her love for her stepson Hippolytus. Later, after being spurned by him, she accuses him of harboring for her the very love he has rejected, causing his father, Theseus, to curse him and banish him from the kingdom. The curse is realized when the innocent Hippolytus is dragged to death by runaway horses.

Spurred by a false rumor of Theseus' death in the early part of the play, Phaedra makes bold to reveal her desire in the excerpt that follows.

[71] From *Phaedra* in *Chief European Dramatists*, edited by Brander Matthews. Reprinted by permission of Houghton Mifflin Co.

PHAEDRA: Ah, yes, for Theseus
  I languish and I long, not as the
   Shades
  Have seen him, of a thousand dif-
   ferent forms
  The fickle lover, and of Pluto's
   bride
  The would-be ravisher, but faith-
   ful, proud
  E'en to a slight disdain, with youth-
   ful charms
  Attracting every heart, as gods are
   painted,
  Or like yourself. He had your mien,
   your eyes,
  Spoke and could blush like you,
   when to the isle
  Of Crete, my childhood's home, he
   cross'd the waves,
  Worthy to win the love of Minos'
   daughters.
  What were you doing then? Why
   did he gather
  The flow'r of Greece, and leave
   Hippolytus?
  Oh, why were you too young to
   have embark'd
  On board the ship that brought thy
   sire to Crete?
  At your hands would the monster
   then have perish'd,
  Despite the windings of his vast
   retreat.
  To guide your doubtful steps
   within the maze
  My sister would have arm'd you
   with the clue.
  But no, therein would Phaedra
   have forestall'd her,
  Love would have first inspired me
   with the thought;
  And I it would have been whose
   timely aid

Had taught you all the labyrinth's
    crooked ways.
What anxious care a life so dear
    had cost me!
No thread had satisfied your lover's
    fears:
I would myself have wish'd to lead
    the way,
And share the peril you were
    bound to face;
Phaedra with you would have ex-
    plored the maze,
With you emerged in safety, or
    have perish'd.
HIPPOLYTUS: Gods! What is this I
    hear? Have you forgotten
That Theseus is my father and
    your husband?
PHAEDRA: Why should you fancy I
    have lost remembrance
Thereof, and am regardless of mine
    honor?
HIPPOLYTUS: Forgive me, madam.
    With a blush I own
That I misconstrued words of inno-
    cence.
For very shame I cannot bear your
    sight
Longer. I go—
PHAEDRA: Ah! cruel Prince, too well
    You understood me. I have said
      enough
To save you from mistake. I love.
    But think not
That at the moment when I love
    you most
I do not feel my guilt; no weak
    compliance
Has fed the poison that infects
    my brain.
The ill-starr'd object of celestial
    vengeance,
I am not so detestable to you

As to myself. The gods will bear
   me witness,
Who have within my veins kindled
   this fire,
The gods, who take a barbarous
   delight
In leading a poor mortal's heart
   astray.
Do you yourself recall to mind the
   past:
'T was not enough for me to fly, I
   chased you
Out of the country, wishing to
   appear
Inhuman, odious; to resist you
   better,
I sought to make you hate me. All
   in vain!
Hating me more I loved you none
   the less:
New charms were lent to you by
   your misfortunes.
I have been drown'd in tears, and
   scorch'd by fire;
Your own eyes might convince you
   of the truth,
If for one moment you could look
   at me.
What is't I say? Think you this
   vile confession
That I have made is what I meant
   to utter?
Not daring to betray a son for
   whom
I trembled, 't was to beg you not to
   hate him
I came. Weak purpose of a heart
   too full
Of love for you to speak of aught
   besides!
Take your revenge, punish my
   odious passion;
Prove yourself worthy of your valiant sire,

And rid the world of an offensive
  monster!
Does Theseus' widow dare to love
  his son?
The frightful monster! Let her not
  escape you!
Here is my heart. This is the place
  to strike.
Already prompt to expiate its guilt,
I feel it leap impatiently to meet
Your arm. Strike home. Or, if it
  would disgrace you
To steep your hand in such pol-
  luted blood,
If that were punishment too mild
  to slake
Your hatred, lend me then your
  sword, if not
Your arm. Quick, giv't.

2. *All for Love*, Dryden, Act V, Scene 1. Although Dryden abandoned the Alexandrine meter of the French Neoclassicists for the blank
verse of Shakespeare, he retained the Neoclassic principle of the Unities
(from Aristotle), and created characters in a heroic mold, which he elevated to contrived nobility of spirit. Additionally, he composed a diction
more sensible to order and decorum than to freedom of release. If he
achieved less height in the Neoclassic form than Corneille or Racine, it
could be because the genre was not truly indigenous to him.

  The example given below will provide an idea of English handling of
the Neoclassic style. Dryden's play, a masterpiece of its kind, deals with
the Mark Antony phase of the Cleopatra story. Defeat, long encouraged
by preoccupation with each other and neglect of affairs of state, now is
the inevitable fate for both Antony and Cleopatra. Knowing that his
enemy Augustus Caesar is triumphant, and tricked into believing that
Cleopatra is already dead, Antony "falls on his sword" and is near death.

(*Enter Cleopatra, Charmion, Iras*)
CLEO. Where is my lord! where is he?
CHAR. There he lies,
  And dead Ventidius by him.
CLEO. My fears were prophets; I am
  come too late.

Of that accurst Alexas! (*Runs to
      him*)
ANT. Art thou living?
   Or am I dead before I knew, and
      thou
   The first kind ghost that meets me?
CLEO. Help me seat him.
   Send quickly, send for help!
(*They place him in a chair*)
ANT. I am answered.
   We live both. Sit thee down, my
      Cleopatra:
   I'll make the most I can of life, to
      stay
   A moment more with thee.
CLEO. How is it with you?
ANT. 'Tis as with a man
   Removing in a hurry; all packed
      up,
   But one dear jewel that his haste
      forgot;
   And he, for that, returns upon the
      spur:
   So I come back, for thee.
CLEO. Too long, you heav'ns, you
      have been cruel to me;
   Now show your mended faith, and
      give me back
   His fleeting life!
ANT. It will not be, my love.
   I keep my soul by force.
   Say but thou are not false.
CLEO. 'Tis now too late
   To say I'm true: I'll prove it, and
      die with you.
   Unknown to me, Alexas feigned
      my death:
   Which, when I knew, I hasted to
      prevent
   This fatal consequence. My fleet
      betrayed
   Both you and me.
ANT. And Dolabella—
CLEO. Scarce

Esteemed before he loved; but
    hated now.
ANT. Enough: my life's not long
    enough for more.
Thou say'st thou wilt come after:
    I believe thee;
For I can now believe whate'er
    thou say'st
That we may part more kindly.
CLEO. I will come:
Doubt not, my life, I'll come, and
    quickly too:
Caesar shall triumph o'er no part
    of thee.
ANT. But grieve not, while thou
    stay'st,
My last disastrous times:
Think we have had a clear and
    glorious day,
And heav'n did kindly to delay the
    storm,
Just till our close of ev'ning. Ten
    years' love,
And not a moment lost, but all im-
    proved
To th' utmost joys,—what ages
    have we lived!
And now to die each other's; and,
    so dying,
While hand in hand we walk in
    groves below,
Whole troops of lovers' ghosts shall
    flock about us,
And all the train be ours.
CLEO. Your words are like the notes
    of dying swans,
Too sweet to last. Were there so
    many hours
For your unkindness, and not one
    for love?
ANT. No, not a minute.—This one
    kiss—more worth
Than all I leave to Caesar.

             (*Dies*)

ROMANTICISM

Romanticism as a movement in the theatre was first expressed in the way plays were written. The dramas of the three great Germans of the eighteenth century—Lessing, Goethe, and Shiller—gave an indication of what was to come. But it was the French who established and gave permanence to the style. Around 1830, Victor Hugo, who today ranks much higher in literature than in drama, led a successful revolt against Neoclassicism.

Idealism was the keynote of this new genre, made explicit by sentiments favoring freedom from restriction, liberty for the individual, and a self-conscious beauty. Emotive and sensory energy in great quantities supplied the drive for this attention-demanding and attention-getting movement. The initial impetus being successful, the style entrenched itself in the works of Hugo, Dumas, and later, Edmond Rostand.

Romantic action likes movement. Of its several outstanding characteristics, vitality must be ranked among the first. Energy, like the unbound spirits of youth, flows into and gives abundant life to all its actions, as if good health, matched by corresponding spirit, must forever have an uninhibited outlet.

Romanticism is self-conscious, but in the sense that its participants are conscious of self in a very positive manner. Because the individual is important, individualities have a right to clamor for attention. In an attractive way the mark of the show-off is always on the Romanticist. He must and he will attract the interest of others. He poses, but without the affectation of the poseur, and if he deliberately sets out to attract attention, it is with confidence that he will merit it, being sure that who he is and what he does is worth noting.

Self-confidence is another of the Romantic's characteristics. Since he is self-confident, it is clear that if his assumption is not justified, if his *savoir faire* is a hope rather than an actuality, he will be no true Romanticist. Not only must he exude a capacity to perform, he must be good enough to bring the performance off with *élan*.

Since so much is at stake, and because he cannot fail, the Romanticist is forever alert. He is robustly sensitive; he is tastefully sensuous. His faculties of eyes and ears are tuned to a high pitch. They tell him of pleasure, they warn him of danger. His appetites in all things are lusty, but he restrains himself from overindulgence in any form—in love as much as in food and drink.

Control is a discipline he imposes on himself. His care for his manners is as marked as his concern for his appearance, self-restraint and careful dress being distinguishing characteristics of good taste. His clothes not only show his sensibility to the dictates of fashion, they also show to advantage the lines of his figure. Even if his clothes are poor or torn, he wears them with an air, investing them with a quality fit to match a king's poise.

He is also possessed of genuine grace. The body, container of so much energy, has extra value for him as an instrument of self-expression. It must be capable of matching in action the aspiration that elevates the soul within, and no one knows better than the Romanticist that it is the spirit that initiates all. Grace is an inner quality as well as an outer manifestation. This makes it possible for even the grosser body to partake in some measure of the graceful and proportioned movement of the Romantic.

Physical Characteristics • The weight is forward on the balls of the feet most of the time. The base is the broad stance of the swordsman or swashbuckler, but there is no coarseness in it. All joints are extremely well articulated, permitting the knees to flex readily and often in the actions of leaping and fighting. Because poise is always present, the torso is erect, the shoulders back and the head up. The elbows are out or tend that way, and the hands often rest on the hips.

All movement is graceful and sweeping, but never random and never filled with extra flourishes—that is left for the fop or the braggart. For example, the hat, be it plumed or be it a topper, comes off with a sweep, but without any extra turns of the wrist. The legs may be crossed when sitting, but always with a consciousness of the full line of the body. Gloves and capes may be worn, but they will be put on and taken off with a sensibility to function that precludes the overdemonstrative movement.

It is easy to overdo the romantic style of acting. This is something the actor must be quite careful about. When a manner already tends toward the extreme, it is a serious mistake to distort it even a little, for then the proportion and the beauty of the style is lost. Fortunately, any overdoing in this genre is immediately apparent—the action will appear melodramatic and sententious—or, in slang, hammy.

Reflecting aspiration and idealization, the Romantic genre forever appeals to those same qualities in all of us. Freedom for release, coupled with expansive movement, offers healthy exercise, especially for the sober player. By its very nature, Romanticism finds a most appropriate home in the theatre.

EXERCISES

1. A pantomimic exercise for women: Dressed appropriately, imagine yourself in doublet and hose, wearing a cape and a peaked hat and carrying a

sword or dagger in your belt. Practice movements of rising suddenly from a seated position, of doffing the hat, of throwing back the cape, of kneeling, of testing the sword in the hand, of leaping onto a bench or straddling a chair or leaning against a table.

2. A pantomimic exercise for men, featuring an imaginary act of legerdemain. Array yourself in a sash, a cloak, a plumed hat, and a pair of gloves; then, two centuries of time having passed rapidly, take off the same pieces as articles of modern clothing—that is, modern gloves, a top hat, a coat, and a formal sash of some noble order.

Examples • 1. *Peer Gynt*,[72] Ibsen, Act III, Scene 4. Before he composed the dramas in the Realistic style on which his title of Father of the Modern Drama rests, Ibsen had already made a notable contribution in the Romantic genre with a verse play, *Peer Gynt*. No character in modern drama revolts more against established order and none creates for himself as idealistic a concept of the all-important self than Peer. In the eyes of others Peer is a ne'er-do-well, a rascal and vagabond; in his own hope-world he is none of these things.

Although outlawed, Peer returns to his home, only to find his mother, Ase, dying. With his never-failing ability, he sweeps her along on a last trip into their own special realm of escape.

Notes

PEER. No, now we will chat together, but only of this and that,—forget what's awry and crooked, and all that is sharp and sore. . . . The bed is short, Let me see;—if I don't believe, now, it's the bed that I had when a boy! Do you mind, dear, how oft in the evenings you sat at my bedside here, and spread the fur-coverlet o'er me, and sang many a lilt and lay?

ASE. Ay, mind you? And then we played sledges when your father was far abroad. The coverlet served for sledge-apron, and the floor for an ice-bound fiord.

PEER. Ah, but the best of all, though —mother, you mind that too? —the best was the fleet-foot horses—

[72] From *Peer Gynt* by Henrik Ibsen, Translated by William Archer, *The Collected Works of Henrik Ibsen*. Reprinted by permission of Charles Scribner's Sons, Publishers.

ASE. Ay, think you that I've forgot? . . .

PEER. To the castle west of the moon, and the castle east of the sun, to Soria-Moria Castle the road ran both high and low. . . . In the Castle the King and the Prince give a feast. On the sledge-cushions lie and rest you; I'll drive you there over the heath—

ASE. But Peer dear, am I invited?

PEER. Ay, that we are, both of us. (*He throws a string round the back of the chair on which the cat is lying, takes up a stick, and seats himself at the foot of the bed.*) Gee-up! Will you stir yourself, Black-boy? Mother, you're not a-cold? Ay, ay; by the pace one knows it, when Grane begins to go!

ASE. Why, Peer, what is it that's ringing—?

PEER. The glittering sledge-bells, dear!

ASE. Oh, mercy, how hollow it's rumbling!

PEER. We're just driving over a fiord.

ASE. I'm afraid! What is that I hear rushing and sighing so strange and wild?

PEER. It's the sough of the pine trees, mother, on the heath. Do you but sit still.

ASE. There's a sparkling and gleaming afar now; whence comes all that blaze of light?

PEER. From the castle's windows and doorways. Don't you hear, they are dancing?

ASE. Yes.

PEER. Outside the door stands Saint Peter, and prays you to enter in.

ASE. Does he greet us?

PEER. He does, with honour, and
pours out the sweetest wine.

ASE. Wine! Has he cakes as well,
Peer?

PEER. Cakes? Ay, a heaped-up dish.
And the dean's wife is getting
ready your coffee and your dessert.

ASE. Oh, Christ; shall we two come
together?

PEER. As freely as ever you will.

ASE. Oh, deary, Peer, what a frolic
you're driving me to, poor soul!

PEER. (*cracking his whip*) Gee-up;
will you stir yourself, Black-boy!

ASE. Peer, dear, you're driving right?

PEER. (*cracking his whip again*) Ay,
broad is the way.

ASE. This journey, it makes me so
weak and tired.

PEER. There's the castle rising before
us; the drive will be over soon.

ASE. I will lie back and close my eyes
then, and trust me to you, my boy!

PEER. Come up with you, Grane, my
trotter! In the castle the throng is
great; they bustle and swarm to the
gateway. Peer Gynt and his mother
are here! What say you, Master
Saint Peter? Shall mother not enter in? You may search a long time,
I tell you, ere you find such an honest old soul. Myself I don't want
to speak of; I can turn at the castle
gate. If you'll treat me, I'll take it
kindly; if not, I'll go off just as
pleased. I have made up as many
flimflams as the devil at the pulpit-
desk, and called my old mother a
hen, too, because she would cackle
and crow. But her you shall honour
and reverence, and make her at
home indeed; there comes not a
soul to beat her from the parishes

nowadays. —Ho-ho; here comes
God the Father! Saint Peter! you're
in for it now! (*In a deep voice*)
"Have done with these jack-in-of-
fice airs, sir; Mother Ase shall enter
free!" (*Laughs loudly, and turns
towards his mother*) Ay, didn't I
know what would happen? Now
they dance to another tune! (*Un-
easily*) Why, what makes your eyes
so glassy? Mother! Have you gone
out of your wits—? (*Goes to the
head of the bed*). You mustn't lie
there and stare so—! Speak, mother;
it's I, your boy! (*Feels her forehead
and hands cautiously; then throws
the string on the chair, and says
softly:*) Ay, ay! —You can rest yourself, Grane; for even now the journey's done. (*Closes her eyes, and
bends over her.*) For all of your
days I thank you, for beatings and
lullabys! —But see, you must thank
me back, now—(*Presses his cheek
against her mouth*) There; that was
the driver's fare.

2. *As You Like It*, Shakespeare, Act III, Scene 2. The setting is the
idyllic Forest of Arden. Rosalind, masquerading as a young man, has met
Orlando, with whom she is in love, and before whom she plays her part
with dash and *élan*, drawing from him the ready admission that he is in
love with—Rosalind.

Ros. . . . There is a man haunts the
forest that abuses our young plants
with carving "Rosalind" on their
barks, hangs odes upon hawthornes
and elegies on brambles—all, forsooth, deifying the name of Rosalind. If I could meet that fancy-
monger, I would give him some

good counsel, for he seems to have the quotidian of love upon him.

ORL. I am he that is so love-shak'd. I pray you, tell me your remedy.

Ros. There is none of my uncle's marks upon you. He taught me how to know a man in love; in which cage of rushes I am sure you are not prisoner.

ORL. What were his marks?

Ros. A lean cheek, which you have not; a blue eye and sunken, which you have not; an unquestionable spirit, which you have not; a beard neglected which you have not. But I pardon you for that for, simply, your having in beard is a younger brother's revenue. Then your hose should be ungarter'd, your bonnet unbanded, your sleeve unbutton'd, your shoe untied, and every thing about you demonstrating a careless desolation. But you are no such man: you are rather point device in your accoutrements, as loving yourself, than seeming the lover of any other.

ORL. Fair youth, I would I could make thee believe I love.

Ros. Me believe it? You may as soon make her that you love believe it, which I warrant she is apter to do than to confess she does. That is one of the points in the which women till give the lie to their consciences. But, in good sooth, are you he that hangs the verses on the trees, wherein Rosalind is so admired?

ORL. I swear to thee, youth, by the white hand of Rosalind, I am that he, that unfortunate he.

Ros. But are you so much in love as your rhymes speak?

Notes

ORL. Neither rhyme nor reason can express how much.

Ros. Love is merely a madness and, I tell you, deserves as well a dark house and a whip as madmen do. And the reason why they are not so punish'd and cured is that the lunacy is so ordinary that the whippers are in love too. Yet I profess curing it by counsel.

ORL. Did you ever cure any so?

Ros. Yes, one, and in this manner: he was to imagine me his love, his mistress, and I set him every day to woo me. At which time would I— being but a moonish youth—grieve, be effeminate, changeable, longing and liking, proud, fantastical, apish, shallow, inconstant, full of tears, full of smiles; for every passion something, and for no passion truly anything, as boys and women are for the most part cattle of this color. Would now like him, now loathe him; then entertain him, then forswear him; now weep for him, then spit at him; that I drave my suitor from his mad humor of love to a living humor of madness, which was to forswear the full stream of the world and to live in a nook merely monastic. And thus I cur'd him, and this way will I take upon me to wash your liver as clean as a sound sheep's heart, that there shall not be one spot of love in't.

ORL. I would not be cured, youth.

Ros. I would cure you, if you would but call me Rosalind, and come every day to my cote and woo me.

ORL. Now, by the faith of my love, I will. Tell me where it is.

Ros. Go with me to it, and I'll show

it you. And by the way you shall
tell me where in the forest you live.
Will you go?

ORL. With all my heart, good youth.

Ros. Nay, you must call me Rosalind.
Come. Will you go?

3. *Additional Suggestions.* Additional suggestions for studies in the Romantic genre: *Maria Stuart,* Schiller; *Twelfth Night* and *Midsummer Night's Dream,* Shakespeare; *Cyrano de Bergerac* and *L'Aiglon,* Rostand; *If I Were King,* McCarthy; *Elizabeth the Queen* and *Mary of Scotland,* Anderson.

The Fop • The fop is an eccentric cousin of the Romantic character. Played entirely by men, he is one who apes his more balanced relative, but is deterred by some quirk of character from having the other's normalcy. Generally the twist in his personality comes from a top-heavy ego that causes him to overdo all his social manners. He has had his vogue in France and England, shining with particular brilliance on the Restoration and eighteenth-century British stage.

He is a wonderful fellow to play. Unaware of his exaggeration as seen by others, he esteems himself as the epitome of grace, fashion, elegance, and wit. All is overdone. He takes his snuff with too much display of his snuffbox, he brings the pinch up to his nose with too much flick of the wrist, and he later brushes his clothes with a too large and lacy handkerchief. When his hat comes off his head we are aware of the hand and the wrist going up, and of the too full sweep of the article coming down, accompanied by a twist or turn of the wrist that gives us an extra flourish.

Yet he is not awkward. Genuine grace is the foundation of all his movements. He cannot help being effeminate, but is never more than that, and it is a mistake to dwell on that characteristic in the hope of gaining easy laughs.

His ego gives him great vitality, which he expends in petty manifestations. He has a curious kind of poise, an attribute that can easily slide into effrontery. And he can have wit. Hungry for attention, he continually poses, and at the same time, as a subconscious cover-up, he affects indifference to the attentions of others.

Physical Characteristics • Physically, the fop is realized by a delicate type of muscular activity throughout the entire body. His assumed attribute of indifference causes his movements to be languid. Lassitude shows itself in his stance and the carelessness with which he lets a chair or divan support his person. The placement of body weight is mostly passive and is shown by resting the body mass on the heel of the back foot when standing and on a somewhat curved spine while sitting, unless an arm, consciously but carelessly draped along the back of a sofa, also assumes a little of his support. On the other hand, when an item of gossip piques his interest his whole body becomes active. He stands, walks, and sits with a very narrow base.

The trunk exhibits the poise he possesses by being quite straight, with abdomen in and chest out. The shoulders are more set than stiff, showing his determination to be recognized as a superior being. The elbows extend out from the torso, favoring a right-angled forearm, which is held part way across the body. A flexible wrist permits the hand to be busy (but not random), touching the clothes, arranging a lace cuff here and calling attention to the elegance of a waistcoat there. Handkerchiefs, snuffboxes, and gloves supply a motivation for restless hand activity, which, on the stage, is more suggested than real.

Liking the feel of fine things, the tactile sense is well developed, consequently the fingertips are alert and practiced in constant contact with objects, resting on what is fancied, drawing away from what is not.

The head, held aloof, favors little turns and twists that break the straight vertical line, which in a more forthright person runs the length of the body. Disdain, superciliousness, and affected unconcern are balanced by avidity of interest, a sensory alertness and an insatiable curiosity, causing the pull up and back of the head to alternate with a forward thrust in which the chin leads and the eyes squint with intensity and blink with excitement. Unless hot on the scent of a piece of gossip or a tasty tidbit of scandal, the brows are lifted and held in that position for a longer period of time than for any other type of character; assumed boredom prompts this action.

The eyelids droop, as befits one who is not moved to give the world too much of his attention, when this mood is upon him. Conversely, they can be held wide in amazement on hearing an unexpected rumor, or can squint in disdain at the sight of a coarse action or object. The mouth goes round when necessary to match the opening of the eyes. Additionally, two other positions are shown by a variance between a pursed and prissy position and the supercilious smile that moves off center and to one side.

When the fop is acting his part in society, the movements of any portion of the body are never gross and seldom large. He is a creature of wonderful contrasts, now languorous in studied unconcern, his eyes focusing on nothing and taking in everything, his hand toying absently with a ring he wishes seen, and then again busy with movements charged with the energy of curiosity or titillated into liveliness by flattery. Egocentric, the fop is always aware of what he is doing, even when he seems least to be so. Ego-hungry, he is never unaware of all that transpires around him.

The fop requires an expert sense of timing of the actor, sharp awareness of the center of interest, an unusual degree of flexibility, boldness in commitment of self to a somewhat eccentric personality, sympathy with a character that has more hungers than satisfactions, and abundant vitality that manifests itself in full freedom of release.

EXERCISES AND ASSIGNMENTS

1. Although she is never called upon to play a fop, the actress can still find profit in exercising in his manner. Both male and female should create and perform a pantomime of a fop in one of these situations: dressing in preparation for morning calls, taking a dish of chocolate at a popular coffeehouse, circling a room at a *soirée*, using a mask, and sharing a snuffbox in a corner while at a gala.

2. Different manifestations of a basic character, Witwoud and Petulant in Congreve's *The Way of the World* demonstrate the fop in action. As an example, or for practice and presentation, see Act III, Scene 3.

3. Other plays with scenes that feature the fop are *Love for Love*, Congreve; *The Man of Mode* or, *Sir Fopling Flutter*, Etherege; *The Plain Dealer*, Wycherley; *The Relapse*, Vanbrugh; *The Careless Husband*, Cibber.

NATURALISM AND REALISM

Here are two terms the distinction between which has plagued students of the theatre for several generations. Both are theatre movements, and both began at approximately the same time. Each had and has much in common with the other, and unfortunately the two are often used interchangeably. Indeed, from one point of view it can be urged that the difference between them is merely academic. Certainly many stage directors use the terms as synonyms, meaning the same thing when they say, "You are too stiff, be more natural in that action," or "Your movement is too artificial, make it more realistic." However, a simple distinction can be made between the two.

Naturalism, like Romanticism, was initiated in Paris. Emile Zola was the leader of the movement. He, like Victor Hugo, was better known as a literary than a dramatic writer. In revolt against both Neoclassicism and Romanticism, the new genre reflected the deep impact made by the surge of scientific thought that was sweeping all of Europe. So wondrously revealing were the discoveries in this new field of human inquiry that the tendency grew to give all credence, in creative as well as materialistic matters, to an objective and scientific way of looking at things. Everything in life, it was believed, could be analyzed, and as a result more accurate knowledge would be gained in the process. Let the stage reproduce a picture of society, the proponents of the new thought said, as the microscope reproduced a view of the teeming world below the level of ordinary eyesight, and a true justification of its place in a country's culture would be made. No longer an agent of escape into entertainment, the drama was to be an instrument of instruction, and demonstrated truth was to be the result.

Une tranche de vie was the cry. Put a slice of life on the stage and let the scientific approach prevail. Don't interpret; reproduce, for only reproduction can be trusted. Do not select and reject until you get a representation of what you wish to say, but show the life of man as it is, for only in the mosaic of detail reproduced exactly can truth be found.

All this meant that the actor was to act onstage as he did in life. It further indicated that little stages and small audiences were necessary, and that sets of living rooms and street corners were to be copied from the real thing. It also meant (horror of horrors) that the player might occasionally turn his back on the audience. It signified that the statuesque postures of Neoclassicism and the sweeping but unnaturalistic action of Romanticism had to give way to truth as revealed in lifelike movement.

For a time Naturalism prevailed. During its vogue a basis was established for the kind of movement employed everywhere in the western world today. Unfortunately, Naturalism was a dead-end street as far as dramatic creativity was concerned. With the artistic essential of selection and rejection disavowed, the actor simply could not express how he felt about what he was doing. Exact reproduction assigned him a mechanical role—and denied him one of his major motivations for going into the theatre—namely, to express what he thought and felt in the extraordinary manner the dramatic manner of self-expression provided.

It is practically impossible for any person living today to say whether there was any real distinction between the Naturalistic and the Realistic acting of the late nineteenth century. There was a notable difference in the way plays were written, as a comparison between the works of Zola and Ibsen will disclose. But it is questionable whether anything more than a modification of the first extremes of Naturalism took place in the transient art of acting when Realism took over, obtaining and maintaining a position not relinquished to this day. If a difference between these blood-brother styles had to be found, it might best be stated in the fact that Realistic acting, while equally concerned with truth to nature, also recognized that acting is a convention, an artificiality, a distortion of the acts of nature as required by the physical properties and limitations of the theatre and the dramatic form of expression.

In short, Realistic acting is the process whereby the positions, movements, and tones executed on stage seem to be as like their primary-source counterparts as is possible while still meeting the requirements of the shared dramatic experience. This is the method of composition Ibsen followed as the pioneer and recognized leader of the Realistic movement. Working in Norway at the same time as Zola was writing in Paris, but living on the periphery of the western cultural world, his ideas required more time to create a response. Once established, however, his work and his manner were marked as permanent, and his position of prominence was secured for his time and ours.

Thus it is that the style of acting you have employed in most of your work has been in the realistic manner. Few, if any, of today's actors employ the restricted form of Naturalism, except those whose need is for the practice of psychodrama rather than sociodrama. Those are the ones who need a strong, self-oriented experience that is *watched* by others— reminiscent of the child who cries to his elders "Watch me, watch me!" —as contrasted with the actors who create an experience that is *shared* with others. Your training has been oriented to the sociodramatic form, that being essential to the communal nature of the theatre.

There is little need for practice in Naturalistic playing—if, indeed, anyone could exactly demonstrate the style. Regarded today, even Zola's work—*Thérèse Raquin* was his most notable play—reads as flamboyantly romantic and melodramatic.

As for Realistic acting, the most activity seen today on the stages of both America and Europe is in that genre. Such has been the concentration in this book on a mastery of the realistic style that a description of its physical characteristics such as has accompanied the previous discussions in this chapter, would be quite redundant. At the same time it must be stated emphatically that excellence in the practice of any other style will serve to increase proficiency in this, the one principal style that probably will be the mainstay of any professional life.

ANTIREALISTIC STYLES

There have been many antirealistic styles of writing for the theatre. There are few antirealistic methods of acting. The form of stage settings in such genres as Expressionism, Constructivism, and Symbolism have all been markedly antirealistic in nature. But it is difficult to denote a clear-cut style of acting representative of any of the above. Consequently, it must be stated that, of all the arts of the theatre, that of acting is the least distorted from the Realistic form, even when employed in an antirealistic drama.

When an actor plays in a Symbolist play, he may have a different sort of line to deliver, he may speed up or slow down his tempo, he may have a radical change of costume and makeup, but the basic patterns of his acting will still take identity from their verisimilitude to realistic movements. There is no set Symbolic way of acting, nor Expressionistic nor Futuristic. Thus, for a great many antirealistic genres, the player's task is more to change the character of his thought and feeling than it is to alter his movement.

Certain antirealistic styles, however, are easily discernible and quite pleasurable to play.

The Mechanical Style • Employable in a pantomime about either toys or modern machines, this manner of moving is known to all of us. The body and its attachments simply recreate the angular, stop-and-go action of a machine, be it clock, typewriter, toy soldier, lawnmower, or huge stamp press. Always the movements of the automaton, controlled by an external power source, are present. Always there is a lack of human warmth; at best only painful attempts are made to achieve some human attributes. The robot, of which there are many kinds, is a prime demonstrator of mechanical movement.

This style is an excellent one for the pantomimist to work on. Calling for precision and control, it also offers a challenge to the imaginative powers of the creator. Whether you endow the subject with human characteristics or attempt to capture what you believe to be the spirit of a machine, variance from the usual routine is called for.

Fantasy • Strictly speaking, there is no such thing as a fantasy style in acting. There is, however, a sizeable number of plays, and good ones too, written in the fantasy vein, and they call for acting suited to the material. Definitely antirealistic, fantasy has many possible shapes. Its title immediately associates the subject with that vast flood of imaginings whereby the human mind finds release from the routine thoughts of daily life. A fantasy idea is an escape idea, and it can go in any one of several directions: our minds can conjure up images of horrible objects, animals, or events, and by the mechanics of the same act visualize scenes and persons of beauty and delight.

The childlike attitude is always a possibility in the creation of fantasy.

Growing out of a state of innocence, or at least of unawareness of the workings of the world, images of the near-perfect and the all-evil indicate something of the simple dichotomy of attitude present in our early years. There is an imaginative stretch in this kind of mental action that permits a wide range of subject material. Less learned, the child is less restricted by the firm facts of reality and so can let the mind go a-conjuring with much more ease than its grown-up brother or sister.

But older minds have need of escape into fantasy, too, as your own experience will testify. Here the employment may be more utilitarian, reflecting the drives, or the need for opposition to drives, of everyday life. The grown-up's fantasy can be benign or horrendous in a life situation and in a dramatic creation.

When you function as an interpreter of fantasy, the challenge is to your ability to catch the spirit of the thing you represent, whether it is a pantomime of a flower coming into bloom, the reading of verse in a children's program, or the creation of a character in Barrie's *Peter Pan*. Movement and tone will be more realistic than anything else; the attitude that informs the action will provide the distinction you seek.

Some plays that feature fantasy-like attitudes are *Aria da Capo* by Edna St. Vincent Millay, the plays of J. M. Barrie, *The Scarecrow* by Percy Mackaye, any play with a dream sequence, and, of course, the increasing number of plays for children's theatre that are coming off the presses.

Examples • Examples of antirealistic plays are: *The Intruder* or *The Blue Bird*, Maeterlinck; *The Spook Sonata*, Strindberg; *R. U. R.* or *The Insect Comedy*, Capek; *From Morn To Midnight*, Kaiser; *The Adding Machine*, Rice; *Blood Wedding*, Lorca; *Peter Pan*, Barrie; *End Game*, Beckett; *The Sandbox*, Albee.

FARCE

Properly speaking, farce is not a style of acting. Unlike the other genres we have discussed, farce is not a movement with a philosophy behind it that motivates a particular form of acting. It is rather a division of the drama, and its beginnings go farther back than the first records of accountable history. When some ancestor of ours, longer ago than can be reckoned, took an inadvertent pratfall and heard the laughter of his fellows, not as mockery, but as a heart-warming stimulus to further action, farce was born. Whether it is a beneficent gift or a wondrous development of human capability, farce has been a boon to man through all the ages of his life. Although it is not a style, the justification for its inclusion here lies in the benefit and the pleasure to be derived from its study and practice.

Farce seems easy, but its practitioners testify that it is difficult. When questioned about the various kinds of acting, the great David Garrick is said to have exclaimed, "Ah, farce—now, there's a serious business." And so it is, which does not mean that it is any the less enjoyable—for all the skill and ability necessary for its successful execution.

For our study of the nature of farce, we must begin with this: Farce is a state of mind, an emotional attitude, one that prompts its owner to snap his fingers at normalcy and social convention and to plunge boldly into the creation of improbable situations, characters, and actions. First, last, and always one must feel the zany to play the zany. Farce is an attitude toward life in which all is exaggerated, and in which nothing is tolerated that is sober, conventional, or serious. Mirth is the aim, abandoned laughter that shakes the physical frame is the goal. We need laughter, which is none the less hearty for all the therapeutic value it contains, that impulsively springs out of matter that is either straight fun or satirical comment.

Whatever the subject, the antic action that depicts an improbable character involved in an incongruous or ludicrous situation contains the core of farce. Filled with unexpected twists and turns of circumstance, the farcical scene moves with a swift pace, too swift for considered judgement to function. If it did not move thus, the whole enterprise would soon have to sober up.

We of the theatre have had a tendency to give the highest place of honor to our serious and tragic works. This is entirely justified, provided we never forget that two masks are used to represent the drama, and that high tragedy has never really stood alone but has always been buttressed or balanced by the more lusty and earthy form of farce. The Greeks knew this, and set up two festivals to honor Dionysus, the god of the theatre. Nor has it been forgotten since. The greatest periods of theatrical history have featured both masks, and sometimes it has been the comic face of farce that has had the higher station, as the history of the *commedia dell'arte* and the works of Molière will testify—Shakespeare can only be said to have matched himself with greatness in both areas. Every generation needs a full allocation of farce and can have it, provided the people of the theatre are willing to go after the disciplined mastery it entails.

More physical and emotional than intellectual, farce requires few nuances of meaning or movement. The desirability of a broad and obvious effect sets the tone and determines the requirements. A sense of and an appreciation for the absurd must be reckoned one of the first components of the farce complex; it is the source that supplies the energy for the improbable activity of the form. Frozen face or ribald grimace, the spirit of exaggerated fun should permeate every effort in this genre, letting the appropriate inner state flow freely in wholesome release.

The next requirement is vitality. The antic gesture of this form demands the most vigorous action of them all. In this case the farceur must truly work at his calling. In heavy costume or in padded clothes, moving under stage lights, the player sweats away the pounds. It is no calling for the weak or indolent actor. Blows that hit and blows that miss and falls that make a fearful sound are all part of the stock-in-trade. The actor who does not feel as if he has put a good day's work into his two or two and a half hours of traffic on the stage has left something out of his playing.

Flexibility, with its concomitant of control, is necessary, and it must be a flexibility as inwardly oriented as it is outwardly shown. In spirit and in body, the requirements of this broadest of comic shapes cause the player to express all manner of thoughts and emotions. Derisive, mocking, sometimes cruel, often sympathetic, wherever man, the social creature, has performed an indiscretion or overreached himself in prideful or pompous action, there farce will choose a subject, the expression of which is bound to call for expert manipulation of any and all parts of the player's body.

An acute awareness of a fast tempo is also essential. In this kind of playing an idea must be broadly stated, without subterfuge or depth, or the humor of the style is lost. Briskness of pace is one of the means by which this is done. In effect, the actors must always be ahead of the audience, allowing no time for the development of reasonable sensibilities.

A sense of timing must be accompanied by an awareness of the need for exactitude in movement. Sloppiness of action ruins comic effects, and movement that is slurred or inept can be hazardous in the rough and tumble of fights, chases, trips, and falls.

A definite part of the technique of farcical playing is allocation of the right amount of time for the creation of effects. The coordination of action and timing must in many cases be as precise as a sequence in a ballet and requires as much time in setting and practicing it. For difficult action units, the use of slow motion is of great value, permitting exactness of coordination not possible in a regular tempo.

If the body is afraid of giving and taking blows, if the spirit is doubtful about the validity of the comic statement, if the personality shies away from the foolishness of playing the fool, the player is bound to find much lacking in his work. Freedom of release is essential, for fun cannot be restricted and still be fun.

Examples • For study and exercise material, Aristophanes, Shakespeare, and Molière are good sources. *The Rivals* by Sheridan provides as many farce scenes as *She Stoops To Conquer*. *The Boor* and *The Marriage Proposal* by Chekhov are outstanding examples of the farcical one-act play. Interestingly enough, Beckett's *Waiting for Godot* employs farce, as do such other theatre-of-the-absurd plays as *The Rhinoceros* and *Oh, Dad, Poor Dad, Etc.*

MIME

America has no pantomime theatre. France does, although it is not called by that name. The art of mime supplies the form and the title for that country's unique style of expression. Derived from the Greek word *mimesis* and coming directly from the Latin term *mime*, its action follows the definition of neither of those words. In type of activity, character, and concept, the French *mime* is closer to the *commedia dell'arte* stage than to any other known form.

Mime differs from pantomime more in degree than in form. Like pantomime, its artistry lies in its disciplines of illusion and in its dynamic, definite, economic, and telling movement. It, too, features solo performers working on a bare stage, presenting characters in situations with genuine originality and remarkable simplicity.

But mime and pantomime are not the same. They differ principally in this: the mime distorts actions more than the generally realistic pantomime does, giving itself greater scope in the expression of fantasy and abstraction. On the other hand, pantomime relates itself to its primary sources in more recognizable forms than does its sister art. Both, of course, are silent. Mime also uses a costume, distorted much as the *commedia* clothes were, to which is added the unique feature of a mask-like makeup. The all-white face is an artistic touch that produces a bland neutrality that at the same time permits great mobility. As a point of departure for the facial movements of any character, the unrelieved features of the mime are hard to surpass.

In mime, movements that are sometimes so tight as to seem angular are also possessed of a singular grace. Sparse in action to the extent that economy of movement seems quite severe, the form still abounds with freedom and flexibility of expression. Sharp, vital, regulated fluency marks a style that lends itself to the creation of Chaplin-like characters as well as to the projection of Aristophanic comments. Always the body of the performer reveals to other theatre folk the ardor of its preparation and the sense of pleasure it takes in its performance.

As training for a career in mime, dance exercises and practices are as practical as the usual forms of actor preparation. The degree of stylization is so marked as to require this. By the same token it is possible that the heightened exaggeration employed by the actor-mime makes his work less susceptible of transfer into the idiom of the realistic stage than almost any other form.

Asking which is the greater art form, mime or pantomime, is both unnecessary and fruitless. In America we have neither, save for a few valiant but scattered individual efforts, yet either would be most welcome.

Chapter 23

The Creative Cycle

Acting is creative because it must synthesize into an ordered whole facts and feelings that in life are often disparate and disordered. The ability to do this is dependent upon (1) accurate observation—seeing things as others do, and also as others do not, (2) independent cognition —freeing the mind to make new thoughts from old patterns, and (3) dynamic imagination—from established order creating new order.

THE CYCLE

A straight line might represent the progress of a manufactured product from its origin to its ultimate destination. A circle would be better to describe the progress of an art product from inception to completion. The difference between the line and the circle is important. The line does not return to itself; the circle does.

If man is primarily concerned with himself, it follows that he is interested in any or all portions of the human story he finds personal and applicable to himself. Because he is a portion of that story, he has at least a latent interest in all of it. If he does not himself possess the impulse, the energy, and the imagination to break through inertia and rouse himself to active expression of this latent interest, he can appreciate and applaud the act when someone else, the artist, does it for him. This is the appeal of the dramatic experience. This is why the spectator comes to the theatre, to find the aid he requires to break himself out of his own static state and over into the audience's kind of active participation. He comes also because the main story told there is primarily about him.

The theatre touches on that story in intense and concentrated fashion. What man has done, is doing, will do in the future are food for the drama. This is a broad sweep of subject material. It is broader than all history, for history must stop with the present. But even as large as this field is, it can be increased, for man is sometimes as interested in the possible as he is in the actual. Add to the above, then, the element of supposition—what man might have done, might be doing, or might do in the future and we have a field of subject matter so vast it almost

371

defies conception. But at some time or other, or in one way or another, the theatre has probed at and touched upon most of it. How can the individual escape inclusion in this vast sweep? He cannot, and he will not, as long as he can see that what is happening onstage bears a personal and unmistakable pertinence to him.

The actor goes to the life around him to gather the information and the inspirations that feed his labors. The characters he creates and the situations in which they are involved must originate in his own experiences, or from the experiences of others he knows. As an artist he has a more acute and better trained perception than the nonartist. He can see not only what the fellow creatures of his society do, but why they do what they do. He can recognize in what context actions are significant, and so recognizing, use that knowledge to form the basis for the truth of that particular portion of the human story he is going to develop.

This, then, is the theatre artist's circle. He draws his materials from the society around him. He translates knowledge of his materials into the particular art form in which he works. When his materials are properly shaped, he sends out the notices that bring the public into the auditorium seats, and gives back his materials to the very people from whom he got them in the first place. The circle is complete, and all the people in the theatre, those out front and those backstage, are glad that this is so. This is the basis on which any art, and the art of the theatre particularly, must exist. Nor does it differ whether the lightest comedy or the heaviest tragedy is being played.

This is the magic cycle. But why magic? Is there something of mystery inherent in the dramatic experience and in the institution we call theatre?

Somewhere along the way, some time in the process of change from the actual to the illusion of the actual, some indefinable element, an element we can never quite catch and hold long enough to mold into the shape of an expressible idea, some tingling element that will not show itself and yet will insist upon being present, enters into the work of creation.

Who knows what extra thing it is the sculptor puts into his stone that makes it more than a copied figure? Who knows what intangible element it is that works into and then out of the mind of a composer and gets down on paper and makes his composition a work of art and not a musical exercise? Who knows what it was that made Thespis, the single man, the more than single man he became when he was Thespis the actor?

Men have sought for ages to catch in words the meaning and the source of the spirit of art. In our own time we still try, and the full answer still eludes us. Our search is interesting and necessary, but it is not critical. What is said and written about artistic creativity is of secondary importance. As long as the magical properties of art are contained in the work itself, the spirit of creation is secure, and the cycle remains unbroken.

Appendices

Appendix A

Pantomime by Parts

The expressive potential of the human form offers challenging possibilities to the actor who desires more detailed information about the dramatic functioning of all parts of the body. The following material[73] is offered as a reference work for those who would undertake such a study. Suggested exercises and assignments are given at the end of each section so that theory may be implemented by practice.

A specialist in any field knows his activity as a whole and at the same time is expert in the manipulation of its parts. Mastery is a necessary feature of expertness. To become a specialist in pantomime, it is necessary to achieve mastery of the individual elements of the art. This requires taking apart units that had previously been carefully put together.

The extent of segmentation required is considerable but not complex. The activity can be divided into two phases: one, the separation of the constructed pantomime into basic units of activity and, two, the division of the actor's body into its components of legs and feet, arms and hands, head and face, and torso and shoulders. The first separation produces a basic *action unit*, the second a basic *body unit*.

ACTION UNITS

An action unit is the smallest segment of a pantomime (or a scene) that has a unity and completeness of its own. This definition rules out of consideration the primary units of a pantomime, namely the single separate movements that, one by one, like the strides in a walk, carry the pantomime forward. Although attention must be paid to these individual movements, it is the unit made up of a series of single movements, those phased to form a unified action, that is the center of interest now.

For example, a pantomime of a teen-ager slipping into the kitchen to steal a piece of party cake contains several clear-cut action units. They are indicated by (a), (b), etc. Note that each is composed of its series of single movements. (a) The pantomimist enters and cautiously approaches an imaginary kitchen door; a hand reaches for the handle, slowly turning it;

---

[73] See "Guidelines for Use," pp. xi-xii.

the door is quickly opened; the player's head peers around the edge to see if the room is empty; satisfied that it is, the body quickly slips through the narrow opening; turning, the pantomimist softly closes the door. (b) Turning again, the player looks at the refrigerator; a smile of anticipation comes to the face; quickly a cross is made; the refrigerator door is opened—but the cake is not there. (c) The player stands motionless, frowning in thought; turning, the eyes check the drainboard, then move from cupboard to cupboard; the look focuses on one set of shelves; again the smile comes to the face; (d) the refrigerator door is closed; the pantomimist crosses to the sink; reaching underneath, the hands bring out a small kitchen stool; crossing again, the stool is placed in front of the special cupboard. (e) There is a pause while the young, would-be thief listens; then the feet step up on the stool and the body is raised to a level with the upper shelves—the cake is there, the smile on the face tells us so. (f) Again there is a pause as the pantomimist listens for sounds of danger; again the action continues as the cake plate is lifted clear; it is held carefully as the body comes down to the floor; it is set on the drainboard and the glass cover is lifted off; the player's eyes shine and the tongue comes out to run along the edges of the lips. (g) Quickly a cross is made to a drawer; a knife is taken out; a return is made to the cake; the knife is held ready to make the first cut; an offstage noise is heard—and here we can interrupt the pantomime to check what has already occurred.

Seven action units were completed, each composed of several single movements. The unit divisions were obvious and the blocks were logical and easy to locate. As a matter of fact, they might have appeared so logical that it seems unnecessary to go to the trouble to set them up in the first place. The important point is, however, that if a specific action of this nature is not taken, general and characterless flow of movement can result, and while a story is revealed clearly enough, it can lack distinction and interest.

The practicality of the action-unit concept to the pantomimist (and later to the actor) lies in the fact that it permits focus of concentration on a unit of manageable proportions. An action unit is like the individual play in baseball, in which several single movements coalesce into one well-defined unit of action. In baseball, the various plays differ in importance and intensity; so do the action units in a pantomime. The significant fact is that each play or basic action unit, when in progress, receives the full concentration of each performer just as if it were the only unit or play to be enacted.

Actors, with equal concern and with just as much at stake, would do well to emulate the situation in baseball in which every player on both teams, on the field or in the dugout, is required as a matter of professional efficiency to follow the action of each unit of play with complete attention. While it is in progress, no matter what its place in the whole scheme, each play (action unit) is *the* important fact of existence in the life of every player.

SUGGESTED EXERCISES AND ASSIGNMENTS

There are four things to emphasize in these exercises: the defined limits of the action unit, the importance of the individual movements within the unit, the smooth flow of continuity between the units, and a full commitment of attention on the part of the player.

Following the model of the cake pantomime, write out two such exercises. For greater concentration, limit the pantomimes to four or five action units. Ideas may be drawn from the following: leaving home, arriving at work, having lunch, skeet shooting, fishing, practicing a new dance step, trying to get comfortable for reading, trying on a new coat or dress.

Follow the writing by performance.

BODY UNITS

The purpose of dividing the body into individual units is twofold: to discover, out of the total number of things the body can communicate by movement what kind of pantomimic action each can best project and, by capitalizing on this knowledge, to increase by practice the expressiveness of each part.

The human body is singularly susceptible to division. Working from those easier of manipulation to the more difficult sections, the units are legs and feet, arms and hands, head and face, and torso and shoulders.[74]

As the first step in finding which function best suits which one of the four body divisions, it is necessary to turn directly to the action of the human form itself.

To begin the process, several commonplace actions should be selected and enacted. After this has been done, notations should be made of the fundamental movements performed. As a result, the functions of each basic body unit will begin to be manifest. Three actions of the kind needed would be to rearrange furniture in a room, finding several things that please and displease; to look for an address on a city street while carrying packages or a suitcase; to check, as a stage manager, the stage's playing area, correcting imaginary faults before calling places.

The findings of such a survey can be checked when they are compared with the material of each of the following sections. (Although the concentration is on the workings of the separate body units, it must be remembered that certain physical and psychological facts pertain alike to all portions of

[74] When performance is attempted, the problem is to confine all center of interest activity to that part of the body being placed in action, letting the rest of the body go into a state of nonactivity or neutrality, or at best responding with the simplest of complementary movements—for example, the eyes watching the hands and arms perform an entire pantomime by themselves. When the center of interest is elsewhere, the arms and hands can hang easily at the side of the body or be put into pockets or held behind the back. If, at any time, the eyes of an audience are compelled to focus on any portion of the body other than the one being featured, the performer has defeated his purpose.

the body—for instance, a young lady is not bold in the face and shy in the legs, a boy does not have the flu in his arms and not in his head, a coarse character does not have gross movement in his hands and not in his head and face. Unless physical injury or abnormality is intended, one area does not contradict another. An exception is found when a character experiences a contradiction—for example smiling while backing away in fear.)

PRIMARY AND SECONDARY FUNCTIONS

Before beginning an investigation of the functions of the basic body units, it must be noted that all portions of the body, when performing in a natural manner, employ both *primary* (major) and *secondary* (minor or complementary) movements. A primary movement denotes a functional action basic to an area, one that is performed better there than elsewhere. Pointing is done best by arm, hand, and finger. It can also be accomplished, but not as well, by a jerk of the head. Consequently, we designate pointing as a primary function of the arm, hand, and finger, and as a secondary function of the head.

You have probably already noted, in your own exploration, that the face expresses emotion best. Yet you can recall that closely clasped hands and twisting fingers also reveal emotional stress. The difference between the movements of these two areas is the difference between primary and secondary actions. When the hands and fingers, used to express an emotional condition, are also the center of interest, it follows that what is ordinarily secondary or complementary then becomes primary.

Sometimes such a distortion is good. When deliberately planned, it can become an action of some distinction, but the execution must be judiciously handled. An example can be given of a fighter at work in a ring. Practically all of a boxer's leg and foot action is of a secondary nature. If a boxing pantomime were to be performed employing the lower limbs only, the pantomimist would have to depend on the power of suggestion to aid his efforts in telling an audience what was happening in the upper, immobile part of his body. Skillfully executed, this could conceivably become an intriguing exercise. This thought, however, must be weighed against the possibility— if the pantomime is performed with anything less than exceptional skill— that the action could result in a guessing contest. It is necessary, therefore, to maintain clarity of thought about the primary and secondary functions of each portion of the body.

LEGS AND FEET

The legs and feet are the action agents of the body. They are the instruments of locomotion, capable of carrying the owner in all directions, forward and backward, from one side to the other, and up and down. The length of stride, the vitality in the muscles, the width of the base, the flex in the knees, the grossness or delicacy of muscular activity, the control of movement—these and other factors, mixed in multiple combinations, permit an unlimited variety of expressive movement. To go directly toward, to back away from, to stand against, to sidestep, to slide, stride, glide, creep, kick, push and run—these are other expressive possibilities of the agents of locomotion. The meaning of the action in the movements is revealed by what the legs and feet do; how the movements are done reveals the character of the doer.

The legs and feet support the body. Themselves weighing less, they hold up many more times their weight in the bulk of body above. Strength is one of their notable characteristics; power rides in every action. The most powerful line in the human body is the line of strength in the upper leg and thigh of the male. We are so used to this condition of potency we seldom recognize the energy exerted and released in every stride of the ordinary walk. The saying *to walk like a king* has connotations of grandeur, command, and dominion in it. The opposite of strength has a similar effect on the whole person, when the legs give way, the rest of the body is potentially impotent.

The legs and feet are the balancers of the body. Themselves occupying but a relatively small portion of floor space, they hold upright a mass of bone and muscle that extends up and out in every direction and encompasses a much larger area of displacement. Motionless or in movement, a precise and rather miraculous control is effected with little trouble to the conscious mind.

A fine or a poor balance is expressive of physical and psychological conditions in a character. When a broad base is employed in position and movement, it generally is associated with gross muscular activity; a narrow base is identified with more delicate action. Contradictions, however, are both rewarding and revealing. A broad base with the weight well forward and the body moving up and down over the balls of the feet is a prime position for the athlete who has agility as well as strength, while the body that is held in balance over the heels of the feet will imply a static condition for any character.

The legs and feet have important roles to play in maintaining personal security. Attack and defense are involved here. The lower limbs assume, with the arms and hands, the major burden in this respect, but with a difference in type of action. Distinctive and revealing are the actions of kicking, pushing, tripping, leaping, and lifting.

The Knees • The knees, together with the balls of the feet, are the body's principal elevators, lifting and lowering the mass above and any additional load the mass might contain. They bespeak vitality and flexibility, reflecting in their vigor and freedom of movement something of the physical state of the whole form. When the weight of the body is forward on the balls of the feet and the knees are bent in a position of readiness for action, the human form has achieved a state of aliveness, expectancy, and vitality difficult to surpass.

In all positions of kneeling the knees are like the feet, performing the same function of providing a base for the body; the same general rules that apply to the one act on the other. Thus, if a broad base is maintained by the feet, the knees will show a base only slightly less broad; this is as true for seated positions as for the action of kneeling. Not only do the knees, in a sitting position, show a broad or narrow base when the legs are held parallel to each other, the same holds true when the legs are crossed.

Inaction • It should not be overlooked that there is expressiveness in the inaction of the feet and legs. When such active agents are motionless, the very fact gives emphasis to the condition. Legs extended in a sprawl or tucked in close to the body or held tightly against the torso with the knees just below the chin are strong dramatic positions. When a person must wait for any reason, if standing, it is the legs and feet that bear the burden, and the placement of the body's weight reveals much about the conditions of waiting. Anxiety, impatience, resignation, three attitudes that normally are best expressed by the head and face, can here be projected with particular effectiveness; this is as true in a seated as in a standing position.

Walks • Walks, with extensions in one direction into running, jumping, and leaping, and retardations in the opposite of creeping, shuffling, and backing, are actions of particular concern to the pantomimist. For one thing, the concern must be for the expressive possibilities inherent in a good stage walk; what the legs and feet do indicate purpose as well as direction. With no intention of making a play on words, it can be said that, in many instances, walks keep a pantomime moving, carrying the work load of the story as agents of locomotion for the center of interest.

Action in a walk can sometimes tell the spectator the location of the scene, showing that the character is moving in mud or on a tightrope, on a sidewalk or in plowed ground, going uphill or down, feeling his way or walking with confidence. At the same time the manner in which these powerful limbs move indicates two other things: (1) what sort of a person it is that moves about—that is, state of health, weight of body, preciseness or slackness of muscular control, age as shown in degrees of vitality in the muscles and in the degree of articulation in the joints; (2) how the person feels about his place in his environment—that is, the sureness or the caution of the step, the pound of the heels, the aggressiveness of a kick, the resignation of a backward step, the bounce or the shuffle of the forward movement, and the tap of impatience.

SUGGESTED EXERCISES AND ASSIGNMENTS

1. Using only a few action units for each effort, practice the following exercises in illusion and control of movement: walking in mud, on a tightrope, in sand and rocks, up and down stairs, across a bog, in water, showing ill health, demonstrating injury, across a ballroom floor.

2. An exercise in characterization for legs, feet, and knees. Conceive a character and illustrate your conception by showing how it would walk, stand, jump,

go up and down stairs, and sit with legs crossed and uncrossed. Use only one action unit to each part of the exercise.

3. An exercise in occupational walks. It is a fallacy to assign certain stock characteristics to either persons or occupations. For all their military bearing, no two marines are exactly alike, nor any two schoolteachers, or farmers. But some occupations, because of the work requirements involved, do cause their adherents to form some special patterns of movement, or, to view the matter from another angle, some occupations, by putting a premium on certain types of physical qualities, attract into their ranks those who have such a physical makeup. Athletics, engineering, and dancing serve as examples.

With these conditioning statements in mind, prepare two walks. In performance, walk across the room (or stage) as one character and return as the other. Each cross should be done in three action units: a walk to stage center, an interruption of one sort or another, a walk off. Here are possible combinations: a nimble sailing-ship sailor—a coarse sailing-ship sailor; a scrubwoman—a majorette; an athlete—a track-walker; a headmistress—a model; a policeman—a bum; a ballet dancer—a WAC.

4. Complete pantomimes for legs, feet, and knees. All other portions of the body are to be in neutral or complementary positions and the center of interest is to remain only on the lower limbs. Characterization is to be strongly emphasized. Evolve your own story. If any aid is required, these one- and two-word suggestions may help to get you started: stream crossing, dark room, dance, corner waiting, edge of crowd, foot bath, shoe fitting, shackles, hopscotch.

Arms and Hands

The most utilitarian of all the divisions of the body, the arms and hands have many functions and serve many purposes. Although the feet contact the earth in a very elemental way, neither they nor any other part of a person relate the body to the environment in the manner the arms and hands do. In ceaseless and uncatalogued ways these flexible limbs perform their multiple functions. As part of a whole person they reveal the character of their owner just as the other sections do, showing physical, mental, emotional, and sensory states of being in a great variety of ways.

Gesture • Gesture is the term used to designate the actions of these members. Applied with equal justification to the expressive movements of other portions of the body, especially the face, the word gesture, in common usage, generally refers to the activity of arms, hands, and fingers.

If the truth were known, it would be found that while we recognize some movements as purely expressive gestures, for the most part we unconsciously think of gesture as an arm and hand accompaniment to speech, used more to support and give emphasis to verbalizations than to be independently expressive. One of the commonest faults in acting is the improper manipulation of these limbs when supporting speech, as manifested by too much movement or too little, by stiffness, or by lack of proper synchronization between utterance and gesture.

Communicators • In pantomime the arms, hands, and fingers are the body's prime communicators. They point directions and they wave instructions. They can make sure and exact descriptions of physical objects of all kinds. They aid in expressing abstract ideas. They were and are employed in the making of language symbols, sketching motions in the air that carry word meanings. (And they write—an action now so usual and so expected the miracle of its execution generally passes unnoticed.)

Militant Units • The arms, hands, and fingers are the principal aggressors and defenders of the body. Their facility of manipulation renders them particularly useful in this respect. In aggression they can hurl objects of many kinds, most of which they themselves have fashioned, and to considerable distances. Nearer, in the close contact of direct combat, they can strike with fist, palm, edge of hand, and elbow. They can grasp an object or a portion of a person to crush, push, pull, and control. In defense they ward off objects and blows. Themselves not nearly so vulnerable, they protect other more delicate parts such as head, eyes, abdomen, and genitals.

For clear, sharp, and immediately recognizable action, militant movement is hard to surpass. In the thrust and parry of physical conflict each action carries its own unmistakable meaning. There is nothing indefinite about the motions of arms that cover and circle the head; they say with great plainness that protection is needed and intended. When a slap is given or an arm twisted, ambiguity is never present. Any number of pantomimes can be built around the activity of arms, hands, and fingers as militant units, each primed for conflict. For example, using arms and hands only, in a pantomime for two, children might fight over a popcorn bowl; or, for comedy, a game of checkers might cause a fight between two old men. In a single pantomime, arms, hands, and fingers might struggle with a home-savings bank to make it give up its contents. The same members might be the paws of a cat in pursuit of a mouse, or they might fight against getting caught in the wheels of a machine.

Liaison Agents • Extensions rather than appendages, the sections of upper arm, elbow, forearm, wrist, hand, and fingers relate the body to the outside world. By touch they make contact. By gesture they can sever communications or connections between a person and his situation or, conversely, signify a desire for a more intense contact with persons or environment. Arms extended, palms facing outward—this is a gesture that tells whatever is there to stand off, stay away. Palm turned in, gesturing inward, and the message is given to advance, come closer. When arms are raised, palms cupped, the request for help we designate as prayer is made. Arms forward but angled out, with palms facing toward each other—this is the signal of welcome, an invitation to come close, be personal, make contact; arms wide and straight out from the shoulders with palm facing forward—a sending out of whatever intensity of spirit we contain; arms folded across the chest—the static condition of one who has arrived at a conclusion and indicates to the outside world that he will stand pat on it.

Because of the bulk of bone and the thickness of muscle contained there, the upper arm denotes strength of a healthy sort, unless age or illness has debilitated the area. For heavy work and large gestures or for forceful action it is the agent to be brought into play. The physical culture person who builds muscles never neglects this section, and the man who does heavy manual labor shows something of his occupation by the way the upper arm hangs down and slightly out from the side of the ribcage.

The elbow occupies three main positions, two of which are extreme. Generally hanging easily at the side, it acts as a hinge and a transition point for the movements above and below. Fulfilling these functions, it scarcely calls attention to itself. But when extended well out from the body and made into a point it unmistakably denotes aggression. A blow from the point can be a forceful action in a stage fight. An attitude of submission is projected when an opposite action is taken and the elbow is held close to the body's side.

The forearm is more easily moved than the upper arm, indicating less strength but more adroitness. Related directly to the hand much of the time, the two form a single semirigid unit for such activity as reaching, pushing, pulling, and pointing.

The wrist, like the elbow an important hinge in the arm, is equally busy. Held straight and made inflexible, it makes the hand an extension of the forearm. When released and permitted full freedom of movement, it becomes one of the most graceful parts of the body. Unless grossness is intended, it always leads the hand for both outward or unfolding gestures and inward for all opposite movements. When used too much by the female it denotes artificiality and affectedness. When too much prominence is given it by the male it indicates effeminacy. Its flexibility or lack of flexibility denotes the existence of the same condition in the physical or psychological structure of the owner's body.

The hands are wonderfully expressive units. With them we can say, without benefit of words, "The back of my hand to you," or "Give us this day our daily bread," or "The hand of friendship is extended." Age, physical condition, and personality structure can be told by these members. Moved as one unit in gesturing they indicate old age, or physical power, or a manual occupation, or individual coarseness. In youth, highly skilled persons, and intelligent people, a large amount of flexibility is usually present. The hand has various meaningful shapes: a fist, a semifist, a cup, a pointer—whole hand or single finger, and a holder. The position and the direction in which the palm of the hand faces is constantly revealing. Innumerable variations can be shown by the opposites of palm out and facing away or palm turned in and brought close to the body, or palm down and facing the ground or palm over and facing up. Better than a catalogue of possibilities is the proof of demonstration. On your own, put the palm into motion and arrive at your own conclusions from the positions of this flexible member and where it faces.

The fingers, exceptionally important to their owners in that the thumb is set in opposition to the other four members, also have innumerable actions as beneficial as they are revealing. They point, pinch, pull, push, snap, scratch, dig, hold, mold, clench, and manipulate. The thumb, unique by position and shape, is a most expressive unit. It has a strength matched only by the forefinger, and it reveals grossness as none of the others can: use it to point a direction, scratch an itch on the face or body or squash an object and you will see why.[75]

The forefinger is the master finger of the hand. When only one finger is required for an action, it is the one that responds. It has more flexibility, strength, and functional value than the others. Opposed to the thumb, it reveals opposition in more than position, having a sensitivity in its skin the other cannot match and capable of a refinement in movement that indicates at least some degree of intelligence on the part of its owner. In life it is used as a pointer; on stage it has the same function. Unfortunately, too many actors think that is its only use, and the wagging forefinger is used, act in and act out, to beat the air in an attempt at emphasis that could be better obtained in less monotonous ways.

The middle and the ring fingers seldom act individually. Each possesses a character of its own, but neither has much opportunity to reveal it. The size of the little finger indicates something of its character. Although it carries its share of the load in lifting and holding objects, when used separately it invariably suggests a delicateness that, if too pronounced, indicates affectation, artificiality, and, in a male, effeminacy. Yet, when working with the other fingers to cup as fragile an object as a baby's face, it can project a sense of tenderness obtainable in few other ways.

The Tactile Sense • The act of touch relates the individual to his environment. The tactile sense works two ways, sending messages in and passing them out. Although all the skin on the limbs is sensitive to contact, it is the pads on the inside and at the tips of the fingers that most surely and clearly tell the nature of the object touched. Was it for safety's sake that the portion of the body that can extend farthest, or that must cradle and hold objects before making use of them, was thus designated for such sensitive development?

At any rate, to touch and tell is one of the prime functions of the fingers. And to touch others and so express to them what is felt inside is another and similar act, but one in which the message goes in the opposite direction. By this means, in which we touch not to receive a message but to give one, we reveal ourselves to the external objects and the persons around us, signifying, in some cases, tenderness and love, care and affection, and in others anger, hate, or ill will.

[75] To arrive at further meanings follow the above actions with a duplicate set performed by the forefinger, and then by the little finger. Are not two things obvious? First, you probably felt the difference among the three by a change in your inner state of being; second, your mind told you what the difference was—two acts necessary to the process of comprehension.

A touch always signifies, or should, an intensification of the relationship between two people; this will be sacrificed or lost entirely if the contact is overdone or too indiscriminately used. A touch is a wonderfully revealing act, so much so it is a matter of acting misconduct to misuse it. A mother touches a child, a child touches a doll, a boy reaches for the hand of a girl, wonderingly lover touches the face of lover, and hands are clasped in sturdy friendship—all these are meaningful contacts. But a socially or politically inferior person does not touch a superior one; onstage casualness should not be permitted to intrude through thoughtlessness into any but a casual relationship.[76]

Holders • Among other functions the turning, twisting, extending, contracting limbs can hold objects. Whether it is finger against finger, finger against thumb, fingers against palm, arm against arm, or arms against body, the delicate yet firm, the intricate yet sure, the complex yet simple act of grasping is a commonplace miracle. Its benefit to mankind is obvious.

The Makers • Last but not least, the limbs that can touch, hold, push, pull, punch, poke, pat, cup, stroke, wave, finger, handle, slap, and jab can also *make*; hands and fingers are the great shapers of objects. Both utilitarian and esthetic, the products of man's handiwork fill the world. Although a pantomimist uses his limbs less to construct things onstage than to perform such other actions as opening doors, touching, turning, and handling objects of all kinds, it still is important to remember that the great and beneficent capability to make any and all sorts of things resides in the fingers and hands.

The Limbs and the Body • So far we have touched on the relationship of a character to his surroundings. Now we consider what happens when the arms, hands, and fingers relate themselves to a character's own body.

Hands and fingers not only move about in the air in the action of gesturing, they contact and play about each other in an interesting variety of ways. They are placed together in prayer, a fist pounds against a palm in frustration or for extra emphasis, one hand is gripped tightly by the other in anxiety, finger plays against finger in idleness. One hand scratches the other, one picks at the other's fingernails, both rub together in anticipation of a coming pleasure, or they lock in repose.

Personal contact continues as the hands and fingers touch or are placed upon or move about the other portions of the body. Observation indicates that the activity is almost continuous. The subtle implications of such contacts are many and complex. The basic meanings, however, are simple and obvious.

The guiding statement in this consideration is this: as a general rule, when

---

[76] When observing primary sources, note with special interest those involving physical contact. See if repetition dulls the act, check whether casualness reduces its importance. Also note those times when the contact is fitting and meaningful and the impact strong, and then judge if the act of physical contact, be it touch, stroke, or blow, is not best reserved for moments of increased intensity, at which time meanings otherwise lost are fully realized.

the hand goes to any one area of the body it identifies itself with the features or characteristics of that area. This is so not only when the limb is used in complementary movement, but even when it carries the center of interest. For example, if the fist must pound against the body, it is bound to be the focus of attention. But when the action is against the forehead it will not mean the same as when the hand is beaten against the thigh, the stomach, or chest. The same is true if the fingers touch an area or a hand rubs against it.

When the hand or fist is placed on the hips or around the thighs, an earthy, vigorous meaning is projected, one that partakes of the strength and vitality of an area where the promise of regeneration is contained and where the terminus of the great muscles of the upper leg is housed.

When the hands move upward a few inches and contact the abdominal walls meanings of a different sort are created. If the arms and hands spread to circle and cover this region, they call attention to the thinness and vulnerability of its muscle casing, and the act signifies protection. Without the circling, and with the hands in contact with the clothing over the visceral region the movement can say "My belly is full, I am well satisfied," and then, with but slight change in the hand action, say, "I hunger, I starve."

Romanticists have long endowed the spot on the chest above the heart as the contact point for expressions of love, tenderness, and affection. Wrong as they are,[77] and right as an iconoclast may be, we cannot break a tradition that has such a conveniently built-in meaning. Therefore, we must accept much of the contact between the hands and the heart area as intended to signify something pertinent to the tender passions.

The relationship between the limbs and the chest area is a different matter. If the arms are crossed and the hands are placed on opposite shoulders another strong protective movement is created. But generally, contact between the two areas indicates an expansion of feelings in the direction of confidence or pomposity.

Hands contact the face quite often, even to the extent that it is unsound to try to give all the reasons why. A couple of generations ago the elocutionists had answers. They used to say, for example, that forefinger placed on temple indicted thought. They were right, it does have that meaning, but no one today dreams of being so blatantly obvious. They had other similar observations to make, but since the execution always made the movement seem like a manufactured thing, their practices have deservedly fallen into disuse. We know that the fingers play around the mouth area in multiple actions. They stroke the nose and touch the forehead and temples in movement that is mainly complementary, as is scratching the head, pulling the ear lobe, and running the fingers through the hair. So active are they in this

[77] The heart is mainly a large, sturdy muscle incapable of initiating any feeling itself, and it only responds as a reacting organ to other more forceful stimuli; it is a gross muscle whose most endearing feature is its methodical and repetitious action.

regard that the pantomimist must be warned of a tendency to both random and covering movements.

Impulse Playing • So far the greater portion of the movements described have been of an unconscious nature—which leads to this point: in all life situations the vast majority of such movements are not consciously motivated. All portions of the body move in response to a subconscious impulse, none more than the arms, hands, and fingers. But onstage a different situation prevails. What was formerly left to chance motivation and unplanned impulse now becomes part of a planned and worked-out creation, one that only seems to be chancy. Indiscriminate and random, life-situation movements must yield, in playing, to a designed discipline. For that reason the nervous feelings of the pantomimist must never betray the owner through the character he creates. And for the same reason fewer movements must say more than is usual off the stage. What comes spontaneously in life must also come spontaneously on stage, but with this difference: the spontaneity is planned and canalized and thereby rendered much more effective.

This is not to say that impulse playing is improper and has no place in any scheme of acting. On the contrary, a response to impulse, coming at any time and on any occasion, is not only beneficial, it is impossible to avoid.

The caution is to be receptive but alert to the impetus an impulse prompts, checking each such spontaneous message against sound dramatic practice. As time goes on there is no doubt that the amount of impulse playing increases. If training is sound, the impulses that form will actually be marks of a well-organized and disciplined creativity. Then it is that creative abandonment within disciplined artistry is possible.

SUGGESTED EXERCISES AND ASSIGNMENTS

All pantomimes are for the arms, hands, and fingers only.

1. As an exercise rather than a complete pantomime, perform a problem of your own creation in which you emphasize the expressiveness inherent in the sense of touch. Introduce the element of contrast.

2. Perform another exercise in which the arms, hands, and fingers work militantly.

3. Create a complete pantomime in the realistic manner. Suggestions: a magic act, a card game, a chemistry experiment, traffic control, in church, in court, on the concert stage.

4. Create a complete pantomime of a fanciful or nonrealistic nature. Example: One hand represents a spider caught within the walls of a sink, the other hand is the drop of water that finally washes the insect down the drain.

HEAD AND FACE

Two areas, one contained within the other, combine to form what is probably the most distinctive feature of the human form. Whenever we think of another person and a visual image shapes itself in our mind, more often than not it is the head and the face that constitutes the subject of our image. Inseparable as they are, we still can focus our attention on each of these areas in single concentration.

The Head • The head is the least plastic and yet one of the most movable parts of the body. Incapable of changing its shape, it still can change its position by horizontal, vertical, and circular motions. Used always as a unit, it is capable of clear and forceful expression.

The primary function of the head in dramatic usage is to denote attitudes. Housing four senses in a small area, sight, hearing, taste, and smell, it assigns the first two to exceptionally heavy dramatic labors. Perhaps, since it is the senses that run the two-way connection between the individual and his environment, and because it is what we learn from our senses that causes us to form responses, we reckon attitude to be the most apt of expressions for the head.

When the head, face forward and at right angles to the line running from one shoulder tip to the other, moves up and down in a directly vertical action, two basic attitudes, one positive, one negative, are expressed. It is easy to see why these dichotomous terms were chosen: a positive attitude is one that is outgoing, moving from its base toward another person or object in expressions of either interest or dominance; a negative attitude is one that does not venture out but stays in, remaining self-contained in an expression of disinterest, fear, or abnegation.

Head bowed, forward of the shoulder line and lowered toward the ground, exposing the vulnerable portion of the back of the neck, denotes the negative act of submission. As with all other basic movements, it must have had this meaning since the beginning of man's time as a social animal. Whether the position takes its significance from the lowering of the head or the deliberate exposing of the neck it is impossible to say. But the movement is used in all phases of life: in sociopolitical and socioeconomic situations, as an act of recognition of superior physical powers, and as a religious symbol. The serf of the middle ages bowed his head to his lord through necessity; we bow and nod to our friends as a courteous gesture, indicating that we would willingly do the others service. Universally, no matter who the god, the adherents of all religions, in penitence or worship, lower their heads in reverence to a higher being.

Raised to its full height without strain and inclined slightly back of the shoulder line, the head shows an attitude at once superior and dominant. If tilted to one side or the other an alteration occurs and arrogance becomes the sign. As a matter of fact it should already have been noted that out of each basic position multiple related expressions develop. At the same time the equally important fact should be recognized that precision in expression is a matter not of a variable distance recorded in feet, but of an alteration reckoned in fractions of inches.

Aggressiveness comes with sticking the chin out. Arrogance follows when the chin is withdrawn slightly and the head is tilted a little to one side, causing slight changes in distance but major changes in meaning. Identified with the opposite extreme, when the head is lowered slightly and the chin is tucked in, attitudes of fearfulness and apology are shown. In the same position, if the head is tilted slightly, doubt is expressed.

The head is turned to look at an object or to listen to a sound, movements that speak for themselves with a simplicity that needs no explanation. But the head turns from side to side or tilts to right or left for other meaningful reasons. The *dis* movements, with their opposites, come in this grouping: disinterest or interest, dislike or like, distrust or trust. In each case the positive action is to move toward (or look toward) the target object. This requires leaning forward. The negative action is to pull back or turn away from whatever displeases or is distrusted or disliked.

There are many head movements of a seemingly complementary nature that actually carry the center of interest. These occur when the head moves in such a way as to cut contact with the outside world the better to concentrate on a mental problem. We bow the head or, alternately and for the same reason, we tilt it back to look at the ceiling as we try to recall a forgotten memory. At the same time, when we wish to establish or to maintain a strong contact with our environment, the head moves into the most favorable position possible for the senses to do their work.

An attitude of attention, one of the positive attributes, is shown by a forward extension of the head or by a pronounced tilt to one side. This last is a movement often seen in animals. When performed by a puppy or kitten it has power to kindle a most emphatic response, thus making it a movement with unique possibilities for stage use.

Quite naturally the head responds to conditions of health or disability as any other part of the body would, moving with strength and a high degree of articulation in the neck when the person is well and his spirits are up, moving in an opposite manner when the reverse condition obtains. In like manner the muscles of the face, the next focus of attention, will move.

The Face • So various, subtle, and complex are the expressions that play upon the features of people everywhere, this area accomplishes the finest and most delicate shades of meaning of which the human form is capable.[78]

Small as the face is in relation to the bulk of the body, its whole area still cannot become the center of interest. Although we are aware of the face as a whole when we look at another person, we can focus upon only one spot at any given time. Attention will generally be centered in one of three areas: the forehead or brows, the eyes and the muscles around them, and the mouth.

---

[78] If you were to be precipitously set down in a foreign land in some distant place on the globe, you would not need the niceties of language to tell you of the friendliness or hostility of your situation. In a moment, if you were confronted by members of the local community, you could judge your condition by the positions and movements of those around you. Nowhere would you focus your attention more continuously than on the faces of the people surrounding you.

We can and do look at the nose and chin, but these relatively immovable features command our attention only in specific instances.

The Forehead and Brows • The forehead, closest to the brain, is identified in its action with the processes of thought. When the brows are raised, horizontal lines are established in the forehead. These indicate either lack of will, or thought. Take the position and see if this checks out. As you do so, try to think your way through a complex problem. Brows lowered and drawn together to form a vertical line in the center and lower part of the forehead denotes an active thought or an act of will. As you do this try to convince yourself that your mind is in repose. Brows knotted but raised halfway between a frown and the horizontal lines say in effect, "I'm puzzled. I'm trying to think it out, but I don't understand it."

Some, trying these movements of the forehead, discover that little, if any, movement can be effected in this area. If this is so because no demand has ever been placed on it, then consistent exercise will soon bring about a change. If, however, the response is small because of the facial structure, the skin between scalp and brows being extraordinarily taut, a certain limitation of expressiveness is bound to result. Even more exercise work than normal is indicated.

The Eyes • Several basic expressions are possible in the eye area, but the first and most important statement is this: the eyes are the most alive and vital part of the body. Capable of unusually quick, diversified, and independent action, not only do they contact environment in a never-ceasing search during all waking hours, but they also become the most used point of focus when looking at another person.[79]

The eyes—eyes, eyelids, brows, and surrounding muscles—either freely and fully open to receive whatever impression is present, or narrow in alertness and caution to reduce the size of the opening that lets the impression in.

When the eyes are frankly open, with no contraction in the side muscles, interest, trust, liking, attention, desire, and similar expressions are indicated. Conversely, brows and lids down and the muscles at the sides contracted denotes caution, distrust, and a questioning state of mind; note that the action is too vital to suggest disinterest. Lids opened wide with little eye movement to one side or the other bespeaks lack of will and goes with the creation of a strong horizontal line in the forehead; a simpleminded person or one dazed from a blow would use this expression. But when the eye muscles are contracted to match the knitting of the brows, a very strong degree of mental activity is indicated.

The contrast when movement in one area seemingly contradicts action in another is not only dramatically strong but conveys a clear and definite meaning of its own. For example, brows raised due to lack of will seem to

---

[79] A multitude of meanings grow out of this last fact. For example, the degree to which we fail to look another person straight in the eye is the degree to which we fear an exposure of self to the other person.

contradict the mental action of caution shown by the contraction of the side muscles in the eye areas. The resultant combination, however, has a very specific meaning: it can indicate that the person is looking into a glare from sun or light, or that the person has a passive interest (note the contradiction) in some external object or event. On the other hand, when the brows are raised and the horizontal line is formed and the side muscles of only one eye are contracted, the resultant squint projects strong distrust, caution, or suspicion.

An important and revealing action is one demonstrating intelligence or its lack in a character. An eye that moves easily, darting in all directions independently of head actions can indicate a high degree of intelligence. Eyes that move only as the head moves indicate an opposite amount of mental capacity. Two contradictions to this last statement must be made. In older persons, when the calcification of bones has made articulation in the joints more difficult and when independent muscular activity is on the decrease, the eye and the head tend to move together, reflecting more of a physical than mental condition. Illness also affects the eyes, as the lackluster appearance of many sick people testifies; this, too, is the result of a physical state and does not necessarily reveal anything about the intelligence of the individual.

The Mouth • To those with a knowledge of theatre history, two of the five mouth positions are quickly recognized. The classic masks of the antique stage are known to most of us. Comedy, with its perpetual lift, and tragedy, with its sustained depression, have become the most frequently used symbols in the field of drama. Add to these two known positions the thin line of the firm mouth, the slack form of the open, the off-center pull to one side only, and the main positions are covered.

We have all laughed and smiled too often for this positive action to require discussion. It would be well, however, to allude in passing to the never-ceasing need for spontaneity in acting a pantomime. Nowhere is this more simply and more satisfactorily revealed than in the human smile. Nowhere in the body will the impulse from an inner state manifest itself with such directness and clarity. Nowhere will the activating power of external positions and movement, even when arbitrarily imposed, effect as immediate and unmistakable an inner response.

Spontaneity can seldom be practiced as an acting exercise more effectively than in the momentary or sustained creation of a smile. Try turning a spontaneous smile on and off at will, letting both the inner and the outer state be charged with immediacy when smiling and fully released when not. Alternate this exercise with the act of sustaining the smile, keeping the condition spontaneously in force for extended periods of time. Do not let the inner freshness lapse or the outer aliveness fade.

The negativeness of the pulled-down corners of the mouth is well known. Although this action is often performed, it usually is not executed with the fullness given to the smile. It is just as well, for as full a movement downward as upward would result in a decidedly unpleasant grimace. The mask of tragedy exaggerates what is in reality only a slight—but strong enough—movement.

Other mouth movements are read with ease. Determination is in the compressed lips that form a thin line across the lower part of the face. The slack and open mouth indicates both amazement and unintelligence—amazement is a momentary block to a mental action. The off-center and one-sided smile is really a smirk, an indication of a smile that is not meant to be a smile at all, a contradiction containing a critical comment that says, in effect, *I could smile, if it were not that I do not like what you are or what you are doing.* Such an expression always has the element of criticism inherent in it.

Many singular actions are performed in the mouth area, and each carries its own meaning. We pucker our lips for the kiss of kinship or friendship—we do not pucker for the kiss of passion. In a different kind of action our lips draw tight and form an O as complementary movement to the pain of an injury. In another complementary movement we purse our lips and extend them forward during moments of introspection or while exerting efforts of memory. Occasionally, in moments of extreme emotion having a content of fear, we uncover our teeth as an animal might bare its fangs. To express other and quite different feelings we smack our lips in pleasure or lick them in anticipation of what is to come. And lip action can combine with the wrinkling of the nose to show distaste or repugnance.

SUGGESTED EXERCISES AND ASSIGNMENTS

1. As an exercise, match head movements to facial expressions to show three different combinations of attitudes and feelings.

2. Give four expressions that develop out of differing combinations from the three areas of forehead, eyes, and mouth.

3. Also as an exercise, set up a pattern of your own on the model of this suggestion: Listen to something that puzzles you, see it and feel pleasure, look more closely and express doubt, suddenly become alarmed at what you see; follow this with a marked fear that gives way to a realization that a good joke, pleasurable enough to cause laughter, has been played on you.

4. Perform an exercise centering on the activities of tasting and smelling, with appropriate facial reactions included.

5. Do a complete pantomime for the head and face, drawing your subject matter from the actions that are primary to this area. A few ideas may spring from these random phrases: at a tennis match, watching an operation, a place of worship, bobbing for apples, a bird watcher, a sleepy student, a doubting Thomas.

TORSO AND SHOULDERS

The torso and shoulders, limited in action for obvious physical reasons, are seemingly the least expressive of the four major divisions of the body. But this area does have major statements of a revealing character to make. They are found in the relationships between the positions of abdomen, chest, and shoulders. Posture is the word used to describe the condition that results from each position of these areas, and posture has always been an important consideration in acting.

Housing so many of the vital organs of the body—heart, lungs, digestive tract—and making up so much of the bulk, many of the statements pertinent to characterization will come out of this area. In addition, because we turn toward what we like and turn away from what we dislike, and because we pull a part of the body back from what we fear and advance another part toward what we would impress or dominate, it is possible to state that attitudes also can be shown by the torso and shoulders.

As was pointed out in the chapter on characterization, the lower area of the region works in opposition to the upper. Balance, operating over the plumb line of gravity, requires that this be so. Belly out and upper chest and shoulders back can indicate obesity, pomposity, confidence, superiority, and other such attitudes. Abdomen in and shoulders forward shows a movement of protection or an expression of fear. It can also denote age, ill health, or a state of enervation.

The position of torso and shoulders is important to good carriage. Posture that denotes poise, power, grace, and dignity should be part of the accomplishments of every actor.

SUGGESTED EXERCISES AND ASSIGNMENTS

1. Varying between standing and sitting positions, strike torso and shoulder poses for several different characters, each in the act of having a picture taken.

2. In the greatest challenge to your originality yet, do a complete story for the torso and shoulders only. It will probably be necessary to give what normally are secondary functions a primary emphasis. Here are a few suggestions: a whipping post, a tough steak, a boxing contest, a wrecked car (a problem in lifting), a breathing contest. Pantomimes for two: a shy boy and a shy girl, teacher and pupil, an officer and an enlisted man, duelists.

Appendix B

The Processes of Speech

An unusual number of fortuitous physical arrangements make speech possible. To produce speech, the laws of physics require certain actions in logical sequence. The physical appointments necessary to initiate and carry on those actions are located in the exact areas where each sequential action must take place.

It is a fortunate anatomical fact that the air that supplies oxygen to the body can be used on its outward passage as an activating agent for the production of sound. It is just as fortunate that a ligament, capable of vibrating in such a manner as to form a sound wave, is located in the upper throat where air can be concentrated and controlled. Providentially, in the body area above the sound-producing ligament there are places where a primary sound can be amplified to such an extent that it can be projected a considerable distance. Happily, in that same area there are muscles and bones that, like a chopping machine in a modern processing plant, can act upon the issuing sounds in such a way as to give them differing shapes, thus increasing the number of symbols that can be used to express the expanding sounds of the creators.

Four separate but related processes are synchronized in the above arrangements. Not one of the processes was intended originally to fulfill a speech-making purpose, yet each, in its way, was readily adaptable. We can be grateful to our ancestors that they gave it a primary function in our communication scheme.

RESPIRATION

In order of performance, respiration is the first of the speech processes.

The basic purpose of respiration, bringing oxygen into the body and carrying waste material out, is to sustain life. Its subsidiary function is to provide the ammunition for speech. In both cases two separate actions transpire: *inhalation and exhalation.*

Inhalation occurs as often as a new supply of oxygen is needed by the body. To obtain the air required, the muscles of the chest cavity increase the size of that area; air pressure inside becomes less than that outside, and new air, with its supply of oxygen, pours into the lungs through the nose or mouth.

Inside, the air that will oxygenate and purify the blood passes through lung tissue into the bloodstream. At the same time, waste material, principally carbon dioxide, gathers in the lung sacs. When this balanced exchange is completed, the muscular action of exhalation takes place.

By the expedient of bringing in the walls and raising the floor, more pressure is created inside the chest area than outside, and the air, with its freight of waste material, is forced up through the throat and out by the nose or mouth. It is this last action that is used to produce sound.

Physiology of Respiration • Knowledge of the physiology of respiration will make the actions that must be taken meaningful. Organized from the lowest area to the highest, the parts of the body and their functions in breathing are as follows:

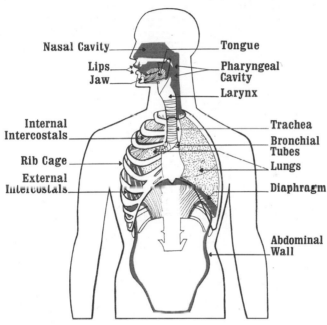

Physiology of Respiration

1. *Abdominal wall.* The outer casing of the visceral region acts as a foundation for the movements of the diaphragm. If the wall is weak, the diaphragm will lack necessary support. The abdominal wall has no direct part in inhalation. But in exhalation, the contraction of a ventral muscle pulls the abdominal wall in, thus permitting the muscles of the diaphragm to relax and move upward to a natural position of rest. The resultant increase of pressure on the lower portion of the lungs is one of the principal actions of exhalation.

2. *Diaphragm.* This member, made of muscles and sinews, forms the

partition that separates the chest from the abdominal cavity. Convex upward in shape, it resembles an umbrella somewhat, without that object's regularity of circumference. The diaphragm is anchored to the backbone in the rear and to the ascending line of the ribs on the sides and in front, causing it to be higher in front than in back.

Its function is to increase and decrease air pressure in the chest cavity. It does this in inhalation by a muscular contraction that pulls the raised center downward, thus lowering the floor of the thoracic cavity and enlarging the space above. In a compensatory action, the walls at the front and sides of the abdomen are forced outward, a movement that can be seen while breathing.

Breath control for dramatic speech requires that the diaphragm stay down longer than usual and return more slowly to its original position. It is an agent of strength and control.

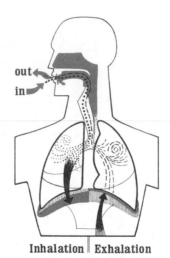

Inhalation | Exhalation
The Diaphragm

Exhalation is the critical portion of the breath process. In it the diaphragmatic muscle relaxes, permitting the center to rise again to its domelike position.

3. *Backbone.* This bonal pillar has no active function in respiration. It serves as anchorage for the diaphragm and ribcage.

4. *Ribcage.* This framework of bone and cartilage encloses the thoracic cavity on the sides and front. Anchored to the backbone in the rear and connected to the sternum in front, it is composed of the three sets of true, false, and floating ribs.

The ribcage both protects the area that houses the heart and lungs and provides a framework for the muscles that control its members during inhalation and exhalation.

5. *Intercostals*. These muscles are the principal activators of the ribcage. There are two sets of intercostals: external and internal.

The external intercostals operate during inhalation, initiating that process in part by a contracting action that causes the ribcage to rise and expand. The internal intercostals function in exhalation by contracting, pulling the ribs down and closer together. Both sets work in exact coordination with the diaphragm. They are also agents of control and strength.

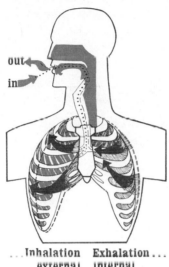

...Inhalation Exhalation...
external internal
intercostals intercostals

The Intercostals

6. *Sternum*. A large flat bone that both protects the contents of the thoracic cavity and acts as an anchor for the muscles and cartilages that operate the ribcage. Its action in respiration is minimal.

7. *Lungs*. Inside the ribcage are two masses of lung tissue. Composed of tiny sacs, the whole structure is a living but inert form that responds in movement only because of the bellow-like action of the diaphragm and ribcage.

The actor's concern with the lungs centers on increasing the capacity of that organ, without, of course, causing such strain as might do injury to tissue.

8. *Bronchial tubes*. The bronchial tubes are the larger air channels leading into the lungs. The closer they are to the windpipe, the larger the size. They are not consciously employed in breath control.

PHONATION

In order of performance, phonation is the second of the speech processes. It is the act that produces human sound, which is the limit of its function; speech comes later.

Phonation takes place in the upper part of the throat and is caused by the action of a column of air moving under pressure past the edges of a sound-producing body, the vocal folds.

Condensation and Rarefaction • Formed like a **V**, and extended across the throat from front to back like a protective valve, the edges of the vocal folds vibrate from the friction of passing air. When air first strikes, each edge moves upward in direct ratio to the strength of the blow. As it does so, it creates a condensation of the air particles in its path, but leaves fewer air particles in the space just vacated, where an act of rarefaction has taken place. The two parts of the movement, condensation and rarefaction, form the two portions of a sound wave.

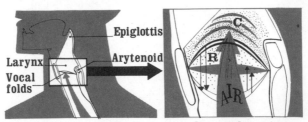

C...condensation
R....rarefaction

Condensation and Rarefaction

In vibration, when the farthest extent of the swing is reached, the natural elasticity of the vocal folds causes the edges of that member to return downward, continuing past the former position of rest until a second limit of arc is reached. Thus a full vibration is accomplished. A vibration is a sound wave, and a sound wave is the initial tone in the speech process.

Fundamental Tones and Overtones • The vocal folds perform like any other vibrating body, by moving as a whole and at the same time in segments. As a rubber band moves up and down when blown upon, the vocal folds vibrate over their whole length from the anchor in the thyroid cartilage in front to the connection to the arytenoid cartilage in the rear. This whole vibration produces the fundamental tone of the sound wave.

But even as the vocal folds are moving as a whole, so are the segments of the cords moving in exact and decreasing divisions of the whole. That is, the two halves of the whole vibrate as if they were whole, and the two halves of those halves do likewise. By halves, quarters, eighths, sixteenths, and so forth, the action continues. This is termed segmental vibration, and its action produces the overtones of the sound wave.

Overtones are of equal importance to the fundamental tone. Their number and strength determine the initial quality of a person's voice. An actor cannot consciously alter the basic structure of his vocal folds, but by thinking about

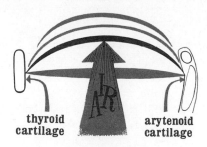

Whole Vibration

The Fundamental Tone

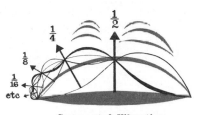

Segmental Vibration

Overtones

the process of phonation and by exercises, he can do much to improve the natural instrument.

Degree of Arc • The stronger the force that strikes the vocal folds, the greater the degree of arc of vibration. The degree of arc determines the amount of strength that can be heard in a tone. This fact establishes the importance of muscular strength and muscular control in the two processes of respiration and phonation.

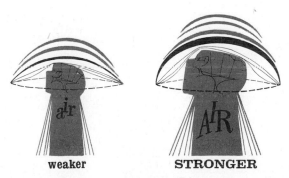

Degree of Arc

Physiology of Phonation • With the exception of the vocal folds, the functions of all other parts of the body involved in phonation are those of support and protection.

1. *Trachea.* The trachea or windpipe is the cartilage-ringed column that runs from the top to the bottom of the throat. It provides a passages for the air going into and out of the lungs.

2. *Larynx.* Two thirds of the way up the throat is the area of the larynx. It contains the five cartilages that support and protect the vocal folds: the cricoid, thyroid or Adam's Apple, arytenoid, cuneiform, and corniculate.

3. *Glottis.* This is the empty space between the vocal folds.

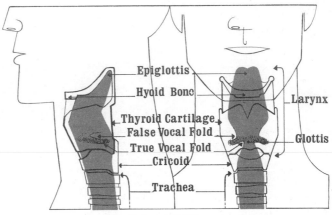

Epiglottis
Hyoid Bone
Larynx
Thyroid Cartilage
False Vocal Fold
True Vocal Fold
Glottis
Cricoid
Trachea

Physiology of Phonation

4. *True Vocal Folds.* The original function of these V-shaped ligaments was to protect the passageway to the lungs. In speech they serve as the vibrating body that initiates sound. Extending directly across the trachea, they relax during respiration to permit the largest possible passage of air. In speech they tense and draw together, thus decreasing the size of the glottis so as to obtain maximum benefit from the passing air. During phonation the length and thickness of the cords vary according to the need to make a tone that is strong or soft, high or low.

5. *False Vocal Folds.* Located immediately above the true vocal folds, the false vocal folds have no other function than protection.

6. *Hyoid Bone.* Situated at the top of the trachea and at the base of the tongue, the hyoid bone serves as an anchorage for muscles and as a protector for the windpipe.

7. *Epiglottis.* This is an elastic cartilage located at the top of the trachea. In swallowing and breathing it functions as a valve to let air in and keep food out of the windpipe.

RESONATION

In this third process, sound waves leave the vibrating body and move upward under pressure past the epiglottis and into the first of the three resonating chambers with which we are concerned.

Resonation is the reinforcement or amplification of tone that arises from the rebounding ability of a sound wave. Striking the walls of a resonating cavity, a sound wave bounces back much as a ball would or as the sound of an echo does, but in exact synchronization with the next vibration. Thus each sound wave is reinforced or amplified many times by the bounding and rebounding of each vibration.

Without the amplification of resonation, an original sound wave would strike the ear as a very flat tone, limited in strength and variety, and decidedly unpleasant in comparison with even the most ordinary of tones.

Once formed, an individual has no control over the rebounding action of a sound wave. He does have the ability to direct it and to create favorable conditions for its amplification. By enlarging the size of a cavity, by controlling the duration of sound, by emphasizing the use of one chamber and avoiding the use of another, he can improve the timbre of his tone as well as bring increased variety into his interpretive work.

Physiology of Resonation • There are only three important resonating chambers involved in this process. In the order of progression upward they are *pharyngeal, oral,* and *nasal.*

The pharyngeal resonating cavity is located at the top of the throat and the back of the mouth. It can be both seen and felt when the sound *ah* is

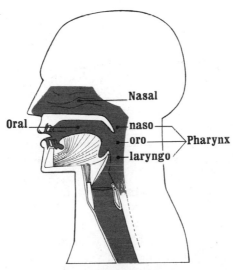

The Resonating Chambers

made. The largest of the resonating chambers, it is of particular importance in the production of an orotund quality. It has three divisions: the laryngopharynx, which begins at the epiglottis and comprises the lower portion of the parent chamber, and in which the resonation that produces the orotund quality takes place, the visible oropharynx, which is located in the upper part of the pharyngeal tube, and the nasopharynx, out of view behind and above the uvula, which is closed off for all but nasal sounds.

The second resonating cavity is the oral. It is the mouth area, roofed by the hard and soft palate, bounded by a wall of encircling teeth and floored by the tongue. More flexible than the pharyngeal, it can change its shape and size to a greater extent. Limited in most persons by the unconscious habit of a lazy or tight jaw, its amplifying and enriching possibilities will work to the benefit of any player who forms the habit of swinging the jaw lower than usual in the formation of all vowel sounds. This cavity best produces a normal or oral quality.

The nasal resonating cavity is located immediately above the roof of the mouth and behind the nose and eyes. Made up of a series of spaces partially closed off from each other by cartilaginous baffles, it acts as both a resonator and a nonresonator, and it can produce both pleasant and unpleasant sounds.

When a sound wave is permitted to pass from the main pharyngeal cavity through an opening behind the uvula directly into the nasopharynx and then the nasal cavity itself, the resultant reverberation produces the unpleasant sound of nasal quality.

But if the sound wave is sent directly into the mouth area, the air in the nasal resonating cavity moves only by the *sympathetic* vibration caused by the action of the roof of the mouth. It is as if, in response to the action of the sound waves in the mouth area below, the floor of the nasal cavity were like a floor in an ordinary room that moved up and down because something below caused it to vibrate. The up-and-down movement would naturally cause the air above to respond in like manner. Thus, a synchronized vibration would amplify and enrich the quality of tone produced. This kind of resonation is essential in support of the pharyngeal resonation that produces an orotund quality; exercises for its development have already been given.

Of minor importance is the effect that occurs when neither direct or sympathetic vibration takes place in the nasal resonating cavity. When blocked off by an act of will or because fluid from a cold has replaced the air in the nasal cavity, a complete lack of vibration in that area produces a denasalized quality. This causes an occasional strange effect. For example, an *m* sounds like a *b*, and the word *means* becomes *beans*.

ARTICULATION

Articulation is a process in which movements of the tongue, jaw, and lips shape resonated sound waves into the vowel and consonant combinations of syllables.

Vowels • For good stage speech the fullness of a vowel sound is as important as its formation.[80] This is a matter of lowering the jaw to increase the degree of amplification by increasing the size of the oral resonating cavity. If this is done, the slight increase of size required of the pharyngeal chamber takes care of itself.

Consonants • It is in the formation of consonants that the articulators are most active. Because of the distance a tone must travel in a theatre, and because of the above-normal intensity of dramatic delivery, special care is required of a player in all articulatory movements.

Good articulation results from the precise actions of lip against lip or teeth or tongue, or of tongue against teeth or roof of mouth. That stage speech may be a pride to the actor and a pleasure to an audience, consummate skill in its execution is essential.

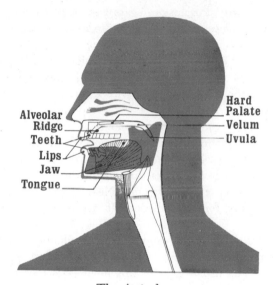

The Articulators

In this regard attention must be paid to beginning and ending consonants, with added emphasis upon the latter. Plosive consonants—*p, b, t, d, k, g*—are the most critical, especially when in a terminal position. Good articulation is more dependent upon the precise formation of these six sounds than upon any of the other seventeen vowels and twenty-one consonants on the usual phonetic list.

The pernicious habit of swallowing the syllables and words at the end of a phrase or sentence is so prevalent among players everywhere that special understanding of the problem is required. A psychological reason is behind

---

[80] American actors should use American pronunciations, unless a specific dialect is called for. Good stage speech is good offstage speech. Unless an interpretation demands a note of affectation, there is no reason to imitate the sounds of our English cousins in the mistaken belief that this is how all actors everywhere should sound.

failure to articulate terminal sounds. Each of us thinks at a much faster rate than he talks. Consequently, a word or phrase or sentence is completed as a thought in about half the time required to articulate the spoken one. The thought finished, the player mentally releases it before the physical action is completed. Thus arises the undesirable habit of permitting terminal sounds to trail off or fade out. Cautioned, the actor uses his audience ear to break the practice.

Physiology of Articulation • The following list names those parts of the mouth area of which the actor should be conscious and informed.

1. *Tongue.* This agile member is the most active of all the articulators and must assume the major responsibility for good articulation. If it is not the principal agent in the formation of a syllable, its position complements the action that occurs elsewhere. Each section—front, middle, and back—is active, forming complete or partial occlusions against the teeth, alveolar ridge, or the hard or soft palate. Laziness or slurred action in its movements means a major loss of clarity in speech.

2. *Teeth and jaw.* The teeth, immobile extensions of the jaws, act as stops against which the lips and tongue play. The single function of the jaw is to increase or decrease the size of the oral cavity according to the needs of vowel formation or consonant enunciation. For good dramatic speech it must be free and flexible well beyond the requirements of ordinary usage.

3. *Lips.* The lips sometimes follow the action of the jaw, but many times they move independently of it. When they must effect a complete or partial closure, or move outward on a lateral line, as in the vowel *e* [i], the actions must be as precise as those of the tongue. Next to the tongue, the lips bear the most responsibility for good diction. If laziness is present, it will be noticeable here.

4. *Alveolar ridge.* This is the gum ridge immediately behind the upper teeth. It is a point of contact for the tongue in many of its important actions.

5. *Hard palate.* The usual term for this member is roof of the mouth. It not only serves as a point of contact for the tongue, it also acts as a sounding board in resonation.

6. *Velum.* When the hard palate loses its rigidity at the back of the mouth, it becomes the velum or soft palate. It is another point of contact for the tongue.

7. *Uvula.* The pendant tip that hangs from the roof of the mouth and moves up and down in synchronization with syllabic formation is termed the uvula. Seldom activated by conscious control, it is one of the few body parts about which an actor need not be concerned, except in cases of nasality.

To conclude, it can be said that articulation is a process whereby the meaning of words is added to the meaning of tone. This action alone adds incalculable scope to vocal communication. As accustomed as an actor is to cautions about poor articulation, the above point should serve to make his awareness forever acute.

Appendix C

Phrasing

Phrasing is the grouping of words to form a unit of expression. Length of phrase is determined by a playwright when he composes his thought units, usually indicated by punctuation. A player, reading both thought content and punctuation, generally follows the implied direction of the author.

As a physical action, phrasing is integrally associated with breath control. Within reasonable limits, no phrase should be lost because air supply is insufficient for length. Inability to coordinate thought and breath results in loss of meaning or loss of words. Synchronized, thought and breath permits the fitting expression of all meanings and intensities.

In delivery the length of a phrase is marked by a pause before and a pause after the expressive unit. As a rule (one that has many exceptions), inhalation occurs during the pause. Thus creativeness of interpretation is associated with techniques of breath control.

In their book, *Improving Your Speech*, Gresham and Gooder illustrate the effect of improper phrasing.

John Smith, / having gone to sea, / his wife asks that you pray for his safety.

John Smith, / having gone to sea his wife, / asks that you pray for his safety.

The Run-on Line. The dramatic use of phrasing in the run-on line is not recommended. Popular in all ages, the run-on line has an attractive, attention-getting quality that endears it to many players. Invariably, however, the run-on line does damage to a playwright's thought units, for the simple reason that it adds the coming phrase to the one just past as though the two were integral to each other. The effect is as if a printer were to run two independent phrases together without benefit of punctuation.

The following illustration of how the run-on line is delivered is as typical as any in dramatic literature. It is from Hamlet's first speech. Punctuated and phrased for clarity, the line reads:

HAMLET: Seems, Madam! / Nay, it is; / I know not seems. . . .

But as a run-on line, it reads.

HAMLET: Seems, Madam! / Nay, it is I know not seems. . . .

Unfortunately, it sometimes appears that a player must choose between clarity of meaning and dramatic effect. Such is not the case, however, for the simple reason that it is as possible to be dramatic with clarity as it is to be dramatic for the sake of an effect. Line readings with clearly marked units of thought give foundation and substance to dramatic delivery. Lines read for effect only have only a surface appeal to sustain the dramatic experience.

Actually, few problems should arise in the ordinary course of dramatic delivery; the establishment of the thought unit as a phrase and the control of breath that energizes its delivery are as easily coordinated on an acting level as they are in usual forms of expression. Beyond that, the difficulties that occur probably will be for one of two reasons.

First, the form of speech, poetry (rhymed or blank verse), for example, or a distinctiveness of style as in such widely separated sources as Greek drama, the *commedia dell'arte*, or Ionesco, may present technical problems in word grouping that make special demands on the breath control capabilities of an actor.

Second, when intensity is present in any degree, extra amounts of energy are required to sustain and project the material. In such cases, the quantity of air needed is in direct ratio to the quantity of energy expended; both the amount of air inhaled and the length of time it is held for use are problems of breath control.

To synchronize breath control with thought units, practice the problems presented in the various passages that follow. You may wish to rearrange the phrasing to suit your interpretation. If so, try to maintain such intervals as offer a challenge to the physical act of synchronization. After the first reading, repeat, taking a breath on every other break, then on each third break.

1. Clear well spring not, /
   Sweet birds sing not, /
   Green plants bring not
      Forth their dye; /
   Herds stand weeping, /
   Flocks all sleeping, /
   Nymphs back peeping
      Fearfully: /
   All our pleasure known to us poor swains, /
   All our merry meetings on the plains, /
   All our evening sport from us is fled. /
   All our love is lost, for Love is dead.

   > Shakespeare, *Sonnets To Sundry Notes of Music, III*

2. CHORUS:
      Cut is the branch that might have grown full straight, /
      And burned is Apollo's laurel bough,

That sometimes grew within this learned man. /
Faustus is gone; / regard his hellish fall,
Whose fiendful fortune may exhort the wise
Only to wonder at unlawful things, /
Whose deepness does entice such forward wits
To practice more than heavenly power permits.

> Marlowe, *Doctor Faustus,*
> final speech

3. Each of the next two speeches is motivated by an intense emotional state. In each the breaks have been spaced at such intervals as will challenge the synchronization of phrasing for thought content with breath-control spans of more than usual length.

Ophelia, alone on stage, has just been the target of more cruel jibes and slanders from Prince Hamlet than she would ever have dreamed that young man could or would utter. As he intended, she now believes him mad, and the belief shocks her even as it saddens her.

OPHELIA.
　O what a noble mind is here o'erthrown! /
　The courtier's, soldier's, scholar's, eye, tongue, sword: /
　Th' expectancy and rose of the fair state,
　The glass of fashion and the mold of form,
　Th' observ'd of all observers, quite, quite down! /
　And I, of ladies most deject and wretched, /
　That suck'd the honey of his music vows,
　Now see that noble and most sovereign reason,
　Like sweet bells jangled, out of tune and harsh, /
　That unmatch'd form and features of blown youth
　Blasted with ecstasy. / O woe is me,
　T' have seen what I have seen, / see what I see!

> Shakespeare, *Hamlet,* Act III, Scene 1

Hamlet, the excitement of having just killed Polonius still upon him, faces his mother with a comparison between the ideal of his dead father, as shown on one side of a medallion, and the less-than-ideal picture of his uncle on the other.

HAMLET.
　Look here, upon this picture, and on this,
　The counterfeit presentment of two brothers. /
　See what a grace was seated on this brow: /
　Hyperion's curls, the front of Jove himself,
　An eye like Mars, to threaten and command, /
　A station like the herald Mercury
　New-lighted on a heaven-kissing hill, /
　A combination and a form indeed,
　Where every god did seem to set his seal,
　To give the world assurance of a man. /

This was your husband. / Look you, now, what follows. /
Here is your husband, like a mildew'd ear
Blasting his wholesome brother. / Have you eyes?
Could you on this fair mountain leave to feed,
And batten on this moor? / Ha! / have you eyes? /
You cannot call it love, for at your age
The heyday in the blood is tame, it's humble,
And waits upon the judgment; / and what judgment
Would step from this to this? / Sense sure you have,
Else could you not have motion; / but sure that sense
Is apoplex'd, for madness would not err,
Nor sense to ecstasy was ne'er so thrall'd
But it reserv'd some quantity of choice
To serve in such a difference. / What devil was't
That thus hath cozen'd you at hoodman-blind? /
Eyes without feeling, feeling without sight,
Ears without hands or eyes, smelling sans all, /
Or but a sickly part of one true sense
Could not so mope. /
O shame! where is thy blush? / Rebellious hell,
If thou canst mutine in a matron's bones,
To flaming youth let virtue be as wax
And melt in her own fire: / proclaim no shame
When the compulsive ardor gives the charge,
Since frost itself as actively doth burn,
And reason panders will.

Shakespeare, Hamlet, Act III, Scene 4

4. Treating thought control and breath control as one and the same thing, phrase the following energized passages to express the exact thoughts and attitudes, as you believe them to be, of the character you read.

HARDCASTLE. So, madam! So I find *this* is your *modest* lover. This is your humble admirer that kept his eyes fixed on the ground, and only ador'd at humble distance. Kate, Kate, art thou not asham'd to deceive your father so?

MISS HARDCASTLE. Never trust me, dear papa, but he's still the modest man I first took him for; you'll be convinced of it as well as I.

HARDCASTLE. By the hand of my body, I believe his impudence is infectious! Didn't I see him seize your hand? Didn't I see him hawl you about like a milk maid? And now you talk of his respect and his modesty, forsooth!

MISS HARDCASTLE. But if I shortly convince you of his modesty, that he has only the faults that will pass off with time, and the virtues that will improve with age, I hope you'll forgive him.

HARDCASTLE. The girl would actually make one run mad! I tell you I'll not be convinced! I am convinced. He has scarcely been three hours in the house, and he has already encroached on all my prerogatives. You may like his impudence, and call it modesty. But my son-in-law, madam, must have very different qualifications.

Miss Hardcastle. Sir, I ask but this night to convince you.

Hardcastle. You shall not have half the time, for I have thoughts of turning him out this very hour.

Miss Hardcastle. Give me that hour then, and I hope to satisfy you.

Hardcastle. Well, an hour let it be then. But I'll have no trifling with our father. All fair and open, do you mind me?

Miss Hardcastle. I hope, sir, you have ever found that I considered your commands as my pride; for your kindness is such that my duty as yet has been inclination.

Goldsmith, She Stoops To Conquer, Act III

Ben Jonson begins *The Alchemist* with a heated quarrel, a falling out between rogues. The alchemist, Subtle, has prevailed upon one Face, a housekeeper (who, for our purpose, could be female as well as male) to let him, Subtle, operate his fleecing game in the house Face is to guard in the absence of the master.

Face.   Why, I pray you, have I
  Been countenanced by you, or you by me?
  Do but collect, sir, where I met you first.
Subtle. I do not hear well.
Face.   Not of this, I think it.
  But I shall put you in mind, sir—at Piecorner,
  Taking your meal of steam in from cooks' stalls,
  Where, like the father of hunger, you did walk
  Piteously costive, with your pinched-horn-nose,
  And your complexion of the Roman wash,
  Stuck full of black and melancholic worms,
  Like powder-corns shot at th' artillery-yard.
Subtle. I wish you could advance your voice a little.
Face. When you went pinned up in the several rags
  Y' had raked and picked from dunghills, before day;
  Your feet in mouldy slippers, for your kibes;
  A felt of rug, and a thin threaden cloak,
  That scarce would cover your no-buttocks——
Subtle.   So, sir!
Face. When all your alchemy, and your algebra,
  Your minerals, vegetals, and animals,
  Your conjuring, coz'ning, and your dozen of trades,
  Could not relieve your corpse with so much linen
  Would make you tinder, but to see a fire;
  I ga' your count'nance, credit for your coals,
  Your stills, your glasses, your materials;
  Built you a furnace, drew you customers,
  Advanced all your black arts; lent you, beside,
  A house to practice in——
Subtle.   Your master's house!
Face. Where you have studied the more thriving skill
  Of bawdry, since.

SUBTLE.   Yes, in your master's house.
  You and the rats here kept possession.
  Make it not strange. I know you were one could keep
  The buttery-hatch still locked, and save the chippings,
  Sell the dole-beer to aqua-vitae men,
  The which, together with your Christmas vials
  At post-and-pair, your letting out of counters,
  Made you a pretty stock, some twenty marks,
  And gave you credit to converse with cobwebs
  Here, since your mistress' death hath broke up house.
FACE.   You might talk softlier, rascal.
SUBTLE.   No, you scarab,
  I'll thunder you in pieces. I will teach you
  How to beware to tempt a Fury again
  That carries tempest in his hand and voice.
FACE.   The place has made you valiant.
SUBTLE.   No, your clothes.
  Thou vermin, have I ta'en thee out of dung,
  So poor, so wretched, when no living thing
  Would keep thee company, but a spider or worse;
  Raised thee from brooms and dust and wat'ring pots;
  Sublimed thee, and exalted thee, and fixed thee
  I' the third region, the high state of grace;
  Wrought thee to spirit, to quintessence; with pains
  Would twice have won me the philosopher's work;
  Put thee in words and fashion; made thee fit
  For more than ordinary fellowships;
  Giv'n thee thy oaths, thy quarreling dimensions,
  Thy rules to cheat at horse-race, cock-pit, cards,
  Dice, or whatever gallant tincture else;
  Made thee a second in mine own great art;
  And have I this for thanks? Do you rebel? . . .
FACE.   Out, you dog-leech! . . .
SUBTLE. Cheater!
FACE.   Bawd!
SUBTLE.   Cow-herd!
FACE.   Conjurer!
SUBTLE.   Cutpurse!
FACE.   Witch!
BOTH.   'Sdeath!

                Jonson, *The Alchemist,* Act I, Scene 1

Appendix D

Articulation Exercises

The passages that follow offer more extensive practice than that given in Part III, Chapter 11.

To master the articulation problems of difficult phrases, first read slowly enough to permit lips, tongue, and jaw to form each syllable correctly. Adequate tempo comes with familiarity. Warm-up action should precede each practice session.

Then a sentimental passion of a vegetable fashion must excite your languid
    spleen,
An attachment à la Plato for a bashful young potato, or a not-too French
    French bean!
Though the Philistines may jostle, you will rank as an apostle in the high
    aesthetic band,
If you walk down Piccadilly with a poppy or a lily in your mediaeval hand,
      And every one will say,
      As you walk your flowery way,
       "If he's content with vegetable love which would certainly not suit me,
Why, what a particularly pure young man this pure young man must be!
                          Patience, Gilbert and Sullivan

Into the street the Piper stepped
Smiling first a little smile,
As if he knew what magic slept
In his quiet pipe the while.
Then like a musical adept
To blow the pipe his lips he wrinkled,
And green and blue his sharp eyes twinkled
Like a candle flame where salt is sprinkled.
And ere three shrill notes the pipe uttered,
You heard as if an army muttered,
And the muttering grew to a grumbling.
And the grumbling grew to a mighty rumbling.
And out of the houses the rats came tumbling:
Great rats, small rats, lean rats, brawny rats,
Black rats, brown rats, gray rats, tawny rats,
Grave old plodders, gay young friskers,
Fathers, mothers, uncles, cousins,
Cocking tail and pricking whiskers,

Families by tens and dozens,
Brothers, sisters, husbands, wives
Followed the Piper for their lives.
From street to street he piped advancing,
And step for step they followed dancing
Until they came to the river Weser
(Where in all plunged and perished!) . . .

The Pied Piper, Robert Browning

HOTSPUR: I cannot choose, sometime he angers me
With telling me of the moldwarp and the ant,
Of the dreamer Merlin and his prophecies,
And of a dragon and a finless fish,
A clip-winged griffin and a moulten raven,
A couching lion and a ramping cat,
And such a deal of skimble-skamble stuff,
As puts me from my faith.

King Henry IV, Part I, Shakespeare

POLONIUS: The best actors in the world, either for tragedy,
comedy, history, pastoral, pastoral-comical,
historical-pastoral, tragical-historical, tragical-
comical-historical-pastoral, scene individable, or
poem unlimited: Seneca cannot be too heavy nor
Plautus too light. For the law of writ and the liberty,
these are the only men.

Hamlet, Shakespeare

HAMLET: The rugged Pyrrhus, he whose sable arms,
Black as his purpose, did the night resemble,
When he lay couched in th' ominous horse,
Hath now this dread and black complexion smeared
With heraldry more dismal: head to foot
Now is he total gules, horridly tricked
With blood of fathers, mothers, daughters, sons,
Baked and impasted with the parching streets,
That lend a tyrannous and a damned light
To their lord's murder. Roasted in wrath and fire,
And thus o'er-sized with coagulate gore,
With eyes like carbuncles, the hellish Pyrrhus
Old Grandsire Priam seeks——

Hamlet, Shakespeare

'Twas brillig, and the slithy toves
Did gyre and gimble in the wabe
All mimsy were the borogoves,
And the mome raths outgrabe.

"Beware the Jabberwock, my son!
   The jaws that bite, the claws that catch!
Beware the Jubjub bird, and shun
   The frumious Bandersnatch!"

He took his vorpal sword in hand;
   Long time the manxome foe he sought—
So rested he by the Tumtum tree,
   And stood awhile in thought.

And, as in uffish thought he stood,
   The Jabberwock, with eyes of flame,
Came whiffling through the tulgey wood,
   And burbled as it came!

One, two! One, two! And through and through
   The vorpal blade went snicker-snack!
He left it dead, and with its head
   He went galumphing back.

"And hast thou slain the Jabberwock?
   Come to my arms, my beamish boy!
O frabjous day! Callooh, Callay!"
   He chortled in his joy.

'Twas brillig, and the slithy toves
   Did gyre and gimble in the wabe:
All mimsy were the borogoves,
   And the mome raths outgrabe.

                  Jabberwocky, Lewis Carroll

Samuel Foote, satirist in Seventeenth-century England, once challenged actor Charles Macklin, who boasted of his wonderful powers of memory, to get the following nonsense speech by heart on the spot. The value of this exercise lies in the need to make the articulators respond immediately to the unexpected word.

So she went into the garden to cut a cabbage-leaf to make an apple-pie, and, at the same time, a great she-bear, coming up the street, pops its head into the shop. "What, no soap?" So he died, and she very imprudently married the barber; and there were present the Picninnies and the Joblillies and Garolillies and the Grand Panjamdrum himself, with the little round button at top, and they all fell to playing the game of Catch-as-catch-can till the gunpowder ran out at the heels of their boots.

. . .

The Cataract strong
Then plunges along,
Striking and raging
As if a war waging
Its caverns and rocks among:
Rising and leaping,
Sinking and creeping;
Swelling and sweeping,
Showering and springing,
Flying and flinging;
Writhing and ringing;
Eddying and whisking,
Spouting and frisking,
Turning and twisting,
Around and around
With endless rebound!
Smiting and fighting,
A sight to delight in;
Confounding, astounding,
Dizzying and deafening the ear with its sound. . . .

And glittering and frittering;
   And gathering and feathering;
And whitening and brightening,
   And quivering and shivering;
     And hurrying and skurrying,
And thundering and floundering; . . .

Retreating and beating and meeting and sheeting;
   Delaying and straying and playing and spraying;
Advancing and prancing and glancing and dancing,
   Recoiling, turmoiling and toiling and boiling,
And gleaming and streaming and steaming and beaming,
   And rushing and flushing and brushing and gushing;
And flapping and rapping and clapping and slapping;
   And curling and whirling and purling and twirling;
   And thumping and plumping and bumping and jumping,
And dashing and flashing and splashing and clashing;
   And so never ending, but always descending,
Sounds and motions for ever and ever are blending,
   All at once and all o'er, with a mighty uproar,
   And this way the Water comes down at Ladore.
The Cataract of Ladore, Robert Southey

Read the following speech with manageable rapidity.

Mrs. Malaprop: Observe me, Sir Anthony.—I would by no means wish a daughter of mine to be a progeny of learning; I don't think so much learning becomes a young woman; for instance—I would never let her meddle with Greek, or Hebrew, or Algebra, or Simony, or Fluxions, or Paradoxes, or such inflammatory branches of learning—neither would it be necessary for her to handle any of your mathematical, astronomical, diabolical instruments;— But, Sir Anthony, I would send her at nine years old to a boarding-school, in order to learn a little ingenuity and artifice.— Then, Sir, she should have a supercilious knowledge in accounts;—and as she grew up, I would have her instructed in geometry, that she might know something of the contagious countries;—but above all, Sir Anthony, she should be mistress of orthodoxy, that she might not mis-spell, and mis-pronounce words so shamefully as girls usually do; and likewise that she might reprehend the true meaning of what she is saying.—This, Sir Anthony, is what I would have a woman know;—and I don't think there is a superstitious article in it.

The Rivals, Sheridan, Act I, Scene 2

The following passage serves a double purpose: as regular practice material and as an articulation check chart. In the latter capacity, the spacing of letters is sufficient to permit identifying circles to be placed where what should be a proper sound is insufficient or deficient.

. . . SINUOUS SOUTHWARD AND SINUOUS NORTH-
    WARD THE SHIMMERING BAND
OF THE SAND-BEACH FASTENS THE FRINGE
    OF THE MARSH TO THE FOLDS OF THE
    LAND.
INWARD AND OUTWARD TO NORTHWARD AND
    SOUTHWARD THE BEACH-LINES LINGER
    AND CURL
AS A SILVER-WROUGHT GARMENT THAT CLINGS
    TO AND FOLLOWS THE FIRM SWEET
    LIMBS OF A GIRL.
VANISHING, SWERVING, EVERMORE CURVING
    AGAIN INTO SIGHT,
SOFTLY THE SAND-BEACH WAVERS AWAY TO A
    DIM GRAY LOOPING OF LIGHT.
AND WHAT IF BEHIND ME TO WESTWARD THE
    WALL OF THE WOODS STANDS HIGH?
THE WORLD LIES EAST: HOW AMPLE, THE
    MARSH AND THE SEA AND THE SKY!
A LEAGUE AND A LEAGUE OF MARSH-GRASS,
    WAIST-HIGH, BROAD IN THE BLADE,
GREEN, AND ALL OF A HEIGHT, AND UNFLECKED
    WITH A LIGHT OR A SHADE,
STRETCH LEISURELY OFF, IN A PLEASANT
    PLAIN,
TO THE TERMINAL BLUE OF THE MAIN.

. . .

YE MARSHES, HOW CANDID AND SIMPLE AND
   NOTHING-WITHHOLDING AND FREE
YE PUBLISH YOURSELVES TO THE SKY AND
   OFFER YOURSELVES TO THE SEA!
TOLERANT PLAINS, THAT SUFFER THE SEA
   AND THE RAINS AND THE SUN,
YE SPREAD AND SPAN LIKE THE CATHOLIC
   MAN WHO HATH MIGHTILY WON
GOD OUT OF KNOWLEDGE AND GOOD OUT OF
   INFINITE PAIN
AND SIGHT OUT OF BLINDNESS AND PURITY
   OUT OF A STAIN.

The Marshes of Glynn, Sidney Lanier

Let meter and rhyme aid articulation in practice on these old English nursery rhymes.

> Hinx, minx, the old witch winks,
> The fat begins to fry,
> Nobody at home but jumping Joan,
> Father, mother and I.
> Stick, stock, stone dead,
> Blind man can't see,
> Every knave will have a slave,
> You or I must be he.
>
> Ink, minx, pepper, drink,
> Bottle full of rotten ink.
> Ink, pink, pen and ink,
> You go out because you stink.
>
> Hoddley, poddley, puddle and fogs,
> Cats are to marry the poodle dogs;
> Cats in blue jackets and dogs in red hats,
> What will become of the mice and rats?
>
> I would if I could,
> If I couldn't how could I?
> I couldn't, without I could, could I?
> Could you, without you could, could ye?
>
> As I walked by myself
> And talked to myself,
>   Myself said unto me,
> Look to thyself,
> Take care of thyself,
> For nobody cares for thee.

I answered myself,
And said to myself
   In the self-same repartee,
Look to thyself,
Or not to thyself,
   The self-same thing will be.

Inter, mitzy, titzy, tool,
Ira, dira, dominu,
Oker, poker, dominoker,
Out goes you.

Intery, mintery, cutery, corn,
Apple seed and briar thorn;
Wire, briar, limber lock,
Five geese in a flock
Sit and sing by a spring,
O-U-T, and in again.

In fir tar is,
In oak none is,
In mud ells are,
In clay none are.
Goat eat ivy;
Mare eat oats.

Articulation and breathing exercises. Use orotund quality with a moderate to rapid tempo.

This is the house that Jack built. (Breathe)

This is the malt
That lay in the house that Jack built. (Breathe)

This is the rat,
That ate the malt
That lay in the house that Jack built. (Breathe)

This is the cat,
That killed the rat,
That ate the malt
That lay in the house that Jack built. (Breathe)

This is the dog,
That worried the cat,
That killed the rat,
That ate the malt
That lay in the house that Jack built. (Breathe)

This is the cow with the crumpled horn,
That tossed the dog,
That worried the cat,
That killed the rat,
That ate the malt
That lay in the house that Jack built. (Breathe)

This is the maiden all forlorn,
That milked the cow with the crumpled horn,
That tossed the dog,
That worried the cat,
That killed the rat,
That ate the malt
That lay in the house that Jack built. (Breathe)

This is the man all tattered and torn,
That kissed the maiden all forlorn,
That milked the cow with the crumpled horn,
That tossed the dog,
That worried the cat,
That killed the rat,
That ate the malt
That lay in the house that Jack built. (Breathe)

This is the priest all shaven and shorn,
That married the man all tattered and torn,
That kissed the maiden all forlorn,
That milked the cow with the crumpled horn,
That tossed the dog,
That worried the cat,
That killed the rat,
That ate the malt
That lay in the house that Jack built. (Breathe)

This is the cock that crowed in the morn,
That waked the priest all shaven and shorn,
That married the man all tattered and torn,
That kissed the maiden all forlorn,
That milked the cow with the crumpled horn,
That tossed the dog,
That worried the cat,
That killed the rat,
That ate the malt
That lay in the house that Jack built. (Breathe)

This is the farmer sowing his corn,
That kept the cock that crowed in the morn,
That waked the priest all shaven and shorn,
That married the man all tattered and torn,

That kissed the maiden all forlorn,
That milked the cow with the crumpled horn,
That tossed the dog,
That worried the cat,
That killed the rat,
That ate the malt
That lay in the house that Jack built. (Breathe)

When you're lying awake with a dismal headache, and repose is taboo'd by anxiety,

I conceive you may use any language you choose to indulge in, without impropriety;

For your brain is on fire—the bedclothes conspire of usual slumber to plunder you:

First your counterpane goes, and uncovers your toes, and your sheet slips demurely from under you;

Then the blanketing tickles—you feel like mixed pickles—so terribly sharp is the pricking,

And you're hot, and you're cross, and you tumble and toss till there's nothing 'twixt you and the ticking.

Then the bedclothes all creep to the ground in a heap, and you pick 'em all up in a tangle;

Next your pillow resigns and politely declines to remain at its usual angle!

Well, you get some repose in the form of a doze, with hot eyeballs and head ever aching,

But your slumbering teems with such horrible dreams that you'd very much better be waking;

For you dream you are crossing the Channel, and tossing about in a steamer from Harwich—

Which is something between a large bathing machine and a very small second-class carriage—

And you're giving a treat (penny ice and cold meat) to a party of friends and relations—

They're a ravenous horde—and they all came on board at Sloane Square and South Kensington Stations.

And bound on that journey you find your attorney (who started that morning from Devon);

He's a bit undersized, and you don't feel surprised when he tells you he's only eleven.

Well, you're driving like mad with this singular lad (by the by, the ship's now a four-wheeler),

And you're playing round games, and he calls you bad names when you tell him that "ties pay the dealer";

But this you can't stand, so you throw up your hand, and you find you're as cold as an icicle,

In your shirt and your socks (the black silk with gold clocks), crossing Salisbury Plain on a bicycle:

And he and the crew are on bicycles too—which the've somehow or other invested in—

And he's telling the tars all the particuLARS of a company he's interested in—

It's a scheme of devices, to get at low prices all goods from cough mixtures to cables

(Which tickled the sailors), by treating retailers as though they were all vegeTAbles—

You get a good spadesman to plant a small tradesman (first take off his boots with a boot-tree),

And his legs will take root, and his fingers will shoot, and they'll blossom and bud like a fruit-tree—

From the greengrocer tree you get grapes and green pea, cauliflower, pineapple, and cranberries,

While the pastrycook plant cherry brandy will grant apple puffs, and three-corners, and Banburys—

The shares are a penny, and ever so many are taken by Rothschild and Baring,

And just as a few are allotted to you, you awake with a shudder despairing—

You're a regular wreck, with a crick in your neck, and no wonder you snore, for your head's on the floor, and you've needles and pins from your soles to your shins, and your flesh is a-creep, for your left leg's asleep, and you've cramp in your toes, and a fly on your nose, and some fluff in your lung, and a feverish tongue, and a thirst that's intense, and a general sense that you haven't been sleeping in clover;

But the darkness has passed, and it's daylight at last, and the night has been long—ditto ditto my song—and thank goodness they're both of them over!

Iolanthe, Gilbert and Sullivan

Appendix E

The Nature of Emotion

Emotion is a normal human condition, internally felt, externally expressed, and occurring irregularly. Always stronger than a unemotional state, it is characterized by a core feeling of excitement. From the excitement nucleus, diverse emotional patterns develop.

Emotions are formed in response to stimuli, to which we react with a series of definite physiological actions. These actions, in their simplest form, follow a standard pattern. Cued in by the element of excitement, certain autonomic changes occur: the blood vessels that serve the visceral region, especially the stomach and intestines, tend to contract at the beginning of an emotional state, but those serving the action muscles of the skeletal frame enlarge, with the result that blood is diverted from digestive to muscular functions; at the same time, nerve impulses step up the tempo of the heartbeat, so that blood pressure increases and the pulse rate quickens; in addition, the rate and intensity of respiration rises above normal, the pupils of the eyes enlarge, and the mouth, temporarily lacking secretions from the salivary glands, tends to become dry. Concurrently, adrenalin hormones, carried in the bloodstream, act upon the liver, so that sugar is changed into blood food, providing more energy for brain and muscles. Some of these activities leave a record in the body, and it is thus that we feel emotion.

When a stimulus occurs, a nervous charge of some strength is always present. It is felt as an impulse to action, and it is this impulse, generally sudden in appearance and carrying above-average amounts of energy, that makes emotion a major motivational force in human behavior. For good or ill, these emotional charges, insisting as they do upon action, are the agents responsible for a large portion of our behavioral patterns.

The Kinds of Emotion

The interaction of motivational force and emotional response is exhibited in its least complex form during the period of infancy. The newborn child, in the first months of its life, separates its reactions into the two broad categories of the pleasant and the unpleasant, the desirable and undesirable, thus identifying its response with one of the main life forces, the seeking and attainment of wishes or goals.

Stemming from the core feeling of excitement, the infant rapidly develops the ability to enjoy the related emotions of delight, elation, and affection, while the unpleasant feelings of distress, anger, disgust, fear, and jealousy also grow.

Later there are rearrangements, but these take place as the individual passes through the processes of learning and maturation that accompany childhood and early adulthood.

Three Basic Emotions • Psychologists have established three main categories of emotion for the adult person: *pleasure, fear,* and *anger.* The correspondence between this list and the three basic attitudes or relationships that have been used throughout this book are immediately apparent: pleasure—going toward life; fear—drawing away from life; anger—standing against life.

In irregular patterns, each of these basic emotions, or its associates, is experienced by all of us many times each day, variation in emotional response being a syndrome of normalcy. In a constant play of feelings, one emotion gives way to another in reaction to changes of stimulus. Or, if the motivation is strong and holds long enough, one feeling dominates for an extended period of time.

In few, if any, cases, however, will the dominant emotion also be exclusive. It is doubtful if there is such a thing as a pure emotion, at least in the sense that one feeling holds isolated sway to the exclusion of all others. In this respect emotions are tolerant; two or more exist at the same time, each one acting as a conditioning factor for the others. Generally, one is dominant.

Pleasure • Pleasure, with its associated feelings of delight, joy, liking and love, is experienced when needs are satisfactorily met, when the energy drive of desire, unrepressed, expends its force to some purpose and something deemed valuable is acquired or achieved. Enjoyment of the emotions grouped in the pleasure category bespeaks temporary or permanent success in some phase of living. Under these conditions optimistic attitudes prevail.

Pleasurable states of being are expressed when movement is psychologically free, within the limits of a character's age and physical condition, when feet willingly point or move toward the object of attention, when arms open wide to release inner feelings, when the head turns toward and the eyes look directly at surrounding persons and objects, when other individuals are brought freely into contact in handshakes and embraces. Such attributes as vitality, grace, dignity, openness, and trustworthiness are associated with this emotional group.

Pleasure-oriented Roles • Toinette and Tony belong unmistakably in this group. Even though both are notorious for the way they fly in the face of authority, their attitudes toward life are positive to the point of enthusiasm. Most of the leading characters in plays of the romantic genre, as well as roles in comedies and musical comedies are pleasure-oriented. Other examples can be drawn from such diverse characters as Prince Hal in *Henry IV*, Part 1, Cyrano de Bergerac, and Henry Higgins in *Pygmalion.*

Perhaps Oedipus towers above all others as the mightiest figure among those who willingly go toward life. Unhappily, in this case, society did not answer with a reciprocal action, for although the direction of his movement was right, the manner of his movement was wrong. Hubris, overweening pride, the greatest of sins according to the Greeks, characterized his attitude toward his people. Willing though he was, and able, his was a case in which the approach and the reception differed.

Fear • Fear, and its associated emotions, generally is indicative of a condition of insufficiency, or what the individual considers insufficiency. A person in this category relates himself to himself, acting as judge of his own capabilities. In his evaluation he finds that he lacks, in some manner, the properties that could insure success for his endeavors and protect him from harm. Fear motivates withdrawal, blocking positive actions before they are attempted.

Although it may seem that anything that threatens one's person or position is the basic cause of fear, actually the substance of fear is found in the inability of the individual to meet a threat successfully; it is the negative factor within rather than the positive one without that stirs this emotion. Shyness, timidity, anxiety, alarm, and awe are some of the less energetic feelings in this category, while dismay, dread, terror, and panic are its extreme forms.

Withdrawal movements are occasioned by fear, so also are those seeking to protect a person or thing. Escape and defense become desirable actions.

Fear-oriented Roles • Hamlet, Prince of Denmark, is the best known of fear-oriented roles. In the basic conflict of the play, Hamlet continuously sits in judgment on his own actions. Struggling with himself more than with any other character, he never wins more than temporary victory. The result is that his main course of action seldom deviates from a progression toward a final and full retreat from life.

Other fear-oriented characters are the Ajax of Sophocles, *Capitano Spavento del Val Inferno* in the *commedia dell'arte* and his Shakespearean counterpart Falstaff, Richard II, Argan in *The Imaginary Invalid*, the Captain in *The Father*, Oswald in *Ghosts*, Emperor Jones, Blanche in *A Streetcar Named Desire*, Eddie in *A View from the Bridge*, and the Old Man in Ionesco's *The Chairs*.

Anger • Anger is the emotional response to frustration. It is provoked by restraints and goaded by denials. Intolerant of defeat, anger denotes an unwillingness to accept the results of blocked desire drives. The actions of other persons or the results of one's own inability are the catalysts that arouse the feeling of anger. Of all the emotions that most motivate antisocial behavior, this is least acceptable to society.

Associated with anger are the companion emotions of pique, aversion, irritation, and bitterness, of loathing, malice, hate, and abhorrence, each stemming from the same source, each energized with a different power, but all a mark of human unwillingness to accept repression or defeat.

Anger-oriented Roles • The Greeks supply us with numerous examples:

Electra, Clytemnestra, Medea, Antigone, Phaedra—all women, and all magnificent characters. Shakespeare matches the Greek with a male set equally great: Richard III, Iago, Shylock, Cassius, Hotspur—and Katherina, the Shrew, must be listed, too.

Modern drama gives us Hedda Gabler, Laura in *The Father*, Liliom—a classic instance, Leonardo in Lorca's *Blood Wedding*, Frank Maurrant in *Street Scene*, Regina in *The Little Foxes*, and Solange and Claire in Genet's *The Maids*.

Appendix F

Stage Properties

The expert handling of stage properties—props—is an obligatory aspect of acting, and is a matter of technical proficiency. Props can work for or against the player, whose skill will determine which shall be the case.

Two statements are applicable to all properties and all situations: Whenever possible, the handling of a prop should be worked into the forward flow of the scene's major action, but if such integration is not feasible, the movements involved in handling the prop should be performed in such a manner that the attention of the audience is successfully sustained for that period of time. The people out front should not have to wait until a hard-to-light cigarette is finally lit, or while a telephone cord is untangled, or until a wrongly tied package is finally opened. It is good practice to introduce a production's props, or facsimiles thereof, into rehearsal as soon as scripts are laid aside.

Here are points applicable to the handling of the most commonly used stage props.

CIGARETTES

1. Have all cigarettes easy of access, either in package or container. Unless so designated in the script, the cigarette should not be the only one there.

2. If a cigarette lighter is to be used, it should be tested before performance. Have a supply of matches at hand in the event the lighter does not work.

3. When a match is to be used, the matchstick is less likely to break in striking if the middle or forefinger is held close to the tip.

4. The delivery of a line should not be delayed by the lighting of a cigarette, unless such action is specifically indicated in the script.

5. The cigarette should always be thoroughly lighted.

6. It is annoying to some members of an audience to see a cigarette extinguished shortly after being lit.

7. An act of smoking should not betray the smoker's inexperience.

TELEPHONES

1. After using a telephone be careful about placing the receiver in the cradle. A receiver that slips or falls or that is placed half on or half off the cradle causes an unwanted distraction.

2. If other players are to use the telephone, the position of the receiver should

be established beforehand. The comic movement incident to placing the wrong end of the phone to the ear is not desirable in a serious situation.

3. When talking over the telephone there must seem to be time for the person at the other end to say what he has to say.

Food

The act of eating on stage can pose some difficult problems, especially if a player must seem to eat heartily or to take large bites, or is under time pressure, or is required to manage unusual foods.

1. To chew or to swallow food during line delivery is difficult. Time the act of mastication so that it fits between the times of delivery.

2. It is possible to seem to take large quantities of food into the mouth when the amount actually is quite small.

3. Food should not be held in the mouth any longer than is necessary.

4. Be wary of spewing food particles when in the act of speaking.

5. It should be known that the British do not hold and use knives and forks as Americans do. The player should also be aware that there is a difference in table manners and the management of silverware in various parts of our own country.

6. A few simple precepts about the management of trays can be of help:

   a. If a character must carry a tray through a door, the posterior of the body and occasionally the feet can control the door's swing. If a door must be opened, there will be more security if the arm is under the center of the tray so that the fingers may clasp the outside edge. In all types of carrying, the objects on the tray should be balanced as to weight.

   b. Arrange the objects to be lifted from the tray so that those that must be taken off first are the closest and easiest to handle.

   c. When stacking dishes to clear a table, organize your movements so that the largest plates are on the bottom. Determine by trial how the dishes can most conveniently be placed on the tray for maximum use of space and safety. Long-stemmed wineglasses will be more secure if placed in the center of a tray rather than near the edge.

If the player keeps such small points as the above in mind during the rehearsal period when the props are introduced, he can save the director and the cast much time by attending to these details himself.

Liquids

1. When pouring liquids—water, wine, tea, or coffee—know from practice the amount to have in the container and the amount to pour. Neither the container nor the receptacle should be so full that spilling is a danger. On the other hand, the amount poured should not be noticeably insufficient.

2. For some perverse reason the audience watches the act of pouring with unusual concentration, and, of course, that is the time when an actor's hands are most likely to betray his nervousness. Sureness derived from sufficient practice is the only answer to this problem.

3. There is a marked difference in the manner in which different wineglasses,

tumblers, mugs, cups and saucers, and so forth, are held. The player should acquaint himself with the proper management of each.

4. If a filled cup or glass is to be carried across stage, the player is wise to follow the example of the trained waiter and not look at what he is carrying. If they are not watched, the arm and hand adjust more easily to the motion of walking.

5. As with eating and smoking, drinking should generally be done between the player's lines.

CLOTHING

1. Clothes, especially those of some bulk or intricacy of design, are among the most bothersome of stage properties. The manner of wearing, carrying, handling, or placing clothes on furniture should be worked out carefully in order to minimize the danger of putting the arm in the wrong sleeve, or of trying to adjust the bottom of a cape to a lady's shoulder, or of frantically searching for a neck scarf under a pile of coats on a clothes tree, or of having the tie of a dress suit ride off the collar and onto the neck of the wearer.

2. Occasionally playwrights do not supply enough lines to cover an onstage costume change. Of course, ad libs can be added to correct the situation, but the inserted comments usually reveal themselves for exactly what they are, bits of filler talk delivered in the hope of distracting the audience's attention from the hurried movements of the costume change. Manual dexterity made certain by practice, and the organization of movement based on logical, time-saving patterns are the surest means the player has to make his business work for rather than against him.

3. One of the notable values to be obtained from a study of this kind is that you can accumulate knowledge of how to manage a large number of small details, thereby decreasing in advance the worry about trivia during dress rehearsal and performance times.

a. When helping another player with coat or jacket, do not put the garment on the other person yourself; hold it open and ready and let him get into it.

b. When tying a tie onstage, determine the length of both ends before the knot is formed.

c. Become thoroughly acquainted with the clasp mechanism on any jewelry that must be taken off or put on.

d. If a coat and hat should be carried offstage, hold the hat and drape the coat over the arm away from the exit door. If the door must be closed after the exit, it is an easy matter to shift both hat and coat to the opposite arm so that the exit may be made without an awkward turn.

e. Male actors wearing dress clothes of any kind should develop the habit of having a fellow player check to insure that coat collars are in place, ties properly knotted up, pocket flaps out, and so on before each entrance. Actresses should do the same thing, taking care to mention any detail that might require special attention.

f. Take gloves off before coats.

g. When hanging up clothes or draping them on furniture, be exact as to placement if they must be worn again in the scene, so that they will be easier to manage when handled again.

Suitcases and Packages

1. Unless comedy is intended, be sure a suitcase is right side up before opening. Also ascertain that it is securely closed before making an entrance.

2. When carrying suitcases or packages, the approximate weight of the props should be suggested by your movement. It is not necessary that the container be loaded with rocks just to make it realistically heavy, although some weight is always a help to the actor.

3. If you do not know the proper kind of a knot to tie when wrapping a parcel, ask for instructions. Knots that do not stay secure can cause embarrassment.

4. If you must open a package, check with the prop man as to the kind of a knot he will tie and how it can best be untied.

The Actor and the Property Master

1. Actors have a special relationship to the property master, being dependent on him for what is often a critical item in a scene's progression. In a well-organized company the property master, or *props* as he is called backstage, has complete control over all set and hand props in the offstage area. Several simple rules pertain here:

1. Unless otherwise directed, plan to obtain your prop directly from the prop man before an entrance, and return any prop to him you bring offstage.

2. Never handle the properties on the prop table, or those placed elsewhere for the convenience of the actors.

3. *Never* handle prop weapons of any kind, *never* use them in mock fights at any time.

4. Such edibles as candy, cookies, and so forth are to be treated as any critical item would be and are to be consumed only as part of the business of a play.

The Breakable Prop

Occasionally it is necessary that a prop be broken onstage. If the script requires that a glass, cup, or vase fall from a table or be dropped by hand, it is usually the duty of the property master to create a "break-away" article, which will come apart on contact with the floor. In such a case the actor's responsibility is to perform the act of dropping the item or of knocking it off the furniture in the manner and the direction desired. The technique of making the seeming accident appear unplanned is to focus attention elsewhere deliberately, so as not to appear to have planned the mischance.

In more violent movements, a player may be required to smash an article such as a cup, plate, or vase. This action, generally called for in moments of emotional intensity, can be difficult and dangerous. The energy of the motion of throwing is such that a break-away prop need not always be prepared. It then devolves upon you to acquaint yourself with both the article and the action, to the extent that you know how to hold and how to throw in a manner that makes the break certain; a bounce rather than a break can occur.

It is a matter of concern that neither members of the cast or the audience be harmed by flying particles of glass or pottery. Two precautionary steps may be taken to insure that no such untoward accident occurs. The first is to make certain that the player involved be able to throw and to hit the target area. It is no disparagement to suggest that actresses take extra care in this matter. The second is to guarantee control of all flying particles by containing the smashed article in the target area. It is, of course, always safer to throw upstage rather than downstage, but this fact does not minimize the necessity to make sure that no fragment goes in an unwanted direction.

The Dropped Prop

In the event that a prop accidentally falls or is dropped to the floor, the player nearest the article or the character to whom the action is most appropriate should immediately pick it up. A dropped handkerchief, spoon, pen, or any other hand prop remains a distraction until it has been retrieved. The action of recovery should be performed in character and as naturally as possible.

Were a glass of wine to be inadvertently spilled or a cup and saucer accidently broken, the matter should be handled onstage as it would be in a life situation by persons possessed of social poise, by effecting remedial actions that are unhurried and unembarrassed. In such a situation there is this to remember: errors are bound to creep into the performance of even the best-prepared play, but their advent should be a signal to the actors to be mentally alert, not emotionally confused. Probably your training has revealed to you the psychologically helpful fact that an audience will accept and respect an actor's appraisal of an unplanned occurrence. If those who are onstage treat an accident in an honest manner, they say in effect to the audience: yes, something has gone wrong, but it was not planned and is not too important, and if you will bear with us, we will shortly rectify the situation and then get on with the more important business of the play.

EXERCISES AND ASSIGNMENTS

1. Working in pairs, create an original situation that will involve the management of one of the prop combinations listed below:

   a. Food, telephone, and three Christmas packages.

   b. A tray with wineglasses and a narrow-necked decanter, cigarettes, and hors d'oeuvres.

   c. A briefcase with books and papers, a pair of shoes, a shirt and a tie that must be put on, and an alarm clock.

2. Prepare and present scenes from the following plays, or any other sequences that can be made into good prop scenes:

   The Red Peppers, Noel Coward, the dressing-room scene with its change of costume and action of eating.

   Fumed Oak, Noel Coward, the food-throwing scene.

   Laburnum Grove, J. B. Priestley, the dining-room scene.

Ah, Wilderness, Eugene O'Neill, Act II, Scene 1.

You Can't Take It with You, Hart and Kaufman, Act II, the scene before the entrance of the Kirbys.

They Knew What They Wanted, Sidney Howard, Act I, the first scene.

Men in White, Sidney Kingsley, Act I, Scene 3 or 4.

The Gentle People, Irwin Shaw, Act III, Scene 2.

The Taming of the Shrew, Shakespeare, Act IV, Scene 3.

Stalag 17, Bevan and Trzcinski; there are several good prop scenes.

Appendix G

Stage Falls and Stage Struggles

Every actor or actress, at some time or other onstage, can expect to faint or to fight. A necessary accomplishment of acting is proficiency in the execution of stage falls and stage struggles. Because both are emotionally motivated and therefore emotionally charged, both falls and struggles can be dangerous. With the common-sense thought of safety in mind, the element of excitement must be balanced by knowledge of procedure, sureness of control, and sufficiency of practice.

Among the least used of major stage actions, falls and struggles generally occur at moments of critical importance. Associated with the element of intensification, both are usually identified with a minor or major climax.

Basic Principles

Knowledge of certain basic principles will aid you in the development of the skills required in this highly specialized segment of your training.

1. The eradication of fear is essential. If knowledge replaces ignorance, there is no cause for the presence of this unstable state.
2. Physical fitness and control are required of all participants.
3. In the case of stage struggles, conflict must give way to coordination, opposition must become cooperation.
4. Knowledge and practice can reduce or eliminate the hazard of injury. Spur-of-the-moment inspirations invite accidents, therefore patterns of movement should be set as definitely and followed as exactly as the routines of a dance sequence.
5. Safety and certainty are most assured by the practice of every assignment in slow motion.
6. Generalized or blurred movement, full of sound and fury but signifying little else, detracts rather than adds quality to a struggle scene.
7. Stage struggles demand constant interplay of action and reaction. Much of the success of your action depends on your ability to govern and bring these elements into play.
8. Properly motivated and well-executed sounds can intensify the excitement of a physical contest.

Stage Falls

A stage fall represents either an unconscious or a conscious action.

An unconscious fall is caused by an act of fainting, a response to internal malfunctioning, or by a blow of some sort, externally applied. In each case the control center of the brain ceases to function and the muscles that sustain the points of bone articulation permit the body to collapse downward, joint by joint, in one fluent action.

The second type of stage fall, in which consciousness is retained, is characterized by loss of muscular control only. A stumble, trip, push, or blow can occasion this fall, as can a spell of physical weakness or a sword or dagger thrust. In any case, the downward movement generally is marked by a mental and physical attitude of resistance, by an attempt not to give way, not to go down; the resistance may be slight or it may be fiercely maintained, as in the manner of a Mercutio who strains with utmost will to sustain a position of pride.

When the actor is free of emotional constraints and physical tenseness, each fall can be performed so that no injury results from body contact with the stage floor. You have proven this fact many times since childhood. If more than your own previous actions are needed as a source of study, the activity of the football player, the gymnast, and, if available, the rodeo rider can provide you with excellent primary-source material. From observation of these specialists you can learn how the relaxed fall and the rolling fall are performed and see how the full force of a fall is broken by the proper handling of arms and hands, legs and feet.

The Plumb Line of Gravity • The predominantly operative element in any kind of fall is the plumb-line pull of gravity. When we cease at any time to exert a counteraction to gravitation, a body mass responds to the downward attraction in as direct a line as possible. Thus, when a person faints— if we exclude the swaying of a dizzy spell that is sometimes a prelude to unconsciousness—the body crumples straight downward. Of course, the human body cannot pile up on a floor as a heap of sand does; it must deviate from the straight line to the extent its length requires, but it does so only as each successive section strikes the floor.

In the case of a conscious fall, the ability to counteract gravity is in some measure retained by the individual. At the same time, since gravitational pull is constant, the need for a performer to force himself downward is eliminated. The violent throwing of the body to the floor, an action dear to and amusingly used by players in what we term old-fashioned melodrama, is obviated.

The Fainting Fall • Relaxation, mental and physical and as nearly complete as possible, is the core condition of this dramatic exercise. The first step in the process of achieving relaxation is to initiate *mental decontrol*. It may be well to discover how easily this can be done by practicing first with the arms and head.

Standing or sitting, stretch one arm directly overhead to its full length, then let it fall of its own accord. If it is truly relaxed, the member will fall loosely, easily, and as directly downward as possible. After several trials, bring the other arm into play. Next, increase the scope of the movement by permitting the head to slump at the same time. After that, and in the same manner, execute the fall itself. Standing upright, pull out the energy plugs and let gravity do the rest.

You will crumple straight down, not like a sack of cement, but like a sack of potatoes, each part making separate contact with the floor—knees, hips, torso, arms and head, loosely, softly, and with a quick, natural flow.

The body drops with equal facility in any direction. On the stage the exact position is usually predetermined by the pattern of the scene's business. If, after your fall, other actors must move to your side, the needs of their business will determine the direction of your movement. Further, if you must later be lifted, the wrong position could add greatly to the hazard of what is always a difficult action.

The Rigid Fall • Completely different in nature and purpose, the rigid fall is nearly always performed as comic business. A farcical movement, it achieves its purpose by breaking the rules of nature in an absurd way. When you perform it, instead of instituting relaxation, you assume a posture of rigidity, falling stiffly over like a piece of lumber. To avoid injury, any one of three things may be done.

1. You may be caught by someone standing nearby before you strike the floor. Falling to the rear or side, rigidity can be maintained even after the catch is made.

2. You may fall straight forward. In this action the hands and arms are interposed at the last moment to break the impact of the fall. The best place to begin practice, if you are not already accomplished, is on the sand of a beach or the grass of a lawn.

3. You may fall straight backward. Clowns and acrobats use this fall extensively. In execution, rigidity is broken at the hips. More of a rolling fall than the others, the impact of the body on the floor is decreased by bending the torso forward as the fall is in progress, with the result that continuous movement is achieved. Like the rolling fall, it emulates the action of a hoop. As soon as the body is prone, the movement is generally ended by raising stiffened legs and then letting them drop flatly down again.

The Conscious Fall • Always the result of an unpremeditated action, the greatest difficulty in enacting a fall resulting from a trip, stumble, or push lies in making the movement appear accidental. To compensate for a tendency to err in this respect two actions may be taken: avoid showing anticipation of what is to come; permit enough loss of balance to occur to make the movement seem reasonable.

If a fall comes as a result of weakness, a body blow, or a sword thrust, the ensuing action takes on more of an aspect of regular stage business than of a sudden collapse. The normal reaction is to maintain mental control as long as possible, with the result that a character goes down, as each part of the body gives way, in a series of movements that still contain some degree of energy.

The Rolling Fall • If a fall occurs when a character is in motion, a rolling fall is indicated. This movement requires both control and flexibility.

The practicality of the rolling fall lies in the fact that the impact of the action is dissipated by continuing movement. The image of a wheel can be helpful here. Visualize the action of a rounded surface striking the floor. Recall that the turning body is not stopped on contact with the floor but continues to move in a direction parallel to it. Thus the force of the impact is quickly dissipated in continuing movement, as it was in the somersault so commonly performed in our childhood.

The rolling fall can be quite spectacular. If there is sufficient momentum, a trip can be turned into a flying somersault in which a player is down and up again in an instant. By its use in either comic or serious business, seemingly violent actions can be used to excite an audience, with no harm to the player.

On occasions when battle scenes are to be played, or when a spectacular incident is needed in a murder mystery, a fall down a flight of steps or from a height can be used to advantage. If the principles of the fainting fall (the sack of potatoes) and the rolling fall (the somersault) are combined, the business can be brought off without harm. To demonstrate the action, imagine a soldier standing high up on a parapet. Suddenly struck by a bullet, he first lets his gun slip from his hands to clatter to the stage floor, an exciting preliminary sound and action in itself. Then he falls off the wall by the simple expedient of moving swiftly, always letting one portion of his body descend before the other, each part either breaking or restraining the rest.

The Stage Lift

The action of lifting a mass of any size or weight from an inert position on a stage floor is a difficult maneuver. As graceful as the human form can be in normal postures, in an unconscious state it is a flabby shape of sprawling limbs and rounded trunk that defy easy handling.

It goes without saying that a player should never attempt to lift a body that is out of proportion to his size and strength. To avoid muscular strain and to decrease the likelihood of an ungainly lurch or awkward slip, you should acquaint yourself with the physical principles that apply to raising any weight.

1. Never perform a lift from an unbalanced position in which the lifter's torso and arms are out of plumb.

2. Begin the lift from as solid a foundation as possible. In most cases a distribution of weight between a foot and a resting knee provides a firm base.

3. Lift on a perpendicular line as much as possible.

4. Employing the large muscles of the legs, lift with the knees rather than the arms.

5. Hold the lifted body close to your own.

6. Once the lifting movement is initiated, maintain momentum by continuing the action to completion.

To gain optimum advantage from the above physical principles, coordinate them with the following physical actions.

1. Make use of the fact that the seemingly unconscious player can aid you in the task ahead. Limp arms and limp neck will direct attention away from other muscles that work in unseen coordination with your own.

2. Secure a firm hold before beginning the lift. Kneel so that one of the inert arms can be placed over your shoulder in such a way that the other player, by locking his arm on your shoulder, can sustain some of the added weight. Reach well under the other's back with your lifting arm so that your wrist and hand may hold firmly to the other side of the chest.

3. Place your knee as far under the back of the other person as possible.

4. To prevent the posterior of the lifted player from sagging, place your arm under the middle or upper portion of the legs. Your unconscious friend can aid you by maintaining a slight rigidity in the lower back muscles.

5. Secure the weight by your upper arms rather than your forearms.

6. Raise the body by straightening your back so that the weight is directly over the base that is the foundation for the lift. Have the knees bear the brunt of the burden. If a pause must be made, rest the inert form on your raised knee after the initial lift and pull the body more firmly to you. When both bodies are balanced over the center of gravity, use the leverage of the knees to come to a standing position.

7. When walking with your burden, lean back far enough to permit the friction between the bodies to relieve some of the strain on your arms.

8. If the body must be laid down again onstage, do not lower it by bending over. Again let the knees, rather than the back, sustain the action.

9. When two persons can be employed to lift an unconscious form, the action is performed more efficiently if the lift is from the sides rather than the top and bottom. When such is the case, both should kneel as close to the body as possible. Locked arms provide more security than individual handholds. Exact timing of the coordinated movement is essential. A simultaneous intake of breath is a good signal for the initiation of action.

10. A comic lift is best performed by assuming unbalanced postures and by instituting an uneven tempo. A lift and carry by wrists and ankles can be good business.

The Stage Slap

The action of slapping the face of another player or of being slapped is one most actors dislike. Yet a slap, because it releases a pent-up emotion, always increases the dramatic intensity of a scene.

A stage slap is an easy, simple action. The palm and fingers of the hand, held almost flat, strike the fleshy part of the recipient's cheek just above the jaw line. The result of the movement is painful only if either of the participants fear its consequences. Anticipation that produces tenseness in either the slapper or the slapped is the main deterrent to a good, clean-cut movement.

There are several *ifs* that go into the execution of a good stage slap. The player who slaps another will be most certain of performing a convincing action and of hitting his proper mark if he achieves good articulation in the joints of arm and wrist, if he accomplishes a free and full arm swing, and if he exerts the necessary amount of vigor. The actor who is slapped will perform his part best if he does not anticipate the blow, and if he does not flinch. He will save himself some hurt if he relaxes the muscles of the face and neck, and if he turns slightly with the blow as it lands.

STAGE STRUGGLES

Whether it is the life and death struggle in *Macbeth*, the wrestling episode in *As You Like It*, the *duel-ballade* in *Cyrano*, the swinging fists of the free-for-all in *Mr. Roberts*, the hair-pulling contest in *The Plough and the Stars*, or the tumbling fun in *Private Lives*, a stage struggle invariably indicates a high point in the dramatic experience.

Shakespeare, with his great fund of dramatic instinct, knew the potential of the stage struggle and used it as a device for intensification of conflict, developing that potential with telling effect in play after play. Molière, following in the tradition of the *commedia dell'arte*, saw the comic possibilities of violent physical actions and exploited them continuously. In the sweep from high tragedy to low comedy there always has been a need for all forms of militant movement.

Stage struggles are of many kinds, varying from a light face slap to the violence of a full body attack between two or more persons. Certain basic principles apply to all forms of physical combat.

Coordination • A stage struggle is not a real struggle, it is only an illusion of one. As a physical conflict, the struggle is strictly a no-contest affair. Struggling actors work together, coordinating their physical actions much as dancers or gymnasts do, but with the exception that their movements create an impression of conflict. This is possible because the rapidity of their movement does not allow the audience time to make a reasonable analysis of the actions witnessed.

In actions of opposition, when muscular force meets muscular force, some elements of realism are employed. In a struggle for balance, for example, each player exerts enough energy to match the attack of the other. Arm can be locked on arm or body can strain against body in an obvious display of conflict. Sword can clash against sword with no question of the force behind the blow. But there is this difference between the real and the sham struggle: in the latter the force is measured beforehand, the direction of attack is known, and one action is balanced against another for calculated effect. In this respect one of the most necessary skills required of the player is the ability to gauge the degree of energy both he and his opposite exert in a struggle. Feeling the power of his opponent, he matches it as required, but he is always aware of the point beyond which he dares not go. It is not unusual that one player, who to all appearances is forcing his opponent down toward the floor, is, in reality, holding him up.

Safety • There are several precautions that can be taken in the interests of safety.

1. In militant movement, each player is obliged to accept the dramatic element of illusion as one of the initial ingredients of his practice. The thought that a struggle is an expression of vindictiveness, or that a hatred shown is a hatred felt, is both repugnant and wrong. Instead, a player's purpose is to be as convincing in action as he is innocent in intent.

2. The element of safety demands that the patterns of movement in any stage struggle be conceived carefully and executed exactly. When this is properly done, physical injury can result only from error. If you or your opponent receive a hurt, it is because one of you has made a mistake.

3. Weak or untrained muscles should be exercised from the beginning of the period of rehearsals so that by opening night they will be fit and prepared.

4. Nervousness or fear on the one hand, or too much enthusiasm on the other, produces a tensed muscular condition that is unresponsive to direction. Such a state throws timing off, causes movements to be improperly executed, destroys the sense of balance, and causes error to breed error. Muscular tension is desirable and necessary, muscular tenseness is not.

5. Dramatic combatants, sharing a foreknowledge of what is to come, should plan defensive and offensive movements as one process. Then, by the simple expedient of giving the initiative to the defensive, they eliminate the element of surprise and at the same time guarantee in the most effective way possible that no hurtful blow or thrust will reach its target. Rapidity of action prevents the audience from realizing that the defensive actor has placed his weapon or his body in the blocking position the moment before the offensive movement arrives.

6. A correct estimate of distance is as essential as an alert sense of timing. In all struggles the manner of making contact determines the distance at which the opponents face each other. For example, fists almost touch, swords overlap, and arms clasp arms or torsos in close embrace. Misjudged distance can cause a sword to cut the air inches or feet short of contact or make a fist fly through the air in a ludicrous miss.

7. From primitive times to the present day aggressive physical actions usually follow a well-defined pattern. With fists or weapons, the opponents first spar in a series of trial actions, testing each other and seeking advantage. Then one takes the initiative and the fight is joined. A few moments of furious activity follow. If a decision is not reached in this first trial, the fighters disengage, either on equal terms or with the advantage to one or the other. After a short but wary pause, the cycle is enacted again. The contest then continues in this pattern to the moment of climax. Containing as it does numberless opportunities for preliminary and main movements and for the interplay of action and reaction, such a series of sequences is made to order for a dramatic build of almost perfect proportions.

8. Exactness can best be assured and injury prevented if the whole sequence is practiced in slow motion until the correct movements become reliably habitual. The sureness established by this practice can be maintained as the tempo of the action increases. Other than continual alertness, no other element insures safety from injury to the extent this one does.

9. Only a foolish actor will take dangerous chances just to make a fight, or himself in a fight, appear to advantage. It is easy to be lured into an attempt at emulation of the swordplay seen on the motion picture screen, but bear in mind that there are two men on the studio lot who can do things most actors cannot. One is the expert athlete who is hired to do the fighting, and the other is the studio cutter, who probably creates the best fight of all.

10. Some contests are governed by official or practical rules and regulations. If the character you play is rated an expert, you must be practiced in such things as proper stance, use of weapons, and the most advantageous movements to make. This book does not purport to speak with authority on any type of combat. However, there are other books that do. The recommendation here is that you turn to such works whenever the occasion demands.[81]

Principal Types of Stage Struggles • There are three main kinds of physical contest used in the theatre: fist fighting, sword fighting, and tussling (wrestling). Each has its variables, but all are covered by a basic set of common-sense rules.

1. *The Fist Fight.* Generally this discussion is of interest only to the actor. The men will note that the term boxing was not used. In most plays, physical combat results from the need to release emotional pressure by the use of fists, unregulated by the Marquis of Queensberry rules.

The problem is to know how to deliver and how to receive an attack. There are two kinds of blows: those that can be received and absorbed without decisive hurt, and those that stop the fight. The first generally land on the arms or torso of the opponent in such a manner or place as to give the suggestion of vigorous activity, but they are not decisive. The second, the decisive blow, is directed at the chin, solar plexus, or the back of the neck. The first group might be called the filler blows of the fight, adding to and filling out the activity. The last is the terminal blow that often ends the contest.

No blow, not even the filler punch, should land with full force. However, there are ways to create the illusion that all blows contain a full quota of energy. One is to soften the blow on contact, taking the force out of the punch at the moment of impact, but not before. If this action is combined with the receiver's ability to sustain some impact without hurt, the blow can be an effective one.

Another way is to use a covering movement. As the offensive blow comes

---

[81] The fine points of such sports as fencing and boxing often do not lend themselves to dramatic action, in which case dramatic necessity will take precedence over fidelity to primary-source material.

in toward its target, a quick shift of a head or body position by either of the players, or the sudden interposition of a reaction character between the combatants and the audience, can cover the actual contact. For example, the player who delivers a blow to the solar plexus moves in close to his opponent by stepping forward with his downstage foot, with the result that his shoulder and back block the audience view of the impact from the swinging upstage arm. On the same principal either the aggressor or defender can cover a blow to the chin by stepping directly downstage of the opponent; thus either one body or the other blocks the view of the audience. The sparring movements inherent in a fight provide ample motivation for assuming these positions.

2. *Swordplay.* For healthful exercise and for the development of grace and muscular fluency, as well as for the acquisition of expert knowledge and skill, it is recommended that the actor and actress enroll in a fencing class whenever possible.

There are several kinds of swordplay in which actors should be proficient: the foil, which concentrates on maneuver and the fencing thrust, with danger only in the point; the épée, which has both point and edge, and combines the fencing thrust with cutting swing; broadsword and shield, featuring pierce and slash against ward and parry; and sword and dagger.

This last is the most difficult and dangerous fight of all, requiring skill in each hand and concentration on both. The sword is held in the right hand while the dagger is grasped in the left, with the blade extending out from between thumb and forefinger. Long-range fighting is done with the sword as in regular play. But when the swords lock, the combatants come close together and the daggers are brought into action.

In swordplay, feint and lunge followed by parry and counterthrust provide a variety of action. Any good manual on fencing will demonstrate the points of attack, which are many, and the actions of defense.

There is a standard and almost traditional movement for the thrust that wounds or kills. It is accomplished by means of a full lunge in which the point of the sword passes the recipient's body on the upstage side, but far enough away from the torso to preclude hurt. As soon as the movement has reached its full length, the blade is laid against the wounded man's side before being pulled back. To heighten the effect of harm, the injured party clamps his arm against the blade, holding it just tightly enough to require a suggestion of effort when the blade is withdrawn. The audience, of course, is aware that no actual wound is made, but, in the hands of a skilled player, the adroitness of the action will add to rather than detract from the illusion.

3. *Tussling.* Tussling embraces all kinds of scuffling actions—pulling hair, slapping, tumbling over furniture, falling down stairs, and rolling on the floor.[82] The actress is concerned with this as much as the actor.

[82] Of all stage struggles, rolling on the floor is the one most likely to be filled with a flurry of random movement and meaningless sounds. At its worst, it is a grossly inefficient kind of action wherein the players emit panting noises and roll over each other in overworked fury.

When the female player fights, she usually tussles, slaps, or pulls hair; on occasion she has been known to bite and scratch as well.

The separate act of pulling hair offers splendid opportunities to any pair of actresses fortunate enough to find such an action in their script. It should be said immediately that no hair need be pulled in this kind of scene. The technique is to grasp a handful of hair in such a way that the butt of the hand and the closed fingers rest on the scalp. With a hand on either side pressing directly against the head, it is possible to move or shake vigorously without causing hurt. To control the center of interest, both actresses should not launch an attack at the same time. It is enough that one tug while the other tries to block the action. An attack on the hair can be balanced by a bite on a hand or an arm.

The act of pushing makes a good opening movement for a female fight. The usual procedure, in which the push or shove becomes a preliminary movement for the resultant struggle, follows a standard cycle: the first push is made, causing an appropriate reaction; on recovery from the reaction, the one pushed retaliates with a similar but more vigorous push of her own; again there is a reaction, which is followed in turn by a recovery and the execution of yet another more energetic push; at this point the fight can be joined.

THE SOUNDS OF STRUGGLE

Tonal sounds are mainly reactions, and are capable of adding greatly to the effectiveness of a scene. In addition to the lines of the script, such vocal responses as exclamations by the combatants and cries of encouragement from the onlookers can be employed to heighten the intensity of the main action.

The sounds resulting from violent action are of two kinds. The first is the sound of a blow striking its target. Although few sounds come when flesh hits flesh in a real fight, the need to hear the sound of a blow often seems necessary in the theatre. Generally the sound is produced by hidden hand movements that strike a thigh or a chest at the same time the contact is made. Either the offensive or defensive player, or a reaction character, can make the sound. It need not be emphasized that precision of timing is important. If the view of a hit is blocked, as it might be, the aggressor's fist may strike the open palm of the defendant, the latter member being held just below the chin. Although this technique is employed more often than any other, it can be a chancy arrangement if not properly performed.

The second kind of vocal sounds are those made by the players as they struggle and strain. Muttered imprecations can help to fill out the general impression of conflict. Vowel sounds that seem to be subconscious responses to the effect of a blow can, in fact, tell the audience just how effective the blow was supposed to be.

Whenever sounds are used, none should be left to an on-the-spot inspiration by the actors engaged in combat. Some pungent modernisms have been known to carry over the clash of arms in Shakespeare, and occasionally small but offensive words have been heard when no such words were intended.

EXERCISES AND ASSIGNMENTS

1. *Lifts.* Perform two lifts, one of an injured but conscious person, the other of an unconscious body.

2. *Stage falls.* Enact the following list of stage falls:

a. A fainting fall, a turning fall as the result of being shot, a fall from a height.

b. A trip or stumble with little momentum, a fall from a violent push, a fast running fall, a rigid fall.

3. *Stage struggles.* In the following exercises for two persons, construct original sequences just long enough to provide sufficient motivation for the indicated actions:

a. A sequence of face slaps.

b. For the men, a fist fight, a tussling match, a sword fight. For the women, a hair-pulling contest that ends in a tussling match.

4. *Suggested scenes:*

a. Women:

The Plough and the Stars, Sean O'Casey—Bessie and Mrs. Gogan, Act II. Hair-pulling and tussling.

The Women, Clare Boothe Luce—Sylvia and Miriam, Act II, Scene 5. Hair-pulling, biting, and tussling.

The White Steed, Paul Carroll, Roseanne and Meg, Act III. Hair-pulling and tussling.

Ring Around the Moon, Fry and Anouilh—Diana and Isabella, Act III, Scene 1. Hair-pulling and tussling.

b. Men:

Mr. Roberts, Heggen and Logan—Mannion and Insigna, Wiley and Stefanowski, Act I. Fists and wrestling.

Romeo and Juliet, Shakespeare—Mercutio and Tybalt, Romeo and Tybalt. Swords, or swords and daggers.

Macbeth, Shakespeare—Macbeth and Macduff, Act V, Scene 8. Swords and shields.

c. Man and Woman:

The Taming of the Shrew, Shakespeare—Petruchio and Katharina, Act II, Scene 1. Whip and tussle.

Private Lives, Noel Coward—Amanda and Eylot, Act II. Tussling.

The Warrior's Husband, Julian Thompson—Antiope and the Greek warriors, Act III. Swords, blows, and tussling.

Index